THE ESSENCE OF
ENTREPRENEURSHIP
AND THE NATURE
AND SIGNIFICANCE
OF MARKET PROCESS

THE COLLECTED WORKS OF ISRAEL M. KIRZNER

ISRAEL M. KIRZNER

The Essence of Entrepreneurship and the Nature and Significance of Market Process

Edited and with an Introduction by

PETER J. BOETTKE AND FRÉDÉRIC SAUTET

LIBERTY FUND

This book is published by Liberty Fund, Inc., a foundation established to encourage study of the ideal of a society of free and responsible individuals.

𒂼𒄄

The cuneiform inscription that serves as our logo and as the design motif for our endpapers is the earliest-known written appearance of the word "freedom" (*amagi*), or "liberty." It is taken from a clay document written about 2300 B.C. in the Sumerian city-state of Lagash.

Introduction and index © 2018 by Liberty Fund, Inc.

Printed in the United States of America

22 21 20 19 18 C 5 4 3 2 1

22 21 20 19 18 P 5 4 3 2 1

Library of Congress Cataloging-in-Publication Data

Names: Kirzner, Israel M., author. | Sautet, Frederic E., editor. | Boettke, Peter J., editor.
Title: The essence of entrepreneurship and the nature and significance of market process / Israel M. Kirzner, Frederic Sautet, Peter J. Boettke.
Description: Carmel : Liberty Fund Inc., 2018. | Series: The collected works of Israel M. Kirzner; 8 | Includes index.
Identifiers: LCCN 2018012305 | ISBN 9780865978669 (hardback) | ISBN 9780865978676 (paperback)
Subjects: LCSH: Entrepreneurship. | Austrian school of economics.
Classification: LCC HB615 .K585 2018 | DDC 338/.04—dc23
LC record available at https://lccn.loc.gov/2018012305

LIBERTY FUND, INC.
11301 North Meridian Street
Carmel, Indiana 46032-4564

B'EZRAS HASHEM

CONTENTS

INTRODUCTION TO
THE LIBERTY FUND EDITION

This volume goes to the heart of Israel Kirzner's most important work, presenting his fundamental papers on entrepreneurial alertness and market process. Kirzner's work has been recognized not only in the world of Austrian economics but also in the field of entrepreneurship studies. Indeed, the last two decades have seen his oeuvre become a cornerstone of that discipline.[1] Many scholars now refer to Kirznerian alertness as one of the important theoretical insights to understanding the entrepreneurial function. This is reflected in the works of Sankaran Venkataraman and Scott Shane who are two significant witnesses to the growing importance of Kirzner's research in entrepreneurship studies. One can credit Kirzner's influence for helping these scholars shift the focus of their discipline away from a strict behavioral approach—which is mostly concerned with defining and understanding the entrepreneurial profile—toward a more cognitive one. Venkataraman's *The Distinctive Domain of Entrepreneurship Research* (1997) and Shane's *Prior Knowledge and the Discovery of Entrepreneurial Opportunities* (2000) are instances of works that have pushed the cognitive approach to entrepreneurship into the foreground. While studying the profiles of entrepreneurs has generated important results, the profession has now realized that it is also crucial to understand how entrepreneurs come to recognize the existence of opportunities. In other words, the fundamental question has become "why do people discover some entrepreneurial opportunities and not others?" (Shane, 2000, 451)

As a result, more and more research is directed toward understanding both the origins of entrepreneurial opportunities and the discovery process. Venkataraman's and Shane's emphasis on entrepreneurial discovery and the role of prior knowledge has become a theme of numerous studies that have sought to shed light on these questions.[2] Some of

1. Kirzner received the Global Award for Entrepreneurship Research in 2006. The prize committee stated: "Kirzner's theory building has had great impact on the development of the entire field of entrepreneurship research, not to mention it has been applied empirically in several adjacent fields."

2. See for instance the papers of Gaglio and Katz (2001) and Shepherd and DeTienne (2005). See also Sarasvathy (2008).

the core views that have emerged in the last two decades in entrepreneurship research are direct applications of the work of Friedrich Hayek on knowledge dispersion and of Israel Kirzner on the entrepreneurial function. In many ways, the Austrian approach has now become part of the foundational landscape of entrepreneurship research. To a large extent, this new direction can be attributed to Kirzner's work and its influence.

The essence of entrepreneurship in Kirzner's work revolves around the fundamental idea that the discovery and exploitation of gains from trade does not take place automatically, but rather stems from purposeful human action. This departs from traditional microeconomics in which existing gains from trade are always known. Instead, Kirzner emphasizes that in order for these gains to be exploited, they first have to be noticed. The essence of the entrepreneurial function rests on this fundamental insight. For decades, this view escaped the mind of economists who did not notice its importance. But researchers in the field of entrepreneurship studies eventually did. In defining the distinctive domain of entrepreneurship research, Shane and Venkataraman (2000) put forward the importance of knowledge dispersion and opportunity recognition as a cornerstone of the new research framework, thereby recognizing the essence of Kirzner's work.

Unlike entrepreneurship research, the mainstream of economic science continued to adhere to deterministic mechanisms and a purposeless view of human action, which led to a rigid framework to explain individual choice. Once individual preferences are assumed and the constraints are known, microeconomics tells us what the individual will do. There is not much "choice" left in this framework, if one understands by choice an element of human action that is not directly under the sway of deterministic forces. Some economists, such as George Shackle (1972), sharply criticized this approach purporting that nothing can ever rigidly determine human decisions. In Kirzner's view, however, Shackle went too far in denying the relevance of the framework that shapes human choices, but he was right in emphasizing the presence of an indeterminate element in human action: the entrepreneurial function. Kirzner built his theory of entrepreneurship by opening up the framework of choice that defines human action, while keeping the system within the boundaries of rational choice theory. In this gap between the straitjacket of deterministic microeconomics and Shackle's kaleidic world lies the essence of entrepreneurship.[3]

Kirzner has been criticized for defining the entrepreneurial function within the context of traditional microeconomics and insisting on the individual's ability to notice what was previously unknown. Can homo agents fit in a framework for homo economicus? Kirzner meets the challenge by relaxing the strict behavioral and cognitive assumptions of traditional theory, while not abandoning the logical structure of market theory and relative price adjustments.

Traditional price theory is caught in a logical conundrum identified by Kenneth Arrow.[4] If economic actors are price takers as postulated in the theory of general competitive equilibrium, then how do prices ever adjust to clear markets? And, furthermore, if we have no theory of price adjustment, then how will markets converge on an equilibrium path from a situation of disequilibrium? As Joan Robinson pointed out long ago, it appears that the only way an economy can reach equilibrium is to be already in equilibrium.[5] The implications of this theoretical lacuna are significant, and threaten the intellectual legitimacy of the entire neoclassical theory of the market economy. Franklin Fisher explained succinctly in his *Disequilibrium Foundations of Equilibrium Economics* (1989) that either we have good reasons to believe that an economy in disequilibrium will find an equilibrium path, or we must abandon neoclassical welfare economics and the conclusions derived about the tendencies toward market clearing, efficiency of decentralized markets, and economic coordination.

In contrast with traditional microeconomics, Kirzner's view of the entrepreneurial function in the market process consists primarily in liberating human choice from its deterministic structure by introducing alertness. Alertness to unexploited gains from trade sets the market process in motion. Thus, the notion of alertness is crucial also because of

---

3. Garrison (1982) contends that Kirzner adopted a middle-of-the-road view of economics.

4. See Arrow's paper, "Toward a Theory of Price Adjustment," in *The Allocation of Economic Resources: Essays in Honor of Bernard Francis Haley,* edited by Moses Abramowitz (1959). See also Arrow (1994).

5. See for instance "History and Equilibrium" and "The Disintegration of Economics" reprinted in volume 5 of her *Collected Works* (1979).

its relationship to market process. Entrepreneurial alertness is critical to Kirzner's development of the theory of the competitive market process, and this theory provides us with the disequilibrium foundations to classical and neoclassical market equilibrium analysis, offering a response to Arrow's challenge.[6]

Starting in 1967 with the publication of "Methodological Individualism, Market Equilibrium, and Market Process," Kirzner's research on the role of the entrepreneurial function led him to reconsider the nature of the market. The logic of market equilibrium implies that participants always act optimally under given circumstances and with perfect knowledge. In this world, prices and quantities reflect a full mutual adjustment of individual plans; there is no ignorance that is not revealed in the current state of the market. Agents are fully aware of the true situation in which they find themselves. Hayek often emphasized that what matters is not so much what happens in equilibrium but what happens on the path to it. If we assume that knowledge is truly dispersed and plans, as a result, are not well coordinated, then the entrepreneurial function becomes a fundamental aspect of the market system. In this approach, the market is a process rather than a state of affairs.

Kirzner's analysis of the market process is in harmony with the general findings of entrepreneurship studies yet distinct from this line of research. Alertness can be observed through personality traits such as self-motivation, self-efficacy, effectuation, and superior risk assessment. Moreover, entrepreneurs (a) constantly make judgments about the future state of the market, (b) are generally creative and innovative, and (c) often invest their own capital in the early exploitation of opportunities.[7] While all these attributes are important, they are not fundamental to Kirzner's view of entrepreneurship. Indeed, the essential aspect of his market process is the persistent alertness of entrepreneurs to hitherto unknown profit opportunities. Because of this defining characteristic of

6. Given the significance of the problem of open-endedness for the enterprise of economics, and the ingenious way in which Kirzner provides an endogenous solution to it, it is our sincere hope that he will one day be honored by the Nobel Prize committee in Sweden for this technical point in price theory.

7. Some economists have criticized Kirzner's view of the entrepreneurial function as being too abstract and not grounded enough in the daily reality of entrepreneurs and organizations. See, for instance, Klein (2008).

entrepreneurs, Kirzner repeatedly emphasizes the idea of the market as a discovery procedure.

This volume contains three sections. The first section presents some of the papers in which Kirzner has defined the essence of entrepreneurship, while the second and third sections include papers on market process theory. Kirzner explores the implications of allowing the entrepreneurial element to exist in the choice-theoretic framework of microeconomics. It is here that we see the full implication of the idea that the discovery of gains from trade is not an automatic and necessary process. These papers, along with his book *Competition and Entrepreneurship* (1973), present the core of Kirzner's view. They also help us see his evolution since the early 1970s, and how he fleshed out his view of entrepreneurship and market process. Note that section two on market process includes papers on growth, development, and entrepreneurial error. It also contains two debates, on the nature of entrepreneurship with Martin Ricketts and on the market process with Stephen Shmanske. The last section presents articles on the subject of supply and demand, including a critique by James Ahiakpor and Kirzner's reply.

ACKNOWLEDGMENTS

We would first like to thank wholeheartedly Israel Kirzner for his unparalleled contribution to economic science. Kirzner's research program has deeply enriched the discipline and has shed light on some of economics' most difficult puzzles. Economists owe him an immense intellectual debt.

The publication of *The Collected Works of Israel M. Kirzner* would not be a reality without the participation of Liberty Fund, Inc. We are extremely grateful to Liberty Fund, and especially Emilio Pacheco, for making this project possible. To republish Kirzner's unique œuvre has been on our minds since our time spent at New York University in the 1990s—where one of us was a professor (Peter) and the other a post-doctoral student (Frédéric). We are thrilled at the idea that current and future generations of economists and other scholars will have easy access to Kirzner's works.

Finally, we wish to thank Emily Washington for her invaluable help in the publication of this volume.

Peter J. Boettke and Frédéric Sautet

REFERENCES

Arrow, Kenneth (1994) "Methodological Individualism and Social Knowledge," *The American Economic Review,* 84 (2), Papers and Proceedings, 1–9.

Arrow, Kenneth (1959) "Toward a Theory of Price Adjustment," *The Allocation of Economic Resources: Essays in Honor of Bernard Francis Haley,* Moses Abramowitz, ed., Stanford: Stanford University Press.

Fisher, Franklin (1989) *Disequilibrium Foundation of Equilibrium Economics,* Cambridge: Cambridge University Press.

Gaglio, Connie M. and Jerome A. Katz (2001) "The Psychological Basis of Opportunity Identification: Entrepreneurial Alertness," *Small Business Economics,* volume 16, no. 2, 95–111.

Garrison, Roger (1982) "Austrian Economics as the Middle Ground: Comment on Loasby," in Israel M. Kirzner, ed., *Method, Process, and Austrian Economics: Essays in Honor of Ludwig von Mises,* Lexington, Mass.: D. C. Heath and Co., pp. 131–38.

Global Award for Entrepreneurship Research. http://www.e-award.org/web/2006_Israel_M_Kirzner.aspx

Kirzner, Israel M. (1967) "Methodological Individualism, Market Equilibrium, and Market Process," *Il Politico* (Pavia, Italy) 32, no. 4: 787–99; reprinted in *Austrian Subjectivism and the Emergence of Entrepreneurship Theory,* Indianapolis: Liberty Fund, 2015.

Kirzner, Israel M. (1973) *Competition and Entrepreneurship,* Chicago: University of Chicago Press; reprinted, Indianapolis: Liberty Fund, 2013.

Klein, Peter (2008) "Opportunity Discovery, Entrepreneurial Action, and Economic Organization," *Strategic Entrepreneurship Journal,* volume 2, pp. 175–90.

Robinson, Joan (1979) *Collected Works,* volume 5, Oxford: Basil Blackwell.

Sarasvathy, Saras (2008) *Effectuation: Elements of Entrepreneurial Expertise,* Northampton: Edward Elgar Publishing, Inc.

Shackle, George (1972) *Epistemics and Economics: A Critique of Economic Doctrines,* New Brunswick, N.J.: Transaction Publishers.

Shane, Scott (2000) "Prior Knowledge and the Discovery of Entrepreneurial Opportunities," *Organization Science,* volume 11, no. 4, 448–69.

Shane, Scott and Sankaran Venkataraman (2000) "The Promise of Entrepreneurship as a Field of Research," *The Academy of Management Review,* volume 25, no. 1, 217–26.

Shepherd, Dean A. and Dawn R. DeTienne (2005) "Prior Knowledge, Potential Financial Reward, and Opportunity Identification," *Entrepreneurship, Theory and Practice,* volume 29, no. 1, 91–112.

Venkataraman, Sankaran (1997) "The Distinctive Domain of Entrepreneurship Research," *Advances in Entrepreneurship, Firm Emergence and Growth,* volume 3, Greenwich, Conn.: JAI Press Inc., 119–38.

THE ESSENCE OF ENTREPRENEURSHIP

ENTREPRENEURSHIP

A solid case can be made for the claim that entrepreneurship has, throughout the history of the Austrian school, been among its central theoretical constructs. In their history of the variety of ways of understanding the essence of entrepreneurship, Hébert and Link (1988, p. 64) refer to the three "distinct viewpoints" in early neoclassical economics (the "Austrian, French and British"). They remark that, "of the three, the Austrian approach proved most fertile for advancing the theory of the entrepreneur." In a paper exploring aspects of the history of entrepreneurial theory, Dolores Tremewan Martin (1979, p. 271) observes that "much of the modern economic analysis . . . is devoid of any serious consideration of the role of the entrepreneur . . . ," but adds in a footnote that "the primary exceptions to this general trend in the literature are found in the writings of the 'modern Austrian economists.'"

In the following pages we will briefly examine some highlights in the history of Austrian theories of entrepreneurship; canvass some contemporary disagreements among Austrians in regard to entrepreneurship; and seek to explain why it was that the Austrians, rather than other schools of marginalist economics, came to assign such importance to the entrepreneurial role.

THE ENTREPRENEUR IN THE EARLIER AUSTRIAN TRADITION

It is well known that it was only in the course of the marginalist revolution that economists came to recognize an analytically distinct role for the entrepreneur. In classical economics—or at least in its dominant British version—there was simply no distinct entrepreneurial function. It was the capitalist upon whom, it appears, the economists implicitly relied to assure fulfillment of the tasks we generally consider to be entrepreneurial. The profit share of income earned by the capitalist, in classical economics, corresponded mainly in fact to what neoclassical economics was to identify as interest on capital. For the classical economists there was no pure entrepreneurial profit, because for them there

From *The Elgar Companion to Austrian Economics*, ed. Peter J. Boettke (Aldershot, U.K.: Edward Elgar Publishing, 1964), 103–10. Reprinted by permission of the publisher.

was no pure entrepreneurial role. It was in the course of the neoclassical development of the theory of the market that economists came to recognize the importance of the function played by the entrepreneur who acquires all the resource services—including those of capital—in order to produce the product to be sold to consumers. During the 1880s and 1890s there emerged a small flood of articles dealing with this entrepreneurial role. It was at this time that the American theorists, J. B. Clark and Frederick B. Hawley, developed their separate theories of pure profit (upon the elements of which Frank Knight was later to build his own more nuanced theory). It was soon after this period that the Austrian J. A. Schumpeter introduced his own theory of the entrepreneur, laying the foundation for his characteristic way of seeing and understanding the capitalist process.

The Austrians were prominent participants in this discovery of entrepreneurship. Carl Menger had already, in his 1871 *Grundsätze,* paid some significant attention, at least, to the entrepreneurial function. In characteristic subjectivist fashion, indeed, Menger (1950, p. 160) emphasized the element of information and the act of will involved in this entrepreneurial function (although, unlike Schumpeter and later Austrians, he saw the exercise of this function as merely a special kind of labor service). During the 1880s his teaching apparently inspired two of his students, Mataja and Gross, each to write his dissertation on the entrepreneurial role. There has been some disagreement among historians of thought concerning the influence exercised by Menger upon subsequent Austrian developments in the theory of entrepreneurship. Streissler (1972, pp. 432f) has maintained that Schumpeter built his own theory of entrepreneurial innovation largely on Menger's foundations. This seems to contrast sharply with Knight's typically dismissive assessment of the influence of Menger's contribution in this respect. (See also Martin, 1979; Kirzner, 1979, chapter 4, for discussions of Menger's concept of the entrepreneur in the context of the subsequent Schumpeterian and Knightian views.) Be this as it may, there seems little ground to doubt that Schumpeter's own emphasis on the entrepreneur was rooted, not in his well-known admiration for Walrasian general equilibrium theory, but in the subjectivist, Austrian legacy he imbibed from Böhm-Bawerk's seminars.

An assessment by the historian of thought of the state of entrepreneurial theory in the economics of 1914 would recognize the importance of the Austrian contributions, but would certainly not pronounce entrepreneurial theory to be exclusively or even predominantly the province of the Austrians. The bulk of the prewar literature on entrepreneurship and on entrepreneurial profit was certainly contributed by economists of other schools. Yet general mainstream interest in this branch of economic theory was to decline sharply following the war. Knight's work would of course represent a magisterial contribution to the identification of the entrepreneurial role and to the understanding of pure entrepreneurial profit. It offered a crystal-clear articulation of the distinction between the utterly certain Walrasian world of perfectly competitive equilibrium and the real world of radical, inescapable uncertainty. But the progress of mainstream neoclassical economics in the succeeding half-century was virtually to ignore the implications of this distinction. Even among Knight's own disciples microeconomics came to mean, in the second half of the twentieth century, the theory of markets in complex competitive equilibrium, with no possibility of pure profit, and none of the uncertainty which calls forth the special characteristics of the Knightian entrepreneur. It was during this period that understanding of the entrepreneurial role became, if only by default, more or less an exclusively Austrian concern. It was in the economics of Ludwig von Mises that this was most obvious.

ENTREPRENEURSHIP IN MID-TWENTIETH-CENTURY AUSTRIAN ECONOMICS

What Mises contributed to the theory of entrepreneurship may not be immediately obvious to the superficial reader of his works. Although the index to his *Human Action* (1949) demonstrates the importance of the entrepreneur for Misesian economics, a reader may be excused for concluding that what Mises had to say about the entrepreneur was not exactly pathbreaking. The nuances which separate the Misesian entrepreneur from the Schumpeterian or the Knightian might well appear to be only of marginal significance, but the truth is that it is indeed the role which Mises assigns to the entrepreneur which sets Misesian economics so decisively apart from mainstream mid-twentieth-century economics. And the modest revival of the Austrian approach during the past two decades must be seen as recognition of the valuable character of precisely this aspect of the Misesian system.

What sets the Misesian system apart from mainstream neoclassical economics is the Misesian portrayal of *the market as an entrepreneurially driven process:*

The operation of [the factor] market is actuated and kept in motion by the exertion of the promoting entrepreneurs, eager to profit from the differences in the market prices of the factors of production and the expected prices of the products . . . The activities of the entrepreneurs are the element that would bring about the unrealizable state of the evenly rotating economy if no further changes were to occur . . . The competition between the entrepreneurs . . . reflects in the external world the conflict which the inexorable scarcity of the factors of production brings about in the soul of each consumer. It makes effective the subsumed decisions of the consumers as to what purpose the nonspecific factors should be used for and to what extent the specific factors of production should be used. (1949, pp. 331, 335)

It was in the course of the famed inter-war debate on the possibility of economic calculation under socialism that Mises's entrepreneurial view of the market process came to be crystallized and subsequently clearly articulated. As Lavoie has emphasized, it was appreciation for the entrepreneurial character of the market process which enabled the Austrians to see the fallacy of quasi-market "solutions" (such as those of Lange and Lerner) to the calculation problem. This writer has argued that Hayek's important contributions to the calculation debate, although couched in terms of utilization of knowledge rather than in terms of entrepreneurial discovery, ultimately reflect, at least implicitly, a similar understanding of the market process.

In fact the novelty of the Misesian perception of the market as a continuing process of entrepreneurial competition is mute evidence of the drastic decline, in mid-twentieth-century mainstream economic thought, of awareness of the entrepreneurial role. As Baumol has observed, the entrepreneur had virtually disappeared from the theoretical literature. And it was indeed the Misesian emphasis on the entrepreneurial role which inspired subsequent Austrian interest in the theory of entrepreneurship.

THE MISESIAN ENTREPRENEUR FURTHER EXPLORED

Much of this subsequent Austrian interest has been reflected in the present writer's work seeking to articulate more definitively the essential characteristics of the Misesian entrepreneur, and to demonstrate how central these characteristics must be for an understanding of the competitive process. As one writer has put it, the "leitmotif" of this work has been that "the exploitation of the gains from trade will not take place automatically. To achieve the advantages of co-ordination through exchange requires first that these potential gains are noticed. The entrepreneurial role is to be 'alert' to as yet unexploited gains from trade" (Ricketts, 1992, p. 67).

Mainstream economics has of course always assumed that exploitation of gains from trade *will* take place automatically, as soon as the gains exceed the relevant costs. This assumes that all opportunities for winning pure gain are instantly perceived and exploited. It follows that the market outcomes, at any given instant, must necessarily be understood as embodying the fulfillment of the most exacting conditions for equilibrium. Each economic agent in the market must, at each instant, therefore be assumed *not* to be grasping for pure profit (since all such opportunities for pure profit have *already* been grasped and eliminated). This has forced mainstream microeconomics into a straitjacket in which all decisions being made at each instant are, somehow, automatically fully coordinated ("pre-reconciled") with every other decision being made in the system. This has restricted modern microeconomics to strictly defined states of equilibrium. This has, in turn, had the consequence that the notion of *competition* has had to mean, not any process during which competing market participants struggle to get ahead of one another, but a state of affairs in which any such struggle is both unnecessary and inconceivable.

By liberating economics from the assumption that all opportunities for pure gain have already been captured, this Misesian-inspired perspective on markets permits us to see market processes as ones in which such opportunities—hitherto overlooked—come to be perceived and exploited. This has opened up an entirely fresh dimension for economic activity, a dimension necessarily missing from an equilibrium-bound microeconomics. This new dimension is that of entrepreneurial *alertness* and entrepreneurial discovery. Whereas traditional economics has operated in a framework in which outcomes can be attributed to either (or a mix of) (a) deliberate maximizing choice, or (b) pure luck, this entrepreneurial perspective draws our attention to a third possible (and, in general, necessary) source for observed outcomes. This third source is *discovery*, in which unfocused, unspecified, purposefulness—a generalized intentness upon noticing the useful opportunities that may be present within one's field of vision—in fact yields discovered opportunities (which may then be subsequently exploited in maximizing choice fashion). Such discovery cannot itself be characterized as rational, maximizing choice (in the way in which deliberate cost-conscious *search* activity has been treated in the theory of information literature) because, prior to the moment of discovery, the potential discoverer is perceived not to have any specific search objective or search procedure in mind and is (therefore) not seen as weighing the likely benefits of a successful find against the costs of necessary search. (In fact his discovery may consist in *realizing* that he *has* before him a promising opportunity for profitable search.) Nor can a discovered opportunity be entirely attributed to pure luck. Although, to be sure, the objective existence of the opportunity itself (prior to its discovery but at a point in space and time likely to result in discovery) may (disregarding the philosophical reservations one may have concerning the "existence" of an unperceived opportunity) be seen as entirely a matter of luck, its discovery must, at least in part, be attributed to the alertness of the discoverer.

The notion of entrepreneurship as the alertness necessary for the discovery of opportunities has had important implications for the positive understanding of market processes, and for ethical judgments concerning the moral status of market outcomes. The positive theory of the competitive market process has come, in this line of modern Austrian economics, to mean the sequence of market trades and acts of production which can be attributed to the succession of entrepreneurial discoveries generated by disequilibrium conditions. To compete means, in this framework, to perceive an opportunity to serve the market better (than it is currently being served by one's competitors). This view of the function of the entrepreneur has been central to the modern Austrian appreciation of free markets, and to its understanding of the perils of interventionist public policies.

These Austrian insights concerning the role of entrepreneurial discovery have also revealed the *discovered* character of pure entrepreneurial profit. This has permitted an ethical view of the possible justice of such profit in a manner not open to mainstream economics (for which pure profit is likely to appear to have been enjoyed by the entrepreneur strictly as a matter of his good luck). This insight has been explored in Kirzner (1989).

ENTREPRENEURSHIP: SOME CONTEMPORARY
AUSTRIAN DEBATES

Although the central features of Misesian entrepreneurship are, by and large, accepted within modern Austrian economics, certain features emphasized in this writer's expositions of it (as outlined in the preceding section) have been challenged during recent years by a number of Austrian economists, as well as by others. (One line of modern Austrian work, *not* dealt with in this section, is that identified with the late Ludwig Lachmann. That work has sharply questioned the equilibrative character of entrepreneurship which is central to the Misesian view.) We may group these debates around two related themes.

Creativity

The "alertness" view of entrepreneurship appears to separate entrepreneurship from any genuinely creative activity. To be alert to an opportunity would appear not to include anything except noticing that which is *already* fully developed, merely waiting to be grasped. A number of modern Austrians have been unhappy with such implications. See also Ricketts (1992).

Uncertainty

The "alertness" view of entrepreneurship has been understood by its critics effectively to abstract from uncertainty. To define entrepreneurship in terms of *seeing* opportunities, it is held by the critics, seems to identify it exclusively with success: to define it in terms apparently impervious to the very possibility of entrepreneurial loss. Yet surely such possibility of loss cannot be separated from the exercise of entrepreneurship. As soon as entrepreneurship is extended from simultaneous arbitrage to intertemporal arbitrage, uncertainty inevitably enters the picture. All this has suggested to the critics that the essence of entrepreneurship be sought in such qualities as *imagination* (White, 1976) or *judgment* (High, 1982).

In his more recent writings the present writer has attempted to meet some of these criticisms. He has of course agreed that uncertainty is inseparable from the entrepreneurial function in the context of ongoing time; so that it is indeed the case that the futurity of entrepreneurial activity must entail both judgment and imagination. Entrepreneurial alertness, in regard to opportunities the profitability of which lies in the future, cannot be exercised without imagination of that which does not yet exist, and without judgment concerning which of today's active forces is likely, in the course of time, to dominate the others. To concur warmly in these valid and important observations, is not, however, to retreat from the insight that the essence of all entrepreneurial action is the perception of opportunities—offering profit in the present, the near future, or the distant future. To recognize that alertness in a world of uncertainty may call for good judgment and lively imagination does not surely, affect the centrality of the insight that entrepreneurship refers, not to the deliberate exploitation of perceived opportunities, but to the alert perception of opportunities available for exploitation.

Rather similar considerations relate to the criticisms which see the emphasis on alertness as being blind to the role of creativity in the entrepreneurial role. Surely, such criticisms run, what the entrepreneur does, in so many cases, is not so much to perceive a given opportunity as to imaginatively *create* that which nobody had hitherto dreamed of. To such criticisms it seems appropriate to respond that, while the opportunity to be discovered is often indeed the opportunity to be created, this truth should not obscure the more fundamental insight regarding entrepreneurship. This insight is simply that for any entrepreneurial discovery creativity is never enough: it is necessary *to recognize* one's own creativity. In other words, an essential ingredient in each successful creative innovation is its innovator's vision of what he can creatively accomplish.

The point in these responses to the critics is that, while the entrepreneur operates under uncertainty, and therefore displays imagination, judgment and creativity, his role is not so much the *shouldering* of uncertainty as it is his ability *to shoulder uncertainty aside* through recognizing opportunities in which imagination, judgment and creativity can successfully manifest themselves.

AUSTRIAN ECONOMICS AND THE ENTREPRENEURIAL ROLE

The centrality of the entrepreneur in Austrian economics, virtually since its inception in 1871, appears to be no accident. If one accepts *subjectivism* as being the unifying thread which has characterized the Austrian economic tradition throughout its history, then the centrality of entrepreneurship seems eminently understandable. Mainstream economics, with a lesser emphasis on subjectivism, has been prone to presuming that the mere objective presence of the possibility for gains from trade is sufficient to ensure their exploitation. Economic agents are presumed to maximize in terms of the opportunities which exist, without any concern regarding any possible gap between the opportunities which exist and the opportunities which are perceived to exist. Market prices are interpreted as the outcomes consistent with a state of the world in which all market participants are maximizing in respect of the opportunities objectively inherent in the actions of all their fellow participants. There is no need, in such an analytical scheme, for any role specifically geared to ensuring that the opportunities perceived in fact tend to correspond to what is objectively available. There is no need for any role specifically geared to explaining any process through which market outcomes might tend to come to express actual (as against possibly erroneously perceived) mutual possibilities—since no possibility of such a gap is entertained.

It is in a consciously subjectivist mode of analysis, such as that of the Austrian tradition, in which the possibility is taken seriously that agents may be seeking to maximize within erroneously perceived frameworks, that scope for entrepreneurship can easily come to be recognized. Within such a tradition an emphasis upon knowledge and ignorance, imagination and discovery has indeed emerged naturally and organically. Despite the changes over time in Austrian entrepreneurial constructs, and despite contemporary Austrian marginal disagreements concerning the essential entrepreneurial functions, it seems reasonable to attribute the perennial Austrian interest in the entrepreneur to the tradition's consistent subjectivist thrust.

BIBLIOGRAPHY

Hébert, Robert F. and Albert N. Link (1988), *The Entrepreneur: Mainstream Views and Radical Critiques*, 2nd edn, New York: Praeger.

High, Jack (1982), "Alertness and Judgment: Comment on Kirzner," in Israel M. Kirzner (ed.), *Method, Process and Austrian Economics, Essays in Honor of Ludwig von Mises*, Lexington, Mass.: D. C. Heath.

Kirzner, Israel M. (1979), *Perception, Opportunity and Profit, Studies in the Theory of Entrepreneurship*, Chicago: University of Chicago Press.

Kirzner, Israel M. (1989), *Discovery, Capitalism, and Distributive Justice*, Oxford: Basil Blackwell.

Martin, Dolores Tremewan (1979), "Alternative Views of Mengerian Entrepreneurship," *History of Political Economy*, 11, (2), summer, 271–85.

Menger, Carl (1950), *Principles of Economics*, translated and edited by J. Dingwall and Bert F. Hoselitz, Glencoe, Ill.: Free Press.

Mises, Ludwig von (1949), *Human Action*, New Haven: Yale University Press.

Ricketts, Martin (1992), "Kirzner's Theory of Entrepreneurship—A Critique," in Bruce J. Caldwell and Stephan Böhm (eds), *Austrian Economics: Tensions and New Directions*, Boston: Kluwer Academic.

Streissler, Erich (1972), "To What Extent Was the Austrian School Marginalist?" *History of Political Economy*, 4, fall.

White, Lawrence H. (1976), "Entrepreneurship, Imagination and the Question of Equilibration," ms., published in Stephen C. Littlechild, *Austrian Economics*, vol. III, Aldershot: Edward Elgar, 1990, pp. 87–104.

ENTREPRENEURS AND THE ENTREPRENEURIAL FUNCTION: A COMMENTARY

It is by now notorious that for many decades economic theorists virtually ignored the entrepreneurial role. Their models were peopled by agents who displayed few of the characteristics of—and encountered few of the problems faced by—the flesh-and-blood entrepreneurs whom we know both from business and economic history and from everyday casual observation. It has been gratifying during the past few years to witness the reawakening of interest in entrepreneurship among scholars working in several disciplines.[1] The chapters in this book offer us the opportunity to assess the progress made among scholars in economic theory. These chapters were written by outstanding economists; each aims to advance understanding on some aspects of entrepreneurial activity in a variety of institutional contexts. It is with much interest, therefore, that we examine these chapters to discover the extent to which entrepreneurship has become a vital area of study, and to savor the fresh insights into the entrepreneurial role that this new work has perhaps inspired. This chapter consists of the reflections precipitated by one such examination.

This writer would be less than candid if he did not express—along with his admiration for these contributions—a certain sense of disappointment. Each chapter is a conscientious and competent—even brilliant—exploration of its chosen topic within the overall theme of entrepreneurial behavior. Yet, for all their virtues, it appears that these chapters have pushed out the frontiers of the economics of entrepreneurship only slightly. It is apparent that we still have far to go before any recognized and useful economics of entrepreneurship will be part of the settled body of modern economic thought. The road to be traveled before we can hope to reach such a stage, moreover, promises to be rocky and treacherous. What is a matter for concern is not so much that the distinguished contributors to this book lack any commonly shared understanding of what the essence of entrepreneurship *is*, as that they hardly recognize the importance of a clear and satisfactory analytical identification of pure entrepreneurial activity. In the light

From *Entrepreneurship*, ed. Joshua Ronen (Lexington, Mass.: Lexington Books, 1983) 281–90. Reprinted by permission of the editor.

of this observation, it comes as no surprise to note that these chapters lack a unifying theme. They all relate, of course, to some aspect of entrepreneurship. But because the term "entrepreneurship" does not necessarily mean to one writer what it means to another, and because little attention is paid here to the definition of entrepreneurship as such, the sense of a lack of theme remains. It may be helpful, before discussing the elusive essence of entrepreneurship, to consider why modern economics has, until now, avoided paying the entrepreneur any attention at all.

THE ENTREPRENEUR AND ECONOMIC ANALYSIS

One would think that the figure of the entrepreneur, the active businessman, would be one of the last features of capitalist society to escape notice. The active businessman may be more or less innovative, more or less daring, more or less energetic—but he is still the figure in the market to whom one looks for energy, daring, and innovation. The seething activity in the market that we associate with energetic, bold, and innovative decisions is an item in the capitalist scene that is both striking and characteristic. How, then, have these seemingly essential features of the market society succeeded in effacing themselves for so long from the analytic picture constructed by economic theorists?

A plausible explanation for this puzzle might run as follows: The seething market activity that we associate with energetic, bold, and innovative decisions has been, in an important sense, precisely the element in the market from which it is necessary for economic analysis to abstract. After all, it is this activity that appears to defy all efforts at imposing an orderly, systematic analytical framework upon market phenomena. The vision that economic theorists brought to their work was that, *in spite of* the seemingly rudderless course of entrepreneurial events, market phenomena were nonetheless ultimately constrained and guided by systematic market forces. Beneath the facade of apparently unpredictable, energetic, bold, and innovative business activity, there resides a system of powerful coordinating forces to which, sooner or later, the seemingly free decisions of market participants must, willy-nilly, conform. It is the given underlying conditions of production and the given patterns of consumer preferences that, in the last analysis, govern market phenomena. To understand how such governance is exercised, it was *necessary* for theorists to ignore the superficial agitation of market phenomena, and to search for the underlying powerful realities that truly dominate the course of market events.

From this perspective, equilibrium analysis in economics constitutes a special kind of analytical feat—the discernment and explication of regularities that are masked from the eyes of the superficial observer by the apparently unsystematic gyrations of prices and of the quantities of resources and output. From this perspective, attention to the activities of the entrepreneur not only is unnecessary to the economic analysis, but in fact is a hindrance. It is reasonable, therefore, to assess Schumpeter's pioneering work on the entrepreneur in terms of this explanation for the neglect of the entrepreneur.

For Schumpeter, casual observation revealed that the capitalist process over the years was a series of spasmodic, discontinuous changes. The discontinuity of the changes that make up this process contrasts sharply with the theoretical picture of the "circular flow"—a picture that Schumpeter himself spelled out in detail[2] as the foundation upon which to construct his theory of (discontinuous) development. Schumpeter's appreciation, on the one hand, of the Walrasian theory of general equilibrium (the theoretical model of the circular flow) and on the other hand, his awareness of the need for a theory of dynamic, discontinuous development, together guided his own prolific contributions from his *Theory of Economic Development* (1911) and *Business Cycles* (1938) to his *Capitalism, Socialism, and Democracy* (1942). For Schumpeter, the Walrasian theory was the highest theoretical achievement in economics;[3] yet throughout his career, he was impatient with his colleagues for failing to see how limited equilibrium theory is, and how inadequate it is for understanding the *process* of capitalist development. For Schumpeter, a full understanding of capitalism thus required an appreciation of the way the Schumpeterian-entrepreneurial theory of development is superimposed upon the Walrasian theory of the circular flow.

From the perspective outlined above, it can be seen that Schumpeter fully accepted the need to pierce the agitated surface of capitalist reality to perceive the powerful forces beneath that bring about the circular flow. What impelled Schumpeter to focus analytical attention on the entrepreneur—and what sets him apart from all of his contemporaries who failed to understand the entrepreneurial role—was his perception that this agitation on the surface of capitalist reality is *more* than just fuzzy noise. What appears as functionless agitation from the perspective of equilibrium theory emerges, in the Schumpeterian vision, as necessary steps in the process of creative destruction that constitutes capitalist development. Thus, Schumpeter's vision permitted him to have, so to speak, the best of both worlds. On the one hand, he could endorse Walrasian general equilibrium theory by abstracting from entrepreneur-driven market agitation; on the other, he was able to perceive in that agitation an important—indeed essential—feature of the capitalist process.

However, the developments in twentieth century general-equilibrium and growth theories have perhaps made it *less* easy for economic theorists to focus attention on the entrepreneur than it was for Schumpeter. After all, modern extensions of equilibrium theory to include interaction between intertemporal, multiperiod decisions offer a vision of intertemporal growth equilibrium with respect to which Schumpeter's process of discontinuous development, too, must appear as fuzzy noise. The modern effort to discern the true underlying forces governing the course of economic activity through time thus calls for a resolute disregard of the surface discontinuities occasioned by precisely the entrepreneurial innovations that were, for Schumpeter, the essence of capitalism.

The current resurgence of interest in the theory of entrepreneurship recognizes, we hope, that such resolute disregard—whatever its merits might be for limited purposes—should not be maintained so consistently that it prevents us from seeing important systematic market forces arising out of entrepreneurship. Our discussion of these matters suggests a classificatory framework for possible theories of entrepreneurship. It will be useful to set forth this framework as a background for appraising the various approaches represented in this book.

THEORIES OF ENTREPRENEURSHIP: FOUR LEVELS

The discussion in the preceding section suggests that we can identify four levels at which one might, in principle, develop theories of entrepreneurial activity. Moreover, the essence of entrepreneurship at one level of theory might not be very useful at one of the other levels. Let us return to the flesh-and-blood entrepreneur—one of those, perhaps, interviewed by Joshua Ronen.

A flesh-and-blood entrepreneur takes decisive action along a variety of dimensions. He forms companies, he introduces new product lines, he initiates new techniques of production, he cuts prices, he strikes out for new markets, he seeks sources of finance, he innovates new forms of internal organization, he brings in new personnel, he reassigns existing personnel. It is not difficult to imagine the degree of agitation injected into the market by these kinds of activities. The economic theorist might grapple with these activities, or with their market consequences, at one or more of four levels:

1. The economic theorist might try to fit the decisions of this entrepreneur-businessman into the standard theory of the profit-maximizing firm with full relevant information. Each innovation, each pricing change, would then be viewed as a simple profit-maximizing reaction to some apparent shift in the arrays of revenue and production possibilities that confront the firm. Such a theoretical perspective rules out error (or the spontaneous discovery of earlier error), and also surprise. It can, with more or less difficulty, be stretched to include the decisions made by the firm to acquire additional information. However, the degree of information sought and possessed—and thus the degree of ignorance accepted— is at all times viewed as optimal. At this level, the theorist seeks to explain the firm's decisions within the theory of the profit-maximizing firm. For this level of entrepreneurial theory, the term "entrepreneur" simply connotes the imagined center of profit-maximizing decision making. This decision maker is assumed to possess, at all times, full relevant information, including full information concerning the worthwhileness of seeking additional information and full information concerning the sources of such information.

2. The economic theorist might recognize that, at a second level, the decisions of our entrepreneur-businessman cannot be fitted into the standard theory of the firm without unacceptable artificiality. At this level, the theorist recognizes that such human qualities as leadership, boldness, energy, persistence, resourcefulness, creativity, and judgment can crucially affect the decisions taken. There are, obviously, great variations between different would-be entrepreneurs with respect to these human qualities. This makes it highly implausible to view decisions as simply the calculated solutions to maximization problems presented by objective sets of data equally and fully perceived by all entrepreneurs. Instead of seeking to understand the decisions of our entrepreneur-businessman in terms of profit maximization, this second level of theory will seek a framework that transcends maximization. At this level, the theorist would seek theories that explain where their springs of creativity come from, and under what circumstances they will assume Knightian uncertainty,

or what makes them notice opportunities overlooked by others, and so on. For this level of entrepreneurial theory, the essence of entrepreneurship might be seen in any one (or in a combination) of many characteristics generally present in entrepreneurial activity. One theory might see the essence of such activity, for example, in its innovativeness, and might then construct a framework to account for different degrees of innovativeness. (Such a theory, of course, might be a psychological theory rather than a purely economic theory.) Such a theory might show how the degree of innovativeness is affected by economic constraints, regulatory climate, and the like. Another theory might see the essence of entrepreneurial activity in its speculative aspect, and might then trace the psychological or other lines of causation that govern the businessman's willingness to venture into the unknown.

3. A third level for the theoretical explication of entrepreneurial activity might address, not the determinants of the decisions of entrepreneurial individuals, but rather the *market consequences* of such decisions. Schumpeter's was a theory at this level of analysis. Such a theory views entrepreneurial activity as superimposed upon an equilibrium pattern of nonentrepreneurial interacting decisions. Without seeking to account for the particular creative, innovative, or speculative decisions of individual businessmen, a theory at this third level might, for example, illuminate the extent to which market phenomena, in fact, fail to correspond precisely to the conditions consistent with equilibrium. Thus, for Schumpeter, the activity of entrepreneurs is seen as disrupting the circular flow of equilibrium.

For this level of theory, the essence of entrepreneurship will probably be identified by a particular market phenomenon thought to be specifically generated by entrepreneurial activity. For instance, Schumpeter, who links his entrepreneur with dynamic, discontinuous market innovations, sees "creative destruction" as the essence of entrepreneurship: the entrepreneur can break away from the standard mold, initiate change and innovation. The point is that at this level, one's view of the entrepreneur is likely to be related to the ultimate market-theoretical purposes for which he is to be analytically deployed.

4. The fourth level at which a theory of entrepreneurship might be attempted is, like the third, not primarily concerned with the decisions of entrepreneurial individuals. It, too, is concerned rather with the market consequences of these entrepreneurial decisions. However, at this fourth

level, such market consequences are not seen as superimposed upon an otherwise equilibrium world. Indeed, one does not take at all for granted that the market would at all times be in equilibrium in the absence of entrepreneurially driven agitation. At this level, the theorist considers the possibility that entrepreneurial activity is not merely a disturbing fuzzy noise masking the true, dominating forces of market equilibrium, but that such agitative activity might, in fact, be the only element on which we can rely to steer market decisions toward an equilibrium pattern. For a theory successfully sustaining this latter possibility, entrepreneurially driven market agitation is not a ruffled surface beneath which can be discerned the true balance of forces in equilibrium. Rather, the economists' vision of the market in equilibrium is relevant only to the extent that agitation leads eventually toward it.

At this fourth level (as at the third level), one's perception of the essence of the entrepreneur will depend a great deal upon the particular theory of market process for which the entrepreneur is being deployed. In work directed to this level of theory, the writer has identified pure entrepreneurship as consisting of pure alertness to as yet unexploited—because unnoticed—opportunities.[4] The purely formal sense in which the notion of alertness is used is closely linked with the fact that alertness, in that work, accounts for the equilibrative character of the market process.

ENTREPRENEURS AND ENTREPRENEURS

Our classificatory schema has not only suggested a variety of different levels at which the economic theory of entrepreneurship can be pursued; it has suggested further that the theorist's analytical conception of entrepreneurship can depend on the level at which the theorist is pursuing his investigation. The flesh-and-blood entrepreneur of everyday encounter is a bundle of complex motivations, potentials, and perceptions. The ways in which his decisions can be tackled by the theorist are correspondingly multiple. Over the centuries, indeed, economists have identified the entrepreneur in a wide variety of different ways:

1. Many economists referred to entrepreneurial activity—at least part of the time—as merely a specific kind of labor service. Thus, some writers (including Say, Mill, and Roscher) see pure entrepreneurial profit as no more than a kind of wage.

2. For many other economists, the essential feature of the entrepreneur is his assuming the risk (or of the Knightian uncertainty) involved in

business ventures. These economists include Cantillon, a pioneer entrepreneurial theorist, as well as Mangoldt, the major nineteenth-century profit theorist, and the prominent U.S. profit theorists F. B. Hawley and Frank Knight.

3. For yet another group of writers, including Say and, of course, Schumpeter, the essence of entrepreneurship is its innovativeness. The Schumpeterian entrepreneur, as we have seen, is an innovator, the initiator of discontinuous change.

4. For some economists, again, the core of the entrepreneur is his location between different markets. The entrepreneur thus serves as a middleman or arbitrageur, buying resources cheaply and selling output more expensively.

5. An important additional view of the entrepreneur is that he is essentially a coordinator, organizer, or gap-filler. An early statement from J. B. Clark along these lines was echoed independently in recent years by T. W. Schultz.

Besides these five quite distinct, major alternative definitions of pure entrepreneurship, a number of other attempts can be found in the literature. Here, the entrepreneur has been seen (among other things) as

6. providing leadership;

7. exercising genuine will;

8. acting as a pure speculator;

9. acting as an employer;

10. acting as a superintendent or manager;

11. acting as a source of information;

12. being especially alert to opportunities as yet overlooked in the market.

A particular writer sometimes appears to endorse more than one definition of the term at the same time. Sometimes the writer wishes to stress that it is this conjunction of several disparate functions that is essential to the entrepreneurial role. In other cases, the writer holds that one attribute of the entrepreneur is implied by a second attribute, and that only the latter attribute is in fact the essential defining characteristic.

Let us turn now to the chapters in this book. From the perspective of the classificatory schema outlined earlier, these chapters have rather different degrees of relevance to entrepreneurial theorizing. We shall take them up, very briefly, in rough order of *increasing* relevance.

ON THE QUESTION OF THE RELEVANCE,
OR BLACKNESS, OF BOXES

Oliver Williamson's exhaustive and fascinating account of organizational innovation provides us with an excitingly plausible transaction-cost framework for understanding the history of organizational change. Unfortunately, it throws little light on the nature or consequences of entrepreneurial endeavor as such. The entrepreneur is not merely an elusive figure in Williamson's paper; he is absent entirely. Instead, there is an impersonal process of organizational change that tends to somehow conform to requirements dictated by transaction-cost efficiencies.

The impressive chapters by Kenneth Arrow and by Jerry Green and John Shoven add valuably to our understanding of the constraints governing the innovative process. They suggest interesting implications for the ways in which the market determines the size of the firms in which innovations are developed and introduced, and how the market selects ideas to be financed. The focus, however, is not on the activity of entrepreneurs, but on the innovative process. The innovative process is, of course, important, and we expect it to offer scope for entrepreneurial activity. However, an understanding of entrepreneurial activity or its implications is not necessarily advanced by analyses of innovative processes from which consideration of entrepreneurial behavior—except perhaps in its most limited sense of maximizing behavior—is virtually excluded from the outset.

Abram Bergson's encyclopedic study of decision making under labor participation presents us with the challenge of considering what the entrepreneurial possibilities are when the enterprise is "labor-managed." Professor Bergson identifies entrepreneurial behavior with risk taking (with some supporting role for innovation). He offers us a thorough account of the Yugoslav institutional environment, together with an imaginative exploration of the way in which the goals of the labor force are likely to be translated into the decisions of the enterprise they manage. However, it is doubtful that this study can help significantly in understanding the springs of entrepreneurial behavior in *any* institutional setting, or the implications of such behavior upon market processes.

William Baumol has given us an elegant and resourceful method of attacking the problem of how to arrive at systematic conclusions about so elusive an entity as entrepreneurship. In so doing, Professor Baumol has put his finger on the "analytic intractability" of entrepreneurship with brilliant precision. No matter what the specific definition one adopts for entrepreneurship, it is inherently not routine—it defies analysis because of its very nature. Baumol, therefore, avoids a futile frontal assault on the problem. Instead, he turns pragmatically to suggest that one might obtain interesting results by considering that the very success of entrepreneurship might create opposition to it, leading to governmental restrictions on the exercise of entrepreneurship. Professor Baumol can certainly extract interesting implications from this ingenious idea. Yet one is left somehow feeling that this model of the entrepreneurial process was made possible only, as it were, by accident (an idea of which Professor Baumol's alertness has enabled him to take full—and altogether legitimate—advantage). The essential features of the entrepreneurial process have not been captured by this model. The blackness of the box labeled "entrepreneurial activity" is so utterly impenetrable that the very label calls forth challenge. How would Professor Baumol's model change, one wonders, if one replaced that label by another reading simply "business"?

Professor Ronen's paper is an enormously ambitious attempt to distill every ounce of information from his in-depth interviews with real, honest-to-goodness, successful entrepreneurs. Ronen has skillfully organized that information so as to focus on just about every possible angle of interest to potential entrepreneurial theorists. Moreover, his notes and references provide a highly useful guide and key to a rapidly expanding literature in economics as well as other disciplines. Yet Ronen's contribution runs into a fundamental conceptual problem. His interviews are with flesh-and-blood entrepreneurs, not with analytical abstractions. Still, one must subject the resulting raw information to some analytical sifting process if we are to focus on the entrepreneurial elements in this information without being distracted by nonessential, nonentrepreneurial trivia and irrelevancies. Therefore, we must begin our absorption of the interview material with some prior theoretical preconceptions. Ronen senses this at a number of points in his paper, but does not appear to be prepared to face up to the problem directly. After all, the definition one wishes to employ for the essence of entrepreneurship must grow out of the level at which one's theory is being pursued and out of the purposes for which one's theory is being envisaged.

THE ECONOMIC THEORY OF ENTREPRENEURSHIP

That the concept of entrepreneurship remains elusive is, after reading these chapters, more apparent than ever. The writer is emboldened, therefore, to offer a suggestion. As was explicitly acknowledged by Professor Baumol (and was implied, at least, in virtually all the chapters in this book), a frontal theoretical attack on entrepreneurial decision making is doomed unless one artificially and unhelpfully straps it to the Procrustean bed of maximization theory. In other words, referring to the fourfold framework developed earlier (and dismissing the first "maximizing" level, for obvious reasons), one is led to abandon all but the third and fourth levels as avenues for theoretical exploration in economics. Perhaps the practitioners of other disciplines can, in their continued work, offer more and more insights into the roots of successful entrepreneurial decision making. But for economists, the most fruitful task is that of pursuing the implications, *within market processes,* of entrepreneurial activity—that is, economists should work at developing theory at the third and fourth levels. The writer believes that consistent work at these levels will continue to prove its value. Despite our reservations concerning the chapters in this book, they, too, contain much of significant help in this regard. We have much reason to be grateful to Professor Ronen and his distinguished collaborators for their courage in pioneering in so difficult an area.

NOTES

1. For a recent collection of papers on entrepreneurship and entrepreneurial research contributed mainly by noneconomists, see Kent, C. A., Sexton, D. L., and Vesper, K. H., *Encyclopedia of Entrepreneurship* (Englewood Cliffs, N.J.: Prentice Hall, 1982).

2. Schumpeter, J. A. *The Theory of Economic Development* (trans. R. Opie), (Cambridge, Mass.: Harvard University Press, 1934), p. 64 note. The first German edition was published in 1911.

3. Schumpeter, J. A. *History of Economic Analysis* (New York: Oxford University Press, 1954), p. 827. See also O'Donnell, L. A., "Rationalism, Capitalism, and the Entrepreneur: The Views of Veblen and Schumpeter." *History of Political Economy* 5 (Spring 1973): 199–214.

4. See Kirzner, I. M., *Competition and Entrepreneurship* (Chicago: University of Chicago Press, 1973); and Kirzner, I. M., *Perception, Opportunity, and Profit: Studies in the Theory of Entrepreneurship* (Chicago: University of Chicago Press, 1979).

One of the leading themes running through modern discussions of the nature of and causes for pure entrepreneurial profit is that of unanticipated market conditions.[1] Ignorance and superior knowledge, uncertainty and prescience, are the ideas, intimately bound up with economic change, that have been linked, in a variety of ways, with the notions of opportunities for pure profit, of pure profit captured, and of pure loss suffered. One aspect of this linkage is the subject of this chapter: the relative places to be accorded to "sheer luck" on the one hand, and to superior "entrepreneurial ability"[2] on the other, in the winning of pure profit.

To be sure, this question of luck versus ability is of importance in discussing most other questions likely to be asked concerning profit. Of the fifteen questions that Professor Shackle asks about profit, and that form the framework for his classification of different possible profit concepts, there are very few, it appears, that do not in some degree turn on this basic issue of luck versus ability.[3] My present focus will, however, be upon this issue itself, except for one other closely related question. This other question is that expressed by Shackle, in his fifth question, when he asks whether or not profit can be "imputed to a factor of production through the marginal productivity of that factor."

The significance of the issues we will be examining extends far beyond the analysis of profit itself. Moreover, we will be concerned with certain apparent paradoxes surrounding pure profit, but the paradoxes relate also to far broader theoretical questions concerning the market process. I have elsewhere been concerned to promote the view of the market that recognizes the central role of the entrepreneur, and especially the uniquely entrepreneurial character of the dynamic processes that make up the market.[4] This view emphasizes as the distinctive aspect of entrepreneurial activity its inability to be compressed within the equilibrium conception of the market. It might then appear that this "entrepreneurial"

Presented at a session of the meetings of the American Economic Association, held at Chicago, August 1978. From *Perception, Opportunity, and Profit: Studies in the Theory of Entrepreneurship* (Chicago and London: University of Chicago Press, 1979), 154–81. © 1979 by The University of Chicago. Reprinted by permission.

view of the market process entails that the relationship between entrepreneurial activity, however defined, and pure profit, be altogether different from that which links a factor of production to its equilibrium, marginal-productivity-determined factor share of output. This entrepreneurial view of the market process appears to suggest, therefore, a strong inclination toward a refusal to see pure profit as able to be captured, regularly and systematically, through some endowed entrepreneurial ability.

But this same entrepreneurial view of the market process can be shown to suggest a precisely opposite inclination. If the market process is to be understood as in any sense systematic, it will surely not do to envisage the activities of the entrepreneurs whose activities are the immediate constituents of each new step in the market process as in principle unconstrained by the realities of the underlying market phenomena. It will not do to imagine entrepreneurial activities being carried on without the conscious aim to capture pure profit opportunities embedded in these realities, or to understand that profit is in fact won not by deliberate intent, but by sheer luck. So that the entrepreneurial view of the market process seems to imply a strong inclination toward recognizing entrepreneurial ability as a unique talent systematically capable of locating and pursuing pure profit opportunities.

It is with the paradoxical flavor of these reflections in mind that we take up our inquiry. We shall discover, as it turns out, that this paradoxical flavor is inherent in the very notion of entrepreneurial profit, properly understood. So that, far from being disconcerted by these paradoxical reflections, we shall find ourselves enjoying deeper and clearer insight into the nature of entrepreneurship and of entrepreneurial profit.

SOME ELEMENTARY THOUGHTS CONCERNING PROFIT

It will be helpful, in pursuing our inquiry, to keep firmly in mind certain elementary and well-understood ideas on profit. These will serve to direct our inquiry at the very same time that they might appear to deepen the paradoxical flavor of the foregoing paragraphs.

1. *With complete knowledge, pure profit is impossible.* Suppose item a can be sold to consumers at a price r, while this same item a can be purchased or produced by the seller at a cost s (with $s<r$), when s includes all outlays needed to make a available to consumers. Under these conditions we must, it is obvious, be supposing less than perfect knowledge. Were those selling a at the total cost s (or those selling the inputs the sum of

the costs of which are s) aware that other buyers are prepared to pay r (with $r<s$) for a, they would not be selling for as little as s. Again, were those buying at the high price r aware that they could themselves obtain a for a lower price s (with s covering all needed outlays), it is clear that they would not be buying at the higher r price. The opportunity for and the realization of pure profit rests, it is evident, upon imperfect knowledge.

2. *Pure profit tends to be ground down to zero by competition.* Where in fact some entrepreneurs are buying a (or the input services needed to produce and deliver a) at a price below that at which they are selling a, this profit situation will attract other entrepreneurs whose competition will tend both to raise the low cost of acquiring a, and to lower the high price obtained from the final buyers, until the price differential is eliminated. It is upon this insight—that pure profits provide the incentive for market action that results in the elimination of profit—upon which economics depend for Jevons's Law of Indifference. It is upon this insight that economists rely for their understanding of the universal tendency for the "value of the original means of production to attach itself with the faithfulness of a shadow to the value of the product."[5]

In other words, pure profit is the link between imperfect and perfect knowledge: *on one hand, it is generated by ignorance; on the other, it provides the incentive for realizing the truth.* One who has captured profits has acted in accordance with realities that the market had hitherto failed to recognize. His profit has been won by breaking away from the ignorance that previously prevailed as conventional wisdom. As entrepreneurs attracted by the profits so obtained move to take advantage of their availability, the market in general comes to be pulled and nudged to take proper account of the underlying, and hitherto overlooked, realities.

PROFITS AND THE LAW OF INDIFFERENCE

It is clear, then, that a pure profit possibility can exist only because, and to the extent that, full conformity with the Law of Indifference has not yet been attained. Jevons stated his Law of Indifference as asserting that "in the same open market, at any one moment, there cannot be two prices for the same kind of article."[6] This statement refers, of course, to the state of equilibrium; during the market process tending to generate this equilibrium state, two prices for the same article may indeed exist, and it is the difference between them that is pure profit. Moreover, Jevons stated his Law only in the context of the "same kind of article." But the reasoning upon which Jevons's Law rests clearly applies with equal force to any goods, however physically dissimilar they may be, which the market considers to be completely equivalent. Thus, in particular, if a complex of productive services can together suffice to generate a produced commodity, then economists rely upon an extension of the law of indifference when they assert a tendency for the sum of input prices to equal the price of output.

Thus pure profit of *any* kind can exist only while the tendency toward the fulfillment of Jevons's Law of Indifference, broadly interpreted, has not yet been completed. And, again, it is upon the tendency for pure profit to be eliminated by competition that the tendency toward the fulfillment of Jevons's Law itself depends. The question whether entrepreneurial profit is to be attributed to pure luck or to a special kind of ability turns out, then, to concern the way it is discovered that the market has placed inconsistent valuations upon different samples of what, broadly conceived, amount to the same good. Should we argue that such discovery of inconsistent market valuations is indeed a matter of pure luck, then the immediate question would raise the difficulty of asserting a tendency toward the fulfillment of Jevons's Law that relies on pure luck for its systematic achievement. On the other hand, should pure profit be seen as the market-determined reward for the exercise of the special ability of discovering inconsistent market valuations, then it seems we will have painted ourselves, once again, into that uncomfortable equilibrium corner from which we had hoped to be freed by recognizing the entrepreneurial character of market processes.

THE INDIVIDUAL AS ENTREPRENEUR

I contend that considerable light can be thrown on these issues by careful analysis of the insight that, in an important sense, each human decision is an entrepreneurial decision. "In any real and living economy," Mises remarked, "every actor is always an entrepreneur."[7] The entrepreneurial element in human action, one may argue,[8] is that element in individual decision making that cannot be pressed into the standard "maximizing" model of the decision. So long as one views the human decision as consisting only in working out the mathematical solution to the problem of allocating *given* scarce means among a multiplicity of ends, each of given relative importance, one has assumed away the entrepreneurial element in human action. To see the individual as entrepreneur one must—as

Mises did—see the decision as encompassing also *the very identification of the ends-means configuration itself,* within which action is being conducted.

We shall discover that analysis of individual "entrepreneurship," exercised in situations to which the possibility of winning pure entrepreneurial profits *in the market* is irrelevant, will be helpful in organizing our thinking about the role of entrepreneurs in markets. Let us then consider a series of different cases of economic gain, each of which does not depend on *market* opportunities, and determine for ourselves which, if any, of them constitute a "pure profit" that may be associated with the Misesian element of entrepreneurship asserted to be present in all individual action.

INDIVIDUAL GAIN AND PURE (CRUSONIAN) PROFIT

1. Robinson Crusoe has a tree. Without action on his part, the tree yields fruit. Crusoe, who had in the beginning owned only the tree, now has both the tree and the fruit. Crusoe may appear to have "gained" fruit, but clearly this kind of gain has nothing to do with entrepreneurship. In fact, if the yield was correctly anticipated, Crusoe already valued his tree to reflect the full value of the expected fruit. When the fruit finally emerges, then, nothing new has been gained (abstracting, for the present purposes, from all time-preference considerations). Most important, since the fruit is forthcoming without Crusoe's action or decision, it cannot be linked to any entrepreneurial aspects of Crusoe's actions. The unfolding of fully anticipated sequences of events offers nothing new; fully anticipated income derived automatically from capital possessed does not bear the character of entrepreneurial profit. If, on the other hand, the yield was *not* anticipated, then the case belongs to the broader class of cases to be discussed in the next paragraph.

2. Crusoe does not own any tree or, if he owns one, does not realize its fruit-bearing properties, but is suddenly presented by nature with fruit without having undertaken any actions to produce or secure the fruit. This is a windfall gain. Because this gain did not result from any action on his part, this too cannot be linked with any entrepreneurial element in Crusoe's personality. Crusoe has received an unexpected gift from nature; that is all. (A special case belonging under this heading of windfall gain is that in which Crusoe undertakes an action—for example, climbing a tree to look far out to sea—without realizing at all that his action will yield him fruit. Then, even though the gained fruit must be seen as caused by

Crusoe's action, it nonetheless clearly still represents, from Crusoe's own perspective, an unexpected gift from nature; no element of entrepreneurial profit is present.)

3. Crusoe has become aware of the certain opportunity to convert a lesser-valued good into a more highly valued good. He can, let us fancifully say, turn one apple into two apples by a costless wave of the hand, or—more plausibly—he can, by laboring in his apple orchard, convert hours of time, valued cheaply at their worth as leisure, into bushels of highly valued apples. If the possibilities of conversion are indeed assured without shadow of doubt, then no entrepreneurial profit is to be discovered in this kind of case. The efficient deployment of means to achieve given ends is simply a matter of maximizing; it calls for nothing entrepreneurial in Crusoe's character. Indeed, Crusoe will tend to value means so as to reflect precisely the value of the ends to which they are sure to lead. If low-valued means can produce high-valued ends, this itself—as Menger showed so forcefully over a century ago—transforms the low-valued means immediately into high-valued means. If one apple were to be able to produce two apples without delay, then the value attached to any one apple would be that attached to the infinite progeny of apples that each apple can thus instantaneously generate. Precisely because there is no entrepreneurial aspect to Crusoe's strictly allocative decision, that is, because the results aimed at are believed to be completely within reach, the value of the means already fully anticipates the value of the end—leaving no scope at all for any profit differential.

4. A case that to some extent overlaps the preceding one is the following. Crusoe finds himself confronted with the necessity to choose between two packages, one containing a single apple, the second containing two apples. (This case thus differs from the preceding case in that no *physical conversion* of a lower-value package into the more highly valued package is considered here. The preceding case can therefore be reduced to an example of the present case by abstracting from the physical conversion central to the preceding case—for example, by seeing the decision to labor in order to produce apples as simply a choice between one package, of leisure, and a second package containing apples.)

Since we may assume that Crusoe will prefer two apples over one apple, he will of course grasp the two-apple package and is thus better off by one apple than he would have been if he had taken the one-apple package. It might then be argued that this one-apple margin is a gain of sorts.

By rejecting the opportunity of enjoying one apple, at the economic cost of one apple, Crusoe is able to enjoy two apples. Crusoe's decision might therefore be described as a profitable decision, yielding two through the sacrifice of only one. But reflection should convince one that no element of entrepreneurial profit is present in this case. Once Crusoe's preference ranking of two apples over one has been accepted as a datum, the decision to select the higher-ranked package is nothing more than a mechanical exercise, calling for no entrepreneurial element at all. And, as we shall see, there is nothing here that might represent a margin of profit generated by inconsistent valuations of the same item. Since in this case there is no conversion of means into ends, there can be no question of the value of means being lower than that of the ends. There is simply one package of lower-valued ends, and a different package of higher-valued ends; this offers no scope for profit.

None of the cases we have considered have qualified as examples of a gain captured by individual entrepreneurship. Where, as in case 2, what was gained was not aimed for, it was certainly not captured; it fell into Crusoe's lap. Where, as in case 3, what was gained had been anticipated with complete confidence and certainty, its capture called for no exercise of entrepreneurial imagination, initiative, or determination. Reflection showed that the other cases considered represent examples of gain—if indeed they display any element of gain—that would be inevitably enjoyed by beings endowed with no entrepreneurial potential at all.

To see how the individual human agent wins entrepreneurial profits, in the Crusoe context, we must introduce the possibility of *erroneous valuation*. Crusoe spends his time uneconomically catching fish, we are told in elementary economics, with his bare hands. One day he begins a net-making or boat-building undertaking. Textbooks focus on the saving-investment aspects of this process of roundabout production. But let us ask why Crusoe begins to build his boat today rather than yesterday, assuming no change in accumulated capital since yesterday. The answer must surely be that it is only today that Crusoe has persuaded himself that building a boat is a better use of his time than catching fish. Nothing has changed since yesterday except that Crusoe has discovered that his time is more valuably spent in building the boat than in catching fish. He has discovered that he had placed an incorrectly low value on his time. His reallocation of his labor time from fishing to boat-building is an entrepreneurial decision, and, assuming his decision to be a correct one, yields pure profit in the form of the additional value discovered to be forthcoming from the labor time applied. This pure profit is not a windfall gain but was deliberately captured. Nor, as in case 3 cited above, was it a gain that could have been captured without the exercise of entrepreneurial alertness. A mechanical, economizing Crusoe who maximized his welfare yesterday, as far as he knew, by allocating his labor time, as he had done since time immemorial, to catching fish with his hands cannot, ceteris paribus, be imagined to do anything different today. To take notice of the possibility that yesterday's welfare maximization be seen today as being a misallocation, one must introduce the possibility of error and of its entrepreneurial discovery.

INDIVIDUAL PROFIT AND MENGER'S LAW

Much of what has been considered in the preceding section can be usefully restated in terms of an insight that we owe chiefly to Carl Menger. Perhaps the central idea running through Menger's *Grundsätze* is that men value goods according to the value of the satisfactions that depend on possession of those goods. More generally, Menger's Law—as we may call this insight—draws attention to man's propensity *to attach the value of ends to the means* needed for their achievement. It is Menger's Law that, in a definite sense, is responsible for the absence of scope for entrepreneurial profit in many of the cases—particularly case 3—discussed in the preceding section. Since the value of ends comes to be attached to means, it follows that, so long as the law operates, no gain in value can be obtained in the course of successful achievement of goals through appropriate deployment of means.

But, clearly, Menger's Law operates only within the context of a given perceived framework of ends and means. During the process by which acting man arrives at his awareness of the ends-means framework within which he is operating, there may be ample scope for the reevaluation of means. It is only after one has settled down to a definite perception of the ends-means environment that Menger's Law comes fully and finally into its own. When Crusoe discovers that his time may be more valuably spent in boat-building than in fishing, he has discovered that the ends achievable with his time have higher value than the ends he had previously sought to achieve. Since Crusoe had valued his means (time) at the lower value of those earlier ends, his new allocation of his time to more valuable goals signifies that Menger's Law is *violated at the instant of entrepreneurial discovery*. The value Crusoe has until now attached to his time is *less* than the value of the ends he now seeks.[9] This discrepancy is, at the level of the individual, pure profit. "The difference between the value of the end attained and that of the means applied for its attainment is profit."[10] To be sure, the very entrepreneurial act of reallocating time for fishing to boat-building implies the reevaluation of the time itself. Once the old ends-means framework has been completely and unquestionably replaced by the new one, of course, it is the value of the new ends that Crusoe comes to attach to his means; Menger's Law ensures this. But, during the instant of an entrepreneurial leap of faith, the instant of daring the new line of production, there is scope for the discovery that, indeed, the ends achieved are more valuable than had hitherto been suspected. *This* is the discovery of pure (Crusonian) entrepreneurial profit.

Although reference has been made to the *instant* of entrepreneurial discovery, it should be clear that in many cases the transition from an old accepted ends-means framework to reasonable confidence in the relevance of a new framework may be far from instantaneous. Thus the final discovery that Crusoe's time is indeed more valuable than hitherto suspected may come with assurance only long after the instant of the initial entrepreneurial decision to switch production. Indeed, during the time when Crusoe's entrepreneurial judgment is being vindicated, Crusoe may come to hold entirely new views concerning the future. So that *each one of his actions* will be taken entrepreneurially; that is, *at no time* will Crusoe have yet fully and confidently adjusted his valuation of means to the ends aimed at by his actions. Individual profit may be a continual phenomenon; Menger's Law may in fact never hold completely; it may represent nothing more than a tendency.

CRUSONIAN PROFIT, ENTREPRENEURSHIP, AND KNOWLEDGE

In considering his actions, whether prospectively or in retrospect, man is very much concerned with the precise relationship between means and ends. He searches for an understanding of how means combine to achieve ends. He seeks to attribute results to causes. It is upon this attribution that, prospectively, he depends, according to Menger's Law, for his valuation of resources. Unless, as in case 2, he has received a gift from nature, Crusoe attributes his consumption enjoyment to his own actions in deploying definite resources that were at his disposal. To what, one may ask, should Crusoe attribute that portion of his successfully achieved ends that corresponds to entrepreneurial profit?

Notice that while Crusoe will in one sense indeed, quite correctly, attribute the results achieved to the physical resources technologically responsible for them, there is another sense in which he may well feel that such attribution will be less than completely justified. Crusoe will, after all, be well aware that, until the moment when he decided to give up fishing to build his boat, the same resources would in fact *not* have yielded the boat. Clearly, to attribute the boat entirely to these resources is to overlook some vital ingredient, other than the services of Crusoe's unchanged physical resources, without which the boat would not have been forthcoming. What is this other ingredient? At first glance this ingredient might appear to be Crusoe's *knowledge*. Before he realized (knew) the possibility and productivity of boat-building, Crusoe lacked the essential ingredient needed to build his boat. After somehow acquiring the relevant knowledge, Crusoe finds himself in a position to build his boat. He may then attribute his boat—and the superior catch of fish the boat eventually makes possible—not only to the physical resources that go into boat-building, but also in part to the information on boat-building technology and on boat productivity in catching fish upon which he based his decision to change his plan of production.[11]

Moreover, our understanding of the way Crusoe's knowledge may be seen as an essential ingredient in the complex of resources that produced the boat raises a fundamental difficulty for our notion of Crusonian profit. Earlier, we ruled out, as possible examples of pure Crusonian profit, cases in which Crusoe's gain was a simple gift from nature, and also cases in which grasping the gain involved no entrepreneurial judgment or imagination. We ruled out both windfall gains and gains achieved through mechanical resource allocation under certainty. We found true profit only in the case where Crusoe spontaneously discovered a new, superior use for his resources. But, if Crusoe's knowledge is seen as a genuine resource, then it must surely appear that we are, by this very insight, forced to surrender our example of Crusonian profit.

For it must surely appear that, once Crusoe has in fact arrived at his new knowledge, his use of the knowledge in the form of building a boat differs in no respect from his use of the other (physical) resources that went into the boat. So that one might argue that Crusoe's transition from catching fish manually to building his boat came in two separate stages, *each of which fails to display an example of pure profit.* First, one may point out, Crusoe enjoyed a windfall gain in the form of the acquisition (by gift from nature) of a new resource, namely the information, knowledge, and vision needed to build his boat. Second, once having acquired this valuable resource, Crusoe proceeds to put it to deliberate use (in exactly the same way as he deploys his physical resources) in boat-building. The first of these two steps, being the result of no deliberate action on his part, provided, like all cases of windfall gain, no example of profit. The second step, though a deliberate act on his part, was so deliberate as once again to rule out profit. The higher value of the superior catch made possible by the boat is then simply to be attributed to the new knowledge Crusoe now possesses. This higher output value appears, then, to correspond simply to the true Mengerian value of the resources responsible for it at the margin. Without these knowledge resources, output would have been smaller. With the knowledge, output is larger. The knowledge itself was acquired by sheer luck, a windfall gain. No profit seems to be present at any stage of this fish story after all.

The truth is that the difficulty, for the identification of pure Crusonian profit, discussed in the preceding paragraphs offers, in fact, a valuable opportunity to clarify the entire notion of pure profit. The difficulty is only an apparent one. A discussion of the source of this apparent difficulty can be most helpful in further elucidating the highly elusive and subtle profit concept.

Let us notice that our difficulty arose entirely out of the two stages into which we analyzed the Crusoe boat-building example. And, indeed, if it were always possible, without doing violence to the very nature of the case, to distinguish sharply between Crusoe's acquisition of his new knowledge, and his deliberate deployment of that knowledge, our problem would be insoluble. Crusonian profit would have disappeared.

But such a dissection is not possible without destroying the essence of the situation under analysis. Neither chronologically nor logically may we, in general, separate the deliberate action Crusoe undertakes from the entrepreneurial vision that inspires that action. This assertion requires us to review briefly the notion of human action and its relationship to mechanical maximization (allocation).[12]

It was Lord Robbins[13] who made modern economists familiar with the notion of the allocation of given scarce means among given competing ends. Since, in this concept of Robbinsian economizing—or, in subsequent parlance, maximizing—both ends and means are given, it is clear that the activity of economizing arises only *after* that extra-Robbinsian process has been completed during which ends and means have come to be identified and perceived. In the activity of economizing itself, therefore, there can be no room for flashes of discovery, for sudden illuminations of insight, or realization, or of awareness. While the Robbinsian framework does not preclude a later discovery that the given ends-means framework is incorrect and must be replaced, this process of the discovery of error itself occurs, somehow, *outside* the Robbinsian human laboratory.[14]

Contrasted with this concept of Robbinsian economizing is that of human action, a concept we owe to Mises.[15] The notion of Misesian human action sees the human decision as essentially "entrepreneurial"—that is, *inseparably combining* the allocation aspect of action with the entrepreneurial vision and imagination that inspires action. As Lachmann appears to suggest, this Misesian view of the human decision has much in common with the work of Shackle.[16] In this view, to analyze action purely in terms of maximization-allocation techniques is to rob human decision making of something essential to it. From this Mises-Shackle viewpoint, the notion of purely maximizing activity is at best a limiting case, describing a hypothetical situation from which *all* Knightian uncertainty is imagined to have been exhausted. But human action never does occur in such a vacuum. The analysis of human action must therefore recognize that its allocative aspects express only one side of the human decision. Entrepreneurial vision permeates and suffuses all human action; allocation is itself *embedded* in entrepreneurial vision, initiative, and determination.

From this perspective, Crusoe's action in quitting manual fishing and transferring his labor to boat-building, must be seen as embodying, simultaneously and in an inextricably intertwined manner, both the element of deliberately exploiting an available opportunity and the element of permitting himself, in undeliberate fashion, to follow his entrepreneurial hunch. In following this hunch, rather than sticking to yesterday's time-honored groove, Crusoe may, if his hunch is correct, capture results that were hitherto beyond his reach. To impute this gain simply to his deliberate action—identifying, as a resource within his possession, his vision of the future—is to do violence to Crusoe's decision. The gain he wins is to be linked, surely, with that undeliberate adoption by

Crusoe, at the instant of decision making, *not* chronologically before that moment, of the entrepreneurial hunch responsible for his success. In this sense it is quite true that pure Crusonian profit cannot be wholly separated from the element of sheer good fortune. Crusoe's adoption of his hunch is not to be explained as the calculated position taken by the deliberate maximizer-economizer. Crusoe cannot take credit for having correctly calculated his view of the future course of events.[17] But, again, this admittedly undeliberate element in Crusoe's adoption of the fortunate hunch does not qualify the capture of the resulting gain as a windfall gift from nature. A windfall gift occurs when Crusoe gains something without lifting a finger toward it. In our case, Crusoe gains the superior catch, made possible by his boat, because he *acted on his hunch*. Crusonian profit emerges as the result of human action, that is, of deliberate planning to implement the entrepreneurial hunch adopted only at the very instant of action itself.

Menger's Law, as we have called it, operates continually toward wiping out pure Crusonian profit. As the outcome of Crusoe's actions vindicates the hunches on which they were based, Crusoe comes to view these hunches less and less as daring, innovative guesses about an uncertain future, and more and more as the settled knowledge concerning a stable environment. Crusoe's actions, in continuing to exploit his now-established knowledge of his environment, express less and less the entrepreneurial element present in all human action and come more and more to resemble those limiting cases of deliberate action (in the face of *given* ends and means) discussed by Robbins. The results Crusoe continues to enjoy—more fish caught per day—partake less and less of the character of pure Crusonian profit and more and more of that of the deliberately exploited opportunity in a hypothetical world without change and uncertainty.

INFORMATION, HUNCHES, LUCK, AND ABILITY

Our discussion permits us to make some further observations concerning Crusonian entrepreneurship that, like the entire analysis of Crusonian entrepreneurship and profit, will be most helpful in our later analysis of entrepreneurship and profit in the *market* context.

We notice, first, that whether or not Crusoe views his knowledge as simply another resource that must be deployed to achieve a result depends on the degree to which he sees that knowledge as settled or as uncertain information. A piece of technological information about boat-building, about whose correctness Crusoe has no doubts at all, will not be seen as a hunch and will be valued according to Menger's Law.[18] It may be said that Crusoe is well aware that he possesses this kind of information; he will deploy and value it in the same way as he may be imagined to deploy and value other resources he believes are definitely at his disposal. But concerning Crusoe's hunches and his visions in the face of a changing, uncertain environment, it cannot be said at all that Crusoe knows he has a hunch or a vision of the future. He does not act by deliberately utilizing his hunch about the future; instead, he finds that his actions reflect his hunches. One who possesses lumber and potential labor time may decide to build a boat with them. It is his hunch about the future that inspires this decision; his hunch is *never* an *ingredient* involved in the deliberations that control action. One does not decide to use or not use one's hunches concerning the exploitation of a pure profit possibility; after all, to decide not to use a hunch would reveal that the hunch simply did not exist. One does not refrain from exploiting a truly perceived opportunity for pure gain.

In other words, it turns out, the essence of entrepreneurial vision, and what sets it apart from knowledge as a resource, is reflected in Crusoe's lack of self-consciousness concerning it. Crusoe does not "know" that he possesses a particular vision, in the sense of being aware that that vision is at his disposal to be used or not. To be sure, Crusoe may, as we have seen, gradually come to be aware of his vision. When he does, that vision ceases to be entrepreneurial and comes to be a resource. Moreover Crusoe's *realization* that he possesses this definite information resource may *itself* be entrepreneurial. As soon as he "knows" that he possesses an item of knowledge, *that* item of knowledge ceases to correspond to entrepreneurial vision; instead, as with all resources, it is Crusoe's belief that he has the resources at his disposal that may now constitute his entrepreneurial hunch.

Further, the element of sheer good fortune we have noticed in Crusonian entrepreneurship should not be misunderstood and should not be emphasized out of proportion. It is true that Crusoe does not arrive at his view of the world merely by deliberate calculation of the solution to a mathematical problem. It is true that we know far too little about the forces—cultural, sociological, or psychological—that go to shape the world view, the entrepreneurial vision, and the awareness of any given individual. But we do know that all human beings—albeit in varying degrees—come to entertain views about their environment and about their future that are not wholly out of line with the facts as they subsequently unfold. Entrepreneurial vision may not be arrived at deliberately, rationally, but neither is it arrived at purely by chance. In fact, as I have argued elsewhere, it is an implication of the purposefulness of human action that tends to ensure, in some degree, that opportunities come to be noticed.[19]

It is not to be denied that different individuals appear to differ in the successfulness with which they become aware of the opportunities available to them. Certainly insofar as Crusoe has been blessed with an alert temperament, he must attribute much of the success in his hunches to his good fortune in enjoying such a temperament. On the other hand, Crusoe's awareness of his temperament will not constitute awareness of a resource at his disposal waiting to be deployed. As we have seen, Crusoe is never aware that he possesses specific entrepreneurial insights.

It follows that while Crusoe's successful entrepreneurial decisions incorporate deliberate action on his part, they also reflect fortunate entrepreneurial hunches, for which he can claim no credit; and yet Crusoe's success is nonetheless far more than sheer luck. The superficially paradoxical flavor of this conclusion mirrors, of course, the paradoxes raised at the outset. Our discussions concerning Crusonian entrepreneurship have, I hope, adequately explored the paradox at Crusoe's level. We are now in a position to transfer our insights into entrepreneurship from the individual to the market. Before doing so, it may be useful to summarize some of our conclusions concerning Crusonian entrepreneurial decisions. I do so by asserting the following propositions:

ENTREPRENEURSHIP: THE CRUSOE CONTEXT

1. The Robbinsian economizing-allocation-maximizing view of the decision is a construct that excludes the entrepreneurial aspect of human action.

2. Real human action, however, in a world of uncertainty, is never purely Robbinsian; every action incorporates, to some degree, the entrepreneurial element.

3. In the limiting case of pure Robbinsian maximizing decision making, Menger's Law operates fully. No element of value in the results of action remains unimputed to the resources deployed. No Crusonian profit is therefore possible.

4. Because Crusonian entrepreneurship occurs against a background of uncertainty, change, and error, Menger's Law is unlikely to hold completely at any given time. Crusoe, while deciding entrepreneurially to deploy resources toward a hoped-for new result, will not yet have fully valued the resources according to that still very uncertain result. Pure Crusonian profit is present here.

5. The entrepreneurial vision that inspires Crusoe's action is not to be credited to Crusoe's present or earlier success in Robbinsian calculation. The element of sheer good fortune in entrepreneurial success may enter here.

6. Crusoe does not, in the course of making his entrepreneurial decision, consider the entrepreneurial vision that inspires his action as a resource available for deployment. He does not know that he possesses entrepreneurial knowledge.

7. Consequently, Crusoe does not, as would be required by Menger's Law were Crusoe to have regarded his vision as a deployable resource, attach a marginal productivity valuation to his possession of that vision.

8. As experience confirms Crusoe's entrepreneurial hunches, these hunches tend to be viewed as deployable resources; Menger's Law tends to come into fuller application, thus continually grinding away at Crusonian profit, which profit is continually re-created as Crusoe grapples with the possibilities generated by the emergence of continually fresh opportunities.

9. Crusonian profit emerges when Crusoe attaches dual valuations to economically identical or equivalent items, most especially attaching a lower value to a bundle of resources than to the results they are to produce.

10. At any given moment, Crusoe is unaware of the opportunities he is overlooking. Just as Crusoe does not know that he possesses entrepreneurial vision (see point 6), so Crusoe is not aware that he is ignorant of the opportunities he fails to exploit.[20]

11. From the point of view of superior entrepreneurial insight, the wrong decision will appear, in the Robbinsian sense, as an inefficient misallocation of resources.

12. The tendency of purposeful human beings to become aware of available opportunities tends, with greater or lesser rapidity, to eliminate misallocation, error, violations of Menger's Law, and the occurrence of possibilities for pure Crusonian profit (and see point 8).

INDIVIDUAL AND MARKET: THE PARALLELISM

Although we have pursued at some length the Misesian insight that individual human action is entrepreneurial in character, our real purpose in doing so was to shed light on more conventional interpretations of the notion of entrepreneurship. In economics, the term entrepreneur is generally understood, of course, to refer not to an aspect of all human decisions, but rather to a special analytical or actual market role. The entrepreneur is the one who buys in one market in order to resell, possibly at a considerably later date, in a second market. Entrepreneurial profit occurs when the price paid for an item in the first market is lower than that received in the second market. Where the entrepreneur-producer buys resource services and sells their product, we see him as having bought at a low price in one market something that can, without further effort of inputs of any kind, be translated into the output sold at a higher price in a second market.

We shall argue that there is a remarkable parallelism between the entrepreneurial element in individual action, and the role of the entrepreneur in the market.[21] In fact, as we shall discover, each of the twelve summary propositions regarding Crusonian entrepreneurship has its exact counterpart proposition with respect to the market. To perceive this, it will be helpful, as preliminary, to draw attention to certain key ideas at the level of the market that correspond to similar key ideas at the level of individual human action.

1. Corresponding to Robbinsian economizing at the level of the individual, we have market general equilibrium. At both the individual and the market levels, the key idea here is perfect coordination. Robbinsian allocation coordinates activities directed at a variety of goals so as to fit them into a single overall pattern imposed by the given hierarchy of ends. General equilibrium in the market depends on the successful coordination of all individual market activities so that no single plan need fail to be carried out.

2. Corresponding to what we have called Menger's Law at the level of the individual, we have Jevons's Law of Indifference in the market. Menger's Law tends to ensure that means come to be valued by the individual according to the ends they serve. The Law of Indifference tends to ensure that the market prices for resources reflect accurately and fully the prices of the outputs these resources produce.

3. Corresponding to Crusonian profit at the level of the individual, in markets we have profits made possible by price differentials for the same, or economically equivalent, items.

4. Error, in the case of Crusoe, means overlooking available production or consumption opportunities. At the level of the market, error means, at least in its most superficial sense, that some market participants are buying (selling) at prices higher (lower) than the prices at which others are in fact buying (selling). Price differentials are evidence of market error.

With these correspondences in mind, let us now simply restate each of the twelve propositions in a form that will relate them directly to market rather than to individual situations.

ENTREPRENEURSHIP: THE MARKET CONTEXT

1°. The model of general market equilibrium is a construct that excludes any possibility for market entrepreneurship.

2°. Real markets, however, are never equilibrium markets; every market incorporates entrepreneurial activity.

3°. In the limiting cases of general equilibrium, the Law of Indifference operates fully. No resource complex sells at a price less than the full value of its output. No entrepreneurial profit is possible.

4°. Because markets are not, in fact, in general equilibrium, the Law of Indifference is unlikely to hold completely at any given time. The market will not, at a given moment, have fully valued all units of resources at the value of output these resources are able to yield. Opportunity for pure entrepreneurial (market) profit exists.

5°. The superior entrepreneurial vision, alertness, and drive that inspires the capture of market profits has not (as have, for example, produced means of production, or other resources) been deliberately supplied in the market in response to market demand.

6°. The market has not, in fact, in any given case of market profit, recognized either the very existence of or the need for these qualities of vision, alertness, and drive. Were the market to have recognized the need for and the availability of these qualities, the market would have treated these qualities as simple factor services, in a manner fully consistent with general equilibrium. Services that have been hired, must be presumed not to be entrepreneurial.

7°. The market does not, therefore, attach marginal productivity prices to the uniquely entrepreneurial human qualities able to spot gaps in the fabric of market prices. Profits are not a factor income.

8°. As successful market entrepreneurship reveals the disequilibrium in market prices, prices are pushed toward the general equilibrium pattern; the Law of Indifference tends to come into fuller application, grinding away at pure entrepreneurial (market) profits. On the other hand, in a continually changing world, disequilibrium continually reasserts itself, creating anew a continual series of price differentials, with consequent pure profit possibilities.

9°. Market entrepreneurial profits emerge when the market displays more than a single price for the same or economically equivalent items, especially when the market values a complex of resources at a sum below what the market is paying for what these resources can produce.

10°. During disequilibrium there is no market demand for the entrepreneurial qualities needed to spot and eliminate pure price differentials. Were the market to know that such a need existed and how it could be filled, it would already have wiped out those price differentials. (See also point 6°.)

11°. From the perspective of the model of full general market equilibrium, the disequilibrium market may be seen as falling short of fulfilling some postulated relevant social norm. For example, the disequilibrium market may be seen as having erroneously failed to achieve fuller coordination among the preferences of market participants. Or, less precisely, the disequilibrium market may, from the perspective of Pareto optimality, be judged as "misallocating" social resources.

12°. The powerful tendency of the market to discover and eliminate unjustified price differentials tends continually to eliminate the market errors (mentioned in point 11°), departures from compliance with the Law of Indifference, and the possibilities for winning pure entrepreneurial profits in the market (and see point 8°).

MORE ON MARKET ENTREPRENEURSHIP
AND INDIVIDUAL ENTREPRENEURSHIP

The preceding sections have emphasized the remarkable parallel between the element of entrepreneurship as exercised within the framework of strictly individual human action and entrepreneurship as it manifests itself as a specifically market phenomenon. This parallel raises the following question: To what extent, if any, is it necessary, for the exercise of entrepreneurship (in the *market* sense) and for the capture of entrepreneurial profits (again in the market sense), to depend on the entrepreneurial element in *individual* human action? This question deserves some elaboration; and, as is so often the case, such elaboration will help considerably in arriving at the answer to our question.

We have seen that scope for market entrepreneurship is created by the conditions of market disequilibrium, conditions that consist in the emergence of more than one price for identical, or economically equivalent, items. Entrepreneurs are attracted into the market by the pure profit opportunities reflected in such price discrepancies; they tend to buy where the price is low and sell where the price is high, initiating forces that tend to drive prices together. We inquire whether the economic decision making these market entrepreneurs engage in must necessarily display, in an essential way, those entrepreneurial aspects of all human action to which so much of this chapter has (following the hint of Mises) been devoted. We know that microeconomics has, in its standard presentation, abstracted from the Misesian, entrepreneurial element in individual decision making. A good deal of microeconomics has attempted to imagine a market consisting entirely of Robbinsian maximizers. What we ask is whether this kind of abstraction necessarily fails to come to grips with the phenomenon of market entrepreneurship. A positive answer to this question would mean that the phenomenon of market entrepreneurship is not merely *parallel* to the entrepreneurial element in individual action, but in fact depends on the latter element for its own existence.

The grounds for thinking that perhaps market entrepreneurship *does* so depend on the entrepreneurial element in individual decision making are fairly easy to see. The opportunity for the exercise of market entrepreneurship, specifically the presence of two market prices for equivalent items, reflects the erroneous expectations of market participants. Were market participants to have anticipated the price discrepancy, it would already have been grasped at by eager profit-seekers, whose competition would soon have eliminated it. For market participants to replace an erroneous perception of market prices by a more correct one, one must depend, surely, on their capacity to become aware of the errors in their earlier perceptions. One must, that is, depend on something other than man's propensity to maximize and to allocate against the background of given perceptions; one must depend on the entrepreneurial aspect of individual human action—on man's capacity to become alerted to changed conditions. Certainly our understanding of man's entrepreneurial potential enables us to understand the systematic process by which the market operates through entrepreneurs' continual grasping of opportunities for market profit.[22] But it is not quite enough to show that the entrepreneurial element in individual human action may be sufficient to generate examples of market entrepreneurship; we must still ask whether this element is necessary for this purpose. Perhaps market entrepreneurship may occur without special dependence on the entrepreneurial aspect of human action? Two possibilities may be considered.

1. Let us take up the first possibility that a market participant has somehow already become aware with certainty of the existence of a price discrepancy, of the opportunity to grasp pure profit. Any subsequent action by him to grasp the profit opportunity would not be considered entrepreneurial. Since his action consists simply in grasping an *already* perceived opportunity, it would fit entirely into the Robbinsian model of maximizing man. And yet, from the market perspective, his activity would be truly entrepreneurial, consisting in taking advantage of the multiple-price situation created by the errors of others.

This possibility cannot be dissolved merely by pointing out that from the Mises-Shackle viewpoint the very notion of man acting without any element of entrepreneurship is ruled out, so that even one "convinced" of the existence of a price differential must be seen as being sufficiently uncertain about his convictions, at least, to render his profit-grasping action entrepreneurial in the Crusoe sense. This way of treating this possibility will not do because the question raised inquires whether market entrepreneurship depends *in an essential way* upon the individual entrepreneurial element. Showing that the possibility here considered does find room for such an element does not yet convince us that this element is essential to the market entrepreneurship the possibility sets forth.

But this possibility can surely not be sustained. Let us consider the market participant at the instant of his arbitrage. We must ask why he has not undertaken this profitable activity earlier, since we were told that, even before his profit-grasping action, our participant had become certain that it was worthwhile.[23] The only explanation must be that our participant was, up to the present, *not* completely convinced of the profitability of the situation. The possibility cannot, then, be considered valid. Entrepreneurial activity in the market has not yet been shown to be possible without invoking the capacity of individual market participants to perceive things differently from the way they had previously seen them. A second possibility, however, cannot be dismissed so easily.

2. This possibility is that a market participant, having no inkling of a future rise in price, buys when the price is low. At a later date he finds himself able to sell at a substantial profit. Surely this case is one of true entrepreneurial profit in the market sense. Yet the profit cannot be attributed to the market participant's entrepreneurial perception of the higher price that will eventually be available in the second market. From his individual perspective, his gain can appear as nothing but a windfall. And we saw earlier that a windfall gain, not attributable to the individual's purposeful activity, is not entrepreneurial profit in the individual sense.

Now it *may*, of course, happen that while our market participant had no inkling that the price would rise, he nonetheless realized that it *might* rise. And his action in buying may have reflected his judgment that the price would not fall. So his act of purchase *may* perhaps be seen as entrepreneurial in character, with any resulting gain qualifying as entrepreneurial profit, not only from the market perspective, but also from that of the individual himself. Presumably this is what Shackle had in mind when he declared that he inclined to the view "that any windfall realized receipts to which any degree of potential surprise less than the absolute maximum . . . was attached, ought not to be classified as due to pure luck."[24]

But this does not rule out the possibility of cases in which our market participant is astonished by the price rise. In such cases, as Shackle observes, where the windfall receipts carried the "absolute maximum potential surprise," they ought surely to be classified as due to pure luck.

Here, then, we have indeed discovered a class of cases in which profit in the market sense does *not* coincide with profit and entrepreneurship in the individual sense. Without individual entrepreneurship, market profits *may* yet be captured. What should be emphasized, in spite of the validity of these cases, is that this kind of "lucky" market entrepreneurship cannot be relied upon systematically to grind away profit margins, to bring about the tendency toward the full application of the Law of Indifference, or to tend to eliminate lacunae in social coordination. So that while individual entrepreneurship is not absolutely necessary for entrepreneurship to be exercised in markets, it is upon individual entrepreneurship that we must necessarily rely for any systematic process of market equilibration.

Now it cannot be denied that pure luck plays a most significant role in determining the fortunes of market participants in general and of market entrepreneurs in particular. For this reason it becomes easy to see all market profits as generated fortuitously by unanticipated change. This, in essence, was Knight's view of the world. But our discussion will have made it clear that *besides* those entrepreneurial profits won by sheer luck, the market displays entrepreneurial profits captured by the deliberate exploitation of opportunities glimpsed by individual entrepreneurs. Let us now return to the fundamental questions concerning pure profit raised at the beginning of this chapter; in this I will confine myself to those market profits that qualify, at the same time, to be classified as entrepreneurial profits also from the perspective of individual acting man.

LUCK AND ABILITY

In examining Crusonian profit, we found it expressed an intertwining of apparent good fortune and of ability. Crusoe's profit, we discovered, was deliberately grasped at, so that it could not be treated as a simple windfall gift from nature. Yet, at the same time, Crusoe's deliberate grasping after Crusonian profit could not be seen as merely the natural product obtained by the use of available resources. The product of Crusoe's labor, under settled conditions, may be seen as the outcome of his ability as a laborer. But the profit won by Crusoe in a changing world, we saw, came to him as a result of an inextricable combination of deliberate planning and undeliberately adopted hunch. It was incorrect, we found, to categorize all kinds of gain as falling exhaustively into two classes: gains flowing naturally and inevitably from the deliberate application of resources already possessed, and pure windfall gifts from nature. Human action, we found, undertaken in the face of the uncertainty of a changing world, achieves results that fit into neither of these categories.

It follows, therefore, insofar as market profits are derived from the entrepreneurial aspects of the individual human agent capturing these profits, that market profits, too, will not fit into either of these two categories. Market profits of the kind under discussion will not be attributable to sheer luck, since they resulted from the exercise of deliberate profit-seeking individual action. On the other hand, market profits will not be able to be linked absolutely with some special assured ability possessed by the entrepreneur. Entrepreneurs, as discussed earlier, do not see themselves as deliberately deploying their vision and alertness in the same way as they deploy their other resources. Nor does the market identify any specific ability to discover and profit from price discrepancies. The essence of entrepreneurship, we found, amounted to unawareness both by the entrepreneur himself and by the market in general that he in fact possesses the resources of vision at all.

All this should help us understand why the capture of pure entrepreneurial profits in the market will appear, paradoxically, to the outside observer, to reflect *both* sheer luck, *and* some apparent human capital element unique to successful entrepreneurs. Sheer luck will appear to play a significant role because market profits may indeed result, without exercise of the entrepreneurial element in individual human action, from fortuitous change. The link between the capture of market profit and some apparent entrepreneurial ability is to be understood because different individuals certainly differ in their ability to perceive opportunities entrepreneurially. What we must insist on is only that the *entrepreneurial* character of the vision under consideration here, renders it incorrect to see profit as the inevitable gain flowing naturally from the application of a possessed resource. The apparent paradoxes cited at the outset, we now see, are derived from the very nature of the entrepreneurial element with which we are attempting to grapple.

SHOULD MARKET PROFITS BE SEEN AS A FACTOR RETURN?

This is, of course, an old question. Schumpeter discussed the advisability of treating market entrepreneurship as a special category of productive factor.[25] Shackle raised the corresponding question concerning market profits: May they be seen as the marginal productivity return to a factor? This chapter should have provided grounds for refusing to recognize entrepreneurship as a factor and, therefore, for refusing to see market profit as a marginal productivity return. Both at the Crusoe level and at the market level, it should now be clear, entrepreneurship is not to be treated as a resource.

At the individual, Crusoe level, we have seen, the human agent does not "deliberately deploy" his entrepreneurial hunches; he simply has them, and they propel him into action. Menger's Law, therefore, never gets a chance to be applied; Crusoe never sees his hunches as means that can be applied to achieving given ends.

At the market level, we have seen, the market never recognizes entrepreneurial ability in the sense of an available useful resource. Were it to do so, there would be markets in which this factor service was hired, with its price rising to reflect its full productivity, ruling out scope for pure market profit.

The essence of individual entrepreneurship is that it consists of an alertness in which the decision is *embedded* rather than being one of the ingredients *deployed* in the course of decision making. This sets it altogether apart from being a class of productive factor.

Quite analogously, and consistent with the parallelism that was seen to exist between individual and market entrepreneurship, the market does not "demand" the services of entrepreneurs. Market entrepreneurship reveals to the market what the market did not realize was available or, indeed, needed at all. It is essential, in this context, that what is won by market entrepreneurship cannot be construed as a marginal productivity return *either* from the perspective of the market *or* from that of the individual human agent who acts to capture market profits.

NOTES

1. See for example F. H. Knight, "Profit," in *Encyclopedia of the Social Sciences* (New York: Macmillan, 1934); J. F. Weston, "Profit as the Payment for the Function of Uncertainty-Bearing," *Journal of Business* 22 (April 1949): 106–18; J. F. Weston, "The Profit Concept and Theory: A Restatement," *Journal of Political Economy* 62 (April 1954): 152–70; M. Bronfenbrenner, "A Reformulation of Naive Profit Theory," *Southern Economic Journal* 26 (April 1960): 300–309. See also I. M. Kirzner, *Competition and Entrepreneurship* (Chicago: University of Chicago Press, 1973), pp. 75 ff.

2. For an important recent treatment of entrepreneurship emphasizing its human capital aspects, see T. W. Schultz, "The Value of the Ability to Deal with Disequilibrium," *Journal of Economic Literature* 13 (September 1975): 827–46.

3. G. L. S. Shackle, *Decision, Order and Time in Human Affairs* (Cambridge: Cambridge University Press, 1969), pp. 252 ff.

4. Kirzner, *Competition and Entrepreneurship*.

5. J. A. Schumpeter, *The Theory of Economic Development* (Cambridge: Harvard University Press, 1934, trans. from German edition, 1911, by R. Opie), p. 160.

6. W. Stanley Jevons, *The Theory of Political Economy* (1871; reprinted Penguin Books, 1970), p. 137.

7. L. Mises, *Human Action*, 1st ed. (New Haven: Yale University Press, 1949), p. 253.

8. See Kirzner, *Competition and Entrepreneurship*, pp. 30–43 for more extended discussion of this; see also later in this chapter.

9. Menger was fully aware of the possibility of error in valuation. See C. Menger, *Principles of Economics*, trans. and ed. J. Dingwall and Bert F. Hoselitz (Glencoe, Ill.: Free Press, 1950), p. 120.

10. L. Mises, "Profit and Loss," in *Planning for Freedom* (South Holland, Ill.: Libertarian Press, 1962), pp. 125 ff.

11. So that we must, it seems, modify our earlier statement that eventually Menger's Law will ensure that the full value of the superior catch comes to be imputed to the physical resources that go into building the boat. Menger's Law, it now appears, will impute the output value to the *entire* resource complex, with Crusoe's new knowledge seen as an integral component of that complex.

12. See further Kirzner, *Competition and Entrepreneurship*, pp. 30 ff.

13. L. Robbins, *An Essay on the Nature and Significance of Economic Science* (London: Macmillan, 1932; 2d ed., 1935).

14. It is true, of course, that within the concept of allocation it is possible to incorporate the deliberate search for and discovery of new information that may alter the perceived ends-means framework. Such search occurs *within* some accepted (original) framework of ends and means. The assertion in the text refers to spontaneous discovery of error in the framework.

15. It is of some interest that Robbins's own concept owed a good deal to Mises; see *Nature and Significance*, 2d ed., pp. xvi, 16, n. 1.

16. L. Lachmann, "From Mises to Shackle: An Essay," *Journal of Economic Literature* 14 (March 1976): 54–62.

17. Of course, the element of fortune that enters here relates not to the circumstance that external events luckily turn out to fit Crusoe's hunch, but to the circumstance that Crusoe luckily adopted the hunch that correctly envisaged the future.

18. Of course there are well-known special problems in valuing a resource able to be used again and again without wear and tear. See, e.g., Mises, *Human Action*, p. 128.

19. See chap. 2.

20. See chap. 9.

21. For an earlier—albeit incomplete—recognition of this parallelism, see my *Competition and Entrepreneurship*, pp. 31 ff.

22. See Kirzner, *Competition and Entrepreneurship*, chap. 2, for a discussion of this process.

23. If it is argued that our participant *anticipated* a price differential that he proceeded to exploit at the first instant of its occurrence, then the question in the text may need to be reworded to refer to profitable activity in the relevant forward markets.

24. Shackle, *Decision, Order and Time*, pp. 267 ff. I am indebted to Professor S. C. Littlechild for this reference.

25. Schumpeter, *Theory of Economic Development*, p. 143; see also F. Machlup, *The Economics of Sellers' Competition* (Baltimore: Johns Hopkins Press, 1952), pp. 226 ff.

CREATIVITY AND/OR ALERTNESS: A RECONSIDERATION OF THE SCHUMPETERIAN ENTREPRENEUR

The purpose of this chapter is to reconsider the difference between Schumpeter's portrayal of the entrepreneurial role and my own, earlier (1969, 1973) portrayal of that same role.[1] In 1969 and in 1973, in the course of developing my own understanding of the entrepreneurial character of the competitive, equilibrative market process, I emphasized these differences as I then saw them. Schumpeter's entrepreneur, I pointed out, was essentially disruptive, destroying the preexisting state of equilibrium. My entrepreneur, on the other hand, was responsible for the tendency through which initial conditions of disequilibrium come systematically to be displaced by equilibrative market competition. The outcome of the present reconsideration will be, not a thoroughgoing "reconciliation" of these two conceptions of the entrepreneurial role—I still believe that these views are, at least in part, contrasting ones—but a clearer understanding of how each of these apparently conflicting views can be seen as plausible and realistic; and how each can usefully advance economic understanding (of respectively different aspects of the capitalist economy).

The central theme of this reconsideration can be expressed in the following four propositions:

1. For understanding the psychological profile typical of the real-world entrepreneur as we know him, Schumpeter's portrayal is valid and accurate.

2. For understanding the "creative destruction" which Schumpeter sees as the central and distinguishing feature of the capitalist system, Schumpeter's portrayal is valid and essential; to the extent that policy objectives include the stimulation of such creative destruction, careful attention will indeed have to be paid to that Schumpeterian psychological profile to which we have referred.

From *The Driving Force of the Market: Essays in Austrian Economics* (New York and London: Routledge, 2000), 239–57. Reprinted by permission of Springer; the original source is *Review of Austrian Economics* 11 (1999): 5–17.

3. For understanding the equilibrative tendency of markets in general, my own view of the entrepreneur as alert to opportunities (created by, or able to be created by, independently initiated changes) is valid and significant.

4. To see the entrepreneurial role of a real-world entrepreneur as essentially that of being "merely" alert to opportunities created (or able to be created) by independently initiated changes, is not *necessarily* inconsistent with a Schumpeterian perspective on the activity of that same entrepreneur (which sees him as aggressively and actively initiating change).

THE ENTREPRENEUR AS I SAW HIM IN 1973

My 1973 book, *Competition and Entrepreneurship*, sought to offer an Austrian (i.e., a Misesian) perspective on markets which would highlight the dynamically competitive character of the market process. In that process markets tend continually (in the face of equally continual exogenous changes in the relevant independent variables) toward equilibrium, as the consequence of continually stimulated entrepreneurial discoveries. These discoveries are discoveries of earlier errors made in the course of market exchanges. As a result of those earlier errors, market participants have been led (i) overoptimistically to insist on receiving prices that are "too high" (to enable them to sell all that they would like to sell at those prices) [or on paying prices that are "too low" (to enable them to buy all that they would like to buy at those prices)]; or (ii) overpessimistically to enter into transactions that turn out to be less than optimal in the light of the true market conditions as they in fact reveal themselves (e.g., a buyer discovers that he has paid a price higher than that being charged elsewhere in the market; a seller discovers that he has accepted a price lower than that which has been paid elsewhere in the market). The first of these latter two consequences of error (i.e., of errors of overoptimism) leads inevitably to frustrated plans: would-be buyers return home without having bought goods, would-be sellers return home with their unsold goods (in spite of the fulfillment of the conditions needed for mutually gainful exchange to be feasible among potential buyers and sellers). The second of the aforementioned two consequences (arising out of overpessimism) expresses itself as the phenomenon of unexploited pure profit opportunities (the same good is being sold at different prices in different parts of the same market). The entrepreneurial role is that of alertly noticing ("discovering") where these errors have occurred, and of moving to take advantage of such discoveries, and thus of nudging the market systematically in the direction of greater mutual awareness among market participants. (Since equilibrium is the state in which all market participants are, in effect, fully and correctly aware of what all others are doing, the entrepreneurial discovery process is one whose tendency is systematically equilibrative.)

This perspective on the entrepreneurial role and of its equilibrative character was articulated, in my 1973 book, primarily in the simplest of contexts, i.e., in markets for single commodities, within a single time period. For the purposes of that work I believed it important deliberately to abstract, for the most part, from the complications introduced by consideration of production, and of the passage of time. Readers of that work may be excused for concluding that phenomena associated with innovative production and with the uncertainty that accompanies time-consuming processes of production (and certainly time-consuming innovative processes of production) are basically irrelevant for the entrepreneurial role as portrayed in that work.

The entrepreneur who played the equilibrative role for me in 1973, fulfilled his essential function not by introducing new products, or technologically more efficient methods of production (in fact he was not a producer at all)—but simply by noticing earlier errors (manifested, most importantly, by the availability of pure profit opportunities existing in the multiple-price-for-the-same-good situation generated by those earlier errors). The emphasis was thus on the entrepreneur as the person who alertly (but "passively") simply *noticed* the opportunities generated by the earlier errors, which errors were seen as arising from unanticipated, independently caused changes in underlying market circumstances.

Indeed, in that 1973 work (based on insights first developed in a 1969 paper) I was careful to distinguish sharply between the entrepreneurial role as I saw it, and that role as portrayed by Schumpeter. Let us turn to see how I presented that distinction.

THE SCHUMPETERIAN ENTREPRENEUR—AS I SAW HIM IN 1973

It was important for me in 1973 to emphasize the differences between Schumpeter's entrepreneur and my own, because a superficial reader of my exposition of the dynamically competitive market process might easily and understandably be misled by the very significant parallels between my exposition of that process and Schumpeter's understanding of the competitive process. Schumpeter had vigorously rejected the orthodox emphasis on the perfectly competitive market.[2] He emphasized the entrepreneurial character of real-world dynamically competitive processes.[3] In these respects my own expositions of the competitive process (expositions based on my understanding of Ludwig von Mises's monumental 1949 work, *Human Action*) overlapped considerably with those of Schumpeter.[4] Yet, as we shall see, my ("Misesian") understanding of the market economy differed significantly from Schumpeter's understanding of capitalism as a "perennial gale" of "creative destruction." In seeking to clarify this difference I found it convenient to draw attention to the different roles played, within these different expositions of the competitive process, respectively, by the entrepreneur.

For Schumpeter "the essence of entrepreneurship is the ability to break away from routine, to destroy existing structures, to move the system away from the even, circular flow of equilibrium. . . . For Schumpeter the entrepreneur is the disruptive, disequilibrating force that dislodges the market from the somnolence of equilibrium."[5] The primary consequence of Schumpeter's entrepreneurship was the long-run economic development of the capitalist system.

The opening up of new markets, foreign or domestic, and the organizational development from the craft shop and factory to such concerns as U.S. Steel illustrate the same process of industrial mutation . . . that incessantly revolutionizes the economic structure *from within,* incessantly destroying the old one, incessantly creating a new one. This process of Creative Destruction is the essential fact about capitalism.[6]

The Schumpeterian entrepreneur is a *leader* (contrasted with the many "imitators" who follow the innovative lead of the entrepreneurs). All this contrasted, I pointed out, with the way I saw the entrepreneurial role. For me the essential element in that role was its potential of impinging on an initial state of disequilibrium, and, through alertly noticing ("discovering") those errors of which this state consists, moving equilibratively to correct them. I pointed out[7] that Schumpeter's exposition was "likely to generate the utterly mistaken view that the state of equilibrium can establish itself without any social device to deploy and marshall the scattered pieces of information which are the only sources of such a state." (I also drew attention to Hayek's work[8] in regard to the role of mutual ignorance in disequilibrium, and to his critique of Schumpeter in the latter's seeming to fall prey to precisely that "mistaken view" mentioned in the preceding sentence.)

The contrast between the two views was concisely reflected in my following complaint concerning Schumpeter's view of entrepreneurial activity:[9] "Instead of entrepreneurs grasping the opportunities available, responding to and healing maladjustments due to existing ignorance, the entrepreneur is pictured as generating disturbances in a fully adjusted circularly flowing world in which all opportunities were already fully and familiarly exploited." The contrast between Schumpeter's view and my own, which I saw in 1969 and in 1973, came to be variously commented on by several writers during subsequent years. A number of valuable insights emerged from these comments.

CONFLICTING APPRAISALS OF THE "CONTRAST"

One reaction was to treat the contrast which I had perceived between Schumpeter's view and my own as exaggerated. "Superficially," Hébert and Link[10] declared in 1982, "the Kirznerian entrepreneur appears to be the antithesis of the Schumpeterian entrepreneur, but fundamentally their differences are more apparent than real . . . one vision seems to complement the other."[11] This complementarity consists in the circumstance that, while Schumpeter's innovating entrepreneur is responsible for creating disequilibrium "in the first place," it is the "Kirznerian" entrepreneur who "springs into action upon recognizing a disequilibrium situation." One gathers from Hébert and Link that, while the differences between the two views are real, they arise not from two fundamentally inconsistent views of the economic process, but from the necessarily different emphases relevant to the two parts of the same market process, to which these views respectively pertain. (What is not made clear, however, is how a single economic function, the entrepreneurial function, can be simultaneously identified with two contrastingly different sets of characteristics.)

Two other papers have similarly perceptively criticized the sharpness of the contrast drawn between Schumpeter's view and my own. Donald J. Boudreaux[12] argues that *both* Schumpeterian and Kirznerian entrepreneurs should be seen as equilibrating (since both tend to push the market toward fulfillment of as yet unfulfilled potential). The different views should be seen as complementary: Schumpeter usefully draws attention to dimensions of improvement in product quality (dimensions which

Boudreaux believes to be necessarily outside any picture based on my own entrepreneurial discovery process); Kirzner, on the other hand, usefully draws attention to the equilibrative sense in which all social opportunity-grasping, including (by extension) Schumpeterian innovation, can be perceived.

Young Back Choi, after a discussion (rather similar to Boudreaux's) in which the similarities between Schumpeter's entrepreneur and my own are emphasized, reaches the following conclusion: "the concern over whether the entrepreneur is equilibrating or disequilibrating [seems] similar to the debate whether a glass is half-full or half-empty."[13] What Choi means is that the two views are not so much complementary (referring to different segments of the same market process) as in fact *identical* (differing only as a result of "a difference in perspective" reflecting merely "what Schumpeter and Kirzner take as the basis"[14]).

Brian Loasby, like several of these above-cited writers, considers the possibility of complementarity between the two views of the entrepreneurial role, but is led to dismiss it. "Kirzner's entrepreneur profits by assisting cohesion, Schumpeter's by disruption. Each might be regarded as providing opportunities for the other; yet they do not fit together all that well. They are linked to quite different conceptions of profit, and to substantially different conceptions of the working of the economy."[15] Elsewhere he has emphasized the differences as follows: "Whereas Kirzner's entrepreneurs respond to changing data, Schumpeter's cause the data to change."[16]

Stephan Boehm, too, tends to agree with existence of irreconcilable differences between the two views. "Schumpeter's and Kirzner's entrepreneur share a number of characteristics, but they are outweighed by some important dissimilarities."[17]

Affirmation of the contrast which I emphasized in 1973 (between Schumpeter's view of the entrepreneur and my own) does not, however, imply acceptance of my own characterization of the entrepreneurial role. In fact a number of writers generally sympathetic to a Misesian view of the competitive market process, have felt uncomfortable with my emphasis on the entrepreneur as "passively" noticing (and profiting by) independently created changes that have occurred in the data. The Schumpeterian view of the aggressive, active, innovative entrepreneur appears, to these critics, to be too faithful a portrayal of real-world business entrepreneurs to be given up simply in order to achieve the somewhat obscure analytical purposes claimed on behalf of my own entrepreneurial portrait. A number of these critics seem to have been particularly disturbed by what they saw as my deliberate abstraction from uncertainty. Because Mises himself emphasized the place of uncertainty in the context of entrepreneurship, and because the boldness needed to grapple confidently with uncertainty seems more similar to the aggressiveness of Schumpeter's entrepreneur (the success of whose innovations must be inextricably bound up in the uncertainty of an open-ended world) than to the passivity of the Kirznerian entrepreneur—these Misesian critics tended to be critical of my own characterization of the entrepreneur.[18]

ENTREPRENEURSHIP AND UNCERTAINTY

In a 1981 paper[19] I sought to address these criticisms by exploring the role of uncertainty in Misesian entrepreneurship. The relevance of such an exploration to the differences between Schumpeter's entrepreneur and my own can be recognized by noticing that I introduced my exploration with the observation[20] that the character of the market process is, for Mises, "decisively shaped by the leadership, the initiative, and the driving activity displayed and exercised by the entrepreneur." Clearly, I wished to emphasize that the uncertainty which envelops entrepreneurial activity evokes these "Schumpeterian" qualities of "leadership, initiative and driving activity." Although no explicit mention was made, in that 1981 paper, of the contrast which I had earlier emphasized as existing between Schumpeter's entrepreneur and my own, the issues discussed in that paper, concerning the place of uncertainty in entrepreneurship, are profoundly significant for the "reconsideration" in which the present paper is engaged. Because my 1981 paper was concerned with the role of uncertainty, it deliberately extended my earlier discussions of entrepreneurship from the single period (in which uncertainty can be, in one sense, ignored)[21] to the multi-period case (in which scope for uncertainty must be granted). It was this extension which implied, in addition, recognition for imagination and innovativeness:

> [T]he futurity that entrepreneurship must confront introduces the possibility that the entrepreneur may, by his own creative actions, in fact *construct* the future as *he* wishes it to be. In the single-period case alertness can at best discover hitherto overlooked current facts. In the multi-period case entrepreneurial alertness must include the

entrepreneur's perception of the way in which creative and imaginative action may vitally shape the kind of transactions that will be
entered into in future market periods. . . . To be a successful entrepreneur one must now possess those qualities of vision, boldness, determination and creativity.[22]

Some comments upon this paper seem to wish to assert that it may
have misleadingly understated the extent to which it acknowledges, in
effect, the inadequacies which earlier critics found in my 1973 exposition.[23] They read that (1981) paper as constituting a rather significant
modification of my earlier position—a more significant modification
than I was apparently prepared to admit. Some further clarification may
be helpful. The truth is that (while the extension presented in my 1981
paper did permit explicit attention to the psychological characteristics of
Schumpeter's entrepreneur that were absent from my own 1973 entrepreneur) it was not (and is not) my understanding of the extension from
single-period to multi-period entrepreneurship that it entails any modification of my conception of the entrepreneurial role. The key to that
conception is, following Mises, to recognize the arbitrage element in all
entrepreneurial activity, whether single-period or multi-period.

In discussing pure entrepreneurial profit Mises pointed out that
what is responsible for such profit "is the fact that the entrepreneur who
judges the future prices of the products more correctly than other people
do buys some or all of the factors of production at prices which, seen
from the point of view of the future state of the market, are too low."[24]
The crucial element in intertemporal entrepreneurship is thus captured
in the entrepreneur's perception of a price gap between present inputs
and (appropriately discounted) future output. My 1973 work found it
expedient to focus upon this, the essential feature of entrepreneurship,
through the device of abstracting from all other aspects of the real-world
exercise of entrepreneurship. This device consists in imagining how
entrepreneurship might be exercised in a world in which all those other
aspects are imagined to be absent—i.e., in a single-period world without production and without the uncertainty that arises from awareness
of futurity. It was certainly not the intention, in deploying this analytical
device, to deny that in the real world of production and (consequently) of
multi-period decision-making and radical uncertainty, entrepreneurship
is exercised only by calling upon the entrepreneur's qualities of boldness,

innovativeness and creativity. Conversely, in extending the single-period entrepreneur to my 1981 multi-period context, it was not the intention to modify what I understood to be the Misesian conception of pure entrepreneurial activity, viz. the perception (and thus the inevitable grasping) of a divergence between two prices at which the "same" item can be bought and sold. In recognizing how (in order to act entrepreneurially in the uncertain context of time-consuming production possibilities) the entrepreneur will need to display qualities of boldness and creativity, there was no intention (and no need) to see these qualities as essential to the pure entrepreneurial role, as that role enters into our analysis and understanding of the market process. In acknowledging that, for Mises, the uncertainty within which the entrepreneur operates is an essential defining condition for the situations in which scope for entrepreneurship exists, there was no intention (and no need) to see boldness and creativity as anything more than the psychological qualities needed in order for the entrepreneur effectively to recognize, in peering into the future, those pure price differentials in which prospective entrepreneurial profits are to be won. (Consider the factor service "labor." For many real-world employment situations [perhaps all], the psychological profile of a successful laborer will include the quality of "obedience." Yet this does not require us to *define* the laborer's decision to sell labor, in terms of obedience. We simply define the essence of the laborer's decision as that of selling his human services.) Perhaps this can be more clearly expressed in the following assertions: (a) Were we to be able to imagine a world without uncertainty in regard to the future, we would (as Mises taught us) be unable to find scope in that world for pure entrepreneurship. With the future knowable with certainty, we could hardly imagine those errors being made that create the scope for entrepreneurship in our own, open-ended, world. (b) Entrepreneurship, in the context of production possibilities, consists in one's conviction that one has perceived earlier errors in the market to have created a differential between the price at which one can buy inputs and the price at which it will be possible to sell outputs. (c) While psychological and personal qualities of boldness, creativity, and self-confidence will doubtless be helpful or even necessary in order for a person to "see" such price-differentials in the open-ended, uncertain world in which we live (with "seeing" defined as necessarily implying the grasping of the opportunity one has seen), the analytical essence of the pure entrepreneurial role is itself independent of these specific qualities.

So that while the explicit introduction of uncertainty into my portrayal of the entrepreneurial context[25] certainly fleshes out and improves that portrayal ((a) by bringing it closer to the real-world context, and (b) by relating that context to Mises's own explicit insistence on the presence of uncertainty as the defining feature of that context), it does *not* embody any change[26] in the pure, analytical conception of the entrepreneur who, in my 1973 work, was responsible for the tendency toward market equilibration. The equilibrative properties of entrepreneurial activity still consist purely in perceiving price differences. Aggressive, creative or other "Schumpeterian" characteristics often or typically displayed by successful real-world entrepreneurs, play no analytical role in the dynamically competitive market process driven by entrepreneurial activity.

THE SCHUMPETERIAN ENTREPRENEUR RECONSIDERED

Despite this insistence (my critics may consider it obstinacy) on my part in asserting that my 1981 paper did not (contrary to a number of commentaries upon it) represent any essential modification of my earlier understanding of the entrepreneurial role, it must certainly be recognized that that paper encourages a far more sympathetic appreciation, on my part, for the Schumpeterian entrepreneur. Once we permit the multi-period character of real-world entrepreneurial behavior to be explicitly considered, the relevance of the active, aggressive characteristics of Schumpeter's entrepreneurs becomes understandable and important. Entrepreneurial alertness, in this essentially uncertain, open-ended, multi-period world must unavoidably express itself in the qualities of boldness, self-confidence, creativity and innovative ability. In order to make a discovery, in this world, it is simply not sufficient to be somehow more prescient than others; it requires that that "abstract" prescience be supported by psychological qualities that encourage one to ignore conventional wisdom, to dismiss the jeers of those deriding what they see as the self-deluded visionary, to disrupt what others have come to see as the comfortable familiarity of the old-fashioned ways of doing things, to ruin rudely and even cruelly the confident expectations of those whose somnolence has led them to expect to continue to make their living as they have for years past. Recognition of all this is no doubt responsible for the difficulties which my critics had with my earlier discussion of the pure, alert entrepreneur without these Schumpeterian characteristics. Perhaps it was this which led them to read my 1981 paper as a belated concession to the inadequacy of my earlier simple notion of the entrepreneur as merely the ("passive" but alert) noticer of hitherto overlooked changes—a concession compelled, they believed, immediately one takes the step of extending analysis of entrepreneurial behavior beyond the highly artificial context of the single period.

Our discussion in the preceding section of this paper will, I trust, have made it clear how I can both eat my cake and have it (i.e., recognize how the multi-period world requires its entrepreneurs to display the Schumpeterian qualities, while still maintaining that it does not require me to surrender one iota of my earlier view of the entrepreneurial role as one of pure, alert, discovery of hitherto overlooked, exogenously created, changes.) To be sure, the entrepreneurial exercise of alert prescience calls for aggressive, bold, creative, leadership qualities. But this simply means that the seer who can imagine how the world might be improved by a radical innovation, but who lacks the needed boldness and initiative (to shoulder the risks which he would have to assume in order actually to introduce this innovation to reality in a world fraught with uncertainties)—has in fact not yet really discovered an available, attractive opportunity for innovation. If he has not seen that opportunity in so shining a light that it drives him to its implementation in spite of the jeering skepticism of others, and in spite of the possibility of its ultimate failure—then he has not really "seen" that opportunity. To imagine how, under hypothesized conditions, (not confidently believed to be in fact feasible), a true opportunity might exist, is not yet to have seen that opportunity as a tempting available option. For the possibility of genuine "alertness" in the multi-period, uncertain world, that alertness must indeed express itself in the boldness, self-confidence, and daring of the Schumpeterian leader. My "obstinacy" consists in my continuing to insist that what is important for analytical purposes is not these leadership qualities in themselves, but the pure "alertness" which these qualities express and sustain.

ENTREPRENEURIAL INNOVATION— COORDINATIVE OR DISRUPTIVE?

It may be helpful, in this regard, to consider an objection which many have raised in the past in regard to my emphasis on the coordinative tendencies set in motion by (successful) entrepreneurship. This objection has deeply worried a number of otherwise sympathetic scholars, in regard to my notion of the entrepreneurial role. Surely, they argue, every successful entrepreneurial venture constitutes a shock to the market, more or less severely disrupting the existing plans of those who, failing to anticipate these changes, have invested all or parts of their careers in the methods of production which the new venture is about to displace. We may grant, the objection concedes, that this shock may be seen as beneficial to the consumers; but surely, they claim, these benefits to the consumer are obtained only through drastically *dis*coordinating and frustrating the plans of those in the displaced industry. To pronounce these disruptive shocks as essentially coordinative and equilibrative, as I have, is to twist language outrageously. My use of language in this way, my critics tend to believe, is not unrelated to my obstinate refusal to recognize (as Schumpeter did) that successful entrepreneurship is indeed disruptive, to concede that while the destruction it sets in motion may indeed be "creative," it is destructive nonetheless.

To see why and how I believe it possible and accurate to insist on my use of the term "coordinative" to describe the entrepreneur's behavior, it will be useful to focus on an example of bold, creative, innovative Schumpeterian entrepreneurship responsible for a dramatic technological breakthrough, revolutionizing an entire industry. Consider the invention and innovation of the automobile in the United States. This innovation, we may be sure, devastated the livelihoods of many who had built their entire careers around the horse-drawn carriage industry. Virtually overnight, we may be convinced, enormous loss of value occurred in capital investments that had been made in that industry; large numbers of skilled professional workers in that industry find that the market value of their skills has fallen catastrophically. Yet, while understanding how Schumpeter can focus on the creative destruction which this successful and dramatic entrepreneurial innovation has wrought, I maintain that we must, at the same time, recognize the coordinative quality of this innovation, *even in regard to the horse-drawn carriage industry.*

The truth surely is, we now see with 20/20 hindsight, that the horse-drawn carriage industry, for all its placid, normal-profitability over many decades, was an industry in grave disequilibrium *before* the automobile actually appeared. This was so, we now realize, in that the means (and even, in a sense, the technology) to replace expensive, inconvenient, time-consuming horse-drawn transportation by lower-cost, convenient and rapid motorized transportation was available at an acceptable cost, at the very moment when the horse-drawn carriage industry (as far as the superficial vision of the person in the street could discern) seemed normally prosperous and secure. The truth is, we now know, that the investments made in physical and human capital were *mal*investments. The value of the output of the horse-drawn carriage industry was, as we now know, far lower than the value which the market *at that very moment* would have been prepared to place upon the outputs of comparable inputs directed into an automobile-producing industry.

The consumers paying substantial prices for (what we now know to have been) inefficient and inconvenient horse-drawn transportation were in fact "wasting" their money; opportunities, as yet unnoticed, existed for far superior motorized transportation to be provided at prices that would have been highly attractive to many consumers. Production was, in this sense, being conducted inefficiently; capital and labor were being misallocated—invested and specialized in directions and skills that were (in the light of the true conditions which hindsight reveals to have existed) utterly mistaken.

The brash, bold entrepreneurs who introduced the automobile to the U.S. market indeed set in motion market movements which, in one sense, disrupted the plans of many investors and workers in the industries they displaced. But their doing so, we now see, constituted not an act of destruction in itself, but one which *revealed* the wastefulness and the misallocated character of the enormous volume of investor and labor decisions that mistakenly committed resources to the horse-drawn carriage industry. The superficial placidity of the situation in that industry on the eve of the emergence of the automobile was indeed just that, merely superficial. The truth, as we now know, is that it was an industry sitting on a powder keg waiting to explode. The essential entrepreneurial contribution of the automobile pioneers was unmistakably to make clear what that disequilibrium situation really was. Those entrepreneurs alertly saw better ways of using resources; their putting into effect the productive possibilities they saw was coordinative in the sense that it brought the pattern of resource allocation into a higher degree of coordination both with the true pattern of technological possibilities and the pattern of consumer preferences, than had the leaders of the horse-drawn carriage industry. While we can readily understand how, at a superficial level, it seems obvious that it is the actions of the automobile entrepreneurs that have directly destroyed the capital and labor-skill values built up in the horse-drawn carriage industry, we must recognize that, at a deeper level, these losses, while as yet unnoticed, had already occurred at the times the investments (in the horse-drawn carriage industry) were made. From this perspective, the automobile entrepreneurs can no more accurately be described as the agents of "destruction," than can the physician whose diagnosis sends an apparently healthy person (undergoing a routine medical examination) to hospital with a newly identified severe heart condition be described as having ruined that patient's health.

SEMANTICS AND SUBSTANCE

We may readily grant to my critics[27] that a certain semantic ambiguity is partly responsible for the possibly overemphasized differences (between Schumpeter's views and my own) which I had asserted in 1969 and 1973. As I had recognized as early as 1963,[28] so long as one can imagine that "there are *always* unknown technological possibilities that future generations will discover," we can describe a market system as necessarily always being "in a state of disequilibrium, with respect to the infinity of knowledge that is beyond (contemporary) human reach." While this use of the term disequilibrium would permit us to see each and every "Schumpeterian" technological innovation as "equilibrating" (as I appeared to wish to argue in 1969 and 1973), such a semantic usage is neither required nor necessarily advisable. Ordinarily we do describe as an equilibrium that Walrasian state of affairs which fully and adequately incorporates all currently available technological knowledge. Surely, then, Schumpeter was not out of order in seeing entrepreneurial technological innovation as disruptive and disequilibrating. It must seem that my insistence on seeing even Schumpeterian entrepreneurial activity as coordinative and equilibrative, does involve a confusing and unfortunate use of language.

The following may permit me to plead non-guilty to this latter offense. There *is* an important sense in which we must indeed see the entrepreneur who achieves Schumpeterian technological revolutions, who engages in what Schumpeter valuably identifies as "creative destruction," as (Schumpeter's use of language to the contrary notwithstanding) equilibrative. This sense is that in which we wish to understand the *economic* forces at work in generating such technological revolutions. Schumpeter correctly identified the economic forces so responsible as being driven by entrepreneurial activity. What Schumpeter's use of language (i.e., his identification of this activity as disruptive and disequilibrative) obscured,

I maintained (and still maintain), is that this entrepreneurial activity is, after all (and most significantly) stimulated and motivated by the possibility of winning pure profit. What Schumpeter's use of language (and indeed his "vision" of how capitalism works) obscured, is that the entrepreneurial activity with which he is dealing is, at a deep level, responding to the conditions of the market. To fail to see that the entrepreneurs in the automobile industry were responding to the economic inefficiencies and resource misallocations (and the resulting profit opportunities) already present in the horse-drawn carriage industry, is surely to fail to see a most important aspect of the market process. My 1973 book was built on the idea that it is this aspect of the market (present but overlooked in Schumpeter's account of long-run technological change) which is responsible for that tendency for market equilibration which is at the very core of economic understanding—even in the imagined world in which technological change is absent.

I believe the foregoing permits me to sum up the "reconsideration" undertaken in this chapter, by simply reiterating the four propositions announced at its very outset:

1. For understanding the psychological profile typical of the real-world entrepreneur as we know him, Schumpeter's portrayal is valid and accurate.

2. For understanding the "creative destruction" which Schumpeter sees as the central and distinguishing feature of the capitalist system, Schumpeter's portrayal is valid and essential; to the extent that policy objectives include the stimulation of such creative destruction, careful attention will indeed have to be paid to that Schumpeterian psychological profile to which we have referred.

3. For understanding the equilibrative tendency of markets in general, my own view of the entrepreneur as alert to opportunities (created by, or able to be created by, independently initiated changes), is valid and significant.

4. To see the entrepreneurial role of a real-world entrepreneur as essentially that of being "merely" alert to opportunities created (or able to be created) by independently initiated changes, is not *necessarily* inconsistent with a Schumpeterian perspective on the activity of that same entrepreneur (which sees him as aggressively and actively initiating change).

To put the matter somewhat differently: The reconsideration here undertaken indeed permits us to see how both the Schumpeterian view of the entrepreneurial role and my own view can both be simultaneously accepted. Schumpeter is concerned to enable us to see, from the outside, as it were, what constitutes the essence of capitalism (viz. its being characterized by continual technological change driven by innovative, creative entrepreneurs). My own focus on the entrepreneur was inspired by the objective of enabling us to see the inside workings of the capitalist system (its ability to offer pure profit incentives that can evoke entrepreneurial perception of available opportunities—some [but not all!] of which opportunities may consist in the potential for technological revolution [implementation of which calls for the "Schumpeterian" qualities of boldness, initiative, and creativity]). To the extent, however, that Schumpeter's language and his picture of capitalism lead us to see the placid, old-fashioned-technology world as one in which actions have long come to be fully and efficiently mutually and smoothly coordinated, with no "gaps" crying out for alert entrepreneurial notice—until the placidity is rudely disrupted by exogenous "entrepreneurial" creative innovation, I must continue to assert that my own view of entrepreneurial activity permits and requires us to see a quite different picture even in that very same sequence of Schumpeterian events.

NOTES

1. Although the objective of this chapter is to throw light on the nature of the entrepreneurial role (rather than to clarify what this writer "really meant" in earlier, almost forgotten writings), it does focus distressingly abundantly, upon some of that earlier work. I can only apologize for this.

2. Schumpeter (1942, 1950, pp. 103ff.).

3. Schumpeter (1942, 1950, p. 84).

4. On this see also Kirzner (1990, pp. 245–49).

5. See Kirzner (1973, p. 127).

6. Schumpeter (1942, 1950, p. 83).

7. Kirzner (1973, pp. 73ff.).

8. Hayek (1945, 1949).

9. Kirzner (1969, 1979, p. 118).

10. Hébert and Link (1982, p. 99).

11. In a recent paper (Holcombe, 1997) Professor Randall G. Holcombe states that "at least a part of the difference between Schumpeter's and Kirzner's views might be semantic, based on different understandings of the meaning of the word equilibrium."

12. Boudreaux (1994).

13. Choi (1995, p. 62).

14. Ibid.

15. Loasby (1982, p. 224).

16. Loasby (1989, p. 178).

17. Boehm (1990, p. 229). See also McNulty (1987, pp. 536ff.) ("Schumpeter's entrepreneur is a disequilibrating force . . . Kirzner's entrepreneur plays an equilibrating role."). See also Ricketts (1994, pp. 63ff.).

18. See e.g., Greaves (1974); Hazlitt (1974); White (1976); High (1980); see also High (1990, p. 41).

19. Kirzner (1982, 1985, ch. 3).

20. Kirzner (1982, 1985, p. 40).

21. Although the single-period context (upon which my 1973 discussion of entrepreneurship focused) permits us to "ignore uncertainty," this is *not* inconsistent with Mises's insistence that (as my critics pointed out) the entrepreneurial role can be defined only in the context of uncertainty. What Mises meant by that insistence, it is my understanding, was that scope for entrepreneurial discovery (of errors being made by others) cannot be imagined to exist except in a world in which "sheer ignorance" (i.e., undeliberate, costlessly removable ignorance which "inefficiently" remains after all *known* worthwhile, cost-benefit-calculated efforts have been made to remove known ignorance) is essentially present. In the world in which we live the element within it which creates scope for such sheer ignorance is the uncertainty of the future. Were the future to be "determined" (and thus essentially knowable), the only ignorance of it which would remain would be "efficient" ignorance (i.e., ignorance the costly removal of which would be seen as not worthwhile). My device, in 1973, of focusing on the single-period context for entrepreneurship, required the deus-ex-machina-*assumption* of the possibility of sheer ignorance in that context (*without* the multi-period uncertainty which renders sheer ignorance plausible or inevitable in the real world). The analytical core of the 1973 treatment is, I believed (and still believe), identical with that which Mises develops in his own treatment of entrepreneurship in the multi-period real world.

22. Kirzner (1982, 1985, pp. 63ff.).

23. Hébert and Link (1982, pp. 97ff.), High (1982).

24. Mises (1962, p. 109).

25. That portrayal did point out very explicitly that uncertainty was being deliberately abstracted from (see Kirzner, 1973, pp. 86ff.).

26. Although Professor Vaughn disagrees with much of my position, she has recognized the essentially unchanged core of that position over the years. See Vaughn (1994, pp. 148ff.). For a disagreement with Vaughn on this, see Rizzo (1996, pp. xviiiff. and fn 7).

27. For references see above, notes 11, 12, 13.

28. Kirzner (1963, p. 258 fn).

REFERENCES

Boehm, Stephan (1990) "The Austrian Tradition: Schumpeter and Mises," in Klaus Hennings and Warren J. Samuels (eds) *Neoclassical Economic Theory, 1870–1930*, Boston/Dordrecht/London: Kluwer.

Boudreaux, Donald (1994) "Schumpeter and Kirzner on Competition and Equilibrium," in Peter J. Boettke and David L. Prychitko (eds) *The Market Process: Essays in Contemporary Austrian Economics*, Aldershot: Edward Elgar.

Choi, Young Back (1995) "The Entrepreneur: Schumpeter vs. Kirzner," in Peter J. Boettke and Mario J. Rizzo (eds), *Advances in Austrian Economics*, Vol. 2, Part A, Greenwich, Conn., and London: JAI Press.

Greaves, Percy L., Jr. (1974) Review of Kirzner (1973), *Wertfrei*.

Hayek, Friedrich A. (1945) "The Use of Knowledge in Society," *American Economic Review* XXXV(4), reprinted in Hayek (1949) *Individualism and Economic Order*, London: Routledge and Kegan Paul.

Hazlitt, Henry (1974) Review of Kirzner (1973), *Freeman* 24.

Hébert, Robert F. and Albert N. Link (1982) *The Entrepreneur, Mainstream Views and Radical Critiques*, New York: Praeger.

High, Jack (1980) Review of Kirzner (1979), *Austrian Economics Newsletter*.

—— (1982) "Alertness and Judgment: Comment on Kirzner," in Israel M. Kirzner (ed.), *Method, Process and Austrian Economics, Essays in Honor of Ludwig von Mises*, Lexington, Mass.: D. C. Heath.

—— (1990) *Maximizing, Action, and Market Adjustment, An Inquiry into the Theory of Economic Disequilibrium*, Munich: Philosophia Verlag.

Holcombe, Randall G. (1997) "The Origins of Entrepreneurial Opportunities," unpublished manuscript, Florida State University.

Kirzner, Israel M. (1963) *Market Theory and the Price System*, Princeton, N.J.: Van Nostrand.

—— (1969) "Entrepreneurship and the Market Approach to Development," reprinted in Kirzner (1979).

—— (1973) *Competition and Entrepreneurship*, Chicago: University of Chicago Press.

—— (1979) *Perception, Opportunity and Profit*, Chicago: University of Chicago Press.

—— (1982) "Uncertainty, Discovery, and Human Action," in Israel M. Kirzner, *Discovery and the Capitalist Process*, Chicago: University of Chicago Press.

—— (1990) "Commentary" on Stephan Boehm.

Loasby, Brian J. (1982) "The Entrepreneur in Economic Theory," *Scottish Journal of Political Economy* 29.

—— (1989) *The Mind and Method of the Economist, A Critical Appraisal of Major Economists in the Twentieth Century*, Aldershot: Edward Elgar.

McNulty, Paul J. (1987) "Competition: Austrian Conceptions," in John Eatwell, Murray Milgate, and Peter Newman (eds) *The New Palgrave: A Dictionary of Economics*, Vol. 1, London: Macmillan.

Mises, Ludwig von (1949) *Human Action, A Treatise on Economics,* New Haven, Conn.: Yale University Press.

——— (1962) "Profit and Loss," in Ludwig von Mises (ed.) *Planning for Freedom and Other Essays and Addresses,* 2d ed., South Holland, Ill.: Libertarian Press.

Ricketts, Martin (1994) *The Economics of Business Enterprise—An Introduction to Economic Organization and the Theory of the Firm,* 2d ed., New York and London: Harvester Wheatsheaf.

Rizzo, Mario J. (1996) "Introduction: Time and Ignorance After Ten Years," in Gerald P. O'Driscoll and Mario J. Rizzo (eds) *The Economics of Time and Ignorance,* 2d ed., London and New York: Routledge.

Schumpeter, Joseph A. (1942) *Capitalism, Socialism and Democracy,* New York: Harper and Row (reprint, 1950).

Vaughn, Karen I. (1994) *Austrian Economics in America—The Migration of a Tradition,* Cambridge: Cambridge University Press.

White, Lawrence H. (1976) "Entrepreneurship, Imagination and the Question of Equilibration," unpublished manuscript.

THE ALERT AND CREATIVE ENTREPRENEUR:
A CLARIFICATION

When I was awarded the 2006 FSF-NUTEK International Award for Entrepreneurship and Small Business Research, I certainly appreciated the great honor which this award implied for my work on entrepreneurial theory. But, I must confess, I was at the same time somewhat puzzled. This Prize, I had understood, was for work exploring the elusive sources of the entrepreneurial decision. Such work, it was hoped, may throw light on the secrets of successful entrepreneurship. Successful entrepreneurship plays an enormously significant role in driving economic development, growth, and in the achievement of the prosperous economy. It is therefore important to identify the human qualities that make for successful entrepreneurs, and the social and economic conditions needed to promote the emergence of successful entrepreneurship. This Prize, I understood, was thus part of a broad research initiative that might lead to public policies and educational programs that would in turn stimulate and encourage the entrepreneurial potential latent in society, and thus bring about the desirable economic results which successful entrepreneurship can generate.

But my own work has *nothing* to say about the secrets of successful entrepreneurship. My work has explored, not the nature of the talents needed for entrepreneurial success, not any guidelines to be followed by would-be successful entrepreneurs, but, instead, the *nature of the market process set in motion* by the entrepreneurial decisions (both successful and unsuccessful ones!).[1] So that the thrust and character of my work on entrepreneurial theory did not, it would seem, fit the framework for this Prize. Hence my initial puzzlement, referred to above. This paper seeks (a) to identify more carefully the sense in which my work on entrepreneurial theory does *not* throw light on the substantive sources

IFN Working Paper 760 (Research Institute of Industrial Economics, Stockholm, Sweden, 2008). Reprinted by permission. The article also appeared in *Small Business Economics* 32 (2009): 145–52. doi:10.1007/s11187-008-9153-7. © Springer Science and Business Media, LLC. Reprinted by permission of Springer.

1. For the purpose of this paper, "my work" refers primarily to Kirzner (1973), but also secondarily to papers included in Kirzner (1979, 1985, 1992, 2000).

of successful entrepreneurship, (b) to argue that a number of (sympathetic) reviewers of my work have somehow failed to recognize this limitation in the scope of my work (and that these scholars have therefore misunderstood certain aspects of my theoretical system), (c) to show that, despite all of the above, my understanding of the market process (as set in motion by entrepreneurial decisions) *can*, in a significant sense, provide a theoretical underpinning for public policy in regard to entrepreneurship. So that perhaps my work *can* be fitted into the framework for this Prize, after all.

I have always emphasized that my own contribution is simply an expansion and deepening of insights articulated by my teacher, Ludwig von Mises. Yet, as we shall see, much of the following discussion relates to the similarities and the differences between my own portrayal of the entrepreneurial role, and that of Joseph A. Schumpeter 1912, 1942 in his celebrated, pioneering work on entrepreneurship. Although I have made earlier attempts to clarify these similarities and differences,[2] I believe that this further attempt is still needed to clear up what I see as a certain confusion in the literature.

This paper thus addresses the somewhat embarrassing need to clarify what this writer himself meant in earlier writings. I trust that this exercise in intellectual navel-gazing will be received with patient tolerance. There *is* a need to clarify the differences between the Misesian and the Schumpeterian understandings of the entrepreneurial market process. And perhaps the required character of a Prize Essay may soften, if not entirely excuse, the charge of excessive and exclusive focus upon the writer's own work.

INDIVIDUAL DECISIONS AND MARKET OUTCOMES

It is, of course, basic to the microeconomic understanding of market phenomena, that such phenomena can be traced back to (and in fact consist of) individual market decisions. Changes in relative prices, changing patterns of outputs, changing methods of production, are all explained fully by referring back to individual consumers, resource-owners, and producer market decisions. Equilibrium microeconomic theory traces states of market equilibrium back to decisions made in the context of known, given and unchanging patterns of underlying variables (i.e., consumer tastes,

2. See Kirzner (1982, 1999).

resource availability, and technological knowledge). As is well known, in such equilibrium theory there is no scope for and no possibility of entrepreneurship. The introduction of entrepreneurship into the microeconomist's theoretical universe, opens up a new world in which there is scope for such disequilibrium phenomena as pure profit and loss, technological discoveries, innovation (other than the outcomes of planned research), and dramatic shifts in patterns of production. But one feature of microeconomic equilibrium theory does, of course, survive into the world of entrepreneurial change, viz. that market phenomena consist of the individual decisions of market participants (only that now, in the disequilibrium world, we have admitted entrepreneurial decision making into our system).

For entrepreneurial theorizing based on Schumpeter's pioneering work, this has meant that (besides the "mechanical" constrained maximization governing decisions in the equilibrium world) we can now pay attention to the specific qualities which generate successful entrepreneurial decisions. Such qualities, emphasized by Schumpeter, include boldness, imaginativeness, and creativity. The Schumpeterian entrepreneur does not passively operate in a given world, he *creates* a world different from which he finds. He introduces hitherto undreamt of products, he pioneers hitherto unthought of methods of production, he opens up a new market in hitherto undiscovered territory. In so doing the entrepreneur is, in the Schumpeterian view, pushing (what might otherwise have been) an equilibrium market, *away* from equilibrium. His creativity *disrupts* what would otherwise have been a serene market. Because neo-Schumpeterian theory recognizes how important entrepreneurship is for economic growth, theorists have come to focus on the roots of the Schumpeterian qualities of the boldness and creativity, in order, hopefully, to understand how to stimulate entrepreneur-driven economic development—development that might jolt somnolent, poorly performing economies out of their present serene (but poverty stricken!) ruts. This explains the perceived need for a broad research program (mentioned at the outset of this paper) on the determinants of successful entrepreneurial decisions, in order to promote relevantly fruitful public policy.

THE ENTREPRENEUR AS EQUILIBRATOR

In my earlier work on the entrepreneur (particularly in my 1973 book) based on insights articulated by Ludwig von Mises, I drew attention to a different way of seeing the impact of the individual entrepreneurial decision upon the market phenomena of the real world. In this perspective, the entrepreneur is not seen as *disturbing* any existing or prospective states of equilibrium. Rather he is seen as *driving the process of equilibrium*. In this process the market is, as it were, gravitating (through entrepreneurial activity) *toward* the hypothetical state of equilibrium (that is, the state which, in the [impossible!] absence of autonomous, exogenous changes in the underlying variables, might have eventually emerged). In my 1973 work this way of seeing the consequences of entrepreneurial behavior opened up an innovative way of understanding the *active, competitive process* (which, as is well-known, had been assumed away entirely in the then dominant equilibrium models of perfect [and monopolistic] competition). Moreover, in order to be able to focus more clearly upon the nature of the equilibrative competitive-entrepreneurial market *process*, my 1973 work deliberately abstracted from speculative market decisions. As a result, the entrepreneur who dominated my 1973 book did not *need* to be creative at all; he simply had to be *alert* to price differentials which others had not yet noticed. (Thus he had, for example, to be alert to ways of profitably producing existing-type goods by using existing, but as not yet widely known goods.) The central feature of successful entrepreneurship (i.e., entrepreneurship able to "notice" pure price differentials, and thus to move, equilibratively, toward their elimination) was thus *not* creativity (but alertness to already existing, but as yet widely unnoticed changes).

In order to identify the manner in which the market consequences of my entrepreneurs differ from those emphasized in Schumpeter's work, I emphasized how my entrepreneurs can be seen as responsible for equilibrating market movements (such as changing prices), in the *absence* of dramatic changes in product specifications or in production methods. My entrepreneurs were engaged in *arbitrage*, acting entrepreneurially even when they might *not* be seen as Schumpeterian "creators."

In so emphasizing the difference between Schumpeter's theory of entrepreneurship and my own, I was motivated by my primary scientific objective. This was to understand the nature of the market process—even in its *simplest* conceivable contexts. The truth was (and is!) that standard microeconomic theory, because of its focus on competitive equilibrium, has been unable to account for the most basic of market-theoretical principles. Even in the simplest Marshallian demand-supply context, standard theory has not been able to explain how markets systematically gravitate toward the equilibrium states (relevant to the given conditions of those markets).[3] The key to understanding the market process is to understand the dynamic character of market competition. But the neoclassical focus on perfect competition as an equilibrium *state of affairs* prevented appreciation of this insight. It was not until Hayek's pioneering, but insufficiently appreciated work on the dynamically competitive market as a process of mutual discovery, that Austrian economics was able explicitly to grapple with this embarrassing hiatus. It was particularly in the work of Ludwig von Mises that this writer discovered, in the Misesian entrepreneur and in the Misesian dynamically competitive process, what he believed (and believes) to be the true solution. My 1973 work was written in order to spell out this solution. For this purpose it was not necessary (and in fact it would have been a distraction!) to dwell on the qualities needed for creative (Schumpeterian) entrepreneurship. Quite the contrary, it was necessary to show how the systematic competitive entrepreneurial market process can be traced back to entrepreneurial decisions and even these do *not* display Schumpeterian equilibrium-disturbing creativity.

Not only did my work abstract from the creativity of real-world entrepreneurs, it did not even aim to explore the roots and the determinants of individual entrepreneurial alertness. Its focus was upon the dynamic competitive-entrepreneurial process *driven* by such alertness. It was only because the nature of this process is seen more clearly by paying attention to entrepreneurial alertness, that it was necessary to identify its presence in the individual decision. At any rate I certainly did not throw any light on "how to be alert." It would thus seem that my work hardly fits within any broad research program concerned with the secret of entrepreneurial success. Hence the puzzlement mentioned at the outset of this paper.

In retrospect it is possible to see how all this led to certain significant misunderstandings on the part of a number of scholars who commented on my work. Certainly this writer must, because of his imperfect expository technique, bear much of the blame for this misunderstanding. Subsequent sections of this paper will explain how these misunderstandings arose. They will clarify the extent to which, *in spite of* the contrast with Schumpeter which I emphasized in 1973, the

---

3. For a candid, sophisticated recognition of this failure, see Fisher (1983).

truth is that my understanding of the dynamic market process certainly can (and should!) also encompass the consequences of Schumpeterian entrepreneurship.

CREATIVITY AND/OR ALERTNESS: THE MISUNDERSTANDINGS

My emphasis on the entrepreneur as the agent driving the competitive-equilibrative forces of the market, focuses attention on the entrepreneur not as a creator, but as being merely *alert*. His equilibrative role stemmed, not from his autonomously *introducing* change into existing market relationships, but from his ability to notice, earlier than others, the changes that have *already* occurred, rendering existing relationships inconsistent with the conditions for equilibrium. The discrepancies which the entrepreneur notices, appear in the form of profit opportunities. It is the entrepreneurial-competitive grasping of such perceived opportunities which drives the market toward the (relevant new) equilibrium configurations.

Now in the real, multi-period, world, all this takes the form, of course, of entrepreneurially *speculative* activity. As Ludwig von Mises (whose ideas I was, explicitly, expounding and developing) put it (von Mises 1952, p. 190): "What makes profit emerge is the fact that the entrepreneur who judges the future prices of the products more correctly than other people do buys some or all of the factors of production at prices which, seen from the point of view of the future state of the market, are too low. . . . This difference is entrepreneurial profit." Notice that Mises makes no reference to entrepreneurial innovation, creativity, or the like. He refers only to the entrepreneur's ability to "see" future prices more correctly than others see them. My early work, seeking to distil this core insight of Mises' entrepreneurial view of the market, presented this entrepreneurial alertness in the context of the simplest, pure arbitrage, model—in which, *for this stated expository reason,* no scope for creativity was needed at all.

In retrospect it is perhaps not surprising that this generated the misunderstanding referred to above. What some readers understood was that in my theory, in contrast to that of Schumpeter, the *real-world* entrepreneur operates purely as a "passive" noticer of already-occurred changes. It came to be thought that the real-world market entrepreneurial process which my theory was intended to explain, did not move as expressing the creative, innovative leaps of faith by visionary entrepreneurs impatient with the status quo. Rather, it was understood, my theory saw the movements of real-world capitalism as merely the adjustments made by passively alert entrepreneurs, quick to grasp the pure profits generated by errors of others.

This understanding somehow crystallized into the conclusion that my work claims the existence of two *alternative, mutually exclusive* ways of seeing the dynamic, entrepreneurial real-world capitalist process: (a) a Schumpeterian view of this process as a series of disruptive episodes of "creative destruction," one driven by creative, innovative, entrepreneurial ventures, or (b) as a view, attributed to this writer, in which movements are seen as equilibrative entrepreneurial *reactions* to autonomous changes in the underlying supply and demand conditions. Entrepreneurs are to be seen *either* as bold, disruptive innovators, *or* as passively alert, harmony-restoring *responders* to already-occurred changes.[4]

It is not difficult to see how readers might resist accepting such a claim. (And, of course, they would be absolutely right in doing so, if any such claim had in fact been made!) Casual observation surely confirms Schumpeter's insights into entrepreneurial creativity. Anecdotal evidence surely abounds to assure us that in real-world capitalism change often, if not always, *begins* with entrepreneurial outside-the-box thinking regarding newly invented products, newly devised production techniques, and

---

4. Among those who challenge the sharpness of the contrast (which they read me as maintaining) between a "Schumpeterian" understanding of the real-world entrepreneurial-capitalist process, and the "Kirznerian" understanding—and who challenge, in particular, the claim (which they believed me to have made) that only one of these two understandings corresponds to reality—see Hébert and Link (1982, p. 99) and Boudreaux (1994). See also Loasby (1982, p. 224; 1989, p. 178). Holcombe (1998, p. 57) has argued that Schumpeter's views reflect his interest in economic growth, while my view reflects a focus on (short-run?) resource allocation. In several important papers Holcombe (1999, 2003) has perceptively explored the interface between Schumpeter's view and my own. He has valuably argued for an extension of my own approach that might show how an "alertness"-understanding of entrepreneurship can lead to the recognition that it is entrepreneurship itself (*responding* to discovered opportunities) which, by creating market possibilities, generates yet further entrepreneurial opportunities. The capitalist process can thus be seen as an entrepreneurially driven series of opportunity creations. In this section of this paper, in referring to the unhappiness of critics (with the sharp distinction [held to be claimed by myself] between Schumpeterian creativity and entrepreneurial alertness to existing opportunities), I have in mind an underlying theme which, I believe, pervades the literature cited in this footnote. Important contributions to this literature are also Fu-Lai Yu (1998, 2001).

innovative penetration into hitherto untapped market territories. At the same time it is equally apparent that some entrepreneurial profit is indeed attributable to alert awareness of already-occurred changes in consumer preferences, changes in the availability of already-in-use resources, and the like. Apparently, there must be scope for *both* a creative ("Schumpeterian") entrepreneur (one who *generates* pure profit) *and* a "passive," alert ("Kirznerian") entrepreneur (one who *snuffs out* given profit opportunities by promptly exploiting them).

Moreover, it can be argued, it seems reasonable to see the full dynamic of the capitalist system as being the outcome of *two* distinct kinds of entrepreneur-driven changes. A ("longer-run"?) dynamic reflecting the creative genius of Schumpeterian entrepreneurs, can be seen to exist alongside a ("short-run"?) dynamic in which "passive" (merely alert) entrepreneurs tend constantly to bring markets into alignment with new conditions and possibilities (including those opened up by the imaginative, creative, Schumpeterian innovators). So that acceptance of a possible (short-run?) equilibrative role for merely alert entrepreneurs (as elucidated in my work) does *not* require us to reject the Schumpeterian emphasis upon creativity (as, it was believed, my work does require).

CREATIVITY AND/OR ALERTNESS: A CORRECTIVE CLARIFICATION

But the truth is that views reflected in the preceding section have not fully understood my position. The "merely alert" entrepreneur identified in my work was never intended as an *alternative* to the creative, innovative Schumpeterian entrepreneur. (It was only the *equilibrative impact* of the alert entrepreneur that was contrasted with the distinctive impact which Joseph Schumpeter attributed to the activity of the creative entrepreneur.) My 1973 exposition of the role of the merely alert entrepreneur was deliberately couched in the context of the very simplest theoretical model (it was thus constructed to be able to abstract not only from the *creative* element in real-world entrepreneurship, but even from the speculative element).[5] But this did *not* imply any denial of the creativity of (or, the

---

5. I have been criticized, by other Austrian economists, for failing to emphasize (as Mises himself did emphasize) the speculative element in entrepreneurship. The present discussion should help dispel the misunderstanding which underlies this criticism. See also Kirzner (1985, p. 44).

speculative element in) real-world entrepreneurship. It did not deny that, as a result of such creativity and speculation, the dynamics of capitalism can be seen as including movements (*away* from existing stable patterns of relationship) toward new, hitherto unimagined patterns for possible equilibration.

What I had glimpsed in 1973 was an insight which still remains largely unseen by economists. This was that *the entrepreneurial-competitive market process which Ludwig von Mises had identified was driven by entrepreneurial perception of profit opportunities "waiting to be grasped."* To be sure, such opportunities "exist" in the real world only in the speculative sense (i.e., they can be *realized* only in the future). But in a very relevant sense they "exist" *now*. That is, *to the entrepreneur who sees such an opportunity,* it appears in the form of an opportunity to buy and to sell at different prices. Granted, the opportunity to sell, at least, is one that will come into full reality only in the future. But, once again, to the entrepreneur who, piercing the fog of futurity, does *now* see that opportunity, it exists for him in virtually the very same sense that opportunities simultaneously to buy and sell currency profitably in different foreign exchange markets exist *now* for the pure arbitrageur.

Once the pure arbitrage element is recognized to exist in the speculative activities of entrepreneurs, the road is open to yet another recognition. This is the recognition that the bold, creative, innovative entrepreneur, too, is at a yet higher level of abstraction, also engaged in arbitrage. What he "sees" is that, by assembling available resources in an innovative, hitherto undreamt of, fashion, and thus perhaps converting them into new, hitherto undreamt of products, he may be able (in the future) to sell output at prices which exceed the cost of that output to himself. In *all* its manifestations, entrepreneurship identifies arbitrage opportunities; the entrepreneur's activities, like those of all arbitrageurs, tend to squeeze out those arbitrage-profits opportunities he has noticed (and which "alerted" him to their existence). He tends to drive up the prices in the markets in which he sells.

There is, of course, a profound philosophical question as to whether it is legitimate to see speculative entrepreneurial profit opportunities as "waiting" to be grasped. Certainly one may wish to say that in "seeing" such possibilities, the entrepreneur is in fact *creating* them—rather than simply grasping that which already exists. My 1973 exposition, however, was not concerned with such almost-metaphysical questions. It was aiming at a down-to-earth understanding of the dynamic market process—one which clearly consists of movements *responding* to (existing or future) profit opportunities and somehow, but quite surely, succeeding in tending to eliminate imbalances in market activities. As Bastiat had pointed out more than a century earlier, the great city of Paris *does* get fed. Despite the absence of any central agency coordinating the flows of different foodstuffs into the metropolis, the market does, whether we understand it or not, succeed to a significant extent, in coordinating these flows. My 1973 work glimpses the explanation for all this in the role of entrepreneur seen *in his essential role of arbitrageur.*

To see things in this way did not (as the critics have somehow understood) mean that I was in any way denying the elements of boldness, creativity, and innovativeness which, in the real world, certainly do characterize entrepreneurial activity. Rather, my theory sees the Schumpeterian entrepreneur—with all his brash creativity—as being the agent who is *responding* to *existing* imbalances in the market. To be sure, to label a world as being in imbalance as compared with some hypothetical world operating with as yet undreamt of technological breakthroughs may seem to be using hindsight to stretch language. Yet, once these breakthroughs will have become commonplace, it will indeed seem retrospectively appropriate to describe the earlier, primitive, situation, as one pervaded by waste, one "waiting" to be corrected. The advantage to using language emphasizing alert perception of what "is," rather than language emphasizing the bold creation of what as yet does *not* exist, is that the language of alertness enables us to see with clarity that there is a single explanation for all market movements. Such movements consist of entrepreneurial actions aiming to grasp perceived pure profit opportunities. Such pure profit opportunities present themselves in a dizzying multitude of forms—*all* of them consisting of *price differentials.* Such price differentials may exist in simple single-commodity or single-resource-service contexts, in which space- or knowledge-barriers have permitted price discrepancies to emerge. They may exist in intertemporal markets in which today's resource services do not accurately reflect the future strength of demand for the products being produced by these services. And, of course, (the most important for the Schumpeterian vision), price differentials may occur in contexts in which the entrepreneurs who are today buying resource services, do so in order to introduce dramatically more efficient methods of production.

My point was (and is) to draw attention to *the* key Misesian insight. This is that *all* these price differentials (*both* attributable to Schumpeterian creativity *and* those present in the simplest of arbitrage contexts) can and should be seen as examples of entrepreneurial-arbitrage activity. Such activity drives prices systematically in directions tending to eliminate the price differentials (i.e., the opportunities for pure profit) which are, always, the sparks which ignite entrepreneurial attention, drive, and creativity.

CREATIVITY, ALERTNESS AND PUBLIC POLICY: PUZZLEMENT DISSOLVED

We may go even further—in a direction which may perhaps help dissolve the puzzlement referred to at the outset of this paper. It is not merely the case that Schumpeterian creativity can be comfortably subsumed under the category of alertness (and thus be illuminatingly seen to be, in a sense, a *response* to earlier errors). It can be suggested, I will maintain, that a focus on the "alertness" aspect of (*all*) entrepreneurship, can help us understand how public policy may help promote that very Schumpeterian *creativity* (which I certainly do acknowledge, must be the major component of future dramatic leaps in economic development). Once we recognize the "alertness" element in Schumpeterian creativity, we must also recognize that the way in which policymakers understand the market economy, is likely to carry enormously significant implications for encouragement or discouragement of entrepreneurial creativity.

The essence of alertness is, after all, not efficiency of choice within an already perceived given framework. Alertness does not refer to diligence in research. (Research can occur within a given knowledge framework.) Rather, alertness refers to a sense of what might be "around the corner," i.e., the sense to notice that *which has hitherto not been suspected of existing at all*. We know very little that is systematic about what "switches on" alertness (to notice that which has been staring one in the face, but of the existence of which one has had no inkling. After all, we cannot deliberately search for something of whose very existence one has no inkling.) But it does seem intuitively obvious that alertness can be "switched *off*" by the conviction that external intervention will confiscate (wholly or in part) whatever one *might* notice. Surely what excites one antenna to "see" that which has hitherto entirely escaped one's attention, is the general sense that something of value may be within reach, if only one knew what it was. Surely, it is the general prospect of pure entrepreneurial profit available for the taking that inspires entrepreneurial alertness. Public policies which to any degree deaden the excitement inspired by the prospect of pure entrepreneurial profit, must surely, lower the level of entrepreneurial alertness.

To be sure, creativity is much more than alertness. But the creativity that drives profit-winning entrepreneurial behavior is a creativity that embraces alertness too—alertness to present and future price patterns, alertness to new technological possibilities, and alertness to possible future patterns of demand. Public policies which tend to promote alertness, *are* policies which tend to promote creativity.

So that elaboration of Misesian insights into the pure-arbitrage-character of the entrepreneurial decision *can* be fitted into a research program aiming at the encouragement of vigorous, creative entrepreneurial economic development, after all.

REFERENCES

Boudreaux, Donald (1994), "Schumpeter and Kirzner on Competition and Equilibrium." In Peter J. Boettke and David L. Prychitko (eds.), *The Market Process: Essays in Contemporary Austrian Economics*. Aldershot: Edward Elgar.

Douhan, Robin, Gunnar Eliasson and Magnus Henrekson (2007), "Israel M. Kirzner: An Outstanding Austrian Contributor to the Economics of Entrepreneurship." *Small Business Economics* 29(1–2), 213–23.

Fisher, Franklin M. (1983), *Disequilibrium Foundations of Equilibrium Economics*. Cambridge and New York: Cambridge University Press.

Fu-Lai Yu, Tony (1998), "Economic Development in Latecomer Economies: An Entrepreneurial Perspective." *Development Policy Review* 16(2), 265–80.

——— (2001), "Entrepreneurial Alertness and Discovery." *Review of Austrian Economics* 14(1), 47–63.

Hébert, Robert F. and Albert N. Link (1982), *The Entrepreneur. Mainstream Views and Radical Critiques*. New York: Praeger.

Holcombe, Randall G. (1998), "Entrepreneurship and Economic Growth." *Quarterly Journal of Austrian Economics* 2(1), 45–62.

——— (1999), "Equilibrium versus the Invisible Hand." *Review of Austrian Economics* 12(2), 227–43.

——— (2003), "The Origins of Entrepreneurial Opportunities." *Review of Austrian Economics* 16(1), 25–43.

Kirzner, Israel M. (1973), *Competition and Entrepreneurship*. Chicago: University of Chicago Press.

——— (1978), "The Entrepreneurial Role in Menger's System." *Atlantic Economic Journal* 6(3), 31–45.

—— (1979), *Perception, Opportunity and Profit. Studies in the Theory of Entrepreneurship.* Chicago and London: University of Chicago Press.

—— (1982), "The Theory of Entrepreneurship in Economic Growth." In Calvin A. Kent, David L. Sexton and Karl H. Vesper (eds.), *Encyclopedia of Entrepreneurship,* Englewood Cliffs, N.J.: Prentice-Hall.

—— (1985), *Discovery and the Capitalist Process.* Chicago and London: University of Chicago Press.

—— (1995), "The Subjectivism of Austrian Economics." In Gerrit Meijer (ed.), *New Perspectives on Austrian Economics.* London and New York: Routledge.

—— (1992), *The Meaning of Market Process.* London and New York: Routledge.

—— (1997), "Entrepreneurial Discovery and the Competitive Market Process: An Austrian Approach." *Journal of Economic Literature* 35(1), 60–85.

—— (1999), "Creativity and/or Alertness: A Reconsideration of the Schumpeterian Entrepreneur." *Review of Austrian Economics* 11(1–2), 5–17.

—— (2000), "The Limits of the Market: the Real and the Imagined." In Israel M. Kirzner (ed.), *The Driving Force of the Market—Essays in Austrian Economics.* London: Routledge.

—— (2002), "Comment on 'A Critique of Kirzner's Finders-Keepers Defense of Profit.'" *Review of Austrian Economics* 15(1), 91–94.

Loasby, Brian J. (1982), "The Entrepreneur in Economic Theory." *Scottish Journal of Political Economy* 29(3), 220–41.

—— (1989), *The Mind and Method of the Economist.* Aldershot: Edward Elgar.

Mises, Ludwig von (1952), "Profit and Loss." In *Planning for Freedom and Other Essays and Addresses.* 2d ed. South Holland, Ill.: Libertarian Press.

Schumpeter, Joseph A. (1934), *The Theory of Economic Development.* Cambridge, Mass.: Harvard University Press.

—— (1942), *Capitalism, Socialism and Democracy.* New York: Harper & Row.

All of us like to peer into the future. We are all curious to know now what we, or perhaps our grandchildren, eventually will see and experience. And not unnaturally, we look to the practitioners of our intellectual disciplines to help provide this desired prescience. If our thirst for informed future gazing is deep in respect to the physical universe, it is virtually unslakable in respect to the social and, particularly, the economic environments. We look to our social scientists, and in particular to our economists, to tell us what the future holds in store. Surely, we reason, if only we understood how the economic world works, we should be able to know now what the future outcome of economic processes is likely to be. And the more thoroughly and profoundly we understood these workings of the economic world, we assume, the better equipped we would feel ourselves to be to provide accurate and specific forecasts of future economic conditions, and the longer would be the future period for which we would believe our forecasting ability to hold scope.

I believe that my discussion of the role of entrepreneurship in the workings of the economic system will, in this sense, prove somewhat paradoxical. I shall in fact attempt to show that the future course of a capitalist economy does indeed depend crucially upon the present and future exercise of entrepreneurship. However, the more thoroughly and profoundly we understand the way entrepreneurship shapes and determines economic phenomena, the *less* well equipped we must recognize ourselves to be to make detailed forecasts of the shape of things to come. In fact, I shall argue, it is precisely this recognition of our inability to foresee the course of the future entrepreneurial process that constitutes a significant deepening of our understanding of the way the world works.

For an economics in which the role of entrepreneurship is not acknowledged (and it is now being admitted that much of received economic theory is guilty of just this failure), the possibilities for forecasting must appear much more promising. But the better we understand the

From *Discovery and the Capitalist Process* (Chicago and London: The University of Chicago Press, 1985), 150–68. The original source is *Entrepreneurship and the Outlook for America*, ed. Jules Backman (New York: Free Press, 1983). Reprinted by permission of the author.

manner in which entrepreneurial discoveries generate economic progress, the more humble we practitioners of economic science ought to become. This of course does not mean that our understanding of entrepreneurship actually weakens our ability to know the future accurately; rather, it reveals to us how arrogant and illusionary it would be (or was) for us ever to claim such accurate foreknowledge. Our appreciation for the entrepreneurial element will thus enable us indeed to understand the future course of capitalism more accurately than we could know it without such appreciation—but less accurately than we would, in our ignorance of entrepreneurship, have *thought* ourselves to be able to know it. Let us explore how an appreciation of entrepreneurship affects our understanding of the future of capitalism.

In the following pages two basic tools in the economist's kit are considered: the economist's notion of resource allocation and the economist's understanding of capitalism as a system of markets at or near equilibrium. I shall argue that, valuable and useful as these notions may be for many purposes, they prove inadequate and even downright misleading for any deeper understanding of the ongoing capitalist process. For such more sensitive understanding, we shall discover, it will be necessary to perceive how the exercise of entrepreneurship sharply attenuates the importance of efficient resource allocation and renders profoundly unhelpful an analytical perception of the capitalist system as being at or close to equilibrium. Moreover, it will turn out, the longer the future period about which we are curious, the more serious and damaging these limitations will prove to be.

THE ALLOCATION PARADIGM

It is fifty years since Lionel (now Lord) Robbins enunciated his definition of the scope of economics in terms of the allocation of scarce resources among alternative goals.[1] Largely as a result of Robbins's brilliant clarification of the issues, economists have learned to focus their attention on the concept of *allocative efficiency*. In other words, economists ask whether, in view of the given ranking of goals desired and the given array of resources available, the operative decisions are such as to ensure that no lower-ranked goal is attained at the expense of any more highly ranked goal. Where the allocation of resources has been in this sense inefficient, the economist is prepared to discuss the importance of reallocating resources from the lesser valued to the more highly valued goals.

Now there can be no doubt that Robbins's formulation has been enormously beneficial for economics. It provided economics with an analytical framework that has been extremely helpful in many ways. It directs the attention of economists to the kinds of questions that, in many contexts, are indeed precisely the questions that do need to be answered. It enabled economists to recognize that their theorems had generality extending far beyond the narrow context of material wealth and welfare (to which nineteenth-century economics had come to be confined). Yet as we shall see, this allocation paradigm has in certain ways proved something of a stumbling block. *Economists have adopted the allocation criterion with such enthusiasm as to apply it to contexts for which it has in fact no relevance.* And particularly where they have indeed applied it in such illegitimate fashion, economists have become trapped in their own paradigm; they have failed to recognize crucial aspects of socioeconomic problems that simply do not fit into the allocation framework.

Thus, in many of our textbooks of elementary economics, undergraduates are taught that economics deals with the problem of how a nation or a society can solve "its economic problem," that is, how it can efficiently allocate "its" scarce resources among "its" competing goals.[2] But of course this involves an altogether questionable extension of Robbins's formulation. Robbins was concerned exclusively with *individual* economizing, or allocative, activity. He did not make the leap from the clear-cut allocation problem as it faces the individual to the altogether problematic notion of allocation with respect to a *society* of individuals. As Professor Buchanan has pointed out,[3] before one can talk sensibly about an allocation problem facing a society, it is first necessary to solve certain highly intractable and well-known difficulties that plague welfare economics. (Thus, unless one is prepared to make interpersonal comparisons of utility, it is not at all clear what one is to mean by the notion of a ranking of the importance *to society* of alternative production possibilities.)

More to the point, perhaps, of our specific concerns here is the circumstance that the allocation paradigm tends to divert attention away from the entrepreneurial function. The very problem that Robbins identified so clearly and so valuably is set up entirely in terms that presume a *given* framework of ends ranked and resources available. Before the economizing agent ever embarks on seeking the optimal allocative solution to the economizing problem, he is presumed to have already identified, somehow, the range of alternative courses of allocative action from among which he may choose. His economic problem, as defined by Robbins, does not encompass the task of *discovering* hitherto unnoticed available courses of action. (It is of course true that one of the *already given* courses of action available may be to undertake a systematic search along specified lines. But the notion of "given available courses of action" has no room for the step that *discovers,* say, that a systematic search may be a potentially useful course of action.) The problem of allocation presumes a given set of ranked goals—it does not consider the possibility of the discovery of additional goals that may be worthy of pursuit or of the discovery that some different ranking of these goals may be in fact desirable. The allocation paradigm presumes a perceived array of available means and a perceived array of technical formulas for the deployment of these means—it does not encompass the discovery of new resources available or the discovery of new technical uses to which they may be put.

In other words, the allocation paradigm, valuable though it is, bears the disadvantage of drawing analytical attention away from the entrepreneurial function of ensuring the continuing awareness of worthwhile goals, of not overlooking available means—of ensuring that desirable opportunities not be neglected by oversight. And serious enough as this disadvantage may be in respect to individual allocation, *it is of even greater potential harm in regard to the (illegitimate) extension of the allocation concept from the level of the individual to that of the society.* To talk of society allocating its resources presumes a given, perceived framework of scarce resources available to society. This way of discussing the economic problems facing society may permit analysis of how such given scarce resources can be optimally deployed, but it diverts attention away from those dimensions for economic activity along which there may occur entrepreneurial discovery of hitherto unanticipated stocks of resources or hitherto unglimpsed possibilities for the technological deployment of known resources. Clearly, the longer the prospective period we are contemplating, the more serious it becomes to overlook the implications of entrepreneurial escape from the instantaneous finity of resources. We shall return to these considerations after taking account of similar questions that should be raised about the second of the basic tools in the "economist's kit" mentioned earlier.

CAPITALISM AND MARKET EQUILIBRIUM

This second tool is the vision of the capitalist economy adopted by mainstream economists which sees it as a system of markets at or near equilibrium. In this view, a free market (that is, pure capitalist) economy achieves fairly close conformity at all times to a configuration of prices which encourages sets of attempted purchases and sales of each input and of each produced consumer good—that can all be successfully carried out without regret and without disappointment. In other words, the activities undertaken by each market participant are such as to permit them all to be sustained. No one produces a commodity and finds it impossible to sell it at a price that justifies its costs of production. No one seeking a commodity with an eagerness financially justifying its production fails to find that it has been produced. All markets clear. All plans made are able to be carried out; no one subsequently regrets not having made a different plan. Or to put the matter somewhat differently, no one is, in the light of the going market prices, tempted to undertake plans that incorrectly anticipate the plans that others (inspired by the same market prices) are in fact making.

Here there can be no doubt that an understanding of the way markets work has, on the whole, been greatly helped by the insight that what occurs in markets is not random or haphazard but is the logical outcome of systematic forces which (if they could work themselves out in unimpeded fashion) can be imagined eventually to generate the above conditions of equilibrium. There is indeed no doubt that most of the market prices we observe have been powerfully affected, at least, by these systematic forces of market adjustment. For many purposes, especially where attention is focused on a small part of the market, it is an excusable simplification for analysis to proceed as if these forces of market adjustment have indeed already fully completed their tasks. Yet it must be pointed out that, to a very important extent, a view which sees the capitalist economy as a system of markets at or near equilibrium is not merely a *simplified* view of capitalism but also a *distorted* view. This view is distorted in perceiving, as the salient feature of capitalism, its being at all times close to the fully coordinated state—when in fact the salient feature of capitalism is surely to be found, rather, in the ceaseless market agitation generated by the continual discovery of *failures* in coordination. Of course it is this ceaseless agitation of the market which is responsible for the considerable coordinative properties which capitalism certainly possesses.

But a view of the market as a sequential, systematic process of continual adjustment, incessantly buffeted and redirected by exogenous changes, is one sharply at variance with the view of it as expressing at all times an approximately fully adjusted state of affairs. This difference is one that more recent critics of orthodox economics have not failed to identify. What is important, for present purposes, is for us to recognize that the responsibility for this distortion with which we have charged the standard, equilibrium view of capitalism rests with its failure to incorporate the entrepreneurial element into its perspective. As soon as entrepreneurial activity is permitted an essential role in the analysis of capitalism, the focus of attention shifts from already completed states of equilibrium to ongoing processes of adjustment and of responsive change.

THE ROLE OF ENTREPRENEURSHIP IN CAPITALISM

In the preceding sections we have observed that the incorporation of entrepreneurship into economic analysis sharply limits the usefulness of two important tools in the standard economist's tool kit. I wish, in this paper, to examine the implications of these observations for our ability to peer into the future course of a capitalist economy. Let us briefly review the meaning and role of entrepreneurship. For our purposes it will perhaps be excusable to set forth by assertion a number of insights and definitions developed more extensively (and less dogmatically) elsewhere.[4]

An individual decision maker exercises entrepreneurship in discovering opportunities for improving his circumstances that have hitherto not been known to him. Such entrepreneurial discovery is a matter not of correct calculation but of correctly perceiving the elements to be considered in performing calculation. In other words, entrepreneurial discovery consists not in achieving efficiency in dealing with a given situation but in alertness to the possibility that the true situation (with respect to which efficiency would be worth pursuing) is in fact different from the situation that had been assumed to be given. A significant aspect of the entrepreneurial dimension of individual decision making is that, along this dimension, the fixity of available resources is no longer absolute. Entrepreneurship consists, in part, in the discovery of hitherto unnoticed reserves of available resources.

In a capitalist economy, the scope for and exercise of individual entrepreneurship correspond, in significant degree, to characteristic features of the market process. Where a market has not yet attained equilibrium, this manifests itself in opportunities for individual entrepreneurial gain.

The discovery and pursuit of such entrepreneurial profit constitute and drive the market process, during which such profit opportunities are ground down by entrepreneurial competition. We may distinguish two levels at which entrepreneurship may be exercised in a capitalist system.

First, at a given date a market economy is likely to be less than fully coordinated *with respect to information currently possessed*. Specific knowledge may at this moment exist in the minds of some market participants. Other market participants may, nonetheless, be engaged in activities that are imperfectly coordinated in light of the availability of this knowledge. Entrepreneurship may be exercised in harnessing this existing knowledge and in this way modifying the pattern of market activities. What the entrepreneur does, in this case, is discover the existence and/or the value of *available* knowledge.

The second level at which entrepreneurship may be exercised in the market is made possible by the circumstance that, at any given date, there presumably exist innumerable useful truths that *might* be known but which, at the moment, are unknown to *anyone* in the market. Entrepreneurship may thus be exercised not through the discovery of existing knowledge but in the discovery of totally new truths or, at least, in the discovery and anticipation of the prospective relative values of resources as they will be affected by future discovery of such new truths.

Both levels of entrepreneurship, it should be emphasized, constitute the discovery of hitherto incomplete coordination. At the first level, a market participant might, for example, be producing at high cost when technology currently available might permit production at much lower cost. The incompleteness of coordination, in such a case, may be illustrated very simply. Imagine two adjacent rooms in each of which a given item is being bought and sold. Because of the wall between the two rooms, participants in each of the two markets are, let us imagine, unaware of the existence of the market in the adjacent room. As a result the traded item sells for $10 in the first room and for $20 in the second. Clearly we have here incomplete coordination of buying and selling decisions. There are those in the first room who might be willing to sell if only the price were, perhaps, as high as $14. At the same time there are those in the second room who might be willing to buy if only the price were as low as $16. Conditions for mutually beneficial trade between these parties clearly exist, yet they are not being applied.

This incomplete coordination with respect to *existing* information is a result of failure of market participants to exploit the arbitrage opportunity created by the difference in price between the two rooms. Entrepreneurship, in such cases, will then take the form of the discovery of this pure profit opportunity—thus driving prices together and eliminating the incomplete coordination that arose from the original imperfect mutual awareness on the part of market participants. The existence of currently available technology that could produce, at a cost of $10, an item selling for $20, represents precisely this kind of scope for entrepreneurship. There might be potential consumers for the item if only it could be produced and sold for less than $16. This possibility indeed exists yet is not being pursued. Producers have apparently not yet discovered that the technology *already* exists for such low-cost production. The entrepreneur who discovers the opportunity of buying all necessary inputs for $10 and selling the output for $20 is correcting the incompleteness of coordination with respect to *currently existing* knowledge.

At the second level, the incompleteness of coordination is of a different kind, but it exists nonetheless. Current market activities may be fully coordinated *with each other* yet be very imperfectly coordinated with future activities *as these will eventually turn out to be informed by as yet undiscovered truths.* The current price of natural gas and the current level of its consumption may be fully coordinated with one another and with other current prices and market activities (informed by the most up-to-date intelligence). Yet this price may be "too high" and consumption "too low" from the perspective (that may, in several years, be provided by technological or other discoveries) of the possibilities, say, of tapping solar energy. Today these possibilities simply do not exist; yet entrepreneurship may be exercised in anticipating their discovery. Entrepreneurial gain here is captured by anticipating price changes in the future that would never emerge simply on the basis of information existing today.

It should thus be observed that at both of these two levels at which we have identified entrepreneurial activity, such activity may be described as making up an equilibrating and coordinating tendency. At the first level, where imperfect coordination existed with respect to existing information, entrepreneurship may be seen as steering present prices and present decisions in the direction of the relevant, coordinated equilibrium configuration. At the second level, where entrepreneurship consists in arriving at or in anticipating wholly novel truths, it may be seen as tending to coordinate present decisions with future decisions and present prices with future prices; entrepreneurship, at this second level, may be seen as nudging the system in the direction of intertemporal equilibrium. But there is an important difference between these two senses on which the entrepreneurial market process "achieves a tendency toward equilibration."

ENTREPRENEURSHIP, EQUILIBRATION, AND THE DETERMINACY OF THE FUTURE

The central theorem of economics, the theorem which permits economists to view market phenomena as the understandable outcome of systematic forces rather than as a random sequence of events, is what demonstrates the equilibrative and coordinative tendencies in the market process. It is this theorem which permits us to feel confident that, sooner or later, a tendency will have asserted itself toward the social integration of all the currently available information scattered throughout the economy.[5]

So it is the entrepreneurial market process which justifies, to some extent, the view that society as a whole tends to achieve a coordinated balance among the innumerable activities of its individual members, *in a manner analogous to the way we view—à la Robbins—each individual as achieving allocative efficiency with respect to the given goals and resources relevant to that individual.* From this perspective the scarcity of resources, including information, available to society, together with the arrays of preferences displayed by the individual members of society, tends to "determine" the allocation of resources within the economy in a manner analogous to that in which each individual's budget allocations are seen as "determined" by his preference rankings and the array of resources available to him. So it is the fixity and scarcity of existing societal resources that is, in part, the source of whatever "determinacy" economic science enables us to perceive in observed market phenomena.

Now this presents us with a certain paradox. We saw earlier that it is our recognition of the entrepreneurial element that limited, in my view, the significance of the concept of efficient resource allocation (which serves for many economists as the central theme of their discipline). In addition I questioned the possibility of applying the concept of allocative efficiency to a society as a whole, arguing that the concept as expounded by Lord Robbins was one that had reference strictly to individual choice. Yet, as indicated in the preceding paragraph, economic analysis does surely demonstrate the tendency toward the achievement of coordination within a society, at least analogously to the coordination achieved by the efficiently allocating individual economizer. And, paradoxically, it is precisely the operation of the entrepreneurial element (the recognition of which *limited* for us the significance of the allocation concept) that provides some justification for the treatment of society as a whole as achieving a balanced allocation of resources.

The discussion in the preceding section can throw further light on these matters: in exactly the same way that the recognition of the entrepreneurial element in individual action limits the relevance of the concept of individual allocative efficiency, we shall see that the recognition of the second level of those previously discussed, at which entrepreneurship is exercised in a market economy, limits the sense in which the economic achievements of a market can be grasped in terms—even as metaphor—of allocative efficiency. Let me try to clarify what by now must appear to be a somewhat confusing picture; I offer several summary observations.

1. Entrepreneurship as exercised through the market is responsible for its equilibrative and coordinative tendencies. While the ceaseless *operation* of entrepreneurially driven market forces underscores the inadequacy of the view of the market as at all times at or near equilibrium, nonetheless it is the results achieved by these forces that constitute whatever "allocative balance" a society may be thought to possess.

2. This "allocative balance" achieved in a market consists in reality, as Hayek showed, of the social integration of the innumerable scraps of existing information that are present in scattered form throughout society. The degree of social integration thus entrepreneurially achieved is what justifies, to a limited extent, the metaphorical treatment of an economic society as analogous to the Robbinsian allocating, economizing individual.

3. Yet the same entrepreneurial spirit that stimulates the discovery in the market of the value of information *now* existing throughout the market also tends to stimulate the discovery or "creation" of *entirely new* information concerning ways to anticipate or to satisfy consumer preferences. The entrepreneurial process at this second level is what drives

the capitalist system toward higher and higher standards of achievement (quite apart from the economic progress, resulting from the systematic accumulation of invested capital, that is fully consistent with the coordination of *existing* information).

4. While, in a special sense, this progress in the capitalist economy arising from the entrepreneurial discovery or creation of totally new information may also be described as coordinative, nonetheless it represents an *escape* from the limits imposed by the finite and scattered information possessed at earlier dates. In other words, in the context of this "long-run" entrepreneurial progress of the capitalist system, the metaphor of society as analogous to the Robbinsian economizing individual can no longer be sustained at all. The entrepreneurial discovery by an individual of new goals to pursue and new availability of resources cannot be subsumed under the allocative, maximizing model of individual decision making. In precisely the same way, the progress achieved by a capitalist system as a result of entrepreneurial discovery of totally new social opportunities renders totally inoperative the metaphor of the market as an efficient allocator of resources within the constraints of existing, limited resources.

At the outset of this chapter I announced my intention to show that recognition of the entrepreneurial element in capitalism would make it less and less possible for us to correctly anticipate specific information regarding capitalism's future course. We can now see why this must be so. Whatever limited determinacy may be ascribed to the market economy derives from the market's equilibrative propensities. To the extent that the market integrates existing scattered information concerning wants, technology, and available resources, it may be argued that the market's future course is determined by that existing stock of information. But to the extent that the market can, through long-run entrepreneurial discovery, transcend the limits of any existing constraints of knowledge, its future course becomes wholly indeterminate. We may argue, with great confidence, that under capitalism entrepreneurial discovery will disclose new arrays of social opportunities—but precisely because these are wholly new opportunities *created* by entrepreneurial discovery, they cannot be seen in any sense as the *inevitable* outcome of the entrepreneurial process. Our confidence in the creativity of entrepreneurship does not in any way suggest a determinate pattern in such creativity.

TECHNOLOGICAL ADVANCE AND
ENTREPRENEURIAL DISCOVERY

I should perhaps pause to emphasize that the long-run entrepreneurial process upon which I have rested my thesis for the future of capitalism is *not* quite the same process as is usually associated with technological advance. It is certainly often recognized that the long-run capacity of a capitalist system depends crucially on the rate of technological advance. As long ago as 1871 Carl Menger, founder of the Austrian School of Economics, wrote:

> The quantities of consumption goods at human disposal are limited only by the extent of human knowledge of the causal connections between things, and by the extent of human control over these things. . . . Nothing is more certain than that the degree of economic progress of mankind will still, in future epochs, be commensurate with the degree of progress of human knowledge.[6]

It would be possible to concur with Menger's prediction and yet argue that this prediction can be accepted within an "allocation" framework. That is, it would be possible to see advances in technological knowledge as the results of deliberate investment in search activity undertaken entirely within the perceived possibilities available at each date. Investment in R&D may, on this view, be seen as merely a special kind of investment that does not require us to transcend the "maximizing" model for an understanding of market outcomes.

The view advanced here is much closer, in this respect, to that of Schumpeter, who was thoroughly persuaded, of course, of the critical and creative role of entrepreneurship in capitalist development. In his vision, entrepreneurial activity is continually keeping "the capitalist engine in motion" through "the new consumers' goods, the new methods of production or transportation, the new markets, the new forms of industrial organization that capitalist enterprise creates."[7] This activity continually "revolutionizes the economic structure *from within* . . . destroying the old one . . . creating a new one. This process of Creative Destruction is the essential fact about capitalism."[8]

What I wish to emphasize is that this entrepreneurial process, because it cannot be captured within a Robbinsian maximizing framework—even one explicitly arranged to consider maximizing and allocation within a prospective multiperiod framework—is *in principle* beyond the scope of detailed prediction. But this does not mean we have nothing to say about the general character of this entrepreneurial process that so defies detailed prediction.

ENTREPRENEURSHIP AND THE FUTURE OF CAPITALISM

The position I desire to convey can perhaps best be articulated by comparing it with that of a new book just published (1981) by Princeton University Press. In this book, *The Ultimate Resource*, its economist-author, Professor Julian L. Simon, adopts a provocatively unorthodox stance with respect to the likelihood of increasing resource scarcity and economic difficulties in the long-run future. Contrary to the prevalent view that "we are entering an age of scarcity in which our finite natural resources are running out, that our environment is becoming more polluted, and that population growth threatens our civilization and our very lives,"[9] Simon maintains vigorously that:

> [The] standard of living has risen along with the size of the world's population since the beginning of recorded time. And with increases in income and population have come less severe shortages, lower costs, and an increased availability of resources, including a cleaner environment and greater access to natural recreation areas. . . . Contrary to common rhetoric, there are no meaningful limits to the continuation of this process. . . . There is no physical or economic reason why human resourcefulness and enterprise cannot forever continue to respond to impending shortages and existing problems with new expedients that, after an adjustment period, leave us better off than before the problem arose.[10]

Simon's theme parallels my own in certain respects, although it is couched in different terminology. Yet certain differences between the two themes should perhaps be pointed out. As I have argued, Simon maintains that for long-run purposes economic resources should not be treated as finite. "We see the resource system as being as unlimited as the number of thoughts a person might have."[11] The "ultimate resource" for Simon is "people—skilled, spirited, and hopeful people who will exert their wills and imaginations for their own benefit, and so, inevitably, for the benefit of us all."[12] A number of the optimistic observations made by Simon, for example, concerning food supplies and population growth, are strongly reminiscent of Schumpeter's spirited debunking forty years ago of the stagnationist thesis.[13] (Somewhat surprisingly, Simon appears not to refer to Schumpeter throughout his book.) Simon's message, although couched in different terms, parallels my own: the notion of society's being constrained in scarce, given resources, as is the individual in the Robbinsian framework, is not a useful idea in predicting long-run trends in capitalism.

But whereas in my own treatment of this theme I have placed great emphasis upon the notion of *entrepreneurship*, Simon nowhere, as far as I can discover, uses this term in his discussions. Simon appears to rest his case for optimism upon his analysis of past economic performance and upon his general faith in the imagination and resourcefulness of human beings. Moreover, Simon's confidence in these respects is so great as to lead him to make specific, highly optimistic forecasts.[14] My own grounds for challenging the premise of long-run finiteness of resources has been more cautious and depends heavily on the scope permitted by the institutional environment for the free exercise of entrepreneurship.

Whereas Simon appears not to pay much attention to the institutional environment in which his forecasts are to have relevance, my own discussion points very much to the crucial importance of a capitalist framework. In the simplest sense of the term, of course, entrepreneurship—free enterprise—has scope only under free market capitalism. So the possibility of escaping from the long-run constraints of scarce resources through a series of horizon-expanding discoveries would appear to require a capitalist environment. Yet, on the other hand, it might be argued that in the broad sense of the term the concept of entrepreneurship is not necessarily confined to capitalism; after all, central planners may exercise entrepreneurial imagination, creativity, and discovery for the benefit of the socialized society. For my purposes here, it is not strictly necessary to comment on the scope for entrepreneurial discovery in a planned society; but several brief observations are in order insofar as the issue relates to the future of capitalism.

I have argued elsewhere[15] that the scope for entrepreneurship cannot, in general, be disengaged *from the prospect of winning entrepreneurial gain.* For a hitherto unperceived opportunity to be noticed by a potential entrepreneur, it is of great importance that the potential entrepreneur believe that any opportunity he perceives will somehow redound to his own benefit. This line of argument tends, of course, to point to the importance, within capitalism, of freedom of entry into markets and of untrammeled opportunity to gain from entrepreneurial opportunities perceived.

The relationship between entrepreneurship and the future of capitalism is thus a two-sided one. Only a capitalism in which freedom to grasp opportunities perceived is available to the fullest extent can encourage the fullest flowering of entrepreneurial discovery and creativity. On the other hand, it is the exercise of such long-run entrepreneurial creativity and discovery that permits us to see the economic system as liberated from the scarcity constraints that would compress us into an allocation framework.

We are not able to chart the future of capitalism in any specificity. Our reason for this incapability is precisely that which assures us (if not quite on the same grounds as Simon or with the same degree of specificity of optimism) the economic future of capitalism will be one of progress and advance. The circumstance that precludes our viewing the future of capitalism as a determinate one is the very circumstance in which, with entrepreneurship at work, we are no longer confined by any scarcity framework. It is therefore the very absence of this element of determinacy and predictability that, paradoxically, permits us to feel confidence in the long-run vitality and progress of the economy under capitalism.

NOTES

1. See Lionel Robbins, *An Essay on the Nature and Significance of Economic Science*, 2d ed. (London: Macmillan, 1935), pp. 12–16.

2. For examples see W. J. Baumol and A. S. Blinder, *Economics, Principles, and Policy* (New York: Harcourt Brace Jovanovich, 1979), p. 45.

3. J. M. Buchanan, *What Should Economists Do?* (Indianapolis: Liberty Press, 1979), pp. 20–22.

4. See Israel M. Kirzner, *Competition and Entrepreneurship* (Chicago: University of Chicago Press, 1973), and idem, *Perception, Opportunity, and Profit:* (Chicago: University of Chicago Press, 1979).

5. Cf. F. A. Hayek, "The Use of Knowledge in Society," *American Economic Review* 35, 4 (September 1945): 519–30; reprinted in *Individualism and Economic Order* (London: Routledge and Kegan Paul, 1949).

6. Carl Menger, *Principles of Economics* (1871; translated by J. Dingwall and B. Hoselitz, 1950; New York: New York University Press, 1981), p. 74.

7. J. A. Schumpeter, *Capitalism, Socialism, and Democracy*, 3d ed. (New York: Harper and Row, 1950), p. 83.

8. Ibid.

9. Julian L. Simon, *The Ultimate Resource* (Princeton: Princeton University Press, 1981), p. 15.

10. Ibid., p. 345.

11. Ibid., p. 347.

12. Ibid., p. 348.

13. Schumpeter, *Capitalism, Socialism, and Democracy,* chap. 10.

14. See Simon, *Ultimate Resource,* pp. 21, 27.

15. Israel M. Kirzner, "The Perils of Regulation: A Market-Process Approach," Occasional Paper of the Law and Economics Center University of Miami, 1978, reprinted in this volume, chap. 6 [see Israel M. Kirzner, *Reflections on Ethics, Freedom, Welfare Economics, Policy, and the Legacy of Austrian Economics* (Carmel, Ind.: Liberty Fund, 2018)]; idem, "The Primacy of Entrepreneurial Discovery," in Israel M. Kirzner et al., *The Prime Mover of Progress: The Entrepreneur in Capitalism and Socialism,* ed. A. Seldon (London: Institute of Economic Affairs, 1980), reprinted in this volume, chap. 2 [see Israel M. Kirzner, *Reflections on Ethics, Freedom, Welfare Economics, Policy, and the Legacy of Austrian Economics* (Carmel, Ind.: Liberty Fund, 2018)].

THE ENTREPRENEUR IN ECONOMIC THEORY

The issue we wish to explore does not directly concern the theory of entrepreneurial behavior itself. It deals, rather, with how the economic theory of the market economy can accommodate the entrepreneurial role. There is an important difference between these two issues. The theory of entrepreneurial behavior—the issue which we are *not* addressing—is not primarily concerned with the coherence or determinacy of the economic *system*. Instead, recognizing, to greater or lesser degree, the difference between the entrepreneur and other market agents, it seeks to understand the factors which govern entrepreneurial decision-making. Recent attempts in the literature toward a useful synthesis of earlier contributions to entrepreneurial theory appear to have *this* objective primarily in mind.[1] It seems not to be a foremost concern, in these attempts, to examine the significance of entrepreneurial activity for the core market processes and outcomes upon which traditional microeconomic theory has focused. What we wish to explore here, however, is precisely this latter concern. We inquire into the ability of the economic theory of the market economy to incorporate (and hence coexist with) the entrepreneurial function. No doubt our own inquiry will not be able to proceed very far without making *some* guesses or assumptions about the decision-making of entrepreneurs. But, for our question, the construction of models of entrepreneurial decision-making can never be more than a preliminary step toward the goal of fitting such decision-making into our theory of markets.

ECONOMIC THEORY WITHOUT THE ENTREPRENEUR

It is now widely recognized that for many decades the core of economic theory was developed with virtually no attention being paid to the existence of entrepreneurs in markets.[2] From the 1930s to the 1970s and beyond, the standard theory presented models of the market economy in which decisions are made by maximizing agents with full effective mutual information (so that no scope existed for entrepreneurial profit-making). These equilibrium models indeed included a "theory of the

From *The Dynamics of Entrepreneurship*, ed. Erik Dahmen, Leslie Hannah, and Israel M. Kirzner (Lund: Lund Business Press, 1994), 45–61. Reprinted by permission.

firm" in which an "entrepreneur" maximized "profit" by arranging appropriate marginal equalities. But the profit referred to in this theory simply consisted of short-run quasi-rents on given capital equipment, not entrepreneurial pure profit at all. And the maximizing decision-maker operating the firm was an entrepreneur in name only. The model constrained his decision-making, in terms of product quality, techniques of production and price, within limits wholly alien to the context in which real-world entrepreneurs characteristically operate. He was free neither to strike out imaginatively with a new quality of product, nor to innovate boldly with any new technique of production. The profit maximizing price-quantity configuration was marked out rigidly by the mathematics of the firm's circumstances, leaving no scope for entrepreneurial competitiveness, drive, and daring. The behavioral and informational assumptions underlying these models assured effortless maximization and virtual omniscience, undisturbed by the harrowing doubts typically inspired by an uncertain world, and immune to the threats posed by aggressive, visionary industrial pioneers.

In earlier versions of neoclassical economics there had been room, at least, to recognize the existence of the entrepreneur and to puzzle over his contribution to the market process. In fact it was the first decades following on the marginalist revolution of the 1870s which saw the most vigorous efforts at disentangling the entrepreneurial function analytically from the other layers of economic activity with which entrepreneurship is typically integrated in the world of flesh and blood businessmen. It was this half-century in which the leading theorists intensively explored the entrepreneurial role, and in which many of the best known approaches to understanding entrepreneurship (including those of J. B. Clark, F. B. Hawley, J. A. Schumpeter and Frank H. Knight) were developed.

But as neoclassical economics became more carefully formalized, as the mathematics of equilibrium theory came more and more to occupy center stage in the exposition of market theory, references to the entrepreneur receded from the micro textbooks. Price theory came to mean equilibrium theory to the exclusion of all else. The theory of individual decision-making came to mean the theory of individual decisions in the context of fully known equilibrium price configurations. The markets in which individual decisions interacted were explored exclusively on the assumption that all these decisions had already—before the curtain rose on the analytics of market theory—somehow come to be fully and mutually adjusted. Price theory came, in this way, to offer a picture of markets in which there was nothing for the entrepreneur to do; the entire theory was built around a concept from which entrepreneurship was excluded.

Careful consideration of mainstream microeconomic theory since the 1930s leads one, in fact, to understand all too clearly why entrepreneurship was so glaringly absent from its models. From the perspective of this theory the phenomenon of entrepreneurship must indeed *have appeared highly dangerous for and inimical to* economic understanding.

The goal of achieving theoretical explanation of market outcomes depends, for mainstream microeconomic theory, upon our being able to claim determinacy for the sets of individual decisions which together make up these outcomes. As the theory came to be formalized in terms of equilibrium configurations, the justification for emphasis on these configurations came to be seen in that it is the structure imposed by the constraints of the equilibrium models which permits us to see its component decisions as rigidly determined. Because we are in equilibrium, individual decisions are constrained to patterns which are, in principle, predictable. Because individual decisions are seen as rigidly determined, it becomes acceptable to see market outcomes as rigidly determined, in turn, by the decisions of which they consist.

For such a self-reinforcing view of markets, the notion of freewheeling entrepreneurs with unpredictable propensities for initiating daring surprises, must appear alarming in the extreme. If we are to explain the real world in terms of our equilibrium models, we must feel confident that the activities of such "unconstrained" decision-makers can fairly be ignored, that the relevant features of the market landscape can be accounted for entirely in terms of the well-behaved, tightly constrained decision-making constructs of our maximizing models. It is not merely that in equilibrium there is no scope for entrepreneurial grasping of pure profit; rather it is that the methodological point of departure central to the entire sub-discipline, is the notion of exhaustive mutual constraint, a notion requiring the exclusion of the unconstrained entrepreneur, a priori.

THE REAPPEARANCE OF THE ENTREPRENEUR

It is now some twenty years since economic theorists have come to feel uncomfortable about the absence of entrepreneurship from their models.[3] A number of circumstances seem to have contributed to this discomfort. First of all, the importance of the entrepreneur in the real world became more and more difficult to ignore. A theory purporting to account for the phenomena of the market without providing any scope for the most obvious of all market participants became harder and harder to swallow.[4] Second of all, the sophistication achieved by microeconomic theorists in analyzing decision-making within all kinds of complicated scenarios involving risk and incomplete knowledge, appeared to offer, in principle, some hope that entrepreneurial decision-making, too, might some day be found to fit into more complex models of individual choice.[5] And, finally, economists were coming to recognize the methodological inadequacies of theories based on the unbuttressed *assumption* of market equilibrium at all times. It came gradually to be recognized that behind any claim of relevance for equilibrium models must lie some theory of how, in fact, equilibrium can be achieved from initial conditions of dis-equilibrium.[6] In recognizing the need for a theory of equilibration, modern theorists have appeared to be rediscovering the perspective of their pre-1930 forebears, for whom the equilibrium concept never did swallow up the entire corpus of the theory of markets.[7] In achieving this rediscovery it was inevitable that the role of entrepreneurs in influencing the course of the market process came to be considered.

A DIGRESSION ON THE SCHUMPETERIAN ENTREPRENEUR

To some extent the reappearance of the entrepreneur was, paradoxically enough, both encouraged and obstructed by the well-established emphasis upon the innovative entrepreneur which Joseph Schumpeter had introduced into mainstream economics. As is well-known, Schumpeter developed his ideas concerning the entrepreneurial role early in his career;[8] he returned to them again and again in his later work. Particularly in his 1942 *Capitalism, Socialism and Democracy*, Schumpeter used his insights concerning the bold, pioneering entrepreneur to challenge the dominance of the perfect competition model, from which such entrepreneurs were excluded. Although he never did succeed in making much of an impact in this regard upon mainstream theory, Schumpeter's work on innovation was sufficiently prominent to keep the idea of the entrepreneur at least alive on the back burner of economic theory. Schumpeter was the prominent exception to our earlier generalization concerning the absence of the entrepreneur from mainstream theory. And there is no doubt that awareness of this prominent exception has played an important part in the recent reawakening of the interest of economists in the entrepreneurial role.[9]

Yet, at the same time, it seems fair to suggest that Schumpeter's work on the entrepreneur has continued to obscure, to some extent, the need for analytical attention to the entrepreneurial role *within the theory of the market*. Our basis for this contention lies in the following circumstance. Schumpeter's entrepreneur never did play a role in the achievement of equilibrium market outcomes. From his first brilliant 1912 exposition of the entrepreneurial role, Schumpeter saw the entrepreneur as the figure which disrupts an achieved state of equilibrium, creating new ideas, new possibilities—in the light of which the market must somehow adjust to some new, currently relevant equilibrium state. Schumpeter's entrepreneur played no role in this newly initiated process of adjustment. The essence of capitalism indeed came to be seen, for Schumpeter, in the capacity of the system continually to generate such processes of "creative destruction." But it must be pointed out that these processes of entrepreneurial innovation operated wholly outside (or between) those powerful Walrasian equilibrium models which continued, for Schumpeter, to govern the capitalist market.

It was thus possible, for a Schumpeterian, to have the best of both worlds: to recognize the dominance of Walrasian equilibrium systems (in which no room existed for the entrepreneur) while at the same time emphasizing the importance of the entrepreneur in continually raising the relevant level of technology (at which Walrasian equilibrium is established). It seems plausible that it was Schumpeter's influence which kept alive the idea of the importance of entrepreneurship in achieving economic growth and development, at the very same time that entrepreneurship was accorded no role at all in the core of mainstream microeconomic theorizing.[10]

ENTREPRENEURSHIP IN EQUILIBRIUM?

One prominent contemporary attempt to reconcile equilibrium theory with the entrepreneurial role has been that of Professor Theodore W. Schultz.[11] His approach is to postulate a special kind of human ability, the ability to reallocate resources in response to perceived disequilibrium. For this special ability there is a demand schedule and a supply schedule. The demand schedule for this ability reflects the incentives provided by the gains to be expected from successful reallocation in the context of the particular disequilibrium under examination. The supply schedule "of services from these abilities depends upon the stock of a particular form of human capital at any point in time and on the costs and the rate at which the stock can be increased."[12] The value of this special ability is then a "function of the demand for and the supply of that ability." This extension of the role of entrepreneurship, as Schultz sees it,[13] emphasizes that the ability to perceive and correct disequilibria is a scarce resource and must be incorporated into models of general equilibrium theory. "Unless we develop equilibrating models, the function of this particular ability cannot be analyzed. Within such models, the function of entre-preneurship would be much extended and the supply of entrepreneurial ability would be treated as a scarce resource."[14]

The implication of Schultz's approach is that entrepreneurial abil-ity ("the ability to deal with disequilibria") can be fitted into our models of general equilibrium without excessive strain. The market will deter-mine, fairly accurately, the equilibrium value of this ability to deal with disequilibria.

At this value the market will respond fairly faithfully by providing the corresponding volume of services of this ability, i.e., the volume marked out by the appropriate supply schedule for this scarce and costly resource. The market will, therefore, at any given moment be enjoying the appro-priate volume of equilibrating services. The system as a whole will be maintained, pretty well at all moments in time, approximately as close to precisely full general equilibrium as it is worth for the market to pay for.

Careful consideration of this approach reveals the limited extent to which it has incorporated entrepreneurial behavior into its theory of mar-ket adjustment. The notion of a supply schedule for entrepreneurial ser-vices suggests a notion of entrepreneurship which somehow squeezes it back into the model of tightly constrained individual decision-making. The idea of a supply schedule for a particular factor service rests on the assumption that the quantity of that factor service that will be offered to the market in response to a particular factor-price is tightly determined. Given this factor price, it is held, we can be sure that each potential indi-vidual entrepreneur will respond systematically and supply a determinate volume of the scarce service. This approach subsumes entrepreneurial behavior under the same categories of predictable, determinate individ-ual decision-making which cover all other supply decisions made in the models of the market economy. But, as already pointed out, this approach leaves out precisely that kind of unpredictable, unconstrained behavior which we generally associate with the world of flesh and blood entrepreneurs, who operate on hunch, on impulse, with daringly aggressive market moves and on the basis of altogether unpredictable fresh ideas.

It will be recalled that the difficulty of incorporating the entrepreneur into the "tight" equilibrium models of microeconomic theory arose because those models required individual decision-making predictably geared to well defined models of individual choice. A proposal to fit the entrepreneur into such equilibrium models by subordinating him to well-defined models of individual choice appears, therefore, to head inevitably toward a collision with our basic notion of the dynamic entrepreneur—as one who is inherently *unable* to be boxed into any model of predictable behavior. Whatever the merits of Schultz's theory of this special ability to deal with disequilibria, then, it does *not* achieve the objective with which we are ourselves here concerned, viz. the incorporation of the entrepreneur, the flesh and blood entrepreneur of the dynamic business world, into the core of microeconomic theory of markets.

ON THE DETERMINACY OF INDIVIDUAL CHOICE

The observations of the preceding section point us toward reconsideration of our central difficulty. Microeconomic theory is built upon the assumption that the individual decision is tightly constrained. Given his preferences, given his available array of options, the decision of the individual agent is seen as rigidly determined. Insofar as the decisions of other agents shape the contours of the options from among which an individual agent may choose, his own decision is rigidly determined by the decisions of others—as the decisions of others are symmetrically determined, in part, by his own decisions. It is, we have seen, only this assumption of mutually determining individual decisions that permits the equilibrium theorist to postulate determinacy in market outcomes. Our problem, we saw, was that this framework necessarily excludes any role for the entrepreneur, whom we have identified as typically unconstrained and freewheeling. We must note that our problem is quite similar to the more general difficulty which Professor Shackle has, for many decades, expounded in regard to microeconomic theory.

This difficulty is that, for Shackle, *no* human decision is *ever* to be seen as rigidly determined by anything else. All human choices are, so to speak, entrepreneurial choices. Each individual choice is, for Shackle, a genuine new beginning, no doubt a response to existing conditions, but in no way mechanically *determined* by them.[15] If we have found difficulty fitting the entrepreneur into the models of mainstream equilibrium, Shackle has found these models to be altogether incoherent in their reliance upon the determinacy of individual choices—a determinacy the denial of which is the foundation of Shackle's perspective on the world of economics.

It is clear that if we were to follow Shackle in this blanket denial, our primary objective in this paper would instantly disappear. The obliteration of the core of mainstream economic theory would instantly render irrelevant any concern with finding a place, within that theory, for the unpredictable entrepreneur. Is there any way, without following Shackle to the extreme of rejecting the main conclusions of the past century of mainstream economic theory, of retaining a place, within those conclusions, for the bold, aggressive and unpredictable entrepreneur? To believe it to be impossible to do so must surely raise serious questions for the real world relevance of the core of modern economics, offering a threat to that theory almost as serious, indeed, as that posed by Shackle's own more obviously destructive questions. The activity of the imaginative, innovative and always surprising entrepreneur is too prominent and too prevalent in the world of business to permit us to explain that world through a theory which can operate only by systematically excluding that entrepreneur.

THE ENTREPRENEURIAL DYNAMICS OF MUTUAL DISCOVERY: AN OUTLINE

In the balance of this paper we shall endeavor to show how we may indeed accept the cardinal conclusions of neoclassical theory, while yet refusing to exclude the entrepreneur from the scope of that theory. We proceed by noting, as many economists have pointed out, that the logic of market equilibrium requires that we buttress the theory of market equilibrium by a theory of market equilibration. It is simply not enough to postulate that the configuration of individual decisions which mark out the equilibrium position acquires its particular pattern due to the mutual constraints which decisions exercise upon other decisions. Such assumed pre-reconciliation of decisions begs the obvious question of how myriads of independently reached decisions came, in fact, to be mutually adjusted.[16]

We note further, following Hayek,[17] that any postulation of a process of equilibration can be illuminatingly interpreted as a claim concerning mutual *learning*. During the course of the equilibration process market participants learn about what other market participants are likely to do. As the process continues decisions may be said to change because they have become more tightly constrained by the decisions of others. But Hayek taught us to understand this to mean that the changing decisions have come to reflect more accurate knowledge concerning these other people's attitudes and endowments. It is true that in the configuration of decisions which make up the unique equilibrium situation, we discern a pattern which is the only such permitting all these decisions to be made simultaneously. So that, mathematically speaking, this pattern can be said to be dictated ("caused") by the mutual constraints exercised by the component decisions. But, as we learned from Hayek, the *course of events* leading chronologically toward this pattern, expresses a quite different chain of causation—one consisting of gradual discoveries concerning the abilities and preferences of others.[18]

We shall argue, therefore, that it is in this discovery process through which equilibrium may come to be approached, that there is scope for entrepreneurial behavior. We shall in fact submit that entrepreneurial behavior is not merely *consistent* with this learning process (so that there is place for entrepreneurs in the economic theory of market equilibration). We shall maintain that entrepreneurial behavior is an indispensible feature of any such discovery process, so that the economic theory of market equilibration indeed *depends* upon entrepreneurial activity. Our intuitive sense that the dynamic entrepreneurs of the business world are indeed powerful players in shaping the course of market events will, in this way, turn out to be vindicated: it is only through their activity that the systematic course of market equilibration in fact proceeds.

In order to lay out a persuasive case for this approach, we must consider with some care what we mean by an initial state of disequilibrium. We shall only then be in a position to grasp what we must mean when we refer to a process of entrepreneurial equilibration.

THE MEANING OF DISEQUILIBRIUM

The need for careful consideration of the meaning of disequilibrium arises from a tendency, within modern microeconomics, to perceive matters in a way which effectively renders the notion of market disequilibrium totally meaningless. From this perspective the world is not merely *assumed* to be in equilibrium at all times (reflecting the traditional claim of equilibrium theory to be the most useful way of *explaining* real world conditions, viz. by postulating that, somehow, the world has at each moment *already* successfully traveled some relevant process of equilibration). Rather this perspective sees the world as *necessarily* being in relevant equilibrium at all times, once all relevant circumstances have been taken into account. What might *appear* at first glance to be a state of disequilibrium (e.g., the coexistence of more than one price in the market for what appears to be homogeneous units of the same commodity) is, from this perspective, rather to be seen as the true state of equilibrium relevant to special circumstances (which our first glance has failed to notice: e.g., these apparently homogeneous units of the same commodity may in fact differ from one another in terms of location, or date of availability, or in the degree to which market participants are aware of their availability). From this perspective it is *impossible* for true disequilibrium to occur, because its occurrence must reflect unaccountable failure of market participants to have acted optimally, under the given circumstances. While market prices and outputs may indeed reflect ignorance of relevant circumstances, even in the approach we are describing, such behavior-in-ignorance is not seen as unexplained, rather it is seen as fully optimal in the light of the costs of obtaining superior information. At all times, in every relevant respect, market participants are acting in ways that are in full mutual adjustment—insofar as it is worth doing so. From this perspective no situation, however temporary, can be described as a discoordinated one, one containing internal inconsistencies, which must be expected to correct themselves. Each and every situation is fully balanced and internally coordinated, in the light of relevant costs of adjustment. Each and every situation must be described as an equilibrium situation, in the sense that each situation fully and accurately reflects the appropriate force of each relevant circumstance. It must be clear that, from such a perspective, any systematic market movements are to be seen, not as equilibrating processes set in motion by any initial disequilibrium, but as a sequence of equilibrium positions generated by systematically, endogenously changing circumstances (such as market-induced reductions in costs of information).

In order to argue, as we have proposed to do, that the entrepreneur makes entry into the world of microeconomic theory, by way of the discovery process which characterizes equilibration, we will find it necessary to reject the point of view which can perceive no genuine situations of disequilibrium. We shall find, indeed, that by spelling out the possibility of genuine disequilibrium we are ipso facto opening up a scope for entrepreneurship. Moreover we shall find that as we create this scope for entrepreneurship in our theory, we are at the same time achieving an understanding of that equilibration process upon which economic theory must necessarily depend for its internal coherence and validity.

For us the possibility of genuine market disequilibrium consists in the possibility—in fact in the very strong likelihood—that at any given moment the decisions of market participants are *not* optimally adjusted either to each other or to external circumstances. Such lack of adjustment is not to be understood as the rational response to costs of adjustment (such as costs of acquiring information), because this would of course mean that there is in fact no lack of adjustment at all. Instead we posit the likely presence of genuine absence of mutual adjustment, an absence that can be "explained," not in terms of rational response to costs, but only in terms of "inexplicable" *error.* In fact our position differs from that which refuses to recognize any possibility for disequilibrium, primarily in our insistence on the possibility and prevalence of genuine error. Genuine error occurs when agents fail to optimize, even within the range of possibilities costlessly available to them. The cardinal assumption of microeconomic theory, that all agents are rational and are continually optimizing in the light of the information costlessly available to them, must be modified to find room for error. Erroneous decisions do not express any failure on the part of agents to seek the optimum; they express, instead, a failure on the part of agents to be aware of the true situation which they face—with this unawareness being the result, not of any deterrent costs of information-acquisition, but simply of "inexplicable" oversight.[19] Market disequilibrium, we maintain, occurs as the expression of such errors on the part of market participants. Equilibration processes, we consequently assert, consist of processes of error-discovery and error-correction. It is here that the entrepreneur enters, with all his boldness, drive and unpredictable innovativeness.

THE EQUILIBRATION PROCESS—
THE MARKET AS DISCOVERY PROCEDURE

The entrepreneur, in our approach, is the market agent with the propensity to notice errors, and with the drive needed to profit by exploiting the opportunities created by these errors. It is because errors by market participants correspond to overlooked opportunities for net gain, that these errors create incentives for their removal. Entrepreneurs who notice these overlooked opportunities are in a position to take advantage of these incentives; these incentives can in fact serve as stimuli inspiring entrepreneurs to notice these opportunities and, by exploiting them, to move the market in the direction of equilibration.

The discovery by entrepreneurs of opportunities created by error is not the same as the deliberate acquisition of costly information. The deliberate acquisition of costly information is achieved through comparison of two well-identified options (the option of learning valuable information at a given cost, and the option of remaining ignorant while not having to incur that given cost). The discovery of an entrepreneurial opportunity occurs by a sudden realization that a totally new, "costless" (net) opportunity for gain is available.

The process of market equilibration thus becomes, not a smooth sequence of ever-optimizing decision patterns, but a sequence of entrepreneurial discoveries (and their exploitation). This sequence, we maintain, does indeed offer a plausible basis for neoclassical postulation of powerful equilibrating forces in markets. And it is consistent, we shall argue, with the kind of entrepreneurial decision-making which we found impossible to fit into the standard models of equilibrium, viz. decision-making reflecting the entrepreneurial propensity to surprise.

If market participants can err today, we can of course not be sure that they will not err tomorrow. So that the mere circumstance of genuine, error-generated disequilibrium does not by itself assure any corrective market tendencies. What permits us to understand the power of corrective market forces is our appreciation for the discovery-incentives displayed by disequilibrium situations. Entrepreneurs are *inspired* to notice errors because to do so is profitable. This kind of incentive-inspiration is sufficient to set in motion sequences of discoveries which tend to eliminate the opportunities which inspired them, moving markets toward the profit-less state of equilibrium. While we must certainly recognize the possibilities in a changing and uncertain world, for entrepreneurial errors and losses, we can nonetheless understand how sequences of corrective changes may be set in motion by entrepreneurial discovery. Nor should we be puzzled by our postulation of systematic market movements as a result of the decisions of unpredictable entrepreneurs. *The simple truth is that any discovery must inevitably appear surprising to those who have not themselves made the discovery.* To recognize that the decisions made by entrepreneurs are not "constrained" (in the way microeconomic theory sees individual decisions as constrained by the mathematics of optimization) is not to maintain that these decisions are wholly random and unsystematic; it is merely to recognize that entrepreneurs may notice (and have an incentive to notice) opportunities that have been overlooked by others.

The characteristic behavior of imaginative, innovative businessmen is entirely consistent with our thesis that their behavior consists of a series of discoveries, sufficient in general to move markets systematically in the direction toward errorless equilibrium.

THE ENTREPRENEUR IN ECONOMIC THEORY

We are in a position to review the course of our discussion. At the outset we asked whether the role of the entrepreneur can be accommodated by the core theory of mainstream microeconomics. The difficulty in achieving such accommodation was due, we saw, to the circumstance that the theory appears to depend entirely on the determinate, constrained character of the decision-making of market agents, while everything we can say about the entrepreneur prevents his decisions from sharing that character. This difficulty was parallel, we found, to the shortcomings which mainstream theory displays to a theorist, such as G. L. S. Shackle, who refuses to acknowledge determinacy in *any* examples of human choice.

Our discussion has demonstrated how a reconstruction of the core of mainstream theory can be achieved, which not only finds a place for entrepreneurial behavior, but in fact depends crucially upon such behavior for its principal conclusions. This reconstruction places the weight of these conclusions not on the mutual constraints governing decisions, which are required by the mathematics of equilibrium conditions, but upon the process of discovery which points the market toward the fulfillment of these conditions. For this process of discovery we rely entirely on the entrepreneurial discovery of opportunities created by the errors of others.

This must be the case, we saw, because discovery of error is not a planned activity resulting from cost-benefit calculations, but an inspired realization which necessarily appears totally surprising to the world at large. The degree of systematicity which we ascribe to market processes arises precisely out of these surprising, unpredictable bursts of entrepreneurial realization. The principal conclusions of mainstream microeconomic theory retain their validity, on this view, not by virtue of any innate validity to the assumption of equilibrium, but by virtue of our confidence in the power of the processes of discovery (tending toward the equilibrium configurations) inspired by the incentives to win pure entrepreneurial profit.

NOTES

1. Among the more important such works are, M. Casson, *The Entrepreneur, An Economic Theory* (Totowa, N.J.: Barnes and Noble Books, 1982), Robert F. Hébert and Albert N. Link, *The Entrepreneur: Mainstream Views and Radical Critiques*, 2d ed. (New York, Westport, London: Praeger, 1968).

2. See below for discussion of one important exception to this generalization.

3. One now classic sign of this growing discomfort was the session on entrepreneurship held at the December 1967 meetings of the American Economic Association. See especially W. J. Baumol, "Entrepreneurship in Economic Theory," *American Economic Review*, 58, May 1968.

4. The work of H. Leibenstein may perhaps be cited in this regard. See H. Leibenstein, "Entrepreneurship and Development," *American Economic Review*, 58, May 1968; "The General X-efficiency Paradigm and the Role of the Entrepreneur," in *Time, Uncertainty and Disequilibrium*, ed. Mario J. Rizzo (Lexington, Mass.: D. C. Heath, 1979).

5. As an example of this work we may cite M. Rothschild, "Models of Market Organization with Imperfect Information: A Survey," *Journal of Political Economy*, 81, November/December 1973.

6. See e.g. K. J. Arrow, "Toward a Theory of Price Adjustment," in M. Abramovitz et al., *The Allocation of Economic Resources* (Stanford, Calif.: Stanford University Press, 1959), Franklin M. Fisher, *Disequilibrium Foundations of Equilibrium Economics* (Cambridge, New York and Sydney: Cambridge University Press, 1983); Israel M. Kirzner, *Competition and Entrepreneurship* (Chicago: University of Chicago Press, 1973).

7. On this see Frank M. Machovec, *The Destruction of Competition Theory: The Perfectly Competitive Model and Beyond* (unpublished doctoral dissertation, New York University, 1986).

8. J. A. Schumpeter, *The Theory of Economic Development* (Cambridge: Harvard University Press, 1934), translated from the German original edition, 1912.

9. An important example of this influence is in the work of R. R. Nelson and S. G. Winter, see especially their *An Evolutionary Theory of Economic Change* (Cambridge: Harvard University Press, 1982).

10. It is of course true that much of the literature of development sharply questioned the relevance of such theorizing for developing countries. But this did not appear so much to be a challenge to the internal validity of these theories as a challenge to their applicability to the developing world.

11. T. W. Schultz, "The Value of the Ability to Deal with Disequilibria," *Journal of Economic Literature*, 13, September 1975, and "Investment in Entrepreneurial Ability," *Scandinavian Journal of Economics*, 82, 1980.

12. Schultz, "The Value of the Ability to Deal with Disequilibrium," op. cit., p. 834.

13. Ibid. pp. 832f.

14. Ibid. p. 843.

15. See many of the writings of G. L. S. Shackle, e.g. *Epistemics and Economics, A Critique of Economic Doctrines* (Cambridge: Cambridge University Press, 1972), pp. 122f, 351f.

16. See A. Coddington, "Creaking Semaphore and Beyond: A Consideration of Shackle's 'Epistemics and Economics,'" *British Journal for the Philosophy of Science*, 26, pp. 151–63, 1975.

17. F. A. Hayek, "Economics and Knowledge," *Economica* n.s. 4, 1937, reprinted in *Individualism and Economic Order* (Chicago: University of Chicago Press, 1948); "The Use of Knowledge in Society," *American Economic Review*, 35, 1945, reprinted in *Individualism and Economic Order*, op. cit.; "Competition as a Discovery Procedure," in *New Studies in Philosophy, Politics, Economics and the History of Ideas* (Chicago: University of Chicago Press, 1978).

18. Cf. Hans Mayer, "Der Erkenntniswert der funktionellen Preistheorien," in *Wirtschaftstheorie der Gegenwart*, vol. II, (Wien: Springer, 1932).

19. See Israel M. Kirzner, "Economics and Error," in *Perception, Opportunity and Profit* (Chicago: University of Chicago Press, 1979).

THE ROLE OF THE ENTREPRENEUR
IN THE ECONOMIC SYSTEM

I. INTRODUCTION

I am deeply honored to give this Inaugural John Bonython Lecture. I shall say things this evening that tend to strongly defend the social significance of the contributions made by entrepreneurs and the entrepreneurial endeavor. However, I shall point out that this significance and the value of these contributions in no way depends on the benevolence, public spiritedness, scholarship, wit, gentlemanly charm or high moral characters of entrepreneurs. Even if all entrepreneurs were crass, selfish and uncouth, we would have to recognize the valuable role they play in society. From this perspective, then, the tribute that is being paid by The Centre for Independent Studies in offering this lecture in honor of so distinguished a figure as John Bonython—gentleman, scholar and public-minded citizen—comes with very special grace.

I had the pleasure this morning of spending some time with John Bonython at his home and a remark that he made has stuck in my memory. I believe it is highly relevant to my lecture this evening. We were examining the fascinating collection of works on Cornish history and genealogy that John Bonython inherited from his grandfather, and we noticed some ink corrections made in one of the books by Sir Langdon on one of the genealogical tables referring to the sixteenth-century Bonythons in Cornwall. John remarked, "The Bonythons have quite a habit of correcting mistakes." I shall return to this remark a little later this evening. But first let me turn to my topic—the role of the entrepreneur in the economic system.

II. HOW WE SEE THE ENTREPRENEUR

The widespread view, certainly in my own country and I believe in Australia too, is that entrepreneurs are extraordinarily bright and greedy individuals whose activities are rather disreputable. And because they are so disreputable, these activities are likely to result in many unfortunate social consequences. Sometimes it is grudgingly conceded that the sheer

Inaugural John Bonython Lecture, July 30, 1984. Reprinted by permission of the Centre for Independent Studies, St. Leonards, NSW, Australia.

vitality and energy of entrepreneurs somehow pushes capitalist societies to higher and higher levels of well-being. Nonetheless, it is usually maintained that all of this must inevitably be accompanied by exploitation and injustice, by the production of shoddy, unsafe products, by monopoly gouging of the consumer, or by violation of consumer preferences through advertising. Moreover, the most tangible evidence of entrepreneurial success, namely the earning of pure profit, is seen as evidence of the unjustified character of entrepreneurial behavior because, after all, profits are not paid in return for any productive service. Since profits consist of revenues over and above what has to be paid to produce the product, they seemingly cannot be explained as a necessary payment. Inevitably, then, the suspicion is that profit must have been achieved through something approaching fraud or cheating, exploitation or robbery.

An analogy that has sometimes been used perhaps best expresses the popular view: the entrepreneurial lust for profit is compared to the windpower that propels a sailboat. It has the power to move the boat, but cannot be relied upon to move it in the right direction. The wind can just as well propel the sailboat onto rocks as bring it into safe harbor. In other words, profit is a powerful motive that drives individuals to activity. It motivates them, it gets things going, but there is no guarantee whatsoever that the pursuit of profit will not lead to a great deal of waste, injustice and unhappiness.

I have a rather different view of the entrepreneur and the entrepreneurial motive in pursuing pure profit. To repeat, I do not claim that entrepreneurs are moral heroes. I claim instead that the remarkable set of institutions that make up the entrepreneurial market system is able to harness important human characteristics, important human attributes, to the benefit of society. To establish this position it will be necessary for us to consider separately and carefully two items. First we shall consider what is entrepreneurship and the nature of entrepreneurial activity, and second we shall consider what we mean as economists by the "public interest."

III.   WHAT IS ENTREPRENEURSHIP?

Who are entrepreneurs and what do they do? We know that entrepreneurs start companies and introduce new product lines, they discover new techniques of production, they strike out for new markets, they seek for new sources of finance, they develop new forms of internal organization, and on and on. But what is the analytical essence of these diverse activities? How can we capture the theoretical core of entrepreneurship that manifests itself in so many diverse, specific tasks? This had turned out to be an elusive question.

In the history of economic thought, in the history of the attempts economists have made to understand entrepreneurship, a variety of suggestions have been proposed concerning the "essence" of entrepreneurship. Some economists have seen entrepreneurship as consisting essentially in the bearing of pure, sheer uncertainty. Others have seen it as consisting in its innovative character. Others have seen the entrepreneur as the middleman linking markets. Others have seen the entrepreneur as providing leadership; others as a source of information. All of these views are represented in the literature by important contributions.

Alertness

In my own work over the years I have found it useful and helpful to focus on entrepreneurial alertness to available but as yet unnoticed opportunities. What the entrepreneur does is identify opportunities for gain that others have overlooked. These opportunities can take the form of all specific activities that we have mentioned. But the essence of all of them is that the entrepreneur recognizes something that others have failed to recognize: that there is an opportunity waiting to be grabbed. It is the alertness of the entrepreneur that leads him to recognize what others and even the entrepreneur himself may earlier have failed to notice.

Observe that the entrepreneur does not possess specific knowledge that others do not possess. What the entrepreneur possesses rather is a sense for discovering what is around the corner. If you like, it is a sense of knowing where to find knowledge. A rather subtle and elusive role; but, I submit, an extraordinarily important one.

Economizing and Entrepreneurial Discovery

The implication of this is that entrepreneurial activity is sharply distinguished from what economists call "economizing" activity. Economizing activity, in the usual sense in which the term is employed by economists, refers to the careful allocation by human beings of their scarce resources in order to achieve optimal results: the maximization of some desired objective. To economize is to adjust to a particular perceived situation in order to avoid waste and ensure efficiency. But this efficiency is strictly relative to a given perceived situation. Economizing does not embrace the discovery of hitherto unperceived opportunities.

Economists often appear to view all human activity as consisting only of acts of economizing, and there is no doubt that economizing activity is of great importance. But the world of human action is far too rich and dynamic to be confined wholly within the bounds of the static economizing model. The world of action must be recognized as including also the dimension of entrepreneurial alertness and discovery. This recognition dramatically changes the face of things. Thus, for example, economists who have focused on economizing have often asserted, as a simple and universal economic truth, that there is no such thing as a "free lunch." A lunch consumed means that some resources have been diverted away from some other potential use. There are no lunches that do not cost resources in this way. But in the entrepreneurial context, in which there are more resources available than had ever been believed, there can be a free lunch. That is what the entrepreneur discovers: totally new opportunities, opportunities that had previously been overlooked. Lunches so discovered have not diverted resources away from other contemplated projects. And indeed the process of entrepreneurial discovery is the revelation of an unending series of free lunches waiting, so to speak, to be noticed and taken advantage of.

I think you will understand now, perhaps, why I found John Bonython's remark earlier today to be so relevant. Like the Bonythons, the entrepreneur is always discovering where errors have been made, and is always alert to ways of correcting those mistakes.

IV. THE PUBLIC INTEREST

Let me turn now to consider what economists should understand and mean by the term "the public interest." After all, we are interested in exploring how the entrepreneurial role can serve the public interest. What is that public interest?

Mainstream Economics

Here again we must be wary of the standard approach that mainstream economics has tended to follow in identifying the public interest. From a standard economic point of view, the public interest has been seen as the achievement by society of an efficient allocation of social resources. It is as if society were a gigantic economizing entity with scarce resources, a given budget, and competing goals. Society would then need an allocation pattern for its resources that would achieve its peak level of goal satisfaction, avoiding any kind of social waste. That is, society would want to avoid any state of affairs, any pattern of resource allocation that might satisfy one set of goals at the expense of some other more important set of goals.

This notion of the public interest that I've associated with standard economics tends to treat society in exactly the same way as standard economics treats individual human acts: as economizing activity that is successful when it achieves its efficiency objective. From this perspective, to say that the market economy fulfills the public interest means that the market is successful in achieving an efficient allocation of resources. It is here that I believe the Austrian tradition to which Hugh Morgan referred earlier can provide illumination and a most helpful alternative perspective.

The Austrian School and Dispersed Knowledge

We need to go back to the work of F. A. Hayek. Over 40 years ago Hayek pointed out that treating society as if it were an economizing entity overlooks a fundamental problem that society confronts before we can even begin to discuss economizing at a social level. The problem is that one of the prerequisites for talking about economizing at a social level is a complete, centralized bank of knowledge about the objectives of society. But in society, this knowledge is clearly and obviously absent. Instead, as Hayek pointed out, the knowledge we have is scattered and dispersed.

Each of us, as members of society, knows certain things. We know about what we ourselves need and what our families need, we know a little about what our neighbors may need. We also know a little bit about the availability of resources in our immediate neighborhood. We don't know a great deal but we do each know a little bit, and the little bits we know as individuals make up a sort of jigsaw puzzle of separate pieces of scattered information. Before we can even begin to think of solving the social economizing problem we have to confront the problem of ensuring that these scattered bits of information are brought to bear on economic decisions so that in fact the knowledge is not wasted. How can we ensure that there will be coordination between these innumerable members of society, all knowing their own things, so that their knowledge can be deployed in the interest of society?

The answer to this question is the great contribution of both Mises and Hayek. The market comes to be perceived as a social instrument that is able to bring into the picture and harness all of these scattered bits of information, thus initiating a process of mutual learning that permits coordination to be achieved. It is important to recognize the drastic change in understanding what this Austrian view entails. We are no longer dealing with the narrow problem of coping with scarcity, but with the much more subtle problem of overcoming the gaps in knowledge that exist throughout society and of transcending the little scarcity problems that confront each one of us.

You may notice the analogy here between this economic task and the task of the entrepreneur that we mentioned earlier. From this perspective the notion of the public interest becomes far more subtle than the one I have identified with the older, standard economic view. The public interest surely depends, from this newer economic point of view, on the ability of society's institutions to transcend these narrow scarcity problems and to mobilize the scattered and initially uncoordinated bits of information. Let us see where the entrepreneur fits into this.

V. THE ROLE OF THE ENTREPRENEUR

We have stated that the entrepreneur engages in perceiving opportunities. What kinds of opportunities does the entrepreneur discover? As far as markets are concerned the entrepreneurial endeavor can be expressed very simply: the entrepreneur perceives the opportunity to buy at a lower price and sell at a higher price, and the difference is pure profit. It is as simple as that. This simple framework can be translated into hundreds of forms and concrete cases. At the level of simple arbitrage, it is buying and selling in different markets at the same time. In judicious speculation, where resources are purchased for their anticipated appreciation over time, such resources are bought in one market today and sold in another market tomorrow, or 10, or 50 years hence. Finally, this bridging of markets is manifest in the creative activities of entrepreneurs who are able to assemble a group of everyday resources and somehow transform them into new products that others have not dreamed of and that consumers value highly. That too involves bridging markets, where the resources are bought in one market and the new product is to be sold in another market.

Markets and Opportunities

The bridging of these markets involves the discovery of opportunities created by errors. These markets would not be separated and the opportunities for profit would not exist if others had not made mistakes that need to be corrected—if others had not overlooked that which the entrepreneur now sees. The price would not, without such error, be lower in one market than it is in the second market, because those who buy at the high price would not do so if they were aware that they could buy at the low price. So that the very phenomenon of pure profit is evidence of earlier error—error that reflects that dispersed knowledge of which Hayek wrote.

But these errors invite their correction. The incentive for the correction of these errors is provided by the error itself because, as we have seen, the error manifests itself in the form of pure profit. That pure profit is the magnet that attracts the attention of the alert entrepreneur—who, I repeat, need not be a moral hero. He needs merely to be able to "smell" where the profits are, because that sense is his alertness to existing error and his pursuit of those incentives is the way he corrects these errors. When the entrepreneur acts to capture profit he bids up the price where it has been low and bids down the price where it has been high, eliminating the price differential. This phenomenon repeats itself in innumerable guises and all types of entrepreneurial endeavor.

In carrying out this role, what is the entrepreneur in fact achieving? He is achieving exactly the kind of coordination and mobilization of scattered information that we were discussing earlier under the topic of public interest. When price differentials are present between markets it means that the knowledge of the individuals in one market is not being brought to bear upon the knowledge of the individuals in the other market, so that buyers and sellers are not meeting each other because they are not aware of each other. The entrepreneur bridges that gap. He notices those scattered bits of information and, by responding to the translation of those errors into profit, he corrects the initial error. His activity tends to solve the problem of dispersed knowledge. In this way the role of the entrepreneur is wholly congruent with the promotion of what we described earlier as the public interest, in the appropriate economic sense of that term.

Requirements of the Entrepreneur

What is required for the entrepreneur to be able to perform the role that we have identified with the public interest? What institutional framework is required, what encouragement does the entrepreneur need? The answer is that he needs no special encouragement; he needs only the assurance that an opportunity perceived will be permitted to be pursued. This is simply freedom of entrepreneurial entry—the absence of obstacles to discovery. Of course, such obstacles tend to be erected by the pressures of those who stand to lose by the entrepreneurial competition of the entrant. In other words, what we require for the entrepreneurial process to be put to work is absence of privilege and freedom of entrepreneurial entry. These are simply two sides of the same coin.

Does Society Benefit?

Let us return to our initial observation concerning the widespread disparagement of entrepreneurial activity. That disparagement, we noticed, is based in large part on the assumption that pure profit is unjustified. Pure profit does not seem explicable or justifiable in terms of effort or the cost of necessary resources. After all, it is pure "gravy," over and above all amounts necessary to bring about the production of what is produced. It is natural, then, that critics of the entrepreneurial system see profit as prima facie evidence of less than honest dealing in some form or another.

In a narrow sense it is quite true that profits are not necessary for the production of a product. Suppose the entrepreneur buys resources for a sum of money. He creates out of those resources a new type and quality of product, a new form of marketing for that product that inspires consumers to buy at a price that leaves the entrepreneur with a handsome profit. Clearly that product could have been produced even if its price was not greater than the price of the resources. But would it have been produced? That kind of judgment with hindsight presumes that we already know what products are needed. The essence of entrepreneurship is, let us remember, that it happens before it has been discovered what consumers need or what can be produced—the product is still around the corner, so to speak.

What inspires the alertness of the entrepreneur is surely the prospect of being able to benefit by the profits that may be embodied in the production of the product. It is hardly accurate to say that those profits were not needed. They were indeed needed to spur the discovery procedure of the entrepreneurial process. In fact, what has happened is that the entrepreneur, in transforming resources into something worth so much more, has created something out of nothing. The usual criteria of economic justice relate to given economic goods. Therefore they do not apply to the case of entrepreneurial profit, which represents a wholly new economic entity that has been created, found or discovered. So far from the "unearned" character of profit being evidence of exploitation or fraud, this character of pure profit points to its invaluable role in inspiring pure discovery and in generating the solution to the social economic problem embedded in dispersed knowledge.

VI.   CONCLUSION

What then is the role of the entrepreneur in the economic system? I think we can sum up our argument by drawing attention to two entrepreneurial functions. The entrepreneur is the agent that spurs society to take advantage of existing scattered and dispersed knowledge. This permits society to enjoy a tendency toward the fullest exploitation of existing resources in terms of today's technological knowledge. It permits society to avoid waste and to successfully negotiate the economizing problems by bridging and overcoming the dispersed character of knowledge. At the same time, the entrepreneurial role also makes a second, related contribution. The entrepreneur and entrepreneurial activity not only spur society to continually become aware of better ways of utilizing existing resources; it is entrepreneurial alertness that generates and harnesses new technological knowledge, and discovers entirely new bodies of resources that had hitherto been overlooked.

The entrepreneurial role is of paramount social significance in ensuring the fullest utilization of existing resources in terms of existing knowledge. It is no less significant in fueling economic growth and development into a limitless future because the entrepreneur, after all, exists to transcend the limits of what has gone before. I submit that a society that prizes these achievements and appreciates them should surely learn to value the crucially important role the entrepreneur plays in the public interest.

THE NATURE AND SIGNIFICANCE
OF MARKET PROCESS

EQUILIBRIUM VERSUS MARKET PROCESS

A characteristic feature of the Austrian approach to economic theory is its emphasis on the market as a *process,* rather than as a configuration of prices, qualities, and quantities that are consistent with each other in that they produce a market equilibrium situation.[1] This feature of Austrian economics is closely bound up with dissatisfaction with the general use made of the concept of perfect competition. It is interesting that economists of sharply differing persuasions within the Austrian tradition all display a characteristic disenchantment with the orthodox emphasis on both equilibrium and perfect competition. Thus Joseph A. Schumpeter's well-known position on these matters is remarkably close to that of Ludwig von Mises.[2] Oskar Morgenstern, in a notable paper on contemporary economic theory, expressed these same Austrian criticisms of modern economic theory.[3]

EQUILIBRIUM AND PROCESS

Ludwig M. Lachmann has indicated that his own unhappiness with the notion of equilibrium primarily concerns the usefulness of the Walrasian general-equilibrium construction rather than that of the simple Marshallian partial-equilibrium construction.[4] But it is precisely in the context of the simple short-run one-good market that I shall point out some of the shortcomings of the equilibrium approach.

In our classrooms we draw the Marshallian cross to depict competitive supply and demand, then go on to explain how the market is cleared only at the price corresponding to the intersection of the curves. Often the explanation of market price determination proceeds no further—almost implying that the only possible price is the market-clearing price. Sometimes we address the question of how we can be confident that there is any tendency at all for the intersection price to be attained. The

Presented at the Austrian Economic Conference held at South Royalton, Vermont, June 1974. From *Perception, Opportunity, and Profit: Studies in the Theory of Entrepreneurship* (Chicago and London: University of Chicago Press, 1979), 3–12. Reprinted by permission of the Institute of Humane Studies; the original source is *The Foundations of Modern Austrian Economics,* ed. Edwin G. Dolan (Mission, Kansas: Sheed and Ward, 1976), 115–25.

discussion is then usually carried on in terms of the Walrasian version of the equilibration process. Suppose, we say, the price happens to be above the intersection level. If so, the amount of the good people are prepared to supply is in the aggregate larger than the total amount people are prepared to buy. There will be unsold inventories, thereby depressing price. On the other hand, if price is below the intersection level, there will be excess demand, "forcing" price up. Thus, we explain, there will be a tendency for price to gravitate toward the equilibrium level at which quantity demanded equals quantity supplied.

Now this explanation has a certain rough-and-ready appeal. However, when price is described as being above or below equilibrium, it is understood that a single price prevails in the market. One uncomfortable question, then, is whether we may assume that a single price emerges before equilibrium is attained. Surely a single price can be postulated only as the result of the process of equilibration itself. At least to this extent, the Walrasian explanation of equilibrium price determination appears to beg the question.

Again, the Walrasian explanation usually assumes perfect competition, where all market participants are price takers. But with only price takers participating, it is not clear how unsold inventories or unmet demand effect price changes. If no one raises or lowers price bids, *how* do prices rise or fall?

The Marshallian explanation of the equilibrating process—not usually introduced into classroom discussion—is similar to the Walrasian but uses quantity rather than price as the principal decision variable.[5] Instead of drawing horizontal price lines on the demand-supply diagram to show excess supply or unmet demand, the Marshallian procedure uses vertical lines to mark off the demand prices and the supply prices for given quantities. With this procedure, the ordinate of a point on the demand curve indicates the maximum price at which a quantity (represented by the abscissa of the point) will be sold. If this price is greater than the corresponding supply price (the minimum price at which the same quantity will be offered for sale), larger quantities will be offered for sale. The reverse takes place when supply price exceeds demand price. In this way a tendency toward equilibrium is allegedly demonstrated to exist.

This procedure also assumes too much. It takes for granted that the market already knows when the demand price of the quantity now available exceeds the supply price. But disequilibrium occurs precisely because market participants do not know what the market-clearing price is. In disequilibrium "the" quantity is not generally known nor is the highest (lowest) price at which this quantity can be sold (coaxed from suppliers). Thus it is not clear how the fact that the quantity on the market is less than the equilibrium quantity assures the decisions of market participants to be so modified as to increase it.

Clearly, neither of these explanations for the attainment of equilibrium is satisfactory. From the Austrian perspective, which emphasizes the role of knowledge and expectations, these explanations take too much for granted. What is needed is a theory of the market process that takes explicit notice of the way systematic changes in the information and expectations upon which market participants act lead them in the direction of the postulated equilibrium solution. The Austrian point of view does, in fact, help us arrive at such a theory.

ROBBINSIAN ALLOCATION AND MISESIAN ACTION

In developing a viable theory of market process it is helpful to call attention to the much-neglected role of *entrepreneurship*. The neglect of entrepreneurship in modern analysis is a direct consequence of the general preoccupation with final equilibrium positions. In order to understand the distinction between a process-conscious market theory, which makes reference to entrepreneurship, and an equilibrium market theory, which ignores entrepreneurship, it will help to compare the Misesian concept of human action with the Robbinsian concept of economizing, that is, allocative decision making.

It may be recalled that Lord Robbins defined economics as dealing with the allocative aspect of human affairs, that is, with the consequences of the circumstance that men economize by engaging in the allocation of limited resources among multiple competing ends.[6] Mises, on the other hand, emphasized the much broader notion of purposeful human action, embracing the deliberate efforts of men to improve their positions.[7] Both concepts, it should be noticed, are consistent with methodological individualism and embody the insight that market phenomena are generated by the interaction of individual decision makers.[8] But the two constructions do differ significantly.

Robbinsian economizing consists in using *known* available resources in the most efficient manner to achieve given purposes. It entails the implementation of the equimarginal principle, that is, the setting up of an allocative arrangement in which it is impossible to transfer a unit of resource from one use to another and receive a net benefit. For Robbins, economizing simply means shuffling around available resources in order to secure the most efficient utilization of known inputs in terms of a *given* hierarchy of ends. It is the interaction in the market of the allocative efforts of numerous economizing individuals that generates all the phenomena that modern economics seeks to explain.

The difficulty with a theory of the market couched in exclusively Robbinsian terms is that in disequilibrium many of the plans of Robbinsian economizers are bound to be unrealized. Disequilibrium is a situation in which not all plans can be carried out together; it reflects mistakes in the price information on which individual plans were made. Market experience by way of shortages and surplus reveals the incorrectness of the original price expectations. Now the Robbinsian framework suggests that the unsuccessful plans will be discarded or revised, but we are unable to say much more than this. The notion of a Robbinsian plan assumes that information is both given and known to the acting individuals. Lacking this information, market participants are blocked from Robbinsian activity altogether. Without some clue as to what *new* expectations will follow disappointments in the market, we are unable to postulate any sequence of decisions. All we can say is: if all the Robbinsian decisions dovetail, we have equilibrium; if they do not dovetail, we have disequilibrium. We lack justification within this framework for stating, for example, that unsold inventories will depress price; we may only say that with excessive price expectations Robbinsian decision makers will generate unsold inventories. As decision makers they do not raise or lower price; they are strictly price takers, allocating against a background of given prices. If all participants are price takers, how then can the market price rise or fall? By what process does this happen, if it happens at all?

In order for unsold inventories to depress price, market participants with unsold goods need to realize that the previously prevailing price was too high. Participants must modify their expectations concerning the eagerness of other participants to buy. But in order to make these assertions we must transcend the narrow confines of the Robbinsian framework. We need a concept of decision making wide enough to encompass the element of *entrepreneurship* to account for the way in which market participants *change* their plans. It is here that the Misesian notion of human action comes to our assistance.

Mises's concept of human action embodies an insight about man that is entirely lacking in a world of Robbinsian economizers. This insight recognizes that men are not only calculating agents but are also *alert to opportunities*. Robbinsian theory only applies after a person is confronted with opportunities; for it does not explain how that person learns about opportunities in the first place. Misesian theory of human action conceives of the individual as having his eyes and ears open to opportunities that are "just around the corner." He is alert, waiting, continually receptive to something that may turn up. And when the prevailing price does not clear the market, market participants realize they should revise their estimates of prices bid or asked in order to avoid repeated disappointment. This alertness is the entrepreneurial element in human action, a concept lacking in analysis carried out in exclusively Robbinsian terms. At the same time that it transforms allocative decision making into a realistic view of human action, entrepreneurship converts the theory of market equilibrium into a theory of market process.

THE ROLE OF ENTREPRENEURSHIP

There have, it is true, been other definitions of the entrepreneurial role. The principal views of the question have been those of Schumpeter, Frank H. Knight, and Mises. I have argued, however, that these alternative definitions upon analysis all have in common the element of alertness to opportunities.[9] Alertness should be carefully distinguished from the mere possession of knowledge. And it is the distinction between being alert and possessing knowledge that helps us understand how the entrepreneurial market process systematically detects and helps eliminate error.

A person who possesses knowledge is not by that criterion alone an entrepreneur. Even though an employer hires an expert for his knowledge, it is the employer rather than the employee who is the entrepreneur. The employer may not have all the information the hired expert possesses, yet the employer is better informed than anyone else—he knows where knowledge is to be obtained and how it can be usefully employed. The hired expert does not, apparently, see how his knowledge can be usefully employed, since he is not prepared to act as his own employer. The hired expert does not perceive the opportunity presented by the possession of his information. The employer does perceive it. Entrepreneurial knowledge is a rarefied, abstract type of knowledge—the knowledge of where to obtain information (or other resources) and how to deploy it.

This entrepreneurial alertness is crucial to the market process. Disequilibrium represents a situation of widespread market ignorance. This ignorance is responsible for the emergence of profitable opportunities. Entrepreneurial alertness exploits these opportunities when others pass them by. G. L. S. Shackle and Lachmann emphasized the unpredictability of human knowledge, and, indeed, we do not clearly understand how entrepreneurs get their flashes of superior foresight. We cannot explain how some men discover what is around the corner before others do. We may certainly explain—on entirely Robbinsian lines—how men explore for oil by carefully weighing alternative ways of spending a limited amount of search resources, but we cannot explain how a prescient entrepreneur realizes before others do that a search for oil may be rewarding. As an empirical matter, however, opportunities do tend to be perceived and exploited. And it is on this observed tendency that our belief in a determinate market process is founded.

ADVERTISING AS AN ASPECT OF THE COMPETITIVE PROCESS

Characterization of the market process as one involving entrepreneurial discovery clarifies a number of ambiguities about the market and dispels several misunderstandings about how it functions. Advertising provides an excellent example on which to base our discussion.

Advertising, a pervasive feature of the market economy, is widely misunderstood and often condemned as wasteful, inefficient, inimical to competition, and generally destructive of consumer sovereignty. In recent years there has been somewhat of a rehabilitation of advertising in economic literature, along the lines of the economics of information. According to this view, advertising messages beamed at prospective consumers are quantities of needed knowledge, for which they are prepared to pay a price. The right quantity of information is produced and delivered by the advertising industry in response to consumer desires. For reasons having to do with cost economy, it is most efficient for this information to be produced by those for whom such production is easiest, namely, by the producers of the products about which information is needed. There is much of value in this approach to an understanding of the economics of advertising, but it does not explain everything. The economics of information approach tries to account for the phenomena of advertising entirely in terms of the demand for and supply of nonentrepreneurial knowledge, information that can be bought and sold and even packaged.

But such an approach does not go beyond a world of Robbinsian maximizers and fails to comprehend the true role of advertising in the market process.

Let us consider the producer of the advertised product. In his entrepreneurial role, the producer anticipates the wishes of consumers and notes the availability of the resources needed for a product to satisfy consumer desires. This function might appear to be fulfilled when the producer produces the product and makes it available for purchase. In other words, it might seem that the entrepreneur's function is fulfilled when he transforms an opportunity to produce a potential product into an opportunity for the consumer to buy the finished product. Consumers themselves were not aware of the opportunities this production process represents; it is the superior alertness of the entrepreneur that has enabled him to fulfill his task. It is not sufficient, however, to make the product available; consumers must be aware of its availability. If the opportunity to buy is not perceived by the consumer, it is as if the opportunity to produce has not been perceived by the entrepreneur. It is not enough to grow food consumers do not know how to obtain; consumers must know that the food has in fact been grown! Providing consumers with information is not enough. It is essential that the opportunities available to the consumer attract his attention, whatever the degree of his alertness may be. Not only must the entrepreneur-producer marshal resources to cater to consumer desires, but also he must insure that the consumer does not miss what has been wrought. For this purpose advertising is clearly an indispensable instrument.

By viewing advertising as an entrepreneurial device, we are able to understand why Chamberlin's distinction between fabrication costs and selling costs is invalid.[10] Fabrication (or production) costs are supposedly incurred for producing a product, as distinguished from selling costs incurred to get buyers to buy the product. Selling costs allegedly shift the demand curve for the product, while the costs of fabrication (production) affect the supply curve only. The distinction has been criticized on the grounds that most selling costs turn out to be disguised fabrication costs of one type or another.[11] Our perspective permits us to view the issue from a more general framework, which embodies the insight that all fabrication costs are at once selling costs as well. If the producer had a guaranteed market in which he could sell all he wanted of his product at a certain price, then his fabrication costs might be only fabrication costs and include no sum for coaxing consumers to buy it. But there never is a guaranteed market. The producer's decisions about what product to produce and of what quality are invariably a reflection of what he believes he will be able to sell at a worthwhile price. It is invariably an entrepreneurial choice. The costs he incurs are those that, in his estimation, he must incur to sell what he produces at the anticipated price. Every improvement in the product is introduced to make it more attractive to consumers, and certainly the product itself is produced for precisely the same reasons. All costs are, in the last analysis, selling costs.

PROFITS AND THE COMPETITIVE PROCESS

The Austrian concept of the entrepreneurial role emphasizes profit as being the prime objective of the market process. As such, it has important implications for the analysis of entrepreneurship in nonmarket contexts (such as within firms or under socialism or in bureaucracies in general). I have already remarked that we do not know precisely how entrepreneurs experience superior foresight, but we do know, at least in a general way, that entrepreneurial alertness is stimulated by the lure of profits. Alertness to an opportunity rests on the attractiveness of that opportunity and on its ability to be grasped once it has been perceived. This incentive is different from the incentives present in a Robbinsian world. In the non-entrepreneurial context, the incentive is constituted by the satisfactions obtainable at the expense of the relevant sacrifices. Robbinsian incentives are communicated to others by simply arranging that the satisfactions offered to them are more significant (from their point of view) than the sacrifices demanded from them. Incentive is thereby provided by the comparison of known alternatives. In the entrepreneurial context, however, the incentive to be alert to a future opportunity is quite different from the incentive to trade off already known opportunities; in fact it has nothing to do with the comparison of alternatives. No prior choice is involved in perceiving an opportunity waiting to be noticed. The incentive is to try to get something for nothing, if only one can see what it is that can be done.

Robbinsian incentives can be offered in nonmarket contexts. The bureaucrat, employer, or official offers a bonus for greater effort. For entrepreneurial incentives to operate, on the other hand, it is necessary for those who perceive opportunities to gain from noticing them. An outstanding feature of the market system is that it provides these kinds of incentives. Only by analysis of the market process does this very important entrepreneurial aspect of the market economy come into view. The real economic problems in any society arise from the phenomenon of unperceived opportunities. The manner in which a market society grapples with this phenomenon cannot be understood within an exclusively equilibrium theory of the market. The Austrian approach to the theory of the market therefore holds considerable promise. Much work still needs to be done. It would be good to know more about the institutional settings that are most conducive to opportunity discovery. It would be good to apply basic Austrian theory to the theory of speculation and of the formation of expectations with regard to future prices. All this would enrich our understanding of the economics of bureaucracy and of socialism. It can be convincingly argued that Mises's famous proposition concerning economic calculation under socialism flows naturally from his "Austrianism." Here, too, there is room for further elucidation. In all this agenda, the Austrian emphasis on process analysis should stand up very well.

NOTES

1. For an elaboration of a number of issues raised here, see Israel M. Kirzner, *Competition and Entrepreneurship* (Chicago: University of Chicago Press, 1973).

2. Joseph A. Schumpeter, *Capitalism, Socialism, and Democracy* (New York: Harper and Row, 1942), pp. 81–106.

3. Oscar Morgenstern, "Thirteen Critical Points in Contemporary Economic Theory: An Interpretation," *Journal of Economic Literature* 10 (December 1972): 1163–89.

4. Ludwig M. Lachmann, "Methodological Individualism and the Market Economy," in *Roads to Freedom: Essays in Honour of Friedrich A. von Hayek*, ed. Erich Streissler et al. (London: Routledge and Kegan Paul, 1969), p. 89.

5. Alfred Marshall, *Principles of Economics*, ed. C. W. Guillebaud, 2 vols. (London: Macmillan, 1961), 1:345–48; Marshall sometimes used the Walrasian approach (ibid., pp. 333–36).

6. Lionel Robbins, *An Essay on the Nature and Significance of Economic Science* (London: Macmillan, 1962), pp. 1–23.

7. Ludwig von Mises, *Human Action: A Treatise on Economics* (New Haven: Yale University Press, 1949), pp. 11–142; on the comparison of Misesian and Robbinsian notions, see Israel M. Kirzner, *The Economic Point of View* (Princeton: Van Nostrand, 1960), pp. 108–85.

8. In the preface to the first edition of his book, Robbins acknowledged his debt to Mises (*On the Nature*, pp. xv–xvi).

9. Kirzner, *Competition and Entrepreneurship*, pp. 75–87.

10. Edward Hastings Chamberlin, *The Theory of Monopolistic Competition*, 7th ed. (Cambridge: Harvard University Press, 1962), pp. 123–29.

11. See the literature cited in Kirzner, *Competition and Entrepreneurship*, pp. 141–69.

HAYEK, KNOWLEDGE, AND MARKET PROCESSES

The recent work of a number of outstanding economic theorists reveals a most welcome, if muted, rediscovery of an aspect of Hayek's work that has for some time been thoroughly—and most unfortunately—neglected.[1] Economists have, it seems, found their way back to that series of remarkable papers written in the 1930s and 1940s in which Hayek addressed himself decisively to the role of *knowledge* in economic theory. In these papers, the analysis of this role was developed with a clarity and power that ought well to have guided the development of subsequent economic thought along lines both fruitful and exciting. The failure of the profession, during the 1950s and 1960s, to follow Hayek's profoundly insightful guideposts must be counted one of the most disappointing features of postwar economic thought. The rediscovery, in the 1970s, of these guideposts raises one's hopes that the lost momentum can perhaps at last be resumed.

For Hayek's own work, both in economics and in the broader range of social thought, his explorations into the role of knowledge have of course been both central and seminal. No examination, such as this paper seeks to offer, of any one aspect of Hayek's ideas on knowledge, dare lose sight of the overarching unity these ideas, in their entirety, confer on virtually all of his far-flung and many-faceted contributions. For this and for other reasons, therefore, it seems convenient and useful to present, at the very outset of our discussion, a brief catalog of the more fundamental Hayekian ideas concerning knowledge. Thereafter we will be able to identify more usefully the particular strand of thought, running through Hayek's views on the economic role of knowledge, to which we wish to direct critical attention.

THE ROLE OF KNOWLEDGE: SOME HAYEKIAN INSIGHTS

1. The notion of the market equilibrium, Hayek explained, depends crucially on the correctness of the expectations members of society hold

Presented at a session of the meetings of the Allied Social Science Associations, held at Dallas, Texas, December 1975. From *Perception, Opportunity, and Profit: Studies in the Theory of Entrepreneurship* (Chicago and London: University of Chicago Press, 1979), 13–33.

concerning each other's actions. For equilibrium, the different plans the members of society have made for action must be mutually compatible. For this to occur, every person's plan must be "based on the expectation of just those actions of other people which those other people intend to perform," and "all these plans are based on the expectation of the same set of external facts, so that under certain conditions nobody will have any reason to change his plans. Correct foresight is then not, as it has sometimes been understood, a precondition which must exist in order that equilibrium may be arrived at. It is rather the defining characteristic of a state of equilibrium."[2] "The statement that, if people know everything, they are in equilibrium, is true simply because that is how we define equilibrium."[3]

2. The process whereby the market is understood to move from disequilibrium toward equilibrium is, it follows, to be similarly perceived in terms of knowledge. The assertion that a tendency toward equilibrium exists "can hardly mean anything but that, under certain conditions, the knowledge and intentions of the different members of society are supposed to come more and more into agreement or . . . that the expectations of the people and particularly of the entrepreneurs will become more and more correct."[4]

3. The economic problem facing society is one that rests on the fragmentation of knowledge. Thus this problem is *not* how to allocate given resources "if 'given' is taken to mean given to a single mind."[5] The economic problem rests on the fact "that the knowledge of the circumstances of which we must make use never exists in concentrated or integrated form but solely as the dispersed bits of incomplete and frequently contradictory knowledge which all the separate individuals possess."[6] The problem is "how to secure the best use of resources known to any of the members of society, for ends whose relative importance only these individuals know." It is a problem of "the utilization of knowledge which is not given to anyone in its totality."[7]

4. The great debate surrounding the relative merits for the economic organization of society, of the market system, and of the centrally planned system, it follows, must perforce come to grips with the problems created by this social fragmentation of knowledge. "Which of these systems is likely to be more efficient depends mainly on the question under which of them we can expect that fuller use will be made of the existing knowledge. This, in turn, depends on whether we are more

likely to succeed in putting at the disposal of a single central authority all the knowledge which ought to be used but which is initially dispersed among many different individuals, or in conveying to the individuals such additional knowledge as they need in order to enable them to dovetail their plans with those of others."[8] And it is therefore Hayek's perception of the market equilibrating process as effectively marshaling relevant information which led him to perceive the market price system as something of a "marvel"[9]—whose counterpart he was unable to discover in the socialized economy.

5. Hayek's insights as an economist into "the fact that no human mind can comprehend all the knowledge which guides the actions of society" led him more generally to an appreciation of "the impersonal processes of society in which more knowledge is utilized than any one individual or organized group of human beings can possess" and in particular toward his own "comprehensive restatement of the basic principles of a philosophy of freedom."[10] It is the essence of civilization that it "enables us constantly to profit from knowledge which we individually do not possess and . . . each individual's use of his particular knowledge may serve to assist others unknown to him in achieving their ends."[11] And indeed the "case for individual freedom rests chiefly on the recognition of the inevitable ignorance of all of us concerning a great many of the factors on which the achievement of our ends and welfare depends. . . . Liberty is essential in order to leave room for the unforseeable and unpredictable; we want it because we have learned to expect from it the opportunity of realizing many of our aims. It is because every individual knows so little and, in particular, because we rarely know which of us knows best that we trust the independent and competitive efforts of many to induce the emergence of what we shall want when we see it."[12]

Listing Hayekian ideas concerning the role of knowledge and of its fragmentation hardly does justice to the degree to which they support his entire system of thought; nonetheless this listing may serve to suggest the broader context within which Hayek's views on the market process are to be understood. It is with the role played in this process by the process of learning—as noted in the second of the listed propositions—that this chapter is specifically concerned. Some general remarks on the nature and significance of market process analysis may help us appreciate Hayek's contribution in this regard.

THE SIGNIFICANCE OF THE ANALYSIS OF MARKET PROCESSES

It must remain something of a riddle for historians of modern economic thought that the mainstream of theoretical literature has, until perhaps the past half-dozen years, virtually ignored the need to explain and to understand the *processes* occurring in the market. For decades theorists were, with extremely few exceptions, content to preoccupy themselves with the conditions for market equilibrium, without giving serious thought to what is to be understood as going on when these conditions do not prevail. For decades economists blithely assumed, in effect, that equilibrium situations are instantaneously attained.[13] As Patinkin has exhaustively documented, Walras's partial recognition of the problem of how the market might proceed toward equilibrium, and his imaginative, if unsatisfying, attempt to grapple with it through a theory of *tâtonnement,* were for three quarters of a century largely neglected by economic theorists.[14] As is well known, Hicks's *Value and Capital* treatment of the stability of equilibrium flatly assumed that adjustment processes are timeless.[15] And even the introduction into economic theory by Samuelson and others during the 1940s of a "truly dynamic" analysis of stability[16] left, as we shall see, the nature of the processes essentially unexplained and the full significance of their analysis only incompletely perceived.[17]

The truth is that the significance of the issue extends far beyond that usually associated with the question of the stability of general equilibrium—or for that matter partial equilibrium—states. Questions of stability turn on the possibility of demonstrating convergence toward the equilibrium state, whatever the context. But a theory of process must establish the determinateness of the course of market events, quite apart from the issue of whether this course of events does or does not tend toward an equilibrium state. Hahn has recently emphasized that the equilibrium concept by itself implies no tendency toward equilibrium. The equilibrium concept implies little more, Hahn writes, than the weak claim "that no plausible sequence of economic states will terminate, if it does so at all, in a state which is not in equilibrium."[18] The significant question, therefore, is whether we can conclude that the market achieves any *systematic* "sequence of economic states" at all.[19] It was this question that was ignored for so long.

The only voices raised in protest, during the decades of exclusive preoccupation with equilibrium, seem to have been those of the "Austrians," Mises and Hayek. Mises vigorously denounced the abuse of the (concededly highly useful) equilibrium concept by theorists who ignored the essentially process character of markets. Again and again he showed how the belief held by theorists that equilibrium states are actually attained led them to misunderstand grossly what markets in fact achieve.[20] For Mises, the essence of a theory of markets must be to explain the forces that generate *changes* in prices and quantities; the equilibrium concept is useful precisely in its offering, in its utterly hypothetical freedom from change, a contrast to the world of incessant change. Hayek's quite independent search for an understanding of market processes is the subject of this chapter. It was in 1936 that Hayek observed that while usual presentations of equilibrium analysis make it appear that the questions of how the equilibrium comes about have been solved, in fact these presentations do no more than assume what needs to be shown.[21] Again, in the course of his pioneering critique of the way theorists had come to use the notion of competition, Hayek unerringly identified the difficulty as arising from the assumption that equilibrium already exists, that "the data for the different individuals are fully adjusted to each other, while the problem which requires explanation is the nature of the process by which the data are thus adjusted."[22]

It is of course true that in discussing competitive markets economists have always implied *some* kind of process. For many decades, this implied process was uncritically expressed as the "law of supply and demand." This was generally understood in terms of the explanation for the course of market price for a given single good; this simple context will suffice for most of our purpose.

When theorists sought to isolate more specifically the dynamics of this competitive process of supply and demand for the single good, they did so generally in what has come to be called the "Walrasian" version of simple stability analysis.[23] Freshman undergraduates have, in this version, been taught for decades that the intersection of the market supply curve and market demand curve yields the price and output toward which the market tends. Should price be below this equilibrium level, students have been told, the excess demand of competing unsatisfied buyers will force price up; if price is above equilibrium excess supply will bring about falling prices. The early discussions of the stability of equilibrium formalized this mechanism as follows:[24]

$$\frac{dp}{dt} = H(q_D - q_S),$$

where

$$H(0) = 0, \quad \text{and} \quad H' > 0.$$

The time rate of price change is declared to be a function of the excess demand generated by the going price. Price moves up so long as there is excess demand; it moves down with excess supply (i.e., negative excess demand); at zero excess demand price does not change. The Walrasian stability conditions (which associate positive excess demand with below-equilibrium prices) are then sufficient to guarantee convergence to equilibrium, provided the demand and supply curves are not themselves shifted by trading at disequilibrium prices. It will be helpful, in pointing out the problems inherent in this kind of process analysis, to spell out some of the well-known elements of the view of the market process this approach implies.

(1) This approach rules out the possibility of more than one price, even in disequilibrium. Each date is associated with one and only one price. (2) At each price, each market participant believes it is possible for him to buy or sell any amount he chooses without the price being changed as a result of his actions. This implication of perfect competition the approach assumes means that each participant reacts passively to price: He is a "price taker." (3) Price changes come about not through the deliberate decisions of any market participants, since everyone is a price taker, but in some unexplained way, such as through the agency of an imagined Walrasian auctioneer. This enumeration points directly to the difficulties that render this approach so thoroughly unsatisfactory. It is a welcome feature of the recent literature on market process that it has clearly recognized these difficulties.

Most disturbing among these difficulties has been the complete absence of explanation of how, lacking the mysterious auctioneer, prices in fact change, in a world in which no participant changes prices.[25] The difficulty, or one very close to it, has also been articulated by noticing that the approach under discussion fails to deduce price changes "as the maximizing response of economic units to changing data."[26] In other words, the theory of market process the approach provides us is not a "choice-theoretic" one and is thus a major departure from the microeconomic method usually associated with price theory. Another widely noted difficulty concerns the logical contradiction entailed in the assumption of perfect competition under disequilibrium conditions. In order to analyze the dynamics of price adjustment, it is "necessary to discard the perfectly competitive paradigm of the producer as price-taker."[27] One cannot, without logical strain, postulate market participants who at all times see themselves as price takers, able to buy and sell all they choose at going prices, while simultaneously discussing the excess demand or supply being continually generated by these prices until equilibrium has been reached. A further difficulty infrequently noticed in the recent literature is that the stability-theoretic approach we have been examining leaves room for only one price at each point in time, even during disequilibrium.[28] Since the disequilibrium markets we know in the real world are not quite as obligingly simple as this,[29] the approach fails to provide an explanation for an important aspect of the market process, namely, how during the course of the process, many prices converge, as entailed by Jevons's Law of Indifference, toward a single price. Moreover, the equilibrating process of price change that the approach postulates, being based on the single-price assumption, begs the question of how this process is to be understood in the context of that *other* converging process we must assume to be simultaneously at work, during which many prices are only gradually being shaken down toward uniformity.

It is against this background of long-time unconcern by economic theorists with the need for an adequate theory of market process that we turn now to consider Hayek's attempt, forty years ago, to throw light on the character of this process.

HAYEK, KNOWLEDGE, AND MARKET PROCESSES

The kernel of Hayek's contribution to an understanding of market processes consisted in his interpreting the assertion that a tendency exists toward equilibrium as meaning "that, under certain conditions, the knowledge and intentions of the different members of society are supposed to come more and more into agreement or . . . that the expectations of the people and particularly of the entrepreneurs will become more and more correct."[30] Equilibrium was defined, for

Hayek, as the state of affairs characterized by universally correct anticipation of the actions of other people. A tendency toward equilibrium
must therefore mean more than a particular converging pattern of
price and quantity adjustments over time; it must mean a systematic
process through which market participants replace sets of plans based
on incorrect awareness of each other's plans by plans in which everyone more accurately anticipates what everyone else intends to do. The
market process must, if it is to be in the direction toward equilibrium,
be a process of mutual discovery.

Hayek pursued this theme further in a well-known paper on the role
of competition in the market process. In that paper, Hayek sharply criticized dominant notions of competition. The truth is, Hayek argued, that
"competition is by its nature a dynamic process whose essential characteristics are assumed away by the assumptions underlying static analysis."[31] The modern theory of competitive equilibrium "deals almost
exclusively with a state . . . in which it is assumed that the data for the
different individuals are fully adjusted to each other, while the problem
which requires explanation is the nature of the process by which the data
are thus adjusted."[32] And Hayek is emphatic in understanding this process as consisting in the discovery and dissemination of relevant information, that information which the theory of competitive equilibrium
unhelpfully assumes to be already known. Knowledge of the lowest costs
of production can be discovered only through the process of competition.
The wishes and desires of consumers cannot properly be regarded as
given facts to producers, "but ought rather to be regarded as problems to
be solved by the process of competition." The knowledge consumers are
supposed to possess cannot be assumed before the process of competition starts; "the whole organization of the market serves mainly the need
of spreading the information on which buyers act."[33]

What happens in disequilibrium is, of course, different from what
happens in equilibrium. During equilibrium, prices and quantities do
not change; in disequilibrium they do. For Hayek the difference is far
deeper. During equilibrium men act on the basis of correct knowledge;
in disequilibrium they are, on the one hand, acting on the basis of partial
ignorance and, on the other hand, engaged in a process of learning.

Hayek's insight into the nature of the market process enables us to
avoid the difficulties that inhere in the simple Walrasian version of stability analysis. There need be no mystery about how prices change during

equilibrium. Prices change because individual market participants have discovered they can do better for themselves by offering or asking prices different from those hitherto prevailing. A buyer who failed to find a seller willing to sell to him at yesterday's prices has learned the need to offer a higher price. A buyer who found that at yesterday's prices he was inundated with the offers of would-be sellers scrambling for his patronage realizes that he can obtain what he seeks at a lower price. A buyer who purchased yesterday at a given price discovers that others were able to buy for lower prices; he has learned that more than one price has been prevailing, and he will adjust his bids accordingly. And so on.[34] Similarly, once the analysis of the competitive process is couched in terms of information discovery, the other difficulties cited in the preceding section can immediately be seen as no longer relevant. All this attests to the power and fertility of Hayek's insight. It was from this powerful insight that Hayek proceeded to make a series of observations concerning economic theory, which it is my purpose to examine critically.

PROCESS ANALYSIS, PURE LOGIC, AND EMPIRICAL SCIENCE

From the distinction that he drew between what is happening during equilibrium and what is happening during the course of the market process, Hayek proceeded to assert the existence of a sharp difference between the epistemological character of equilibrium analysis and that of process analysis. The analysis of equilibrium is identical with the Pure Logic of Choice; it consists essentially of tautologies that are necessarily true because they are merely transformations of the assumptions from which we start. These tautologies by themselves tell us nothing about the real world; they merely elaborate the conditions logically required for the equilibrium state to exist. What enables us to pass from these exercises in pure logic to statements about causation in the real world is only our analysis of the tendency of market processes to lead toward equilibrium. In fact, the only justification for our concern with the fictitious state of equilibrium "is the supposed existence of a tendency toward equilibrium. *It is only by this assertion that such a tendency exists that economics ceases to be an exercise in pure logic and becomes an empirical science.*"[35] And it is Hayek's understanding of the market process as one of learning information that enables him to argue that the assertion of a tendency toward equilibrium "is clearly an empirical proposition, that is, an assertion about what happens in the real world which ought, at least in principle, to be capable of verification."[36] The tautologies of equilibrium analysis "can be turned into propositions which tell us anything about causation in the real world only in so far as we are able to fill those formal propositions with definite statements about how knowledge is acquired and communicated."[37] For Hayek, the asserted tendency toward equilibrium depends upon assumptions "about the actual acquisition of knowledge" in the course of the market process. "The significant point . . . is that it is these apparently subsidiary hypotheses or assumptions that people do learn from experience, and about how they acquire knowledge, which constitute the empirical content of our propositions about what happens in the real world."[38] The assumptions necessary for these empirical propositions differ sharply in generality, Hayek argues, from those upon which rests the Pure Logic of Choice. The latter assumptions are "axioms which define . . . the field within which we are able to understand . . . the processes of thought of other people. . . . They refer to a type of human action (what we commonly call 'rational,' or even merely 'conscious,' as distinguished from 'instinctive' action) rather than to the particular conditions under which this action is taken. But the assumptions . . . which we have to introduce when we want to explain the social processes, concern the relation of the thought of an individual to the outside world, the question to what extent and how his knowledge corresponds to external facts."[39]

We may summarize Hayek's position as consisting in the following propositions: (1) Understanding of the separate plans individuals make, each on the basis of his own knowledge and anticipations, may be sought at a level that involves nothing more than the pure logic of choice. (2) In disequilibrium many individuals will not be able to carry out, or will come to regret their execution of, their plans, because the realized plans of others differ from those which had been anticipated. (3) Our understanding of the configuration of plans that is consistent with equilibrium (i.e., the global set of compatible plans, each of which reflects correct anticipation of the plans of others), is again an exercise in the pure logic of choice. (4) An assertion that the attempted execution of a set of incompatible plans will set in motion a systematic series of plan changes tending toward equilibrium *cannot* be made on purely logical grounds. Such an assertion must depend on a postulated propensity on the part of market participants to learn the correct lessons from their experiences. Such a propensity can be claimed to exist only as a matter of fact; it cannot be derived simply from the logic of conscious human action. (5) The epistemological character of economic theory is thus not uniform. That portion of economic theory that concerns itself with the conditions required for equilibrium is known a priori; it is an extension of the pure logic of choice, possessing no empirical content whatever. That portion of economic theory that attempts to explain the nature of equilibrating market forces possesses the character of an empirical science, since its propositions depend crucially on postulated factual relationships held to govern the way men learn relevant information. Several interrelated observations may be immediately made concerning Hayek's view of the epistemological character of economic theory.

First of all, we note what at least superficially appears to be an important disagreement between Hayek and Mises concerning the character of economics. Hayek is often coupled with Mises as espousing the view of economics as a completely a prioristic body of thought.[40] We have seen, on the contrary, that Hayek took great pains to emphasize his perception of economic science as being, with the exception of equilibrium analysis, empirical science.

We note further, perhaps with an implication casting doubt on the conclusiveness of our preceding observation, that the manner in which Hayek's empirical economic science links the purely logical propositions of economics with the phenomena of the real world is rather different from other perspectives on the same task. Ordinarily, attempts to use pure economic logic in the formulation of empirical statements seeking to describe the real world involve the translation of the formal categories of economic theory into applied form expressing the facts of particular situations. Empirical assertions are derived from statements concerning preferences and choices that are no longer pure, but which rather reflect observed (or postulated) specific patterns of tastes, or technological possibilities.[41] Despite Hayek's remarks about filling formal propositions with definite content concerning how knowledge is acquired, the truth is that propositions about individual plans that continue to presume no specific preference structures and no specific production possibilities must continue to be empty propositions, despite any postulated pattern of learning information. Indeed the empirical element introduced by Hayek not only fails to fill with factual content the empty formal propositions that make up the logic of choice, it leaves these propositions themselves exactly as empty as it finds them. The pure logic of choice explains the decisions a man makes in terms of his preferences and the price and technological constraints he perceives to be relevant to him. These explanations, being purely logical in character, are entirely general. They refer with equal validity to any specific set of preferences and to any sets of perceived prices and technologies. Hayek's empirical element does not, even in principle, provide concrete content to the empty set of perceived prices. It merely assures us that, *were* we to know specifically the various sets of prices individual agents perceived at any one date, we could, on the basis of our factual knowledge of learning processes, know what prices they would expect on future dates. Hayek's empirical element does not, therefore, introduce any specificity into our logical propositions concerning the choices at any given date. It merely provides an abstract pattern within which to *link* the purely formal propositions relevant to choices at one date to the equally purely formal propositions relevant to choices at later dates.

This observation may be presented somewhat differently. Suppose we knew the concrete structure of an individual's preferences at a given date, and we also knew with completeness the precise way that individual's perception of his constraints can be modified by experience. We would not yet, nonetheless, be able to predict his specific decisions at that date until we have, in addition, been provided with factual information concerning his perception of his constraints at that date or at least concerning the perception he had of his constraints at an earlier date, together with a history of his subsequent relevant experience. Hayek's empirical element does not refer to this required additional information. Without it, Hayek's empirical hypotheses concerning the way people learn from experience leave the set of constraints perceived by an individual decision maker as empty as before. What Hayek's empirical element has introduced, therefore, is not a device for translating, even in principle, any of the propositions of the logic of choice into empirical statements; rather, it is a device to explain, on empirical grounds, the way the set of choices made at one date can be seen, ceteris paribus, to follow from the set made at earlier dates.

I do not underestimate the significance of this accomplishment; on the contrary, my principal purpose is to draw attention to the profound importance of these neglected Hayekian insights into the learning process through which the market achieves its tendency toward equilibrium. My observations concerning the special and highly limited sense in which Hayek's empirical element affects the purely logical character of propositions in economic theory, were made to provide a background for a critical examination of Hayek's own understanding of the epistemological implications of his contribution. To this examination we now turn.

ALLOCATIVE DECISION MAKING, HUMAN ACTION, AND MARKET PROCESS

Hayek has offered us a view of the market process that sees it as made up of a succession of two diverse elements, logical inevitability and empirical accident. At any given date, market participants make their buying, production, and selling decisions as determined by their preferences and perceived constraints, with these constraints reflecting the anticipated decisions of others. We understand these allocative decisions in terms of our immediate a priori access to the logic of choice. Owing to the ignorance of market participants, these decisions of a given date will not mesh. As a result, participants will experience market phenomena such as surpluses or shortages that will teach them more accurate information concerning the preferences and decisions of others. The specific lessons market experience will impart are *not* understandable through the logic of choice; they are to be understood by the economist only as empirical regularities—if regularities indeed prevail at all—that happen to be the way they are. Apart from the accident of such empirical regularities, there is nothing in the logic governing the set of choices made by market participants at one date to account for the set of choices they make at future dates. From a strictly logical perspective, the sets of allocative decisions made at different dates are unrelated. They are linked only by the accidents of the learning process. The Hayekian perception of the dynamics of the market process is like a somewhat peculiar motion film made up of a succession of static pictures. Each separate picture itself is entirely understandable in terms of the logic of choice; the changes between each picture and its successor can be explained only in terms of facts ungoverned by a priori considerations of any kind. It is with this dichotomous view of the market process that I will take issue. My position will rely a good deal on the distinction, drawn elsewhere at greater length,[42] between Robbinsian economizing and Misesian human action.

Economizing man engages in allocative decision making within a strictly given framework of ends and means. He "is endowed with the propensity to mold given means to suit given ends. The very concept presupposes some given image of ends and means. . . . Economizing behavior—or, more accurately, its analysis—necessarily skips the task of identifying ends and means. The economizing notion by definition presupposes that this task (and its analysis) has been completed elsewhere."[43] It follows that an analysis confined to allocative, economizing explanations must indeed fail to account for any continuity in a sequence of decisions, since each decision is comprehended purely in terms of its own relevant end-means framework. "With purely allocative explanations, no earlier decision can be used to explain later decisions on the basis of learning; if the pattern of ends-means held relevant by the individual at the later decision differs from that held relevant earlier, then there is, within the 'economizing framework,' nothing but a discontinuity. Such exogenous change has simply wiped out one decision-making situation and replaced it with a different one."[44]

What Hayek contributed was an insight into how continuity can be accounted for in such a sequence of decisions. But, apparently working implicitly within an economizing framework, Hayek was able to introduce such continuity only from outside that allocative framework, from the empirical accidents of the learning process. The pure logic of economic analysis, seen as extending no further than the limits of the economizing framework, could, Hayek argued, be of no assistance in providing an understanding of continuity; the market process must call, for its analysis, on additional, empirical regularities. I will argue that insight into the nature of Misesian human action enables us to see matters somewhat differently.

Human action, in the sense developed by Mises, involves courses of action taken by the human being "to remove uneasiness" and to make himself "better off." Being broader than the notion of economizing, the concept of human action does not restrict analysis of the decision to the allocation problem posed by the juxtaposition of scarce means and multiple ends. The decision, in the framework of the human action approach, is not arrived at merely by mechanical computation of the solution to the maximization problem implicit in the configuration of the given ends and means. It reflects not merely the manipulation of given means to correspond faithfully with the hierarchy of given ends, but also *the very perception of the ends-means framework* within which allocation and economizing is to take place . . . Mises' *homo agens* . . . is endowed not only with the propensity to pursue goals efficiently, once ends and means are clearly identified, but also with the drive and alertness needed to identify which ends to strive for and which means are available.[45]

This drive and alertness can be identified as the entrepreneurial element in human decision making. "In any real and living economy every actor is always an entrepreneur."[46]

For a world of Robbinsian economizers, the market process must indeed seem a discrete sequence of separate states linked, at best, accidentally by the extraeconomic facts of the learning process. But as soon as "we broaden our theoretical vision of the individual decision-maker from a 'mechanical' Robbinsian economizer to Mises' *homo agens,* with the universally human entrepreneurial elements of alertness in his makeup, we can cope with the task of explaining the changes which market forces systematically generate"[47] without necessarily transcending the scope of the analysis of decision making. It will be helpful, in perceiving this, to emphasize the difference between learning facts, and discovering opportunities.

It is, of course, perfectly true that insight into the entrepreneurial element in human action does not by itself assure us that people necessarily learn the correct facts of their situations from their market experiences. While the recognition of universal human alertness provides grounds for presuming learning, it does not, it may seem, guarantee discovery of the truth. Can we be sure that, confronted with a surplus, would-be sellers will realize that they must accept lower prices in the future? Can we be sure that, when more than one price prevails for the same item, entrepreneurs will indeed learn of this and move toward the elimination of the price differential? The very existence of error suggests that men have not learned the correct lessons from experience or, at any rate, have not learned them sufficiently well.

But, having recognized that, despite their alertness to new information, people err, we must nonetheless point out that the alertness we have discovered in human action does carry us further than we may have realized. The entrepreneurial alertness with which the individual is endowed does not refer to a passive vulnerability to the impressions impinging on his consciousness during experience in the manner of a piece of film exposed to the light; it refers to the human propensity to sniff out opportunities lurking around the corner. What the notion of human action gives us is the recognition that people possess a propensity to discover what is useful to them. We have no assurance that a man walking down the street will, after his walk, have absorbed knowledge of all the facts to which he has been exposed; we do, in talking of human action, assume at least a tendency for man to notice those that constitute possible opportunities for gainful action on his part.

It has been the contribution of economic theory to show how markets in disequilibrium offer market participants *opportunities for gain*. The absence of uniform price offers the possibility of pure arbitrage profit; shortages offer alert sellers the opportunity to obtain higher prices than hitherto prevailed, and so on. Our insight that opportunities do tend to be discovered assures us that a process is set in motion by disequilibrium conditions as these opportunities are gradually noticed and exploited. The process by which facts are hammered into human consciousness is not wholly ungoverned by the logic of human action; it fits naturally into the tendency for alert acting human beings to notice what is likely to be of service to them.

This perspective on the learning process that, as Hayek has taught us, constitutes the inner core of the market tendency toward equilibrium provides us, then, with a somewhat different view of its character from that which Hayek himself emphasized so strongly. Our identification of decision making with alert, entrepreneurial human action has provided us with *an explanation for the market process that does not, in principle, depend for its general pattern, upon any extraeconomic factual considerations whatsoever.* The market process emerges as the necessary implication of the circumstances that people act, and that in their actions they err, discover their errors, and tend to revise their actions in a direction likely to be less erroneous than before.

Note that we have not claimed a priori validity for our insight concerning man's propensity to discover opportunities. It is enough, for our purpose, to recognize this propensity as inseparable from our insight that human beings act purposefully. Recognizing that whatever learning occurs during the market process is likely to be a manifestation of man's propensity to discover opportunities, enables us, in fact, to use Hayek's own criteria to question the validity of his dichotomy. For Hayek the regularities governing the way people learn from experience are of a nature "in many respects rather different from the more general assumptions from which the Pure Logic of Choice starts."[48] The first way the latter, more general assumptions are not similar to those relevant to the learning process is that these "more general assumptions" are "common to all human thought. They may be regarded as axioms which define or delimit the field within which we are able to understand or mentally to reconstruct the processes of thought of other people."[49] Our insight concerning the alertness of human beings to information about opportunities renders this alertness fully as integral an aspect of human thought and action as are the purportedly more general assumptions to which Hayek refers.

All this, inconsistent though it may be with Hayek's sharply dichotomous view concerning the epistemological character of the market process, does not, one should observe, deny the relevance of such empirical regularities as may be discovered in the learning process. It is one thing to postulate an equilibrating tendency on the basis of the general character of human action; it is quite another to account for the concrete pattern of events in which this tendency happens to manifest itself. "Economists," Mises remarked, "must never disregard in their reasoning the fact that the innate and acquired inequality of men differentiates their adjustment to the conditions of their environment."[50] It is indeed empirical accidents, such as the differences in the entrepreneurial alertness of different men, that will govern the specific course of market events. But this circumstance does not remove the entrepreneurial, profit-seeking, driving force of the market, which propels this course of events, from the realm of those general assumptions whose relevance Hayek himself was prepared to recognize only in equilibrium analysis. The general logic employed in equilibrium analysis cannot, of course, by itself account for *specific* equilibrium values of prices and outputs; for this, we need additional empirical information. But it is nonetheless the general logic of choice that governs these specific equilibrium values. Similarly, without knowledge of the empirical patterns that characterize the learning processes of specific men, we cannot know the specific course of market events. But our insight into the general propensity of people to be alert to opportunities nonetheless provides us with an understanding of the overall tendencies governing these sequences of market events.

Our recognition of human purposefulness permits us to see the actions of people, the phenomena of social interaction, in terms of a calculus of choice. We explain bald facts in terms of such purposefulness. In the same way, surely, our recognition that human purposefulness embraces alertness to hitherto unnoticed opportunities permits us to see the sequence of market phenomena in terms of the universal propensity to notice what may be useful.

To arrive at empirical propositions concerning the course of market events, it is necessary to fill our general insights into man's propensity to notice opportunities in precisely the same way as the theorems of the logic of choice come to be translated into propositions of empirical science.

PERFECT KNOWLEDGE, ALERTNESS, AND THE EQUILIBRATING PROCESS

Largely as a result of Hayek's work, it is now well understood that neoclassical price theory suffered seriously from its carefree use of the assumption of perfect knowledge. The task of economic theory, we now know, is precisely that of accounting for the way information is brought to bear on the decisions of market participants and on the extent to which the market directs relevant information to those who can make the (socially) best use of it. The assumption of perfect knowledge assumes away the central task of economic theory. In emphatically rejecting the perfect knowledge assumptions we should not, however, lose sight of those considerations that endow such an assumption with its superficial plausibility.

If an activity promises to yield a revenue more than sufficient to cover all necessary costs, *including the costs of buying relevant needed information,* our instinctive reaction as economists is to feel sure that the activity will be carried on. Upon reflection, we are likely to concede that, even if the revenue is sufficient to cover the information costs as well, ignorance may nonetheless block immediate exploitation of this opportunity: no one may yet be aware of the existence of the opportunity at all.[51] Despite this realization, our instinct still assures us that the opportunity will sooner or later be discovered and exploited. The perfect knowledge assumption of neoclassical economics carried this instinctive assurance to altogether unjustified lengths.[52] In rejecting this dangerous assumption, we must take care not to expunge the entirely healthy instinct on which it rested.

The truth is that at any given time people will, on the one hand, be blissfully ignorant of opportunities staring them in the face; on the other hand, they will be delightedly proceeding to exploit newly noticed opportunities of which they had been unaware yesterday. Our instinctive feeling of assurance that profitable opportunities will be noticed should not lead us to treat this tendency as being so powerful as to be instantaneously realized, as is implied in the perfect knowledge assumption. This would cause us to overlook, as neoclassical theory has indeed overlooked, the role of the market process in reinforcing this tendency. We must indeed not take for granted something it is our responsibility to explain. On the other hand, however, we must not consider the possibility of ignorance giving way to awareness as being entirely arbitrary, as a matter on which we can only patiently wait for empirical evidence. We must not fail to exploit to the fullest our assurance that there is indeed a tendency for opportunities to be noticed.

What is significant in all this is that our insight into the existence of such a tendency provides us with an approach to the analysis of equilibrating processes. We need not wait for evidence on the way information comes to spread through a society. We can, instead, employ our logic of choice to identify, within disequilibrium markets, the opportunities for gain that disequilibrium conditions themselves create. Postulating a tendency for such opportunities to be discovered and exploited, we can then explain the way such gradual discovery and exploitation of opportunities in turn gradually alters the pattern of opportunities presented in the market as the process unfolds.[53]

This approach leaves ample room for applied empirical work directed at the specifics of the tendency for opportunity discovery, at the possibility of the tendency's being slowed down by incompetent entrepreneurial activity, and so on. It has been my purpose to argue that such empirical work not be viewed as embracing all or even the principal share of the economics of market processes, that Hayek's pioneering view of market process as being one of information dissemination and discovery be exploited for what it has given us: the guidepost to an entrepreneurial perspective on market processes.

NOTES

1. See especially A. Leijonhufvud, *On Keynesian Economics and the Economics of Keynes* (New York: Oxford University Press, 1968), p. 401; K. E. Boulding, "The Economics of Knowledge and the Knowledge of Economics," *American Economic Review* 56 (May 1966): 1; "Economics as a Moral Science," *American Economic Review* 59 (March 1969): 4; P. J. McNulty, "A Note on the History of Perfect Competition," *Journal of Political Economy* 75 (August 1967): 402; and "The Meaning of Competition," *Quarterly Journal of Economics* 82 (November 1968): 649; J. M. Buchanan,

Cost and Choice (Chicago: Markham, 1969), p. 24; G. S. Becker, *Economic Theory* (New York: Alfred A. Knopf, 1971), p. 214; G. L. S. Shackle, *Epistemics and Economics* (Cambridge: Cambridge University Press, 1972), p. 124; F. Machlup, "Friedrich Von Hayek's Contribution to Economics," *Swedish Journal of Economics* 76 (1974): 514 ff.

2. F. A. Hayek, "Economics and Knowledge," *Economica*, vol. 4 (February 1937); reprinted in *Individualism and Economic Order* (London: Routledge and Kegan Paul, 1949), p. 42. All page references to this article will be from this reprint.

3. Ibid., p. 46.

4. Ibid., p. 45.

5. F. A. Hayek, "The Use of Knowledge in Society," *American Economic Review*, vol. 35 (September 1945); reprinted in *Individualism and Economic Order*, pp. 77 ff. All page references to this article will be to this reprint.

6. Ibid., p. 77.

7. Ibid., p. 78.

8. Ibid., p. 79.

9. Ibid., p. 87.

10. F. A. Hayek, *The Constitution of Liberty* (Chicago: University of Chicago Press, 1960), pp. 3 ff.

11. Ibid., p. 25.

12. Ibid., p. 29.

13. For earlier expressions of concern see K. Arrow, "Toward a Theory of Price Adjustment," in *The Allocation of Economic Resources*, ed. Abramovitz et al. (Stanford: Stanford University Press, 1959); G. B. Richardson, *Information and Investment* (London: Oxford University Press, 1960), pp. 23 ff.; D. Bodenhorn, *Intermediate Price Theory* (New York: McGraw-Hill, 1961), p. 185.

14. D. Patinkin, *Money, Interest and Prices*, 2d ed. (New York: Harper and Row, 1965), pp. 531–40, note B. See also N. Kaldor, "The Determinateness of Static Equilibrium," *Review of Economic Studies*, vol. 1 (February 1934).

15. See J. R. Hicks, *Value and Capital*, 2d ed. (Oxford: Clarendon Press, 1946), p. 336.

16. See P. A. Samuelson, *Foundations of Economic Analysis* (Cambridge: Harvard University Press, 1947), chap. 9 and the cited literature.

17. On this see Arrow, "Theory of Price Adjustment," p. 143. See also Patinkin, *Money*, pp. 539 ff.

18. F. H. Hahn, *On the Notion of Equilibrium in Economics: An Inaugural Lecture* (Cambridge: Cambridge University Press, 1973), p. 7.

19. See also I. M. Kirzner, "Rejoinder," *Journal of Political Economy* 71 (February 1963): 84, note 3.

20. See, e.g., L. Mises, *Human Action* (New Haven: Yale University Press, 1949), pp. 353, 707.

21. Hayek, "Economics and Knowledge," p. 45.

22. F. A. Hayek, "The Meaning of Competition," in *Individualism and Economic Order*, p. 94.

23. For a critical comment on the historical validity of this label, see Samuelson, *Foundations of Economic Analysis*, p. 264 n.

24. Ibid., p. 263.

25. See D. F. Gordon and H. Hynes, "On the Theory of Price Dynamics," in E. S. Phelps et al., *Microeconomic Foundations of Employment and Inflation Theory* (New York: W. W. Norton, 1970), pp. 371 ff.; M. Rothschild, "Models of Market Organization with Imperfect Information: A Survey," *Journal of Political Economy* 81 (November/December 1973): 1285; K. J. Arrow and F. H. Hahn, *General Competitive Analysis* (San Francisco: Holden-Day; Edinburgh: Oliver and Boyd, 1971), pp. 266, 322; for an earlier reference see the article by Arrow, "Toward a Theory of Price Adjustment," p. 43. See also J. M. Ostroy, "The Informational Efficiency of Monetary Exchange," *American Economic Review* 63 (September 1973): 597 and note 2.

26. Gordon and Hynes, "Theory of Price Dynamics," p. 371.

27. R. J. Barro and H. L. Grossman, "A General Disequilibrium Model of Income and Employment," *American Economic Review* 61 (March 1971): 85 n; Gordon and Hynes, "Theory of Price Dynamics," p. 372, note 7; see also M. Rothschild, "Models of Market Organization," p. 1291.

28. Arrow and Hahn, *General Competitive Analysis*, p. 322.

29. It was the phenomenon of price dispersion that was central to G. J. Stigler, "The Economics of Information," *Journal of Political Economy* 69 (June 1961): 213–25. See M. Rothschild, "Models of Market Organization," sec. 5, for models in which equilibrium itself consists of a distribution of prices.

30. F. A. Hayek, "Economics and Knowledge," p. 45.

31. F. A. Hayek, "The Meaning of Competition," p. 94.

32. Ibid.

33. Ibid., p. 96.

34. For a detailed analysis of the kinds of error buyers and sellers can make in disequilibrium, and the kinds of learning processes generated by these mistakes, see I. M. Kirzner, *Market Theory and the Price System* (New York: Van Nostrand, 1963), chap. 7.

35. Hayek, "Economics and Knowledge," p. 44 (italics supplied).

36. Ibid., p. 45.

37. Ibid., p. 33.

38. Ibid., p. 46.

39. Ibid., p. 47.

40. See, e.g., J. M. Buchanan, "Is Economics the Science of Choice?" in *Roads to Freedom*, ed. E. Streissler (London: Routledge and Kegan Paul, 1969), p. 52; see also Buchanan, *Cost and Choice*, p. 24.

41. For an excellent discussion of this issue, see J. M. Buchanan, "Is Economics the Science of Choice?"

42. See I. M. Kirzner, *Competition and Entrepreneurship* (Chicago: University of Chicago Press, 1973), pp. 32–37.

43. Ibid., pp. 33 ff.

44. Ibid., p. 36.

45. Ibid., pp. 33 ff.

46. Mises, *Human Action*, p. 253.

47. Kirzner, *Competition and Entrepreneurship*, p. 72.

48. Hayek, "Economics and Knowledge," p. 46.

49. Ibid., p. 47.

50. Mises, *Human Action*, p. 325.

51. For further discussion on this point see Kirzner, *Competition and Entrepreneurship*, pp. 228 ff.

52. "It seems that that skeleton in our cupboard, the 'economic man,' whom we have exorcised with prayer and fasting, has returned through the back door in the form of a quasi-omniscient individual." Hayek, "Economics and Knowledge," p. 46.

53. For an example of this approach, see Kirzner, *Market Theory and the Price System*.

MARKET PROCESS THEORY: IN DEFENSE
OF THE AUSTRIAN MIDDLE GROUND

The chapters in this book have all, in one way or another, to do with the Austrian view of the market as a systematic process of mutual discovery by market participants. An overview of this Austrian understanding of the market, and of the task of economic theorizing in explicating this process, is provided in Chapter 2. The present introductory chapter has the purposes of reaffirming the thesis that this Austrian approach occupies the middle ground between two more "extreme" positions in contemporary economic thinking, and of defending the viability of this middle ground against some recent criticisms raised by proponents of a radical subjectivism. Identification of the Austrian approach with the middle ground is not merely a matter of doctrinal classification; it will turn out that this identification (and especially a defense of this position against current criticisms) can contribute significantly to an appreciation of what market process theory can offer toward economic understanding. It is because of this contribution that this chapter can perhaps usefully serve to introduce the present volume. I shall call the thesis that the market process approach occupies the middle ground the Garrison thesis.[1]

THE GARRISON THESIS

In a comment on a paper contributed by Professor Loasby to a conference volume a number of years ago, Roger Garrison first introduced the important insight that Austrian economics occupies a position intermediate between two more extreme perspectives in contemporary economics (Garrison 1982). On the one hand we have the mainstream neoclassical perspective, based on the assumption that equilibrium positions are strongly relevant to explanations of real world markets. On the other hand we have the perspective of those (including post-Keynesians) who are profoundly skeptical concerning both the meaningfulness and the real world relevance of the equilibrium models of mainstream

From *The Meaning of Market Process: Essays in the Development of Modern Austrian Economics*, ed. Israel M. Kirzner (New York and London: Routledge, 1992), 3–37. Reprinted by permission of Taylor & Francis Books (U.K.). Cross-references to other chapters are to the original source material.

theory. It turns out, Professor Garrison showed us, that on a number of important issues the Austrians differ from *both* of the (divergent) positions taken by these approaches. Let us take notice of two of these issues; they will be particularly useful for our subsequent discussions.

Knowledge and market coordination

Mainstream economics, Garrison pointed out, has gravitated to one polar position on knowledge. "Perfect knowledge—or perfect knowledge camouflaged beneath an assortment of frequency distributions—has been the primary domain of standard theory for several decades now" (Garrison 1982: 132). (We may add that, in multiperiod models of general equilibrium incorporating intertemporal exchange, this perfect knowledge assumption has been extended, in principle, to knowledge of all future time.) Much of the criticism, from post-Keynesians, Shackle and others, of mainstream economics has taken its point of departure to be the radical uncertainty which shrouds the future. This uncertainty is seen as so impenetrable as to render absurdly irrelevant all those neoclassical theories built up from individual optimizing decisions, assumed to be made between well-defined alternative future possibilities. As Shackle (1972: 465) put it, the "gaps of knowledge" which arise from an uncertain future "stultify rationality" (see also pp. 229f.). Knowledge is not, of course, *completely* absent but, the critics would maintain, there is no way, within a theory of markets, that existing "open-ended" (Shackle 1972: 230) ignorance can be systematically eliminated. (Search is no solution because the "worth of new knowledge cannot begin to be assessed until we have it. By then it is too late to decide how much to spend on breaching the walls to encourage its arrival" [pp. 272f.]). Thus the brute circumstance of ignorance concerning the future actions of other people makes it impossible for markets to induce consistency among individual decisions (Lachmann 1986a: 56f.).

It is here that the Austrian theory of market process takes a position concerning knowledge and possible market equilibration which avoids both these extremes. On the one hand the perfect knowledge assumption makes it pointless to ask how the market process can induce coordination among decisions; such coordination is already implied in the perfect knowledge assumption. On the other hand the assumption of invincible ignorance places the possibility of a systematic market process of systematic coordination entirely beyond reach.

For Austrians, however, mutual knowledge is indeed full of gaps at any given time, yet the market process is understood to provide a systemic set of forces, set in motion by entrepreneurial alertness, which tend to reduce the extent of mutual ignorance. Knowledge is not perfect; but neither is ignorance necessarily invincible. Equilibrium is indeed never attained, yet the market does exhibit powerful tendencies toward it. Market coordination is not to be smuggled into economics by assumption; but neither is it to be peremptorily ruled out simply by referring to the uncertainty of the future.

Volatility of data and the viability of economic science
Mainstream economics, Garrison further pointed out, often appears to occupy a polar position which recognizes no variability in the underlying data at all. At this extreme, "preferences, resource availabilities, and technology, do not change at all. Here, apart from the path dependency issue, the equilibrating tendency is not in doubt. This pole of the spectrum has been the popular stomping ground for neoclassical theorists . . ." (Garrison 1982: 133). On the other hand there is the possible extreme position which sees economic data as being "more volatile than we care to imagine. In these circumstances we can predict not only that the question of an equilibrating tendency would be answered in the negative, but also that economic science . . . would itself be nonexistent" (p. 133). Between these two perceptions of the changing world is that which has nourished the Austrian tradition (and, surely, informed the thinking of most economists). This perception is that the world is indeed constantly changing in unpredictable ways. People die, babies are born, tastes change spontaneously. Resource availabilities change over time; technological knowledge may evolve autonomously. But, it would be insisted, the rapidity and unpredictability of these changes is not, in general, so extreme as to frustrate the emergence of powerful and pervasive economic regularities. It is because these changes are frequent enough to ensure perennial disequilibrium that we need to understand the nature of equilibrating forces. It is because of the possibility, at least, of a benign limit to the volatility of these changes that these equilibrating forces do, at least sometimes, manifest themselves as unmistakable economic regularities. The scope of and possibility for a relevant economic science depends, as Garrison noted, on recognizing not only the variability of economic data but also the extent to which the coordinating

properties of markets may be able to make themselves felt in spite of this variability.

ENTREPRENEURSHIP AND THE AUSTRIAN MIDDLE GROUND

In a paper several years ago (Kirzner 1985a: ch. 1 and fn. 9), which explicitly drew its inspiration from the Garrison thesis, the present writer applied the thesis to locating an Austrian view of the entrepreneur within the spectrum of relevant viewpoints to be found within the profession. Two opposing "extreme" views concerning entrepreneurship were identified.

One view of the entrepreneur sees him as responding frictionlessly, and with full coordination, to market conditions; with pure profit the corresponding reward which these market conditions require and make possible. An excellent example of this view is that provided by T. W. Schultz (1975), for whom the entrepreneur is seen as responsively and smoothly providing a needed service to the market, that of reallocating resources under conditions of disequilibrium. Because this service is valuable there is a demand curve for it. And, because the ability to deal with disequilibria is scarce, there is a supply curve with respect to this service. Thus the entrepreneurial service of dealing with disequilibria commands a market price, as implied by the intersection of the relevant supply and demand curves. It is clear that this Schultzian view sees the market as, in the relevant sense, *always* fully coordinated: the market is always generating the correct volume of services needed to correct incorrect decisions. This extreme view, it must seem, has managed to squeeze entrepreneurship— even though it is defined as the ability of dealing with disequilibrium— back into the neoclassical equilibrium box.

The second "extreme" view of the entrepreneur sees his activity in an almost precisely opposite way. This view is best exemplified by the perspective developed in the profound and prolific work of G. L. S. Shackle. For Shackle entrepreneurship simply cannot be fitted into the framework of equilibrium theory made up of strictly rational decisions (Shackle 1972: 92, 134). More seriously, for Shackle the human choice, in *all* its manifestations, involves (in exactly the same way as entrepreneurship itself does) an "originative and imaginative art" (p. 364), in no sense an automatic response to given circumstances. Thus, for Shackle, recognition of the ubiquity of the entrepreneurial element carries with it extremely damaging implications for the entire body of neoclassical theory. So, far from being able to assimilate a problematic entrepreneurship to an equilibrium theory of unchallenged validity, Shackle finds insoluble problems with equilibrium theory precisely because of its total incompatibility with the entrepreneurial element in human choice.

Between these two extreme views, one seeing entrepreneurship as consistent with equilibrium economics, the second seeing entrepreneurship as utterly destroying the relevance of equilibrium economics, this writer proposed to locate a third ("Austrian") view of entrepreneurship. This third view, developed from Misesian insights by the writer in several earlier works, finds entrepreneurship incompatible with the equilibrium state, but compatible with, and indeed essential for, the notion of the equilibration process.

Pursuing this third view, it was argued, can enable us to salvage elements of important validity from each of the more extreme views. We can, with Shackle, retain our appreciation for the "originative" (i.e., the entrepreneurial) aspect of human choice. Yet we need not surrender the insight concerning the coordinative role of the entrepreneur which was emphasized by Schultz. The third view of the entrepreneur, that recognizing the propensity of the entrepreneur alertly to discover failures in existing patterns of coordination among market decisions, permits us to see how systematic ("equilibrating") market tendencies can be traced back to creative, originative, entrepreneurial alertness.

THE DOUBLE-EXPOSURE OF THE MIDDLE GROUND

It is in the nature of a centrist position to provoke criticism from each of the polar perspectives which it has eschewed. Such centrist positions must then be defended from two quite different sides. Two quite different types of attack may have to be rebutted, calling for simultaneous arguments pointing, it might at first sight appear, in almost diametrically opposed directions. This has indeed been the situation in which Austrian economics has, quite naturally, found itself.

Austrian economists must defend themselves against mainstream neoclassical economists unhappy with the vagueness, the indeterminateness and the imprecision which they see as inseparable from an approach prepared to recognize perennial disequilibrium. At the same time Austrians are placed on the defensive by critics of mainstream neoclassical economics, who are unhappy with the postulation, by the Austrians, of possibly powerful equilibrating tendencies.

Until recently Austrians found it necessary to devote much of their attention to defending themselves against mainstream neoclassical critical concerns. This was rather to be expected. It was, after all, their divergence from that mainstream that was the most obvious feature of the Austrian position. Recently, however, the centrist position of the Austrians has drawn criticism from a different direction, a criticism rooted not in mainstream equilibrium convictions but in the most uncompromising rejection of those convictions. This line of radical subjectivist criticism has assailed the Austrian middle ground position not for its recognition of open-ended uncertainty, of the creativity of individual choice, of the pervasiveness of disequilibrium market conditions, but for what the subjectivist critics have seen as the incompleteness of that recognition.

In particular, this line of criticism has challenged the very possibility of a middle ground position in the arena occupied by mainstream neoclassical theorists and their most radical opponents. If we are prepared to reject the set of constricting assumptions which characterize the equilibrium models of mainstream theory, consistency requires, this line of criticism insists, that we accept the utter irrelevance of these models for economic understanding. If Austrians reject an economics which in effect recognizes only the equilibrium state, they must reject, as well, the notion of equilibration altogether. There can be no halfway house. The middle ground which Austrians seek to occupy does not enjoy the strengths of the two polar positions from which they seek to escape. It suffers, rather, from the inconsistencies arising from the attempt to have the best of two utterly irreconcilable worlds.

The purpose of this chapter is to reaffirm the viability of the Austrian middle ground by addressing, in particular, the line of subjectivist criticism offered by those insisting upon the most complete rejection of the neoclassical paradigm. Such a defense of the Austrian middle ground assumes a special significance in the light of the historical attitude of the Austrian tradition toward the social function of the market.

MARKET COORDINATION AND THE AUSTRIAN TRADITION

The early theoretical contributions of the Austrian economists brought them into sharp conflict with the historicism of the German School. At issue was the validity and relevance of a body of theory proclaiming the existence of important economic regularities. The postulation of economic regularities has implied, throughout the history of economics, certain consequences for the evaluation of the market economy. In the absence of such recognized regularities, a market economy may be perceived as a social system the apparent inadequacies of which invite deliberate corrective measures on the part of a benevolent state. A pattern of income distribution which seems offensive to an intuitive sense of justice can be corrected by appropriate redistributive policies. Market prices which appear, to the eyes of the policy makers or their constituents, to be too high or too low can be corrected by appropriate legislation. It was always the objections raised by the economic theorists which seemed to challenge the effectiveness of such proposed social policies. The existence of economic regularities implied severe limits to the corrective powers of the state. In fact, in the light of these regularities, the apparent inadequacies of the market often turn out to be not inadequacies at all, but unavoidable costs necessary for social coordination. Price controls, far from improving conditions for the consumer or for the farmer or whomever, are shown by economic theory to generate disastrous man-made shortages or gluts. Redistributive taxation policies are shown to generate undesired and undesirable disincentive or incentive effects.[2] The tendency of economic theory to suggest a more sensitive appreciation for the social-efficiency properties of a market system has been so powerful and pervasive over the history of economics as to make economic theory the obvious obstacle to (and enemy of) would-be radical economic reformers (Stigler 1959: 522–32; Zweig 1970: 25). The early Austrian theorists indeed came, not surprisingly, to be identified with a generally classical liberal policy stance (see for example Streissler 1988: 192–204; see also this volume, Chapter 5).

For Carl Menger and his followers the market economy tends to allocate resources and assign incomes according to the valuations of consumers. As Menger (1981: 173) put it, "the *price* of a good is a consequence of its *value* to economizing men, and the magnitude of its price is always determined by the magnitude of its value." Those who object to market outcomes simply do not appreciate the faithfulness and consistency with which markets transmit valuations. "It may well appear deplorable to a lover of mankind that possession of capital or a piece of land often provides the owner a higher income for a given period of time than the income received by a laborer for the most strenuous activity during the same period. Yet the cause of this is not immoral, but simply that the satisfaction of more important human needs depends upon the services of the given amount of capital or piece of land than upon the services of the laborer" (p. 174). Clearly all this results from a theoretical perspective which sees consumer valuations as being quite faithfully translated into market decisions concerning resource allocation and resource prices.

What we wish, indeed, to emphasize is not so much the conservatism, or classical liberalism, of the early Austrian tradition with regard to economic policy,[3] as the extent to which that tradition shared in understanding the powerful and systematic character of market forces. What happens in markets is not haphazard, but the consequence of inescapable economic regularities, expressing themselves in obviously relevant tendencies. Given the institutional framework of the market economy, given an available array of scarce resources, the preferences of consumers must, almost inexorably it appears, result in a particular configuration of methods of production, resource allocation and market prices. It was with respect to this perspective that Austrian economics differed most drastically from that of the German Historical School and of other dissenters from economic theory. And, of course, this perspective was shared not only by the Austrians but by all the turn-of-the-century schools of economic thought. As neoclassical economics advanced in prestige and influence during the first decades of this century, the contrary teachings of the Historical School faded from the center stage of professional atention. It was the shared appreciation for the power of systematic market forces which was the feature common to the various schools of economic theory. The victory of the theoretical approach over the historicist approach was a victory for the recognition of the coordinative properties of the market. In achieving this victory the Austrian economists were prominent. In the now famous inter-war debate concerning the possibility of economic calculation under socialism, it was the Austrian Mises who provocatively asserted that there was nothing, in any program for centralized economic planning, to serve as a substitute for the calculative and coordinative capacities of the market process. And it has been the mid-century extension, by Mises and by Hayek,[4] of the Austrian understanding of the entrepreneurial-competitive market process which has supported the most consistent and profound appreciation for the benign consequences of market coordination.[5] It is against this background of consistent understanding, within the Austrian tradition, of the systematic coordinative properties of the market that we must take note of the thrust of the new line of subjectivist criticism, directed against the Austrian middle ground, that we shall be addressing in this chapter.[6]

THE ATTACK ON MARKET COORDINATION:
PARADOX IN THE HISTORY OF IDEAS?

Although, as noted, the early-twentieth-century developments in economic thought found the Austrians in alliance with the other theoretical schools in neoclassical economics, this alliance began rapidly to unravel toward mid-century. Whereas Mises, in 1932, was able to declare any difference between the various schools to be more a matter of style than of substance, within a few years he was to be emphasizing with some acerbity the substantive differences between the Austrians and the neoclassical mainstream (Chapter 6, pp. 110f., and Mises 1960). The decisive elements in the Austrian approach which rendered it incompatible with the ascendant Walrasian version of neoclassical theory were elements which grew out of a more lively sense for the subjectivism of the Austrian tradition. Mises stressed the autonomy of individual choice, the uncertainty of the environment within which choices are made, the entrepreneurial character of market decisions, and the overriding importance of human purposefulness. Hayek stressed the role of knowledge and discovery as facilitated during the process of dynamic competition. For Mises and Hayek these subjectivist insights in no way compromised the traditional centrality, within Austrian economics, of systematic market coordination and consumer sovereignty. On the contrary, they argued, that it is only by incorporating these subjectivist insights that we can adequately understand the spontaneous, coordinative properties of the market process. We can now perceive the paradoxical character of the new line of subjectivist criticism of the modern Austrian approach, which we are considering in this chapter.

What the critics are calling for is acknowledgment by Austrians that their subjectivist insights—insights enthusiastically applauded by the critics—must inevitably lead to the rejection of precisely those conclusions concerning markets which have been central to the Austrian tradition since its very beginnings.[7] The subjectivist basis for Austrian unhappiness with the mainstream equilibrium paradigm must, according to the critics, inexorably impel Austrians not only to reject the dominance of that paradigm, but also to reject the very notion of market coordination. To be consistent in regard to their subjectivism, Austrians must surrender their traditional appreciation for the contributions of the market. Any hope to stand on a stable middle ground, on which their subjectivism and their appreciation for market subjectivity might coexist, is declared illusory and self-contradictory. Consistent pursuit of Austrian subjectivism must compel the abandonment of Austrian recognition of the social coordinative properties of the free market economy. Let us turn to consider the major arguments offered in this new line of criticism.

SUBJECTIVISM AND EQUILIBRATION: FRIENDS OR FOES?

A good deal of the criticism has been directed at this writer's attempt to restate the Mises–Hayek extension of Austrian theory in terms of an explicitly entrepreneur-driven market process of equilibration (see especially Kirzner 1973 and later work). What renders the market process a systematic process of coordination is the circumstance that each gap in market coordination expresses itself as a pure profit opportunity. It is the existence of these profit opportunities which attracts the attention of alert entrepreneurs. A gap in coordination is itself the expression of sheer mutual ignorance on the part of potential market participants. The profit-grasping actions of entrepreneurs dispel the ignorance which was responsible for the profit opportunities, and thus generate a tendency toward coordination among market decisions. In this way economic theory is able to understand how market prices, market allocation of resources and market distribution of incomes can be understood as the outcomes of a systematic equilibrating tendency—a tendency indeed never completed but, at the same time, never completely suspended. Market phenomena are not to be seen as nothing more than the immediate expression of spontaneously changing preferences and expectations, but as the outcome of a process which, while certainly not completely determined, is nonetheless systematically set in motion by the relevant underlying realities.

In this understanding of the market process, Austrian subjectivist insights play a significant role. It is this role which sets the Austrian theory decisively apart from mainstream neoclassical attempts to understand the market. In the latter attempts many of the subjectivist insights came to be suppressed. In particular, the notions of entrepreneurial creativity and discovery, entrepreneurial alertness to opportunities generated by sheer ignorance, the potential for entrepreneurial injection of surprise, were notions which simply could not be fitted into the neoclassical models. In order to demonstrate a determinate nexus linking market phenomena to the underlying realities, it was necessary for these models to postulate a market mechanism capable of inexorably translating these realities into equilibrium conditions, undisturbed by entrepreneurial surprises and by the vagaries that might be introduced by open-ended uncertainty. For the Austrian view, on the other hand, entrepreneurship emerged not as the foe, but as the indispensable friend, of the notion of equilibration. It is this claim that entrepreneurship can be seen as the very source of the equilibrating tendency that has drawn fire from the critics who wish to deny the viability of the Austrian middle ground. Brian Loasby has been a gently persistent critic in this regard.[8]

Loasby (1982: 122) expresses profound skepticism concerning the ability of entrepreneurs to generate market coordination: "What assurance can we have that entrepreneurial perceptions will not be so seriously in error as to lead them in quite the wrong direction . . . ?" Loasby emphasizes the distinction between entrepreneurial alertness to existing conditions that have somehow escaped attention and entrepreneurial imagination with regard to future possibilities (pp. 116, 119; see also Loasby 1989: 161). With regard to the latter, in particular, Loasby challenges the claim that entrepreneurs can be relied upon to make correct decisions. Their own decisions may in fact frustrate each other's forecasts, and, moreover, there is simply no systematic set of forces to guide entrepreneurs toward making correct, coordinative decisions with regard to the unknowable future. "But while one might be prepared to grant, with some misgivings, that present opportunities are facts, the anticipation of future coordination failures . . . must surely open up the possibility that the entrepreneur will generate, rather than correct, error" (Loasby 1989: 161). Exactly as (at least according to some philosophers of science) we cannot prove that scientific processes must produce true knowledge, so also "Kirzner's endeavours to demonstrate that the market process must work well cannot succeed . . ." (p. 163). Loasby stresses not only the possibility of entepreneurial mistakes in the face of an uncertain future, but also the possibility that entrepreneurs discover profit opportunities through deliberately misleading the consumer (Loasby 1982: 121) or through speculatively purchasing assets "in order to sell them a little later at a higher price to someone who hopes to resell them at a higher price still" (p. 127). Although Loasby recognizes that such skepticism concerning the coordinative properties of the market need not supply immediate justification for government action (p. 121), his conclusion nonetheless is that "it is inherently impossible to use Austrian methods to prove that planning cannot work" (Loasby 1989: 166). The very recognition by Austrians of the circumstances of and importance of "subjective assessments and incompletable knowledge" (p. 166) must, it seems, prevent economists from ascribing any peculiar coordinative virtues to unregulated markets. The very open-endedness of the entrepreneurial economy precludes, it appears, any support, from a subjectivist understanding of that economy, for the notion of a systematic tendency toward market equilibration and coordination.

SUBJECTIVISM AND THE MEANING OF SOCIAL EFFICIENCY

The relationship between market coordination and the attainment of social efficiency has never been a simple one. The history of welfare economics is the history of changing concepts of social economic optimality, as well as of changing evaluations of the success of the market economy in its attainment (see also Chapter 11). But any claims for achievement of social optimality for the market have certainly depended on parallel claims for the systematic achievement by the market of definite outcomes. If market outcomes are wholly indeterminate, nothing systematic can begin to be claimed with regard to the welfare properties of the market economy. Austrian economists, as noted earlier, have generally given a high rating to the degree to which market outcomes correspond to the allocation of resources implied by consumer preferences. Challenges to the validity of claims for equilibrating tendencies thus imply, of course, challenges to Austrians' assertions of market efficiency.[9] The radical subjectivist insights (on the basis of which challenges to the theory of equilibration have been advanced) thus deny viability to the supposed Austrian middle ground not only in regard to positive economics but also in regard to its welfare (and policy) implications.

What emerges from the recent line of subjectivist criticism of Austrian economics considered in this chapter, however, is not merely the rejection of traditional Austrian welfare claims on behalf of the market, but in fact the rejection, in principle, of the very notion of social efficiency on *any* terms and on *any* definition of social efficiency. No matter how it is formulated, it turns out, the notion of social efficiency must be pronounced meaningless, on strictly subjectivist grounds. This rather surprising development deserves some further attention.

Let us immediately distinguish sharply between this subjectivist-inspired critique of the meaningfulness of conventional welfare criteria and that contained in Hayek's celebrated thesis concerning the welfare implications of dispersed knowledge (see Chapter 11). Hayek pointed out the fallacy in approaches to the evaluation of the social usefulness of the market which erroneously assume the relevance, in principle, of complete, centralized knowledge concerning the underlying realities. In a world of dispersed information, Hayek argued, it is idle to measure social efficiency against the irrelevant yardstick of complete information (available, in principle, to, say, a central planning authority) (Hayek 1949b). The subjectivist-inspired critique of the social efficiency notion which we wish to consider here is quite different. It does not rest on the circumstance of incomplete information concerning the underlying realities. It rests, rather, upon the claim that the very notion of "underlying objective realities," in terms of which to evaluate social efficiency, is fundamentally inconsistent with a full subjectivist recognition of uncertainty. Hayek had no difficulty with the notion, in principle, of a social optimum mapped out by the underlying data of preferences and scarcities. He merely declared this optimum not to be the relevant criterion for social policy, since the knowledge needed for the formulation of such an optimum is never given or available to a single mind; the relevant problem facing society is never the deployment of such knowledge concerning the attainable optimum, but rather the mobilization of the bits of information dispersed throughout the economy. But what the subjectivist critics here being discussed wish to question is the very idea of realities in terms of which a social optimum might possibly be defined. Professor Jan Kregel has been explicit in questioning the meaningfulness of the idea of underlying objective realities. He feels that Austrian economists have embraced an inadequate subjectivism (compared with that which characterizes post-Keynesian economics) in not realizing the questionability of these "objective facts."

This questionability, Kregel explains, arises because the future "objective facts" are themselves partly determined by the entrepreneurial actions being taken today (on the basis of expectations concerning these supposedly "objective facts" of the future). Kregel (1986: 160) discusses the impact of this point upon the possibility of equilibration: "There can be no tendency to equilibrium based on a relation between expectations and the objective data of what the consumer will demand and the price he will pay which describes the conditions of equilibrium because the incomes available to consumers will be determined ultimately by the very decisions taken by entrepreneurs on the basis of these expectations. . . . Expectations themselves determine the objective facts of the conditions of equilibrium. . . ."[10] Although Kregel does not pursue his line of reasoning toward a critique of standard concepts of welfare criteria, the implications are fairly clear. To the extent that entrepreneurial activity itself *creates* the future which entrepreneurs wish to anticipate, it seems idle to judge the social optimality of such activity against the yardstick of that objective future. Such an efficiency judgment would make sense only if one could postulate a set of objective future facts (independent of current actions) to which these current actions are seeking to adjust.[11] We shall have reason to return to this radical implication of Professor Kregel's contention later in this chapter.

In a recent unpublished paper James Buchanan and Viktor Vanberg have touched on this issue in a similar vein. The very notion of remediable inefficiency, they argue, rests on the neoclassical view that knowledge of the future is imperfect not because of the intrinsic unknowability of the future but because of ignorance that could, in principle, have been avoided (Buchanan and Vanberg 1990: 11). Full subjectivism, however, requires us to understand the future as undetermined and intrinsically unknowable. From such a subjectivist perspective, the idea of erroneous decision making must appear highly artificial, if not completely incoherent. Buchanan and Vanberg quote with approval (p. 12) the observation by Shackle (1983: 33) to the effect that "unknowledge" of the future is not "a deficiency, a falling-short, a failure of search and study."

The point made by Buchanan and Vanberg recalls the observation insisted upon by Professor Buchanan himself a number of years ago. "In economics," he remarked, "even among many of those who remain strong advocates of market and market-like organization, the "efficiency" that such market arrangements produce is independently conceptualized. Market arrangements then become "means," which may or may not be relatively best. Until and unless this teleological element is fully exorcised from basic economic theory, economists are likely to remain confused and their discourse confusing" (Buchanan 1982). This reference to the "teleological" element, which Buchanan describes as misleading economists to conceptualize an abstract notion of efficiency, apart from the actual progress in which it emerges, calls for a separate section. It represents a special example of the radical subjectivist criticism of modern Austrian economics which is being considered in this chapter.

ON TELEOLOGICAL AND NON-TELEOLOGICAL PERSPECTIVES

Buchanan and Vanberg (1990) develop the distinction between what they call the "teleological" and the "non-teleological" perspectives as follows. In the teleological view "the efficacy of market adjustment is measured . . . in terms of the relative achievement of some pre-defined, pre-existing standard of value" (p. 18). Clearly it is the teleological view which depends upon the conceptualization of "objective facts" (the very notion of which was challenged, we saw, by Kregel), independent of entrepreneurial activity, in terms of which the effectiveness of such activity can be judged. Against this teleological perspective Buchanan and Vanberg argue for "a radical subjectivist understanding of the market" (p. 19) which recognizes the fallacy of visualizing "some well-defined objective that exists independently from the participants' own creative choices" (p. 18). For the non-teleological view "the whole general equilibrium concept is questionable when applied to a constantly changing social world which has no predetermined 'telos,' neither in the pompous sense of a Marxian philosophy of history, nor in the more pedestrian sense of a conceptually definable 'equilibrium' toward which the process of socio-economic change could be predicted to gravitate" (p. 13).

What is significant, for the present chapter, is the assertion by the authors that there is, in their view, "no systematically sustainable 'middle-ground' between a teleological and a non-teleological perspective" (p. 19). One cannot, they claim, simultaneously profess to recognize both the originative, creative character of human choice and any sense in which such a choice can be described as "discovery of error." This writer's attempt to develop a theory of systematic entrepreneurial equilibrating tendencies that is rooted in creative entrepreneurial alertness is pronounced to fail because the "subliminal teleology" (p. 23) implicit in notions of equilibration is thoroughly inconsistent with true creativity. Our defense, in this paper, of the Austrian middle ground will require us to address this criticism. We shall, indeed, argue that creativity and the correction of "error" need not be mutually exclusive categories.

One aspect of the position taken by Buchanan and Vanberg which is sufficiently arresting to demand separate notice is their conviction that a full critique of socialism is impossible within a teleological framework. Both neoclassical and Austrian critiques of central planning, they assert, have failed to identify the core fallacy in the idea of central planning. That fallacy consists in the belief that, given omniscience and benevolence, it would be entirely feasible, in principle, for a central planner to attain the social optimum. This belief is fallacious because "even the planner so idealized cannot create that which is not there and will not be there save through the exercise of the creative choices of individuals, who themselves have no idea in advance concerning the ideas that their own imaginations will yield" (Buchanan and Vanberg 1990: 33). Socialism cannot conceivably become equivalent to "the market as a creative process that exploits man's imaginative potential." What is noteworthy here is that the subjectivist considerations on the basis of which Buchanan and Vanberg denied (just as Kregel denied) the objectivity of those "future facts," in terms of which the effectiveness of markets might be judged, have apparently led them to welfare conclusions quite different from those reached in the preceding section.

In the preceding section we noted that the obvious implication of Kregel's critical insights concerning the "objective facts" of the future is that the very notion of social efficiency (supposedly in terms of the effectiveness with which current activities are adjusted to the requirements imposed by the future facts) loses its meaning. Unless those future facts can be conceived independently of these current activities, we suggested, a subjectivist critic of welfare economics may well challenge the very possibility of any efficiency appraisal (with regard to those future facts). Claims by economists that the market economy is an efficient social institution turn out, we noted, to disintegrate in the light of the questionability of those "underlying realities" necessary to confer meaning upon the notion of social efficiency. Now we have the apparently surprising assertion by Buchanan and Vanberg that challenging the meaningfulness of the "underlying future realities" leads, not to the renunciation of all claims of comparative superiority for the market (relative to socialism), but to the discernment of the core weakness of the socialist idea.

While a detailed critique of this apparently surprising conclusion is only peripherally germane to the central concerns of this chapter, it will be useful briefly to ponder the paradoxes which it seems to raise. On the one hand we are told that the non-teleological, radically subjectivist perspective calls into question any objective standards against which to measure market efficacy; on the other hand we are somehow given to understand that the market economy possesses important merits as a social system—merits denied by definition to socialism—precisely because it promotes the creative imagination of its individual participants. Yet we are given no reason why we are entitled to feel confident that the imaginative creativity of individual market participants is likely to lead to individual (let alone social) well-being, rather than to social (or even individual) disaster. Unless creativity is to be valued for its own sake—regardless of what is created, and regardless of the possibility of different creativities colliding with and stultifying one another—one is left wondering how (in the absence of any meaningful objective facts which might serve to formulate criteria for evaluation) one is able, as economist, to rank a system which fosters creativity more highly than one which does not.

THE SUBJECTIVIST CRITICISM OF THE AUSTRIAN MIDDLE GROUND: A SUMMARY

The radical subjectivist criticisms of the Austrian middle ground position that we have proposed to defend seem to boil down to several key contentions.

Entrepreneurial error

Austrian claims for an equilibrating tendency rest on the assumption that entrepreneurs will tend to discover and grasp pure profit opportunities, thus correcting the market ignorance present in disequilibrium. The critics contend that entrepreneurs may make mistakes (and, especially in regard to the uncertain future, can hardly avoid making mistakes). There can be no assurance that entrepreneurs will systematically tend to reduce market ignorance; the exact opposite may be true.

Underlying realities and the notion of equilibrium

Austrian claims for an equilibrating tendency appear to rest on the notion of a relevant equilibrium configuration, considered to be implicit in the "underlying realities" which constitute the given framework for economic analysis. It is this equilibrium configuration which acts (so the critics appear to understand the middle ground Austrians to be asserting) as a kind of magnet shaping the course of subsequent events. The critics challenge the meaningfulness of such "underlying realities." As soon as we admit the dynamics of time into our analysis, we must recognize that the relevant realities of the future (in terms of which any intertemporal idea of equilibrium must be enunciated) are themselves not "realities" at all (in the sense of having an independent existence to which human activities must somehow be adjusted) but are created by the very activities the consistency of which is under examination.

In general, it appears to be argued, the picture of social history which emerges from a radical subjectivist viewpoint is one entirely inconsistent with Austrian middle ground economics. For radical subjectivism, history is a continual series of Shacklean "new beginnings"; the uncertainty of the future, subject as it is to unceasing injections of sheer surprises, makes it absurd for us to envisage systematic market processes of equilibration. To do so must be judged absurd both because ceaseless injections of surprise must continually abort any incipient equilibrating tendencies and, further, because awareness of the inevitability of such ceaseless injections of surprise must paralyze any entrepreneurial illusions of somehow correctly anticipating the future (or, as noted, even of *defining* that future, as an independent set of facts to be taken into account). The limited subjectivism which sets the Austrian middle ground apart from the neoclassical mainstream is, in this view, so moderate and diluted as to blind middle ground Austrians with regard to the fundamental incoherence of their position. Far from being able to enjoy the best of both worlds, middle ground Austrians have placed themselves in a position shot through with inner inconsistencies.

Let us attempt to clarify the middle ground position of modern Austrian economists in a way that can address these criticisms and show them to be far less formidable than might at first sight appear. It may be useful, first, to dispel some misunderstandings concerning the possibility for (and meaning of) *error* in the Austrian middle ground theory of equilibration.

AUSTRIAN MIDDLE GROUND AND ENTREPRENEURIAL ERROR

Sometimes radical subjectivist critics seem to ascribe to middle ground Austrians the notion that alert entrepreneurs are exempt from the possibility of making errors; they somehow have the capacity of seeing future events correctly. This is certainly *not* the case; or, at the very least, not without careful qualification. First, the Austrian theory of the entrepreneurial

equilibration process relies, as Loasby (1982: 117; 1989: 160–1) has perceptively noted, on some entrepreneurs being more alert than others
(and it is the relative unalertness of the latter which is responsible for
the errors which create the opportunities and the incentives for profit).
Second, the postulation of a tendency for profit opportunities to generate equilibration has not been put forward as an inexorable, determinate
sequence. The emphasis upon the incentive to win profits has not been
intended to deny the possibility of entrepreneurial losses. To show how
entrepreneurial alertness can account for apparently systematic market
adjustments is not, as we shall emphasize again and again, to predict
sure-fire equilibration under all circumstances.

Sometimes radical subjectivist critics ascribe to middle ground Austrians a position which associates entrepreneurial error with a certain
culpability or guilt. Because an error is seen as, in principle, avoidable,
it seems to follow that a failure correctly to forecast the future must be
blamed on carelessness, or something. And therefore, because radical
subjectivists emphasize the intrinsic unknowability of the future, they are
strongly inclined to deny the meaningfulness of the term "error" in regard
to the future. "There can only be 'error' if the future *can* be known. But,
if the future is acknowledged to be created by choices that are yet to be
made, how can it be known?" (Buchanan and Vanberg 1990: 27). It must
be emphasized that, in the Austrian middle ground, lack of "alertness"
with regard to the future need not be blameworthy in any literal sense.
An "error" with regard to the future need involve no carelessness and no
negligence. Certainly the future, especially in the light of the uncertainties
injected by the creativity of future choices, is difficult (if perhaps not quite
entirely impossible) to be correctly guessed at in advance.

In fact it may be contended, from the Austrian middle ground perspective, that the radical subjectivist critics have themselves perhaps *overesti-*
mated the objectivity (the "knowability") of present facts compared with
future facts. Critics who are unhappy with Austrian notions of error in
regard to the future are apparently uncritical of the idea of error in regard
to existing facts. Existing facts are existing facts; an error in regard to any
such fact is seen as a truly avoidable error. Future facts are intrinsically
unknowable; ignorance of future facts is unavoidable and thus considered as no error at all. But existing facts are different. Greater diligence
in search would have revealed the full truth concerning existing facts. So
runs the radical subjectivist insistence on the sharp difference introduced

by the recognition of futurity with all its uncertainty. But, from the middle ground Austrian perspective, ignorance of an existing fact need involve no more blame, no more "avoidability," than ignorance of a future "fact." What is involved, in regard to ignorance of the future, is what this writer has called "sheer" or "utter" ignorance (i.e., one is ignorant of the fact that there is a specific fact which one does not know). Such "sheer ignorance" is, of course, fully possible also in regard to existing facts. One may be completely ignorant of the opportunity to learn about an important fact. Such ignorance—even in regard to existing facts—is not avoidable (in the sense that greater diligence in search could have yielded more complete information) and may be deemed not to involve any carelessness at all. One cannot blame one who is utterly ignorant in this way; one cannot upbraid him for not looking more carefully, for not searching more carefully; after all, he was totally unaware of where to begin searching, of the very opportunity of searching, of the very need to search altogether. If we describe him as having acted "in error," we mean, simply, that he *might* have known the existing facts had he been "more alert."[12] There seems to be no fundamental difference between the capacity to notice an existing fact (concerning which one had previously been in a state of sheer ignorance) and the capacity to "notice" or to sense a future event which one might possibly have taken into account in formulating one's present plans. In the light of subsequent discovery of an existing fact (concerning which one had been utterly ignorant at a time of action) one may retrospectively pronounce oneself to have acted "in error"; it seems entirely consistent for one to pronounce a similar judgment upon one's action which turns out later to have been taken under a mistaken anticipation of the future. If there is a difference between the "alertness" capable of sensing future events and the alertness needed to notice present facts (concerning the very existence of which one has been up to this time utterly ignorant), it must be a matter of degree, not of kind. The "error" involved in overlooking a present fact seems to be no more heinous an oversight than failure to see the shape of future events correctly. And the failure so correctly to see the future must appear, in many cases at least, to be no less an example of error than failure to see what is already a knowable fact in the present.

It will be helpful for us to explore a little further the radical subjectivist position in regard to the utter unknowability of the future, a future in regard to which, it is contended, it is impossible to err.

A WORLD WITHOUT ERROR?

A little thought should convince us that the radical subjectivist denial of the possibility of true error in regard to the unknowable future must lead to quite bizarre implications, implications with which the radical subjectivists must themselves surely feel uncomfortable. We are told that the future is not a rolled-up tapestry waiting to be unfurled, but a void "waiting" to be filled by the creative, originative, unpredictable free choices of human beings (see for example Shackle 1986: 281ff). "The essence of the radical subjectivist position is that the future is not simply 'unknown,' but is 'non-existent' or 'indeterminate at the point of decision' " (Wiseman 1990: 160). So much it is possible for middle ground Austrians to accept with warm concurrence. It is when radical subjectivists conclude directly, from this circumstance of the as-yet-non-existent future, that no future-oriented action can be described as erroneous that the warmth of this concurrence begins to evaporate with alarmed rapidity. We have already seen how this conclusion has been arrived at: if the future does not exist, it is inherently unknowable; if it is unknowable, no action taken can be denounced as having failed to avoid an avoidable disaster; the most disastrous action taken, then, cannot be denounced as an error. Ignorance of the future, Wiseman argues, should not be seen "as leading to 'inefficient' behaviour" but "as an inescapable characteristic of the human condition." To see things differently is to imply "that there is some stock of knowledge about the future which agents 'ought' to have, and some consequent set of decisions that they therefore 'ought' to take, and that it is these that identify an 'efficient outcome' " (Wiseman 1990: 155).

It is at this point that one pauses to take in, with some amazement, what seems to be stated here in the most matter-of-fact tones. The usual, layman's, perceptions of human decisions is that some of them are taken wisely, judiciously, successfully. These are the decisions which, in retrospect, one recognizes as having been crucial to the achievement of some desirable outcome. Other decisions, the usual perception has it, turn out to have been unsuccessful; in retrospect, at least, they are seen to have been mistakes. The issue here is not moral culpability in any simple sense, but recognition, at least from the *ex post* perspective, that the latter decisions were not well attuned to the way subsequent events in fact turned out. Here we have the nub of our apparent disagreement with the radical subjectivists: is it or is it not meaningful to describe a decision as having been appropriate, in the light of subsequent events, or as having been inappropriate? We must press the question a little further. Is it or is it not meaningful for a decision maker to *try* to shape his decision so that it will be able to be pronounced to have been the right decision? Are we really to say that, because, at some philosophical level, the future does not exist, that because it is not "waiting" to be known (since it has yet to be created), it is therefore meaningless for a human being *to seek* to be successful in his future-oriented decisions? The point at issue turns out to be even more troublesome when we consider the idea of economic policy.

Are we really to say that, since no genuine error is conceivable in regard to the future, we are forbidden to distinguish between wise and unwise economic policies? Must we say that while, subjectively speaking, individual and public decision makers may *believe* themselves to be striving to peer ahead in order to make the correct choices, this must, from a more perceptive philosophical perspective, be set down as nothing more than an illusion? Are we really to say that the indeterminacy of the future entails that, since there *is* as yet no future, it is idle even *to attempt* to adjust one's actions to avoid disaster in that future? Does the *in*determinacy of the future lead to precisely that sense of utter helplessness (and hence to the same numbing sense of never having to worry about making a mistake) that must follow from the view of the future as *fully* determined in every respect (regardless of what individuals may believe themselves to be trying to achieve or to avoid)? Must a world the future of which is shrouded in the uncertainties generated by the creativity of human action degenerate into a world in which genuine action is ruled out by the impossibility of error? Surely these are implications which must trouble all subjectivists, of whatever degree of radicalness. George Shackle's life's work on the understanding of how men choose between courses of action *each* of which is associated, in their *imaginations,* with myriads upon myriads of competing hypothesized futures assures us that even the master subjectivist of our time has had no truck with the apparently seductive idea that choice should be recognized as nothing but a chimera, a self-delusion. If the uncertainty of the future has made it impossible to discriminate between more or less advisable courses of action, then choice *has* been reduced to emptiness. "When the decision-maker is free to suppose that any act can have any consequence without restriction, there is no basis of choice of act. The boundedness of uncertainty is essential to the possibility of decision" (Shackle 1970:

224). The very idea of "bounded uncertainty" must mean that the prospective chooser feels entitled to conclude, in spite of the uncertainties he faces, that one course of action appears more likely to be successful than another.

CHOOSING FOR A NON-EXISTENT FUTURE

If we are to salvage the very notion of choice from the impasse threatened by a world without errors, we must clearly insist on several simple but fundamental truths. Without daring to tread in philosophical waters which threaten unwitting economists with minefields about which they may be suffering "sheer ignorance," it is necessary for us to pin down several matters of everyday experience. Because we can *imagine* the future, even a non-existent, unknowable future,[13] we do choose, endeavoring to shape the future flow of events in such a fashion that the free, originating future choices of others can redound to our benefit. We do seek, that is, to tailor our choices to take account of those future events—imagined events—which do not now exist in any sense whatever. And, when the time comes for us to look back upon our earlier exercises in imagination we do, whatever the radicalness of our subjectivism, judge the extent to which our imaginations were helpful. From the *ex post* perspective we do judge our actions as having been the correct ones to have made, or not. We may not judge an "incorrect" action to have been an unwise one, a blameworthy one, in the light of the picture of the world we had at the moment of decision. We may in fact be convinced that, even after our bitter experience, we would now repeat the earlier action (the one now deemed to have been incorrect) were we to find outselves once again in circumstances similar (and with similar pictures of the world) to those in which the earlier decision was made. Yet we will still rue our earlier inability to have somehow conjured up a more prescient picture of the world. The endeavor to make the "right decision," to formulate the "right economic policy" (or, for that matter, the "right foreign policy"), is one which has definite meaning. The non-existent, indeterminate future does not forbid men from imaginatively anticipating what creative acts will fill the future void. And, most significantly, it does not forbid them, with hindsight, from ranking those imaginative anticipations in order of their correctness. All of our *ex ante* endeavors to make the right choice are endeavors to be able, in the future, to stand up to such retrospective judgments successfully. We are *not* satisfied, in making our choices, merely to choose in a way which will not, in the future, be judged to have been rash or overcautious, unwise, and thus *blameworthy*—we seek to choose in a way which will turn out to have been the correct, the successful, choice.

SCOPE FOR SUPERIOR ENTREPRENEURIAL PRESCIENCE

The future does not now exist, but we endeavor to grasp that future somehow in our imaginations. Some of us are more successful at this endeavor than others are. The mistakes, the errors, made by the latter, turn out to constitute the profit opportunities grasped by the more successful. In fact, it is the opportunity for profit so constituted which sparks the entrepreneurial imagination of the more prescient, the more "alert," among human beings.[14] (It is certainly not any equilibrium configuration which operates—as magnet or "telos"—to stimulate entrepreneurial prescience, but rather entrepreneurial errors, in the form of profit opportunities, which attracts anticipatory discovery.) Once we acknowledge the meaningfulness of endeavoring to imagine the future more correctly, we can hardly refuse to recognize the quality of "alertness" (or of more correctly fertile imagination, or of greater prescience—call it what one will) in human beings. We must, that is, recognize something like "entrepreneurial ability," understood as the capacity independently to size up a situation and more correctly reach an imagined picture of the relevant (as yet indeterminate) future. All of us share in this ability to some extent— or we would surely have learned long ago not to bother to make choices at all in a world so full of surprises as to frustrate all our attempts at controlling our lives. But some have higher degrees of this ability—some in some lines of endeavor, others in other lines of endeavor. Economists, psychologists and other social scientists have not developed, as yet, very helpful or extensive theoretical or empirical materials from which to be able to say much about the sources and determinants (if any) of such ability. But to deny its existence is to deny the most obvious of everyday facts of experience.

Moreover, once we recognize scope for entrepreneurial prescience, we cannot avoid acknowledging that it is the "underlying realities" which inspire such prescience, and which thus shape entrepreneurial actions. It is true, of course, that what directly inspire and shape entrepreneurial actions are *imaginations* (of future realities) rather than these realities themselves. But what the alertness of the entrepreneur strives to notice and correctly to imagine are (what will turn out to be) future realities, and it is the *prospective gain offered by these realities* which "switches on" entrepreneurial alertness. It follows therefore that what will turn out to be the future realities are indeed crucially involved in shaping entrepreneurial prescience and thus entrepreneurial actions. It is for these reasons that we shall be arguing that the equilibration process set in motion by entrepreneurial profit-oriented activity is inspired by the underlying realities, after all.

THE PUZZLE OF PRESCIENCE

Yet it must be immediately acknowledged that we have not yet fully grappled with the key problem raised by the radical subjectivists. We envisage entrepreneurs—and, as is well known from the work of Mises and of Shackle, we are *all* entrepreneurs—endeavoring to imagine the future. Yet that imagined future must depend upon their own decisions. The future-to-be-imagined is not the future course of events which would ensue (with all the creativity and novelty of the actions that will make up those events) in the absence of any action by the entrepreneur. The future-to-be-imagined is a future that will include the consequences of the entrepreneur's own present and future actions. The entrepreneur is not seeking to imagine correctly a course of events upon which his own actions will impinge, but the course of events that will, in part, be set in motion by his own actions (which must now be decided upon). It is true that this does not at all prevent us from recognizing, as we have been insisting, that the entrepreneur is endeavoring to express his ability correctly to imagine the future. But it does require us to acknowledge that the future "realities" (i.e., what may eventually turn out to be the realities-to-be-created) which the entrepreneur is endeavoring correctly to imagine are such as to involve some logical knots and conundrums. The entrepreneur is not so much choosing a course of action that shall be *appropriate to the "realities"* as he is choosing among alternative imaginable realities that his prospective action may be initiating. It must be freely acknowledged that the prescience called for, within this scenario, must appear rather different from the simple prescience discussed in the context of a future thought to be substantially determined independently of whatever the prescient person himself may decide to do. The sense in which the entrepreneur's actions are seen to be "responding" to the "realities" is certainly a modified one. Nonetheless, we wish to insist, scope for entrepreneurial alertness and escape from error, and the incentives needed to spark such alertness and escape, can be perceived within this more carefully understood framework in substantially unchanged fashion. Actions taken for the future are taken with the endeavor more correctly to imagine (and profit from) the future.

What may seem, however, to be more troublesome is the question we saw to have been raised by Professor Kregel. In a world in which entrepreneurial prescience takes the form just explained, in a world in which the market process consists of untold series of such interacting entrepreneurial decisions, just how meaningful is it to describe that market process as somehow approximating a trajectory marked out by the "underlying realities" of preferences and resource availabilities? It is one thing to reinterpret, as we have attempted to do in the preceding paragraph, the realities which the decision maker seeks correctly to imagine, so as to recognize their dependence on the entrepreneur's own about-to-be-decided course of action. It is quite another to assert that the resulting series of entrepreneurial decisions and their market consequences are to be seen as constrained, through some "economic law" of equilibration, to the trajectory marked out by the configuration of (present and future) consumer preferences and scarce available resource services (present and future). Surely Kregel is correct in denying any possible "tendency to equilibrium based on a relation between expectations and the objective data . . ." (1986: 160)? How can we salvage the central notion of economic theory, that of the market tending to bring about coordination of market decisions in a manner which, in the light of the objective needs and constraints, avoids waste and inefficiency? To understand this it is necessary to step back and review the simplest notions of coordination in an imagined, stylized context in which we shall largely abstract from the uncertainties introduced by the dynamics of the market process.

THE MEANING OF COORDINATION: THE SIMPLE CONTEXT

Consider a market in which there is a strong, unsatisfied demand for shoes, in spite of the presence of available necessary resources (now being used in other industries of lesser value to consumers). Clearly there is an opportunity for entrepreneurship here. The resources needed to produce shoes could be assembled at a total outlay that would be more than offset by the considerable revenues to be obtained by selling shoes to eager consumers.

Imagine now that a number of entrepreneurs have misjudged the needs of consumers and have erroneously concluded that shoes were not likely to be profitable, but that the production of bicycles *would* be highly profitable. Pursuing their mistaken assessments they have set up factories to produce bicycles, drawing away resources from other (in fact more urgently needed) potential lines of production (such as shoes). Certainly these factories constitute misallocated resources. Suppose now, with these factories in place, their owners encounter a shortage of steel needed for the bicycles. Fortunately an entrepreneur is able to locate a suitable source of steel and to deliver the steel, at a profit, to the bicycle manufacturers. How shall we evaluate this last entrepreneuriual step? Should we say that it is a mistake (since the steel *should* perhaps have been used to help build shoe factories, where an expansion should have been occurring)? Should we say that, in discovering the profitable opportunity offered by the steel shortage in bicycle manufacturing, the steel entrepreneur is failing to respond to the *true*, objective realities (i.e., the strong unsatisfied demand for shoes, in the context of available resources now being wasted on less urgently needed lines of production)? Or should we not rather recognize that, *given the already-committed entrepreneurial errors* of building the bicycle factories, bygones must be seen as no more than bygones—that the relevant realities have now changed? Right now, it *is* an act of coordination to bring together the eager bicycle manufacturers looking for steel with the willing sellers of steel. In other words, a mistake that has been made (i.e., a mistake which resulted in entrepreneurial moves *at odds with* the true underlying realities) may itself change the relevant realities in such a way as to construct valid profitable new opportunities for acts of entrepreneurial coordination in situations which, from the perspective of the *originally* relevant set of realities, must be pronounced to be unfortunate. All this is straightforward and well understood. We shall be able to apply the simple lesson it teaches to the multiperiod market process in which next year's future "realities" will be created by this year's future, unpredictable, creative acts. It was in that context that we were forced to question the relevance (as a "magnet" marking out the trajectory to be taken by the market's process of equilibration) of the key objective realities, preferences and resource constraints. Let us pause to notice some features of our simple shoes and bicycles case.

The entrepreneurship which sees profit in the transfer of steel to the bicycle industry is of course responding to *present* realities. It is no longer in fact the case that the most useful place for this steel is in the shoe industry. Given the capital invested—rightly or wrongly—in the bicycle factories, given the failure to have built shoe factories, the most useful place *now* for the steel is in fact the bicycle industry. The *original* realities (in terms of which the shoe factories "ought" to have been built instead of the bicycle factories) have no relevance *now,* and have, indeed, correctly now failed to influence the allocation of resources. However, it would be incorrect to say that the original realities never did operate, in this scenario, to offer appropriate entrepreneurial incentives. The circumstance that entrepreneurs erred and failed to respond to those incentives should not lead us to say that the only realities which operated to influence entrepreneurial action were those which resulted from the irrevocable mistakes made in building the bicycle factories. The original realities (in which the true strength of consumer shoe demand was greater than that for bicycles) did offer relevant incentives; entrepreneurs simply failed to respond to these incentives—they were not sufficiently alert to recognize the true state of affairs. But whenever and wherever realities exist in the economy, they exercise their influence in offering appropriate profit incentives. Where these incentives, for reasons of insufficient entrepreneurial alertness, are not responded to, the actions taken by entrepreneurs, erroneous as they have been, nonetheless create a new reality which may now and will now exercise its own incentive power to attract the alertness of entrepreneurs to what is *now* called for in terms of social efficiency. Relevant realities always do exercise appropriate influence: as we know from the circumstance of possible entrepreneurial error, such influence may not be sufficient decisively to ensure efficient outcomes. Where they do not, the actual ("mistaken") outcomes achieved now assume their rightful role as the *currently* relevant realities in regard to the identification of the social optimal configurations.

The fact that, in its trajectory as marked out by the initial realities, the market slipped into error does indeed evoke a fresh relevant trajectory. As one period follows another, actual history is thus far from a faithful fulfillment of any one relevant trajectory. But it is always the case, nonetheless, that appropriate entrepreneurial incentives do, at any given moment, offer themselves in regard to the path relevant to the realities *of that moment.* We can now apply these straightforward insights to the more subtle and complex case where the course of equilibration implicit in an initial set of multiperiod realities is complicated by the circumstance that these multiperiod realities are themselves reflections of creative, unpredictable choices that will inevitably be made during the course of the market process—equilibrating or otherwise. We shall be making considerable use of the lessons we have learned in this section concerning the differences between (as well as the common features of) what we have called the "original realities" and the "new" realities which have been created by entrepreneurial mistakes.

THE MEANING OF COORDINATION: THE DYNAMIC CONTEXT

The usual understanding of what is meant by market coordination emphasizes the capacity of the market process to guide entrepreneurial decisions toward a pattern of resource allocation consistent with the realities of consumer preferences and resource scarcities. Subjectivists, radical or otherwise, have pointed out that since entrepreneurial decisions are future oriented the relevant preferences and scarcities must, at least in part, be those perceived to pertain to future dates. Thus the "realities" which supposedly shape entrepreneurial decisions must do so in the form of *expected* preferences and *expected* scarcities. Since, however, today's expectations of future preferences and scarcities must acknowledge that these future preferences and scarcities will themselves be shaped by series of prospective creative, unpredictable decisions on the part of many entrepreneurs, it is difficult, we have seen the radical subjectivist argument to run, to see how today's entrepreneurial decisions can be systematically related to (and appropriately adjusted to) the future arrays of preferences and scarcities (as they will in fact turn out to be). It would seem, surely, that it is more accurate to describe the future realities as having been shaped by today's entrepreneurial decisions than to declare the latter to be geared efficiently to take account of the former. Our discussion in the preceding section can help clear things up. It remains, we shall argue, entirely valid to perceive the market process as tending to coordinate decisions in a manner which takes systematic account of the priorities dictated by consumer preferences and resource scarcities. The middle ground Austrian recognition of the equilibrative and coordinative properties of the entrepreneur-driven and entrepreneur-inspired market process is not, in any essential way, disturbed by our acknowledgment of the indeterminacy of the future at each moment of decision.

Consider an entrepreneur A making a production decision at date t_1 that seeks to anticipate market demand (say, for shoes) at some future date t_{10}. The entrepreneur compares the present value of anticipated shoe revenues at t_{10} with the present relevant t_1 outlays. In so doing he is asking himself whether the revenues to be expected at t_{10} are such as to render the present outlays needed at t_1 erroneously low (i.e., whether the market has failed correctly to assess the true high value of the relevant resources, were they to be directed at t_{10} shoe consumers in the way considered by our entrepreneur). The t_{10} reality that he is assessing is one that will, at least at t_{10}, be an objective one. At t_1 it is an imagined reality. But, as we have emphasized previously, it is the imagined *reality* of t_{10} which inspires and shapes the entrepreneur's decision at t_1.

Suppose now that the entrepreneur A at date t_1 reasons as follows. "The t_{10} demand for shoes that I am wondering about is not something that expresses some future fact of external nature. In part that revenue will depend on what happens to population, to life styles, between now and t_{10}. Perhaps at time t_3 some entrepreneur will introduce a new fashion (say, bicycle travel) that will turn out drastically to affect t_{10} shoe demand." We may distinguish between the anticipated demand for shoes at t_{10} in the absence of bicycles, and the demand to be anticipated at t_{10} in the event that bicycles are introduced at t_3. (For simplicity we shall assume that these are the only alternative scenarios to be taken into account.) Only one of these two states of t_{10} demand will actually be the reality at t_{10}. Either bicycles will or they will not be introduced at t_3. But *both* possibilities exercise their effect upon present decision making. Our entrepreneur A must at t_1 plan his present activities on some perception of what the demand at t_{10} will in fact be. Both conceivable t_{10} "realities" will enter his calculations at t_1. Of course A also knows that the very start of a shoe industry at t_1 may generate changes in consumer patterns of behavior, so that the demand to be expected at t_{10} may not be the same as it might be were A *not* to start the shoe industry at t_1. Nonetheless, in assessing the profitability of beginning now at t_1 A is asking a single question: supposing I begin to build a shoe factory at t_1 in order to sell shoes at t_{10}, will shoe revenues at t_{10} be such as to show that the value of inputs at t_1 has been erroneously low?

Just as in the simple case of the preceding section all relevant realities exercised an appropriate incentive influence upon the entrepreneurial nose for profits, so too in the more dynamic context all relevant imaginable realities exercise their comparable influence. In the preceding section different realities were relevant at different times (when the bicycle factory was built this altered the relevant realities); in the present section (on the dynamic problem) different imaginable realities may simultaneously exercise their influence upon the entrepreneurial nose for profit. But all of them enter, appropriately, into entrepreneurial consideration, to the extent that the entrepreneur is alert enough to take them into account.[15]

In the case of the preceding section the separate realities that, at different times, operate to create entrepreneurial incentives were (a) an "original" reality and (b) a subsequent reality created by a "mistaken" entrepreneurial decision. In the present discussion, too, the arrays of imagined alternative "realities" which operate upon the entrepreneur's future-oriented profit antennae include imagined realities that might be created by "mistaken" (future) decisions. But we must not misinterpret this circumstance.

It is true that the entrepreneur at time t_1, in assessing prospects at t_{10}, takes into account the possibility that those t_{10} prospects may turn out to be the results of erroneous entrepreneurial acts, say at time t_4. But this does not mean that the imagined t_{10} realities which operate on the entrepreneur's incentives at t_1 are *not* the "true" t_{10} realities (i.e., those which *would* be relevant at t_{10} were no entrepreneurial mistakes to have been made earlier that might result in a different set of t_{10} realities). First, the entrepreneur at t_1 does have an incentive to take into account the possibility that mistakes between t_1 and t_{10} will *not* distort the situation at t_{10}. More important, entrepreneurial decisions at t_4 (and at *every* date) have every incentive *not* to be based on error. Thus at all times each and every entrepreneur is operating under the incentives set up by the "true" underlying future realities, *as well as* by the possible "mistake-induced" realities that may turn out to be relevant. Every entrepreneurial mistake creates a prospective intertemporal gap which offers the incentive correctly to anticipate the truth—with that truth reflecting both "original" elements and elements introduced by earlier mistakes (with the latter elements being fully relevant to the genuine coordination needs introduced by those very mistakes).

WHAT MARKET EQUILIBRATION TENDENCIES MEAN

It may seem to critics that our attempt to grapple with radical subjectivist insights has forced us to recognize an equilibration process far more attenuated, far less reliable and meaningful, than that postulated traditionally by middle ground Austrian economists. What we have here acknowledged, it may be held, is that the manner in which "underlying objective realities" exercise their influence upon entrepreneurial production decisions is far less direct and far less reliable than traditional Austrian statements would perhaps suggest. After all, we have recognized that entrepreneurial anticipations have to take into account future conditions, not as they might have been independently of the market process itself, but as they may turn out to be as a result of all the surprises and creativities of which the market process consists. Not only may that process include mistakes galore, that process and those mistakes may so "alter" future conditions as to require present entrepreneurs to anticipate a future that may in fact be quite different from what it might have been in the absence of such a process.

We must certainly be grateful to our radical subjectivist colleagues for compelling us to spell out how the notion of a systematic equilibrating process is to be integrated with our subjectivist understanding of the creativity of choice and the radical uncertainty of the future. Yet, at the same time, it seems fair to insist upon several key points. What middle ground Austrians wish to assert (and it is this traditionally Austrian assertion which provides the common ground which Mises saw in 1932 as being shared by the Austrians and by other schools of economic theory) is that events that occur during the market process are subject to powerful constraining and shaping influences. These influences tend to reflect the relative urgencies of different consumer preferences, and the relative scarcities of different productive resources. Austrians, certainly, have never been under the illusion that the powerful constraining and shaping influence of the market is ever so complete as to ensure attainment, even fleeting attainment, of the equilibrium state. What Austrians have emphasized is the existence of important processes of equilibration. It is of course true that such processes exercise a dynamic of their own, continually modifying the subsequent realities which in turn must serve to set in motion still further segments of equilibrating processes. It is true that human history is far from being a sequence of overlapping sure-fire equilibrating trajectories each unerringly set in motion by relevant objective realities (that can be identified as such apart from these processes themselves). All this is true. Middle ground Austrians have not been in the habit of treating the general equilibrium configuration of market variables as a "magnet" or "telos" with the capacity inexorably to draw actual market phenomena toward them. But, at the same time, they have resisted the temptation to treat market phenomena as only accidentally consistent with underlying objective phenomena. The truth surely is that the sequence of market events can be understood only if we recognize each segment of market history as expressing, at least in part, the systematic coordinative properties of the entrepreneurial process. The degree of importance to be attached to this understanding of market history depends, it must be emphasized, on empirical circumstances. It depends upon the volatility of change in the independent realities; it depends upon the degree of entrepreneurial error, both existing and to be anticipated. The importance of this understanding may thus vary from market to market, from one period in history to another. Although theory insists on the formal validity of the market coordinating process under all relevant circumstances, it does not claim that the tendencies which make up the process operate with uniform power at all times and in all contexts. It is easy to imagine circumstances where the power of the coordinative market process is completely swamped by the volatility of change and by the high incidence of entrepreneurial error. No doubt there have been moments in capitalist history where this has been the case.

But economic science has always proceeded from the important empirical circumstance of economic order. As elementary textbooks have reminded us at least since Bastiat, great cities manage, without a great deal of centralized control, to attract daily provisions in a tolerably orderly way. The market obviously works. That the market works is perhaps the most significant lesson of modern history. Experiences in the past several decades have pressed this lesson into the consciousness of men on both sides of the Iron Curtain. The problem which has always worried theorists is how, without deliberate coordination, can markets *possibly* work. Economic theory has provided the explanation in terms of a theory of market coordination. Austrians, we maintain, have deepened our understanding of that theory by introducing explicit insights concerning entrepreneurial discovery and dynamic competition. These insights reflect the subjectivism of the Austrian tradition. It is only through appreciation for subjectivist insights concerning knowledge and discovery that we can make sense of the dynamic market forces which bring decisions into greater and greater coordination. There is a danger, however, that undue emphasis on the more exotic possible implications of subjectivism may, paradoxically, make it almost plausible to *reject* the central lesson of economic reasoning, the understanding of and appreciation for the market coordinating process. This would be profoundly regrettable.

It is easy enough to show how error may frustrate efficiency and coordination. It is easy enough to show how, once we introduce a multiperiod future during which a continually creative market process may be at work, it must seem almost fantastic to expect entrepreneurs correctly to anticipate the future. What is not so easy is to explain how, in spite of the untold opportunities for error and surprise, the market regularly appears to organize coherent long-range processes of production in profitable ways.

What the theory of the entrepreneur-driven process of market coordination provides is a framework within which to understand how current production decisions can possibly achieve the extraordinary degree of spontaneous coordination which casual experience convinces us that they do. The theory identifies the windows through which discovery of relevant opportunities can illuminate and inform the lattice-work of market decision making. No one needs to be told that these windows may be blurred and obscured, that entrepreneurs may fail to perceive what might be seen through these windows. But once we understand that these windows exist, we can in principle understand how, in spite of the uncertainty of the future, in spite of the cloud of unavoidable ignorance which obscures these windows, opportunities for profit can attract and inspire market actions which turn out to reduce market ignorance and misallocation.

Moreover, once we understand how it is through windows of entrepreneurial opportunity that the light of potential discovery inspires market efficiency, we can understand the Mises–Hayek demonstration of the fallacy of seeking social efficiency *without* the market. We can understand how, by walling up all such windows of entrepreneurial opportunity, central planning dooms itself to operating in a world of sheer ignorance concerning vital, ample and available pieces of information dispersed throughout the economy.

We cannot, as Austrians, follow mainstream neoclassical theory and simply assert perennial equilibrium. Yet we cannot, again as Austrians, follow subjectivist sceptics in denying coordinative properties to the market. We find ourselves, therefore, occupying the Garrisonian middle ground, finding deep understanding of systematic market processes in precisely those subjectivist insights which, if deployed without sufficient care, may tempt one to reject the idea of market coordination altogether.

NOTES

1. Of course Professor Garrison is not responsible for the manner in which his idea is presented and deployed in this paper.

2. See Mises (1966: 2) for the insight that the contribution of classical economics was to show how state policies have systematic, often unintended, consequences (which ought therefore to be taken into account).

3. See Boehm (1985), for some doubts concerning the extent of this classical liberalism.

4. See this volume, Chapter 7, for an account of these developments.

5. See this volume, Chapter 3, pp. 67f., for one contemporary interpretation of the term "Austrian economics" as "free market economics."

6. For earlier contributions defending the Austrian middle ground with regard to positions taken by radical subjectivists, see O'Driscoll (1978) and Garrison (1987).

7. We may add that an implication of this position urged by the critics is that Austrians also reject their traditional commitment to the viability of economic theory (as opposed to historicism). Although Austrian economics began as a sharp reaction against the German Historical School, it is now suggested that something of a reappraisal is in order (see Shackle 1972: 37f., 272f.; Lachmann 1986a: 148).

8. For criticism along similar lines see Wiseman (1990).

9. For an example of such a challenge see Wiseman (1990: 158).

10. See also Garrison (1987) with regard to Professor Lachmann's concurrence with Kregel's position.

11. For recognition of this implication of radical subjectivism, see Wiseman (1990: 155).

12. On the idea of entrepreneurial alertness see further Kirzner (1973: 2; 1979a: Ch. 10).

13. "The future is unknowable, though not unimaginable" (Lachmann 1976: 59).

14. This writer has often talked as if alertness is able to identify *existing* opportunities for future profit. Purists, in both linguistic usage and philosophical consistency, may certainly be excused for expressing unhappiness with such loose or metaphorical use of language in regard to the non-existent future. But the economics of the situation surely depends not a whit on the validity of this use of language.

15. It must be remembered that the theory of entrepreneurial alertness does not operate by having the entrepreneur ponder the comparative merits of a list of alternative future scenarios. Instead the theory posits that, based on the entrepreneur's "alertness," his sense of the future, his attention will tend to be grasped by the relevant profitable future scenario. Our point is that *all* relevant future alternative realities have equal potential for grasping entrepreneurial attention. The greater the degree of his alertness, the greater the likelihood that the "future reality" which will in fact grab his attention will be that which will in fact turn out to be the case.

REFERENCES

Boehm, S. (1985) "The political economy of the Austrian School," in P. Roggi (ed.) *Gli Economisti e la Political Economica*, Naples; Edizioni Scientifiche Italiene.

Buchanan, J. M. (1982) "The domain of subjective economics: between predictive science and moral philosophy," in I. M. Kirzner (ed.) *Method, Process, and Austrian Economics: Essays in Honor of Ludwig von Mises*, Lexington, Mass.: D. C. Heath.

Buchanan, J. M. and Vanberg, V. J. (1990) "The market as a creative process," unpublished manuscript, April.

Garrison, R. W. (1982) "Austrian economics as the middle ground: comment on Loasby," in I. M. Kirzner (ed.) *Method, Process and Austrian Economics, Essays in Honor of Ludwig von Mises*, Lexington, Mass.: D. C. Heath.

——. (1987) "The kaleidic world of Ludwig Lachmann," *Critical Review* 1 (3): 77–89.

Hayek, F. A. (1949b) "The use of knowledge in society," in *Individualism and Economic Order*, London: Routledge & Kegan Paul (originally published in *American Economic Review* 35 (4) (1945): 519–30).

—— (1967a) "Kinds of rationalism," in *Studies in Philosophy, Politics and Economics*, Chicago, Ill.: University of Chicago Press.

—— (1967b) "The results of human action but not of human design," in *Studies in Philosophy, Politics and Economics*, Chicago, Ill.: University of Chicago Press.

—— (1968) "Economic thought VI: the Austrian School," in D. L. Sills (ed.) *International Encyclopedia of the Social Sciences*, New York: Macmillan.

Kirzner, I. M. (1973) *Competition and Entrepreneurship*, Chicago, Ill.: University of Chicago Press.

—— (1985a) *Discovery and the Capitalist Process*, Chicago, Ill.: University of Chicago Press.

Kregel, J. A. (1986) "Conceptions of equilibrium: the logic of choice and the logic of production," in I. M. Kirzner (ed.) *Subjectivism, Intelligibility, and Economic Understanding, Essays in Honor of Ludwig M. Lachmann on His Eightieth Birthday*, New York: New York University Press.

Lachmann, L. M. (1976) "From Mises to Shackle: an essay on Austrian economics and the kaleidic society," *Journal of Economic Literature* 14 (10), March: 54–62.

—— (1986a) *The Market as an Economic Process*, Oxford: Basil Blackwell.

Loasby, B. J. (1982) "Economics of dispersed and incomplete information," in I. M. Kirzner (ed.) *Method, Process and Austrian Economics, Essays in Honor of Ludwig von Mises*, Lexington, Mass.: D. C. Heath.

—— (1989) *The Mind and Method of the Economist, A Critical Appraisal of Major Economists in the 20th Century*, Aldershot: Edward Elgar.

Menger, C. (1981) *Principles of Economics*, New York: New York University Press (originally published as *Grundsätze der Volkswirtschaftslehre*, Wien: Wilhelm Braumüller, 1871: translated and edited by J. Dingwall and B. F. Hoselitz, Glencoe, Ill.: Free Press, 1950).

Mises, L. von (1960) *Epistemological Problems of Economics*, Princeton, N.J.: Van Nostrand (translation of *Grundprobleme der Nationalökonomie*, 1933).

—— (1966) *Human Action, a Treatise on Economics*, 3d ed., Chicago, Ill.: Henry Regnery (originally published as *Human Action*, New Haven, Conn.: Yale University Press, 1949).

O'Driscoll, G. P. Jr (1978) "Spontaneous order and the coordination of economic activities," in L. M. Spadaro (ed.) *New Directions in Austrian Economics*, Kansas City, Kans.: Sheed, Andrews & McMeel.

Schultz, T. W. (1975) "The value of the ability to deal with disequilibria," *Journal of Economic Literature* 13 (3) September: 827–46.

Shackle, G. L. S. (1970) *Decision, Order and Time in Human Affairs*, 2d ed., Cambridge: Cambridge University Press (originally published 1969).

—— (1972) *Epistemics and Economics: A Critique of Economic Doctrines*, Cambridge: Cambridge University Press.

—— (1983) "The bounds of unknowledge," in J. Wiseman (ed.) *Beyond Positive Economics?*, London: Macmillan.

—— (1986) "The origination of choice," in I. M. Kirzner (ed.) *Subjectivism, Intelligibility and Economic Understanding, Essays in Honor of Ludwig M. Lachmann on His Eightieth Birthday*, New York: New York University Press.

Stigler, G. J. (1959) "The politics of political economists," *Quarterly Journal of Economics*, November.

Streissler, E. (1988) "The intellectual and political impact of the Austrian School of economics," *History of European Ideas* 92.

Wiseman, J. A. (1990) "General equilibrium or market process: an evaluation," in A. Bosch, P. Koslowski and R. Veit (eds.) *General Equilibrium or Market Process, Neoclassical and Austrian Theories of Economics*, Tubingen: J. C. B. Mohr, pp. 145–63.

Zweig, M. (1970) "A New Left critique of economics," in D. Mermelstein (ed.) *Economics: Mainstream Readings and Radical Critiques*, New York: Random House.

THE ENTREPRENEURIAL PROCESS

The term *entrepreneurial process* has come to possess two rather distinct, although interrelated, meanings: The two meanings are (1) the process of entrepreneurial competition responsible, in the short run, for the tendencies for the market price of each commodity or input to move toward the respective market-clearing level, for the array of outputs to reflect the pattern of consumer preferences in the light of currently available technological possibilities, and for pure profit opportunities to be ground down to zero; and (2) the process of entrepreneurial discovery, invention, and innovation through which long-run economic growth is stimulated and nourished. The first kind of entrepreneurial process (short-run) is seen as responsible for a continuous tendency toward economic balance and internal economic consistency. The second (long-run) achieves a continual series of steps that together propel the engine of long-run economic growth and development. The second kind of process is the better known than the first and was perhaps most notably discussed in the work of Joseph Schumpeter.[1] Most of this chapter will be concerned with the entrepreneurial process in a sense closer to the second of these two meanings than to the first. However, it is central to my view that a full understanding of long-term entrepreneurial processes will reveal them to be simply a consistent implication and extension of the short-run processes. Although Schumpeter himself did not see the long-run entrepreneurial process quite in this way, I shall argue that the Schumpeterian process can be illuminated by an understanding of the first (short-run) entrepreneurial processes. And I shall argue further that in attempting to formulate policy that should encourage (or at least release) the long-run processes of entrepreneurial discovery necessary for vigorous growth, it will be highly useful to bear in mind the linkages that prevail between these long-run and short-run processes. In other words, the way to permit long-run entrepreneurial growth processes to take off is to recognize and encourage the kinds of entrepreneurial discoveries that make up the short-run processes.

From *Discovery and the Capitalist Process* (Chicago and London: The University of Chicago Press, 1985), 68–92. Republished with permission of Simon & Schuster; the original source is *The Environment for Entrepreneurship*, ed. Calvin A. Kent (Lexington, Mass.: Lexington Books, D. C. Heath & Co., 1984), 41–58. Permission conveyed through Copyright Clearance Center, Inc.

THE NEGLECT OF ENTREPRENEURSHIP
IN GROWTH ECONOMICS

Until quite recently growth economics suffered rather seriously from the neglect of the entrepreneurial role. As Harvey Leibenstein has pointed out, it is one of the "curious aspects of the relationship of neoclassical theory to economic development" that "in the conventional theory, entrepreneurs as they are usually perceived play almost no role."[2] This neglect pervaded not only growth economics but economic analysis in general. It would have been too much to expect an analytical framework that, in regard to markets in general, accorded no special significance to entrepreneurial activity—or in fact any scope for such activity—to analyze growth along entrepreneur-theoretic lines.

As a consequence, conventional thinking about the way economic growth occurs and about the ways it might be enhanced tended to be clouded. Much of the discussion of economic growth and development was, for example, aggregative in tone and approach. The economy was discussed as if it were an integrated economic organism; as if individual decision making by firms, investors, and consumers could be costlessly suppressed insofar as the processes of economic growth were concerned. Certainly no need was recognized for any mutual information among individual participants in the economy.

Moreover, the aggregate economy was seen as rigidly circumscribed by resource scarcity that limited growth possibilities along very definite paths. These scarcity constraints were thought not only to govern the possibilities in hypothetical market economies, but also to delineate optimal growth patterns. Little awareness was displayed that the objectivity of these constraints disappears as soon as it is realized how heavily dependent they are on the assumption that nothing further can be or is likely to be discovered concerning new and better ways of using given resources, or concerning the existence of hitherto unsuspected resources.

An important ingredient in economic growth was recognized to be the continual availability of improved technology. But technological advance was seen as occurring in an inexorably impersonal manner and to be somehow effortlessly and automatically available to all parts of an economy. In particular, the opportunities for growth were seen as marked out, given initial technology, by a clearly defined array of intertemporal investment possibilities that somehow existed apart from any need for them to be discovered, and whose very existence dictated the appropriate growth path. There was no suggestion that the set of opportunities likely to be in fact discovered might in some way depend on the institutional framework within which growth was sought.

It is therefore hardly surprising to find that this earlier growth and development literature not only failed to explore the policies and institutional patterns that might stimulate profit-motivated individual market entrepreneurship; it in fact tended to take for granted that markets were entirely unnecessary for the achievement of growth and that the naturally preferred mode for growth was through wise central planning.

AN ENTREPRENEURIAL VIEW OF ECONOMIC DEVELOPMENT

The view of economic growth and development in this chapter contrasts sharply with that critically described in the preceding section. I will emphasize the *open-endedness* of economic systems. Although I will by no means ignore or deny the prime importance of resource scarcity, either in respect to output at any given date or in regard to the possibilities of increases in output level over time, my emphasis will be on the need and scope for processes of discovery that may in effect render scarcity less overriding in accounting for growth. I will thus be concerned not so much with the ways human beings ensure that every ounce of perceived output possibility is properly exploited as with the incentives to stimulate the perception of possibilities. It is this perception that is responsible for the open-endedness of the economic process. We never know what real possibilities remain to be discovered; we never know what the real limits are to the elasticity of the resource constraints that circumscribe our existence.

In understanding the processes of entrepreneurial discovery that are crucially important for growth, aggregation is a distinct handicap. Treating the economy as a whole and abstracting from the opportunities created by interpersonal error within the system inevitably diverts analytical attention from discovery processes made necessary and possible by such error. Treating growth simply as a phenomenon best achieved through deliberate planning inevitably clamps economic growth into a framework from which open-ended discovery is excluded. To plan is not to discover; in fact to plan presumes that the framework within which planning takes place is already fully discovered. In contrast, I see the unfolding development of a nation's economy over time as a process made up, to a major extent, of the interaction of innumerable individual acts of mutual discovery. An understanding of the institutional climate within which such spontaneous processes of unpredictable mutual discovery can best flourish is central. Let us first examine somewhat more systematically the way entrepreneurial discovery constitutes a unique ingredient in economic growth.

ROBINSON CRUSOE, ENTREPRENEURSHIP, AND ECONOMIC GROWTH

Imagine a "Robinson Crusoe" economy with a low volume of output. We might initially classify the possible reasons for this low level of production (and for Crusoe's consequently low standard of living) in the following manner: (1) Crusoe may command only severely limited resources, thus constraining output to a low level; (2) resources may be available to permit higher levels of output, but these levels are not being attained because of Crusoe's lack of technical knowledge of how to properly utilize the resources available; (3) both the resources to permit higher output and the knowledge necessary to harness the resources may be available to Crusoe, but the higher output is not forthcoming because of Crusoe's ignorance of the availability of the resources, the availability of the technical knowledge needed to utilize them, or both. In terms of this array of possible reasons, it is clear that a process of economic development raising the quantity and quality of Crusoe's output may be the result of any or all of the following: an increased endowment of resources (including an increased stock of capital goods, presumably as a result of deliberate saving and investment); an increased command over the technical knowledge needed to exploit available resources; or discovery of the resources and the technical knowledge that are already available.

Now this way of putting matters is obviously awkward. Technical knowledge is no less a resource for Crusoe than is steel, or labor, or land. Changes in the endowment of Crusoe's knowledge need not, it may be objected, be treated separately from changes in his endowments of other resources. This deliberately awkward classification has been, in fact, employed strictly in order to accentuate an important but often missed distinction—between the technical knowledge needed to utilize given physical resources on the one hand and, on the other hand, *the knowledge that resources are in fact available*. Technical knowledge can be treated as a resource; but knowledge of the availability of resources cannot. There is a fundamental difference between the way changes in the stock of technical knowledge may enter into the explanation of economic development, and the way changes in the knowledge of *availability* of resources enter into such explanation.

Economic development based on growth of Crusoe's technical knowledge may be perceived to occur in the same logically understandable manner as development based on expanded physical resources. Expansion of physical resources may, of course, be either planned or unplanned. In the case of unplanned expansion of physical inputs, as for example when unexpected beneficial changes in climate occur, Crusoe enjoys expanded output by simply continuing to exploit available resources to the utmost. In the more important case of planned expansion of inputs, Crusoe may, by deliberately channeling his productive energies to this end, increase the volume and quality of capital goods, thus generating eventual increases in output flows. Economic growth and development, in these cases, follows for Crusoe from the logic of expanded opportunities made possible by the planned or unplanned available volume of resources. Output possibilities are restricted by the scarce available resources; expansion of resources is followed by exploitation of the now expanded volume of output possibilities.

Growth of Crusoe's technical knowledge, quite similarly, expands the range of productive possibilities. What Crusoe can produce today out of given physical resources with today's technical knowledge is greater than what he could produce with the same resources without today's knowledge. The expanded technical knowledge may have been at least partly unplanned (as has occurred on numerous occasions during the history of technology), or more likely it may have come about at least partly as a result of deliberate investment in research. Growth in technical knowledge expands the range of production possibilities, thus providing an immediate explanation for growth in output.

The key point is that in such cases development consists in the exploitation of expanded opportunities. The volume of opportunities grows, hence output grows. A very large part of economic analysis depends on the postulate that an optimal opportunity that exists is an opportunity that is immediately grasped. From this perspective, growth in the availability of Crusoe's resources, whether consisting of physical inputs or technical knowledge, whether as a result of planned investment or fortuitously increased endowment, provides an immediately convincing explanation for growth in output.

Here lies the important distinction, for explanations of development, between growth in technical knowledge on the one hand and an increased awareness of the availability of resources on the other. For where development occurs as a result of increased awareness of the availability of resources, it occurs *not* because of the availability of new opportunities, but because of expanded awareness of existing opportunities. To understand development that has occurred in this way, it is necessary to escape the economist's assumption that an optimal opportunity that exists is an opportunity immediately grasped. It is necessary to recognize that desirable opportunities may go unnoticed and hence unexploited; it is necessary to understand the entrepreneurial process whereby opportunities that were hitherto existent but unseen become opportunities seen and exploited.

Entrepreneurial discovery of existing opportunities is relevant to an understanding of economic development along two dimensions.

1. At a given point in time output may be less than is possible and desired, because of opportunities that have remained unnoticed. Entrepreneurial discovery of these opportunities makes possible a growth in output.

2. As time goes by, expansion of resources (physical or otherwise, planned or unplanned) expands the range of productive possibilities. For this to be translated into growth in output, it is not enough that these expanded possibilities exist—they must be perceived. Here too entrepreneurial discovery is an indispensable ingredient in economic development.

MARKETS, ENTREPRENEURSHIP, AND
ECONOMIC GROWTH: AN APPARENT PROBLEM

The foregoing Crusonian discussion may be applied, with appropriate modification, to a certain problem in the analysis of growth in a market context. A correct allocation of resources is one that commits each unit of resource to its most highly valued use. An expansion of available resources is presumed to generate expanded output value because we take it for granted that decision makers will tend to correctly allocate the increased resources. This applies to increased technical knowledge no less than to expanded physical resources. If an available unit, say of a scarce raw material, can be utilized in production somewhere in a competitive economy, its market price will, we are taught, tend to rise toward the value of its marginal product in its best use, ensuring that its owner will tend to find it wasteful not to deploy it in that use. Similarly, if a scrap of scarce technical knowledge can enhance the productivity of physical resources somewhere in the economy, potential users of this knowledge will bid for it until its market price tends to correspond to its highest marginal usefulness. But the same market process does not directly apply to knowledge of the availability of resources or, more generally, to knowledge of value.

Let us imagine that a simple, costless operation linking together two items each valued at $1 can transform them into a product worth $12. Clearly this availability of an opportunity for $10 of pure entrepreneurial profit indicates that market participants in general have not realized that this profitable transformation is feasible, or that it is profitable. The market lacks knowledge of the resources available to create $10 of pure profit. Or we may say that the market lacks the knowledge of the true value of the two items of input: the true joint value of these inputs is $12; the market incorrectly believes it to be only $2. Can we, with respect to this missing knowledge, rely on the general market tendency for items to be valued so as to fully reflect their most important uses? Can we assume a tendency for the market to correctly assign full value to this missing knowledge? There are serious logical difficulties involved in any attempt to answer these questions affirmatively.

To assume a tendency for the market to assign full value to the missing knowledge would require that would-be users of this missing knowledge bid for it. That is, we would have to postulate that competing bidders, eager to capture the $10 of profit available through transforming the $2 worth of inputs into $12 of output are prepared to pay for the information that would make such capture possible. This could force up the price of this knowledge of value until it approximates the full $10 that it is capable of generating. But the truth is that we cannot, in this case, assume (as we were able to assume in the case of technical knowledge) that there will be bidders for the missing knowledge.

A moment's reflection should make this clear. Market participants have in general failed to notice that there is a way to transform $2 worth of input into $12 worth of output. In other words, these market participants are not aware that they are overlooking the $10 opportunity of pure profit. Those aware of the inputs place no higher value upon them than $2. Those aware of the high $12 value of the output are aware of no opportunity to achieve such output at an outlay that would make its production available. It is not that market participants feel they lack specific knowledge capable of yielding $10; rather it is that market participants have no inkling that there is anything to be known. In these circumstances we have no right to assume that anyone will be bidding for the knowledge of how to convert the $2 worth of input into $12 worth of output or that potential bidders have any idea of the value of such knowledge.

The source of the $10 profit opportunity resides in the undervaluation by the market of the two inputs, in the existence of unperceived value. The true joint value of the two inputs should be $12; the market values them at $2. The value to any individual of the knowledge of this undervaluation should surely be the full value of the pure profit such knowledge can generate—the full amount of the undervaluation. But, by hypothesis, the market is not aware that any value attaches to knowledge of such undervaluation, since no undervaluation is in fact suspected.

Knowledge of the true value of inputs is thus quite different, in this respect, from technical knowledge. Technical knowledge may be valuable, and potential bidders may assess its value and as a result seek its possession. The knowledge of the true value of inputs may indeed be said to possess value, but this value is of a kind that, by its nature, precludes the possibility of its being able to motivate market participants to deliberately seek it out. *To imagine its being deliberately sought after is to imagine away the source of its value.* The knowledge of value is valuable only if it is not known to be valuable. As soon as the market correctly values the knowledge of value, that correctly assessed value shrinks to zero.

If these conundrums surround the notion of the value of the knowledge of value, then it follows that we cannot rely on competitive market bidding to call forth correct knowledge of value—at least in the way competitive bidding can be relied upon to mobilize productive resources. We cannot, apparently, rely on competitive market bidding to ensure that valuable possibilities will be perceived, that the inputs capable of sustaining these possibilities will be correctly valued. And it is here that we recognize the existence of two distinct avenues along which economic development may proceed: through expansion of opportunities arising through increased availability of resources, or through the discovery of hitherto unperceived opportunities. In practice both strands of developmental causation are intertwined. In order for resources to expand, newly possible opportunities must first be perceived.

These two lines of development differ in important ways, however. Where development occurs through the expansion of opportunities, it may be the outcome of a deliberate planning process to expand the volume of resources through investment in human resources or in physical capital goods. The possibility of such a deliberate planning process permits economic development to be understood as the smooth unfolding of a designed growth path. But with respect to that line of development which arises from the flow of discovery of existing opportunities, no such smooth unfolding of designed growth can be identified. It is impossible to deliberately plan a series of discoveries. Just as we cannot imagine an opportunity being deliberately overlooked unless because of some significant cost of deliberate search that in fact renders the opportunity less than worthwhile after all, so too we cannot imagine a systematic plan to notice that which has hitherto been overlooked. All this means that economic development requires, as part of its explanation, understanding of the entrepreneurial element and of the way this element eludes the analytical tools of standard economic theory.

ALLOCATION, GROWTH, AND ENTREPRENEURSHIP

A good deal of modern economics is concerned with the forces that determine the allocation of society's resources among alternative production possibilities. There were times, in the past at least, when professional economic discussion seemed to draw a sharp distinction between the allocative function of economic systems on the one hand and the process of economic growth on the other. It was as if economic growth presented a series of problems and tasks to which allocative considerations were totally irrelevant. Thus, for example, economists who expressed full confidence in the capacity of markets to allocate society's resources with reasonable efficiency were quick to deny any similar ability of markets to achieve a desirable rate of growth for the economy.[3] The allocative properties of markets apparently failed to include, as an implication, the capacity to successfully lift the total volume of output over time. To use existing resources efficiently called for deploying these resources to avoid waste. To achieve growth, it was held, called for the fulfillment of a quite different task: the steady increase of the total volume of these resources.

This dichotomy appears flawed in several somewhat subtle respects, though it does, of course, possess a certain superficial plausibility. An increase in the total volume of resources available to society is after all not the same as a more effective utilization of the resource volume given at a particular date. Indeed, a case can emphatically be made that to increase the total volume of resources calls for qualities—of an entrepreneurial character—unrelated to those required for calculative, optimizing, allocative activity.

That a market can successfully stimulate the efficient allocation of resources is no guarantee that it can perform similarly with respect to the entrepreneurial activity required for growth. If the economists referred to had wished to draw attention to these important distinctions, there would have been far less the critic could quibble over. Unfortunately this was decidedly not the case. As mentioned earlier, for a long time economists discussing growth virtually ignored entrepreneurship. And for a world in which entrepreneurship in the discovery of new resources (or in the discovery of new uses for already known and available resources) is seen as having no scope, the distinction between allocation and growth is deeply flawed.

In a world of given resources (with no scope for any addition to these resources that might arise from discovery) it should be obvious that growth necessarily arises from a particular (intertemporal) pattern of resource allocation. In exactly the same way that efficient allocation of resources is required in order to ensure that society's scarce resources are directed to the particular basket of current consumption goods judged most urgently required, efficient intertemporal allocation of resources is required in order to express any preference rankings that place higher future levels of well-being above currently higher levels of well-being. Economic growth, in a world of given resources, depends strictly on the rate at which consumption enjoyments are postponed to permit capital resources to be built up or new technological knowledge to be acquired.

There seems little basis to postulate any analytical distinction between allocation processes as they relate to alternative current uses of resources on the one hand and allocation procedures as they relate to alternative temporal production possibilities on the other. It is not at all obvious why a market system acknowledged to achieve effective patterns of resource allocation in the first of these senses should be held incapable of achieving comparably efficient intertemporal allocative patterns.

The sharp dichotomy that seemed to be drawn between economic allocation of resources and economic growth was flawed in a rather more complicated sense as well. It is not merely that economic growth turns out to be merely a special case of the more general allocation problem. As soon as scope for entrepreneurial discovery is acknowledged in the context of economic growth, such scope must be acknowledged in the context of short-run resource allocation as well. Thus, although it appeared, in a world without entrepreneurship, as if allocation economics necessarily embraced—indeed, swallowed up—the economics of growth, almost the opposite seems to occur as soon as the role of entrepreneurial discovery is recognized. As soon as the economics of growth becomes correctly viewed as being in large part the economics of entrepreneurial discovery, it becomes difficult to see the processes of short-run resource allocation as anything but special cases of the more general discovery processes that constitute economic growth.

From this latter perspective, then, the allocation/growth dichotomy is flawed not so much because it overlooks the allocative aspects of economic growth as because it tends to reinforce the neglect of the role of entrepreneurship in both short-run and long-run economic processes.

OPPORTUNITIES, ALERTNESS, AND ECONOMIC PROCESSES

For an analytical perspective in which entrepreneurship and its role are seen as essential elements, the centrality of allocation is highly questionable. Neither at the level of the analysis of the individual economic decision nor at that level concerned with understanding how society's resources are allocated is it possible to proceed without transcending the allocation schema within which economics has so frequently been constrained.[4] Despite the enormously valuable clarity introduced into modern economics by Lord Robbins's formulation (in which economics was rigidly identified as concerned with the consequences of human allocative behavior and which led to the popular notion of economics as being concerned with the ways societies do and should allocate their scarce resources),[5] the truth is that economics can no longer make do with this rather narrow conception of its nature and concerns.

Economists can no longer take it for granted that individual decision makers, or groups, engage in nothing more than allocative decisions against the background of clearly perceived alternatives. Economists must consider that economic processes, and especially market processes, have a profound impact upon the way individuals perceive the options available to them, while the accuracy and sensitivity of opportunity perception itself crucially affects the nature of these economic and market processes that they set in motion. In other words, economic analysis must grapple with the inescapable entrepreneurial element in action and in society.

Individual action is not seen as merely the calculation of the optimum position relevant to a given set of data; it is seen as an attempt to grasp opportunities that the human agent, peering through a fog of uncertainty, judges to be available. The interaction of decisions in markets is not seen as an instantaneous meshing of plans in which the pattern of calculated optima for the participants is such as to permit all of them to be simultaneously sustained. Rather it is seen as an unrestrained, but by no means haphazard, process in which the opportunities perceived to be available are those that have been overlooked by others. In the face of ceaseless and unpredictable exogenous change, the continual pursuit of as yet unperceived opportunities keeps perceptions from straying too far from reality. The role of entrepreneurial alertness in this sequence deserves to be briefly elaborated.

Entrepreneurial theory labors under what appears to be a serious handicap: the specific outcome selected in any particular entrepreneurial decision cannot, even in principle, be predicted.[6] In contrast, the choice made in the course of allocative decision making is, in microeconomic analysis, viewed as emerging errorlessly and ineluctably from the interaction between the agent's objective function and resource and technological constraints. Economic science can, in the case of the allocative decision, claim to account precisely for the action decided upon. But such can certainly not be claimed for the entrepreneurial decision, in which the agent must determine what he or she believes is the relevant environment within which a course of action must be taken.

Economic science is unable to account precisely for the outcome of such entrepreneurial determination. (It should also be pointed out that the purely allocative decision never does occur, and that in fact it is sheer illusion to imagine that economic science can ever provide the kind of precision suggested in microeconomics textbooks.) Yet it is important not to conclude that, simply because the application of the theory of constrained optimization is insufficient to yield precise outcomes, entrepreneurial decision making and the market processes set in motion by such decisions are entirely without guidance.

The truth is that all human decision making is guided by an extremely powerful force—the motivation to see relevant facts as they are.[7] This pervasive pressure to avoid error and to learn from mistakes operates in ways that are far from being fully known. But this powerful instinct is responsible for whatever success humanity has achieved in coping with its environment. To be human is not merely to calculate correctly within an already perceived environment; it is to be able, by peering into a murky present and an even murkier future, to obtain a reasonably useful grasp of one's true situation.

In the market context a correct perception of one's situation calls for a perception not only of physical possibilities and constraints but also of the possibilities and constraints imposed by the actions, present and prospective, of others. The market process consists of a sequence of entrepreneurial decisions, each of which, being only partially correct in anticipating the decisions of others, leaves room and incentive for further mutual discovery. Were such decisions made haphazardly, there would be no basis for claiming the existence of systematic entrepreneurial market processes. Such systematic processes of entrepreneurial discovery are based on the determined, purposeful alertness of market participants.

TYPES OF ENTREPRENEURIAL ACTIVITY

There are many opportunities for alert entrepreneurs. Some are of relevance only for short-run market processes; others hold relevance for long-run processes of growth and development. I will show that, despite the validity of such classification, the nature of entrepreneurial decision making is, at bottom, no different in regard to long-run growth contexts than in regard to short-run contexts.

There appear to be three major types of concrete entrepreneurial activity: arbitrage activity, speculative activity, and innovative activity. *Arbitrage* activity consists of acting upon the discovery of a present discrepancy (net of all delivery costs) between the prices at which a given item can be bought and sold. Such activity involves the discovery of error, since those who sell at the low price are simply unaware of those who buy at the higher price, and vice versa. This discovery constitutes a discovery of an opportunity for pure gain. It is surely the incentive provided by such opportunities that is responsible for the powerful tendency for such arbitrage opportunities to continually disappear. Arbitrage calls for no innovation. In its pure form it calls for no risk bearing and no capital, since buying and selling are simultaneous.

Speculative activity is an arbitrage across time. It is engaged in by the entrepreneur who believes that he or she has discovered a discrepancy (net of all relevant carrying costs and to be revealed through subsequent history) between the prices at which a given item can be bought today and sold in the future. To believe that one has discovered such a price discrepancy is to believe that one has discovered an opportunity for pure gain. There can be no doubt that it is the incentive so provided that inspires entrepreneurs to undertake speculative activity that, if correct, tends to stabilize price over time. Of course such activity is inextricably intertwined with the bearing of uncertainty and also calls for the cooperation of the capitalist to bridge the time gap involved in the speculation. No innovation is required for the activity of the pure speculator.

Innovative activity consists in the creation (for a future more or less distant) of an output, method of production, or organization not hitherto in use. For such activity to be profitable, it will of course be necessary for the innovator to introduce not just any innovation, but one that displays the very same pattern of intertemporal price discrepancy that is identified with speculative activity. Innovative activity, like speculative activity, retains important parallels with the case of pure arbitrage. Innovation calls for the discovery of an intertemporal opportunity that cannot, even in principle, be said to actually exist before the innovation has been created. To talk of the existence of an undiscovered opportunity for an as yet uncreated innovation is merely to engage in metaphor, although it should be pointed out that in important cases the use of such metaphor may be highly instructive.[8] Nonetheless, innovative activity too can bridge a gap between two markets across time, overcoming what at least from a later perspective can be seen to have been error, inspired by the opportunity to grasp the pure gain set up by the relevant price discrepancy.

Alertness is a concept sufficiently elastic to cover not only the perception of existing arbitrage opportunities but also the perception of intertemporal speculative opportunities that can be definitively realized only after the lapse of time, and even also the perception of intertemporal opportunities that call for creative and imaginative innovation. Certainly the concrete manifestation of successful speculative (or of innovative) activity may call for personal and psychological qualities substantially different from those needed to engage in pure arbitrage.

Yet the parallelism among the various kinds of entrepreneurial activity remains. All of them consist of taking advantage of price differentials; all are inspired by the pure profit incentive constituted by the respective price differentials; all are made possible by less competent entrepreneurial activity (the errors of others). In other words, all of them involve *knowledge of value*—with all its attendant conundrums discussed earlier. It is the commonality expressed in these parallels, and in this shared link to the elusive knowledge of value, that I wish to emphasize here.

INCENTIVES, COMPETITION, AND FREEDOM OF ENTRY

A feature common to all kinds of entrepreneurial discovery is the incentive of pure profit, arising out of the respective price discrepancies of which the entrepreneurial opportunities consist.[9] It should be emphasized that this is an incentive rather different from the notion of an incentive in the nonentrepreneurial context. In the nonentrepreneurial context incentives are called for to motivate an agent to engage in some *costly* activity. To provide such an incentive is therefore to arrange that the gross payoff from the relevant activity to the agent be seen to be more than sufficient to offset the associated cost sacrifice. To provide an incentive for a laborer to work is to arrange a wage payment that will prove more attractive to the laborer than, for example, the leisure alternative.

In the context of entrepreneurial opportunities, however, the notion of an incentive is quite different. Incentive in this case is for the discovery of an opportunity for net gain. Were the opportunity already perceived, no further incentive would be required to persuade the agent to exploit it. However little we know about the ways different entrepreneurs discover what they discover, almost all such discoveries would not be made were there not the possibility of personally attractive, desirable outcomes.

For the sequence of entrepreneurial discoveries that constitutes the market process, the system of incentives is spiced and sharpened by the awareness that market opportunities are to be found only where they have been overlooked by others. It is here that entrepreneurial incentives and the conditions required for dynamically competitive markets intersect crucially and fruitfully.

It is now fairly well understood that the dynamic competition upon which market systems rely for their effectiveness calls for only one basic prerequisite—freedom of entry.[10] If incumbent firms are aware that others are free to enter whenever they sense an opportunity for profit, this causes incumbents to concentrate on discovering yet more effective ways of efficiently serving the consumer. This means that the entrepreneurial discovery of better ways of serving the consumer is spurred both by the incentives provided to nonincumbents by their perception of as yet unexploited pure profit opportunities and by the incentives provided to incumbents by the threat of losses that may ensue from the entry of competing entrepreneurs. I will now consider the rather limited public policy implications of the insights into the entrepreneurial process developed thus far in this chapter.

THE ENTREPRENEURIAL PROCESS AND PUBLIC POLICY

The entrepreneurial process is a continuous, endless process of discovery. The opportunities for discovery embrace both those consisting of the discovery of errors by others trading (or expected to trade) in markets now or in the future and the discovery of unsuspected resources or technical feasibilities that constitute genuine innovation.

The solution to society's economic problem (identified by F. A. Hayek as that of the coordination and mobilization of scattered scraps of information) calls for a steady series of successful discoveries. Moreover, once the possibility for discovery is introduced it becomes increasingly apparent that Hayek's coordination problem can, in principle, be extended to cover the opportunities for innovation as well.[11]

> The current price of natural gas and the current level of its consumption may be fully coordinated with one another and with other current prices and market activities (informed by the most up-to-date intelligence). Yet this price may be "too high" and consumption "too low" from the perspective (that may, in several years, be provided by technological or other discoveries) of the possibilities, say of tapping solar energy.[12]

If society has a stake in encouraging the solution to Hayek's coordination problem, this must surely extend to the intertemporal coordination opportunities that can be exploited only by innovative, entrepreneurial breakthroughs. How can society achieve this? What policies can, without incurring unacceptable costs, stimulate or release the potential for discovery that exists in all motivated human beings that make up a society's population?

It should be clear that stimulating the potential for discovery must be a task rather different from that of stimulating or coaxing out a greater supply of a given scarce resource or service. The potential availability of a given scarce resource is usually treated by economists as capable of being expressed by a supply curve. Such a curve relates various potentially available quantities of the resource to the resource prices capable of eliciting these quantities. To command larger available quantities, such a supply curve generally reports, it will be necessary to offer more attractive resource prices. With respect to entrepreneurial talent, however, we are not able to discourse in this fashion. The knowledge of value is never an item deliberately sought after. Nor do those possessing the knowledge of value consciously treat it as a deployable or salable resource.

It is simply not useful to treat entrepreneurship in terms of a supply curve. The exercise of specific quantities of entrepreneurship involves no identifiable cost or required amounts. Yet it is impossible to treat the degree of entrepreneurial discovery prevailing in a society as totally unrelated to public policy. There are two separate ways policy may in principle affect the emergence of entrepreneurial discovery. The first relates to policy that may affect the entrepreneurial attitudes and character of a population. The second relates to policy that may, with a population of given entrepreneurial attitude, stimulate it to be more alert to entrepreneurial opportunities. Arthur Seldon has remarked that the qualities that make for entrepreneurial alertness (such as restive temperament, thirst for adventure, ambition, and imagination) may be nurtured or suppressed. "They are presumably similar in Germany on both sides of the Iron Curtain, in Korea North and South of the 38th parallel, on both sides of the China Sea separating the Chinese mainland from the island of Taiwan, but the results are very different according to the institutions created by government."[13]

Other authors emphasize both access to profit opportunities and security of property rights. The opportunity to obtain profit is by itself not yet sufficient for the emergence of entrepreneurial activity. "The entrepreneur must also be reasonably assured that he may keep entrepreneurial profits that he legitimately acquires. Thus certain institutional practices in a market economy will tend to encourage a high level of entrepreneurial activity, especially (1) a free and open economy that permits equal access to entrepreneurial opportunities, (2) guarantees of ownership in property legally acquired, and (3) stability of institutional practices that establish points 1 and 2."[14] Let us see further what these two kinds of policy goals involve and what, if anything, can be concretely proposed toward their implementation.

Nurturing the Entrepreneurial Spirit

Seldon's references to the Iron Curtain, the thirty-eighth parallel, and the China Sea on the one hand express a conviction that the profound institutional differences that relate to the areas separated by these boundaries have much to do with nurturing or suppressing the thirst for adventure, ambition, and imagination. On the other hand, these references reflect a willingness to recognize the possibility, at least, that ethnic and geographical factors may be important in determining the extent to which a population displays an entrepreneurial attitude.

It should be apparent that in regard to the ways geographic and ethnic factors do or do not affect entrepreneurial spirit our knowledge is woefully meager. Moreover, research effort applied to these questions has been extremely limited. Nonetheless a beginning has been made. Interesting work has, for example, been done by Benjamin Gilad in bringing to bear existing studies that point to a relationship between alternative institutional and cultural environments—particularly as these impinge on the freedom of the individual—and human qualities germane to the entrepreneurial attitude.[15] It remains to be seen whether further research in this area strengthens the insights so far suggested and whether such results offer ideas capable of being translated into meaningful public policy proposals. It is nonetheless worth noting that the conclusions to which Gilad's work points—that economic growth may depend upon the stimulus to the entrepreneurial spirit supplied by an environment of economic freedom—run precisely counter to that implied by earlier economists, who saw economic growth as requiring economic regimentation.[16]

Stimulating Alertness

Research into techniques of stimulating the alertness of a given group of persons is fragmentary and unsystematic.[17] Many discussions of entrepreneurial alertness have relied on the "plain, unremarkable statement of a fundamental facet of human nature" *that human beings tend to notice what it is their interest to notice.*[18] The social significance of a market system does not reside in the beauty of the allocation pattern under equilibrium conditions. Rather, it rests upon the capacity of markets to translate the errors made in the immediate past into opportunities for pure entrepreneurial profit of direct interest to potential entrepreneurs. Features of the institutional landscape that strengthen the linkage between socially significant opportunities and the likelihood and security of associated entrepreneurial gain (such as those proposed by Hébert and Link, note 14 this chapter) clearly improve the chances for entrepreneurial discovery. The linkage between dynamic competition and entrepreneurship is of direct relevance here. The incentives provided by freedom of entrepreneurial entry, as they act on incumbent entrepreneurs and potential entrants, are relevant in devising ways to stimulate entrepreneurial alertness and discovery.

THE DANGER OF TAKING THE ENTREPRENEUR FOR GRANTED

Perhaps the most important contribution that the recent renewal of professional interest in the entrepreneurial process can make toward public policy is to stimulate a general awareness of the grave dangers that accrue from the error of taking the entrepreneur and his role for granted. No doubt there were eras in the history of the development of economic understanding when this kind of error was relatively less critical. No doubt an understanding of the general pattern of results produced by the entrepreneurial process was more important, for such eras, than an understanding of that process itself. But to make the error of imagining that there really is nothing for entrepreneurs to do, that economic processes are somehow propelled without the entrepreneurial spirit and genius for discovery, is to fall prey to a way of thinking that can harmfully affect social policy. To take the entrepreneur for granted is to overlook the dangers of regulatory or fiscal or antitrust policies that block or discourage entrepreneurial entry into perceived avenues for profitable activity. The entrepreneurial spirit, the potential for discovery, is always waiting to be released. Human ingenuity is irrepressible and perennial, and its release requires an environment free from special privileges or blockages of new entrants. For the successful allocative functioning of the market, and for the stimulation of dynamic growth, the entrepreneur must not be taken for granted.

NOTES

1. J. A. Schumpeter, *Theorie der wirtschaftlichen Entwicklung* (Leipzig, 1912); English translation, *Theory of Economic Development* (Cambridge: Harvard University Press, 1934). See also Schumpeter, *Capitalism, Socialism and Democracy* (New York: Harper and Row, 1942).

2. Harvey Leibenstein, *General X-Efficiency Theory and Economic Development* (New York: Oxford University Press, 1978), p. 9.

3. See the statement by Joan Robinson, *Economic Journal* 73 (March 1963): 125: "The strong case for the price mechanism lies in the allocation of scarce resources between competing uses. . . . But no one has ever been able to make out a case (on grounds of economic efficiency) for *laissez-faire* in the sphere of investment." See also Israel M. Kirzner, "On the Premises of Growth Economics," *New Individualist Review* 3, 1 (Summer 1963): 20–28.

4. See also Israel M. Kirzner, "Entrepreneurship and the Future of Capitalism," in *Entrepreneurship and the Outlook for America,* ed. J. Backman (New York: Free Press, 1983), reprinted in this volume, chap. 7.

5. L. H. Robbins, *Nature and Significance of Economic Science,* 2d ed. (London: Macmillan, 1935).

6. G. L. S. Shackle, *Epistemics and Economics* (Cambridge: Cambridge University Press, 1972).

7. Israel M. Kirzner, "Hayek, Knowledge, and Market Processes," in *Perception, Opportunity, and Profit* (Chicago: University of Chicago Press, 1979).

8. Israel M. Kirzner, "Uncertainty, Discovery and Human Action: A Study of the Entrepreneurial Profile in the Misesian System," in *Method, Process, and Austrian Economics: Essays in Honor of Ludwig von Mises,* ed. Israel M. Kirzner (Lexington, Mass.: D. C. Heath, 1982), reprinted in this volume, chap. 3.

9. This and the succeeding sections of this chapter draw on my approach to understanding the role of the entrepreneur as developed in earlier works, especially *Competition and Entrepreneurship* (Chicago: University of Chicago Press, 1973) and *Perception, Opportunity, and Profit* (Chicago: University of Chicago Press, 1979).

10. See Kirzner, *Competition and Entrepreneurship,* pp. 97 ff. See also, D. T. Armentano, *Antitrust and Monopoly: Anatomy of a Policy Failure* (New York: Wiley, 1982), chaps. 1 and 2.

11. F. A. Hayek, *The Road to Serfdom* (Chicago: University of Chicago Press, 1944).

12. Kirzner, "Entrepreneurship and the Future of Capitalism," p. 161.

13. A. Seldon, "Preface," in Kirzner et al., *The Prime Mover of Progress: The Entrepreneur in Capitalism and Socialism,* ed. A. Seldon (London: Institute of Economic Affairs, 1980), pp. xi–xii.

14. R. F. Hébert and A. N. Link, *The Entrepreneur: Mainstream Views and Radical Critiques* (New York: Praeger, 1982), p. 11.

15. B. Gilad, "On Encouraging Entrepreneurship: An Interdisciplinary Approach," *Journal of Behavioral Economics* 11 (Summer 1982): 132–63.

16. See, for example, K. de Schweinitz, "Free Enterprise in a Growth World," *Southern Economic Journal* 29 (October 1962): 103–10.

17. See also N. Balabkins and A. Aizsilnieks, *Entrepreneur in a Small Country* (Hicksville, N.Y.: Exposition Press, 1975), chap. 10; A. V. Bruno and T. T. Tyebjee, "The Environment for Entrepreneurship," in *Encyclopedia of Entrepreneurship,* ed. C. A. Kent, D. L. Sexton, and K. H. Vesper (Englewood Cliffs, N.J.: Prentice-Hall, 1982).

18. A. Seldon, "Preface," p. xvi.

There is a double meaning attached to the word "meaning" in the title of this chapter.[1] The title indicates that, as one objective, we have to distinguish two separate meanings that have been intended by the notion of market process (and, in doing so, to make it very clear which of these meanings is preferred by the writer). As a second objective, we shall attempt to answer the question: "What does the market process mean for human liberty?"; in other words, we shall try to assess the significance of the market process view for an understanding of the free society.

These two tasks that we have set ourselves are by no means entirely separate. As we shall see, one's assessment of the likely economic achievements of a free society depends rather heavily on the way in which one sees the market and, in particular, on the character of the market process that one is prepared to recognize. It may be helpful, in assisting the reader to make his way through the pages ahead, to briefly state the writer's own position in advance. This position can be expressed in the form of a series of assertions: (a) under a system in which private property rights are respected, a free society is one in which economic endeavor flows predominantly through the market; (b) the market is in a continual state of flux and is never in or near a state of equilibrium; (c) this continual flux comprises *two* distinct layers of changing phenomena; (d) one of these two layers of changing phenomena is made up of *exogenous* changes, changes in preferences, population, resource availabilities and technical possibilities; (e) the second layer of change is endogenous—changes systematically induced as market forces move constantly to equilibrate the constellations of forces operating at any given moment; (f) the latter layer of change, consisting of systematic equilibrating tendencies (which never do manage to become fully completed before being disrupted by new exogenous changes) is responsible for the degree of allocative efficiency

From *The Meaning of Market Process: Essays in the Development of Modern Austrian Economics*, ed. Israel M. Kirzner (New York and London: Routledge, 1992), 38–54. Reprinted by permission; the original source is *General Equilibrium or Market Process, Neoclassical and Austrian Theories of Economics*, ed. A. Bosch, P. Kalikowski, and R. Veit (Tubingen: J. C. B. Mohr, 1990), 61–76. © Mohr Siebeck Tübingen. The cross-reference to other chapters is to *The Meaning of Market Process*.

and of growth potential that market economies display; (g) it is to the latter layer of equilibrative change that the term "market process" properly refers; (h) for market processes to work, the essential requirement is freedom for competitive entrepreneurial *entry*; (i) thus complete economic freedom of the individual is necessary if the market economy is to do its work; (j) moreover, the point to be emphasized is not merely that a society of free individuals can (counterintuitively) achieve a measure of coordination, but that—even more counterintuitively—*only* a society of free individuals is able to harness the forces of entrepreneurial competition to make and disseminate those discoveries upon which allocative efficiency and growth depend; (k) this leads directly to the Misesian proposition that only in a market society is it possible to solve the problem of economic calculation; a socialist society, were it to be isolated from contact with market economies, must tend toward inefficiency and economic failure.

As indicated these assertions are *not* universally accepted, even among the small subset of economists who profess a market process view. But in order to develop the position we have here outlined, and to consider the alternative meaning to the idea of market process, we must first briefly contrast the market process view (no matter which variant of it we wish to adopt) with the dominant approach in modern microeconomics—the equilibrium theory of the market.

THE EQUILIBRIUM VIEW OF THE MARKET

For most of the twentieth-century history of microeconomics, economists have, with rare exceptions, understood market phenomena in terms of equilibrium models. In other words, economists have seen the explanations to be provided for market data—prices, methods of production, sizes of industries—as able to be found in the values for these variables that would be consistent with market equilibrium. Take the simplest (and most widely used) example of microeconomic analysis, the perfectly competitive market for a single commodity. In applying this analysis to the market price for any given product, economists start out by assuming that this price is in fact that price at which quantity supplied equals quantity demanded. Underlying this approach is the apparent conviction that equilibrating forces are so powerful that it is an acceptable first approximation to the truth to assume that markets have already, at any given time, attained the neighborhood of equilibrium. Observed changes in market data must, in this approach, be explained as reflecting corresponding changes in the underlying data. Observed discrepancies between the data of a market and the values to be expected on the basis of an adopted equilibrium model are taken to suggest, not any inadequacy in the assumption of attained equilibrium, but rather the possible relevance of some other, possibly more complicated equilibrium model.[2]

This is not the place to develop a complete critique of this dominant equilibrium approach to microeconomics. Nonetheless we mention one of the key objections that have been raised against it. This key objection is that, by concentrating exclusively on states of equilibrium, theory offers no explanation of the equilibrating process itself. As stated earlier, the unstated premise of the equilibrium approach is that equilibration processes are powerful and rapid—but this seems to assume away the task of explaining the nature of such processes. Economists dissatisfied with the dominant approach have become more and more aware of the formidable challenge to economic science which the phenomenon of equilibration poses.[3] As economists have become sensitive to problems of knowledge and learning, and of how these relate to the possibility of equilibration, these economists have become more and more skeptical of approaches which simply assume that equilibration occurs—and occurs instantaneously.

It must be acknowledged that the dominant approach has not entirely failed to address some of these difficulties. But it seems fair to assert that it has addressed these difficulties not by modifying its adherence to the complete equilibrium assumption, but by incorporating new variables into its equilibrium models—in fact, by *extending* the scope asserted for the equilibrium principle. For example, increased awareness of some of the problems raised for equilibrium economics by the phenomenon of ignorance has led economists to include the cost of ignorance-removal (i.e., the cost of learning) into their models. Thus, as it turns out, attention to problems of ignorance has not only not weakened the grip of the equilibrium assumption; quite the contrary, it has *extended* the scope of this assumption. Economists need no longer assume that some necessary process of equilibration has, somehow, rapidly been completed before we begin our work; they may claim that, at each and every instant in time, taking all relevant transactions costs (including the costs of learning) into appropriate account, each market situation *must* necessarily *always* be in equilibrium.[4] To assume otherwise would be to assume that some market participants have failed to take advantage of opportunities for mutual gain through exchange—even when the necessary costs of overcoming ignorance are so low as to render such failure inefficient. For the dominant approach, to admit such possibilities is to admit the unthinkable— irrational behavior.

To sum up, the dominant position in economics has tended to keep equilibrium models at the very center of market theory; it has done so by translating every apparent discrepancy (between the theory and reality) into a more complicated equilibrium theory based on the necessary costs of ignorance-removal.

THE MARKET PROCESS THEORISTS

Market process theorists of all varieties share in common a profound dissatisfaction with the way equilibrium economics looks at the world. Whereas, as we have seen, the latter see market phenomena, at each moment in time, as accurately expressing the balance of forces relevant to the underlying data of that moment, market process theorists see things quite differently. The constellations of prices, product qualities, methods of production and incomes observed at any given instant are not at all taken to be the relevant equilibrium values. (Some process theorists question the very meaningfulness of the notion of "equilibrium values.") Rather these variables are seen, at any given moment, to be subject to changes which market forces are likely to generate—even if we insulate, for analytical purposes, from the impact exercised by exogenous changes in the underlying variables.

Nor are these changes which endogenous market forces are likely to generate seen as mechanically determined by the relative strengths and speeds of these forces. Market process theorists do not conceive of these forces as operating in deterministic fashion. They see them, rather, as understandable only in subtle terms to which dominant microeconomic analysis is singularly irrelevant. For example, equilibrium theorists would approach a phenomenon of a price difference (for what are indeed different samples of the very same commodity) in different parts of the same market by focusing on the costs of learning about the availability of other prices. Once these costs are plugged in, the assumption is that at all times the different parts of the market are in equilibrium with each other. If we find a tendency for such price differentials to disappear, standard economics would explain the rate of disappearance as rigidly reflecting the underlying changes in the costs of learning (about remaining price differentials). Market process theorists, on the other hand, would view the process during which price differentials gradually disappear in much less deterministic terms. As we shall elaborate in more detail later, they would focus on the possibility of learning occurring not through deliberately absorbing the perceived costs of learning but through the phenomena of surprise and discovery. These phenomena, central to market process theory, are simply not reducible to the kinds of problems with which equilibrium economics, based solidly and exclusively on the analysis of rational decision making in a world free of surprises, is equipped to deal.

At this stage we are perhaps ready to identify the alternative versions of market process theory. Let us couch our discussion in terms of (a) the *underlying variables* (UVs), identified conventionally as preferences, resource availabilities and technological possibilities, and (b) the *induced variables* (IVs), consisting of the prices, methods of production and quantities and qualities of outputs which the market at any given time generates under the impact of the UVs. As we have seen, equilibrium economics postulates that at each and every instant the actual market values of the IVs are those equilibrium values predetermined by the relevant values of the UVs. Any apparent discrepancy is explained away by postulating that some relevant UV has somehow been overlooked (as, for example, the costs of overcoming ignorance had been overlooked in earlier equilibrium models). Market process theorists, however, claim that the movements of IVs in the market are *not* fully determined by the values of the UVs. The former retain a degree of freedom with respect to the latter. We may now identify the alternative variants of market process theory we have referred to.

One variant identifies market process as the actual sequence of values of the IVs over time (Lachmann 1986a). Now this sequence, clearly, reflects the *joint* effect of several possible sets of forces for change: (a) the changes in the UVs during this period of time can be understood, even in the market process view, as of course having a continual impact on the sequence of IV values; (b) quite apart from changes in the UVs we can see how any adjustment processes (equilibrating or otherwise) through which given UV values tend gradually to become reflected in IV values can be expected to contribute to the sequence of changing IV values during the period under discussion. By focusing on the joint effect of these sets of forces for change, this first possibility for defining "the market process" thus refuses to accord any real analytical significance to the distinction between these two sets of forces (a) and (b). In Professor Lachmann's terminology the first set of forces are described as disequilibrating changes, the second as equilibrating changes; but the two sets are held to be so intertwined as to defy separate analytical treatment. This is reinforced by the circumstance that, in Professor Lachmann's view, the inevitable presence of disequilibrating changes radically undermines the determinacy of any equilibrating changes that might, in their absence, have been imagined. This is so, in his view, because the presence of the disequilibrating changes renders it impossible for market participants to identify with clarity the steps that need to be taken to achieve equilibrium.

The second variant of market process theory, and the one which this writer believes should be emphasized, defines the market process exclusively in terms of the second of the two sets of forces for change identified in the preceding paragraph. The concept of market process, on this understanding of it, is an analytical one. We distinguish, among the forces causing changes in the IVs, a distinct set of forces unleashed, at each moment, by the *absence* of equilibrium. The changes induced by these forces constitute the market process. These changes would continue to occur, constituting the market process in its purest analytical form, even if, as of a given date, all changes in the UVs were suspended. If we wish to analyze the market process it is therefore most useful to conduct mental experiments against the imagined background of unchanging UVs. In full reality, of course, the market process never does proceed in pure form. Rather, what we encounter over time is a mass of changes in IVs that reflect, in addition, the continual changes in the UVs. Thus these changes in IVs express not just *the* market process, but the total impact of innumerable separate (and possibly colliding) market processes set in motion, at different points in time, by the discrepancies, existing at these respective points in time, between actual IVs and the relevant respective equilibrium values for the IVs. These separate market processes run into one another, colliding with or reinforcing each other, so that the actual sequences of IV values are seen as highly complex outcomes of numerous interacting sets of forces. It is the central tenet of market process theory, under this present variant of it, that, despite the complexities thus introduced by continually changing UVs, the essential character of the market process, as a matter of historical experience, does remain largely intact. In fact, it will be our claim, it is this character of the market process which is the dominant feature of real world market economies; it is through our understanding of this market process that we can understand how market economies work.

For the remainder of this chapter we shall use the term "market process" to connote this meaning of the term, unless we specify otherwise. It may be useful, before proceeding to develop an outline of market process theory (and its significance for the possibility of a prosperous free society), to re-emphasize, in the light of our adopted identification of the notion of market process, how sharply different the market process view of the market economy is from that which we have earlier seen to be the equilibrium theory view of it.

For market process theorists the central thread of change that permits us to understand the market is that of the market process. If we wish to understand the IV values at a given moment, we can do so by referring to the course of the market process until that moment. If we wish to ground our understanding of the market in basic theory, that basic theory must be the theory of what it is that shapes the course of the market process. If we wish to evaluate the significance of the market for human well-being, we must do so by evaluating the impact upon such well-being of the market process. Equilibrium models turn out, for the market process view, to be pictures from which the most important features of the market have been excluded. Such models start by assuming that there is no scope for market processes at all.

THE CHARACTER OF THE MARKET PROCESS

The central feature of the market process, to which we wish to draw attention, concerns the role in it played by ignorance and by discovery. The root insight is that disequilibrium consists in mutual ignorance on the part of potential market participants. We take it for granted that such ignorance cannot persist indefinitely. Sooner or later unexploited opportunities for mutual gain must come to be discovered. It is because the existence of such unexploited opportunities—due entirely to mutual ignorance—are so likely to be eventually discovered that this initial situation is described as a state of disequilibrium.

The market process, then, consists of those changes that express the sequence of discoveries that follow the initial ignorance that constituted the disequilibrium state. We describe this sequence of discoveries as constituting an *equilibrating* process, but we must circumscribe this description by a number of qualifications and cautionary observations. The equilibrating character of the process follows naturally from the circumstance that it is made up, presumably, of corrective discoveries concerning earlier ignorance. Such discoveries lead to the elimination of remaining unexploited opportunities for mutual gain. In the ultimate, when no pockets of ignorance remain, we will be left with a market in full equilibrium. As long as the UVs remain unchanged, the attained absence of ignorance will ensure that all exchanges completed in any one period will be repeated without change in each succeeding similar period. But the equilibrating character of the market process, as we have described it, should not be misunderstood.

First, we emphasize, the fact that the market process is equilibrative does not imply, of course, that equilibrium is in fact ever attained. In any real world, with frequent changes in the UVs, equilibrating processes are continually interrupted by UV changes which initiate fresh, equilibrating processes. None of these processes can be expected to proceed to completion. All that we claim is that the forces for mutual discovery, and for the elimination of ignorance, are constantly at work.

Second, we do not claim that each and every "discovery" is in fact corrective. Many "discoveries" turn out to be mistaken; earlier ignorance may turn out to be increased rather than eroded. Some segments of the market process may thus in fact be disequilibrating. If we maintain, nonetheless, that the market process can fairly be described, in general terms, as equilibrating, this is because of a conviction that in the face of initial ignorance there is a systematic tendency for genuine discoveries, rather than spurious ones, to be made.

Third, the possibility of enhanced error rather than of genuine corrective discovery must certainly gain plausibility as a result of the universal circumstance of continual change in the UVs. Genuine discovery of earlier ignorance does not point unambiguously to improved decision making for the future—since the discoverer must now speculate about the likelihood of new changes.

To emphasize the centrality of equilibration in the market process is not, of course, to concede the appropriateness of equilibrium economics. For reasons already given, market process theorists argue that the major features of the market that call for explanation call for process analysis rather than equilibrium theory. A picture of the world as at all times at or in the neighborhood of equilibrium assumes away far too many important features of reality to be useful for economic understanding. On the other hand, to insist that the real world is unlikely ever to be close to equilibrium is by no means to concede that markets are not powerfully equilibrative. The market process view sees the market as displaying, at all times, the effects of powerful forces encouraging genuine and valuable discovery. This view argues that, to understand how markets work, it is necessary to toe the fine line that rejects both the assumption of constant, instantaneous equilibration and the opposite assumption that the sequence of values of what we have called the IVs is one essentially disengaged from the sequence of UVs.

THE NATURE OF DISCOVERY

In describing the market process as a series of steps correcting earlier ignorance, we do not wish it to be understood that this process consists in a series of deliberate acts of learning. One might indeed describe a sequenced series of deliberate acts of learning as an adjustment process transforming ignorance into knowledge. But the market process is not to be understood on such a pattern. We must distinguish sharply between those acts of discovery of which the market process consists, and the acts of deliberate learning which, unless by accident, form no part of the market process.

A deliberate act of learning occurs when one recognizes one's lack of knowledge, is aware of the way in which this lack can be rectified and at what cost, and believes that the value to be gained by learning more than justifies the costs of learning. The starting point is awareness of one's ignorance—in fact an awareness sufficiently detailed to permit one to identify the specific items of knowledge that one lacks. The endpoint of the learning process is possession of the sought-after knowledge; but such possession involves no essential elements of surprise. When one researches a fact from an encyclopedia, looks up the meaning and spelling of a strange word in a dictionary or examines a street map of a strange city, one need not encounter anything surprising. One knew one's ignorance; one has not been surprised to discover that one had unknowingly been laboring under a misapprehension, that the world turns out to be quite different from what one had anticipated. The kind of discovery steps we have described as making up the market process, on the other hand, are characterized precisely by the surprise involved by the discovery, and by the corresponding earlier unawareness of the nature of one's ignorance. A simple example will illustrate the point.

Consider a market in which two prices prevail for the same commodity in different parts of the same market. Equilibrium theory, of course, would deny such a possibility outright and claim that it can be salvaged only by postulating *different qualities* of commodity (more carefully defined) or the existence of barriers separating the market into *separate* markets. For equilibrium theory such a barrier might be the presence of ignorance that it is costly to remove. Market process theory insists that the possibility of the same commodity selling at different prices within the same market can be entirely accounted for by the phenomenon of costlessly removable unknown ignorance. Unknown ignorance is ignorance concerning which one is unaware. Suppose that one buys fruit for $2, when the same fruit is openly available for $1 in a neighboring store which one has just passed but overlooked. Then it is clear that one might costlessly have been able to know where to buy the fruit for $1, and in fact paid $2 for it only because one did not know of the possibility of costlessly commanding the needed information—in other words, one has suffered from being unaware of one's costlessly removable ignorance. When one discovers that the fruit for which one has been paying $2 is in fact available for $1, this comes as a surprise. The discovery itself cannot, given the circumstances, have been undertaken deliberately; after all one did not know anything existed to be discovered.

When one theorizes that, pursuant to Jevons's law of indifference, such price differences tend to disappear under the impact of competitive market forces, one is postulating, we wish to assert, a series of spontaneous discoveries that tend to eliminate the price differences. We assume that the existence of a price differential will attract notice. People who paid $2 will notice that others have paid $1; people who accepted $1 will notice that others have received $2. Others may notice the possibility of winning pure profit by buying at $1 and selling at $2; the result of these discoveries— none of which has deliberately been searched for—is increased purchases attempted to be made at $1 and increased sales attempted to be made at $2. This leads to the elimination of price differentials. It is not in general possible, we shall argue, to imagine the elimination of such price differentials in the absence of spontaneous discovery. If, for example, we imagine costly steps deliberately taken to search for better prices, then we face the problem of explaining why such steps had not been taken earlier. (One might of course postulate that the sequence of market events systematically lowers the costs of such deliberate search. But one has then left the realm of general theory for that of *ad hoc* assumptions.) Sooner or later one must have resort to spontaneous discovery—even if only the discovery of the possibility of profitable search itself.

The emphasis we have placed on the discovery (rather than deliberate search) character of the market process is of considerable importance. Processes of deliberate search are, in a definite sense, fully determinate. At each point in the search process one knows, as it were, exactly as much as one has chosen to know. The amount one has chosen to know is completely determined by the value of what one might seek to know and by the costs of search. At each point in time one possesses the optimal degree of knowledge (and thus also the optimal degree of ignorance). Were the market process to be of this character it would be a completely determinate process—one fully explicable in terms of equilibrium theorizing. That is, one would not then describe the market process as following a course from disequilibrium to equilibrium, but rather as following a course from equilibrium with a great deal of (optimal) ignorance to equilibrium with a lesser (but, of course, still optimal) degree of ignorance.

What we have been underlining, on the other hand, is that in the market process view the passage leading from many prevailing prices toward a single price is not at all determined, but nonetheless systematic and expressive of a powerful tendency. There can never be a guarantee that anyone will notice that of which he is utterly ignorant; the most complete rationality of decision making in the world cannot ensure search for that the existence of which is wholly unsuspected. Yet we submit that few will maintain that initial ignorance concerning desirable opportunities costlessly available can be expected to endure indefinitely. We recognize, surely, that human beings are motivated to notice that which it is to their benefit to notice. We identify this general motivation with the alertness which every human being possesses, to greater or lesser degree. This omnipresent human alertness makes it inconceivable that market participants can be expected indefinitely to continue to pay more for an item than they in fact need to; or that they can be expected indefinitely to continue to accept less in payment for an item than they are in fact able to command. We are convinced that specifically unpredictable acts of discovery will add up to a systematic erosion of unjustified price differentials. Because of its non-deterministic, non-mechanical character, this market process of discovery does not lend itself to the kind of modeling central to equilibrium economics. Yet the systematic nature of the process requires that we not permit any methodological predilections in favor of formal modeling techniques to obscure vitally important features of the market economy.

UNDERSTANDING MARKETS

All this provides us, in the market process view, with a sensitive understanding of market phenomena that goes significantly beyond the scope of equilibrium economics. The market process view focuses on the incentives offered by disequilibrium market conditions for those discoveries that add up to systematic equilibrative tendencies. It sees these incentives as continually attracting the attention of potentially new competitors; it recognizes that the attention of such new competitors must take the form of entrepreneurial perception of exploitable profit opportunities.

This understanding of markets, then, refuses to see the constant market agitation initiated by jostling competitors and innovative entrepreneurial upstarts as disturbing elements to be filtered out in order to perceive the underlying stable elements corresponding to market equilibrium positions. Rather the market process view sees in this constant market agitation the essential sets of market forces that permit us to comprehend what is happening in markets. This view sees the apparent chaos of market agitation as not chaotic at all; quite the contrary, it is in this apparently chaotic sequence of market events that the market's orderliness resides. The central meaning of the movements which we continually observe in markets is that discoveries are being made concerning overlooked market gaps. Each such overlooked opportunity constitutes at the same time (a) a disequilibrium feature in the market, and (b) an exploitable opportunity for pure profit. It is the incentive offered in the form of pure profit that inspires and motivates those entrepreneurial discoveries that tend to correct earlier features of disequilibrium.

To be sure, the market process view emphatically recognizes that at any given time the market has not yet eliminated all features of disequilibrium—if for no other reason than the circumstance of continually changing UVs. But this view also insists we recognize the character of the forces at all times impinging on the market—forces inspired by entrepreneurial alertness toward opportunities for pure profits.

This way of understanding the market applies, *mutatis mutandis,* both to the short and to the long run. Pure profit opportunities may offer themselves in three distinct forms, which share in common the applicability of the insights of the preceding paragraphs. Pure profit may occur (a) as a result of pure arbitrage, buying and selling simultaneously at different prices; (b) as a result of "intertemporal arbitrage," buying an item at a low price and selling it later at a higher price; and (c) as a result of a creative act of production, buying resources at low prices and selling a product innovatively created out of them later at a high price. In each of these cases pure profit occurs because the market had not been fully adjusted to the possibilities it itself contained (either immediately attainable opportunities or subsequently attainable possibilities). The possibility of winning pure profit motivates the alertness of entrepreneurs and inspires judicious and creative decisions to overcome the initial ignorance of which those possibilities are the market counterpart. The entrepreneurial alertness which notices pure arbitrage possibilities today is fundamentally similar to that which presciently envisages the profit possibilities to be obtained through intertemporal arbitrage. And it is analytically parallel, at least, to that alertness to the possibilities that can be opened up through innovation that inspires the creativity and inventiveness of entrepreneurial producers. The market agitation that expresses these kinds of entrepreneurial alertness is of a single pattern. The kinds of equilibrative process which these respective kinds of market agitation initiate achieve corresponding adjustments in the allocation of resources and of products. Pure arbitrage tends to ensure the exploitation of all available opportunities for mutually profitable exchange; intertemporal arbitrage tends to avoid "wasteful" intertemporal allocation (and thus, where warranted, to build up toward the optimal capital structure); the entrepreneurship exercised in innovative production tends to generate technological progress.

To understand the achievements of the market process in this way should not, we emphasize once again, blind us to the possibilities of entrepreneurial failures. Pure losses, rather than pure profits, may and do emerge. The market process that we have outlined offers a systematic tendency, rather than a sure-fire machine-like trajectory. Moreover the assurance that we feel concerning the overall tendency of the market process is clearly dependent upon the rate at which unanticipated changes in UVs impinge on the market. Were these changes to be so drastic in their volatility and rate of occurrence as to swamp the discovery potential inherent in entrepreneurial alertness, we could hardly expect the market process to manifest itself, in the real world, in a manner able to generate order in the face of apparent chaos. The market agitation thus generated by chaotic change in UVs *could* thus fail to display the underlying tendencies toward orderliness which entrepreneurial processes under less extreme conditions set into motion.

But economic science, from its beginnings, has been moored in the empirical circumstance of markets that do display a certain order. The scientific challenge has been, not to predict an orderliness that has not yet been observed, but to account for the counterintuitive circumstance of observed market order, in the absence of centralized control. It is in meeting this challenge that market theory, ever since Adam Smith, has grappled to achieve an understanding of markets. The market process approach, fully in line with this scientific tradition, sees a significant advance in the understanding of markets as obtainable from insights into the competitive-entrepreneurial discovery process that constitutes, in this approach, the essential core of market phenomena through time.

MARKET PROCESS AND INDIVIDUAL LIBERTY

The market process approach permits us, in fact, to recognize that the counterintuitive character of economists' invisible-hand theorems concerning markets masks an even more surprising discovery. Not only is it the case, as traditional economics has demonstrated since Adam Smith, that market efficiency can prevail in spite of the absence of centralized direction. It turns out, as it happens, that the market process approach shows that such absence of centralized direction is in fact *necessary*, if the kind of coordination (we have seen to be achievable through the market process) is to be attained at all. It is this insight that Mises and Hayek attempted to enunciate in their expositions of the problems of economic calculation that face socialist planners. As has recently been shown (Lavoie 1985a), the failure of post–Second World War economists to appreciate the force, and even the content of the Mises–Hayek position has much to do with their unawareness of the market process view which these Austrian economists—perhaps unselfconsciously—possessed. From an equilibrium approach, the socialist calculation problem appears far from insoluble; once the market process view is understood, the calculation problem assumes far more formidable proportions.

The calculation problem begins, we now understand, from the inevitable circumstance of unsuspected ignorance. This ignorance, as Hayek explained over forty years ago (Hayek 1949b), takes the form of *dispersed information*. The point is that at any given moment opportunities exist for socially significant exchange and production activities. The ingredients for such opportunities consist of pieces of information concerning resources and products which, if brought together in a single mind, could present clearly identifiable opportunities. The problem is that they are not, at the moment in question, present to any single mind. The primary function of the economic system, Hayek argued, is not to "allocate resources efficiently" but, first of all, to overcome the knowledge problem created by dispersed information. The nature of this knowledge problem must, however, be clearly understood; our discussion of the nature of discovery may be helpful in this regard.

The problem created by dispersed information consists, we shall maintain (see also Chapters 8 and 9[5]), not in the circumstance that those who possess some relevant items of information are ignorant of the complementary items of information, but that they are ignorant of their ignorance. Members of an economy possess items of information whose potential value is quite unknown to them, because they have no inkling concerning the availability of complementary inputs, or of complementary information. *This* ignorance means that, even if the costs of search (that might yield the missing pieces of information) are very low, no search will be undertaken. This kind of unknown ignorance, when confronted by central planners, cannot be systematically or deliberately tackled. Planners simply do not know what to look for: they do not know where or of what kind the knowledge gaps are.

And it is precisely this knowledge problem that the decentralized market economy addresses. The existence of unknown ignorance manifests itself in markets as unnoticed opportunities for pure profits. Such opportunities attract the alertness of entrepreneurs. It is the series of discoveries stimulated by such alertness that constitutes the market process. What the market process achieves, then, is systematic coordination of dispersed pieces of information available—but languishing undreamed of—throughout the economy.

It turns out, then, that individual liberty is not merely one element in the definition of a market economy. It turns out that individual liberty is that ingredient in that definition upon which the success of the market process depends. Individual liberty is not a circumstance in spite of which markets work; it is the crucial circumstance which permits the market process to work. All this leads one to add several observations concerning the meaning of individual liberty.

THE MEANING OF INDIVIDUAL LIBERTY

The market process which we have described depends, we have seen, on individual alertness. Such alertness, we have seen, is manifested principally through the exercise of entrepreneurship, but is in fact present, to some degree, in all individual activity. We have emphasized the importance of entrepreneurial entry as the driving force in the market process. But, more generally, this process depends on individual freedom to pursue perceived opportunities, within the limits of property rights, without arbitrary obstacles being placed in one's path. The central idea, for an understanding of individual liberty, lies in the individual's freedom *to identify for himself what the opportunities are* which he may endeavor to grasp. While this may seem obvious and even trite, we should notice that it is only within the market process system of thinking about markets that this aspect of individual freedom becomes clearly apparent (Kirzner 1979a: ch. 13).

Within an equilibrium view of economic activity there really is no scope for this aspect of freedom. For the equilibrium view there is never any question of perceiving opportunities. For this view each individual is assumed, from the very beginning, to find himself confronted by an array of given resources and a ranked series of given objectives. His decision-task is merely the computational one of arranging the disposition of his resources so as to maximize the value of his attained objectives. (Of course this statement of the decision on the equilibrium view recognizes that one of these objectives may be the intermediate objective of obtaining necessary information through search. But we remind ourselves that, on this view, there is no scope for surprise or discovery.) Freedom, under this conception of the individual decision, can mean no more than that it is the decision maker's own preference function, and no one else's, that determines the relevant ranking of objectives. But the market process view that we have articulated points to a far more fundamental feature of freedom, a feature which philosophers have always understood but which economists, under the blinders imposed by equilibrium theory, seem to have lost sight of. This feature is that the free individual has the freedom to decide what it is that he sees. He is free to make his own discoveries (and, of course, to make his own disastrous entrepreneurial mistakes).

The significance of this feature of freedom, for a discussion of the meaning for liberty of the market process, is not difficult to discern. What a free market does is to offer its participants incentives to make profitable discoveries. This central feature of the free market has *two* implications for individual liberty. First, as already noted, it is able to harness individual freedom to generate the systematic discovery process which is the basis for the coordinative properties of the market. Second, by offering the incentive of pure profit opportunities to alert market participants,[6] the market is affording an outlet through which an essential element of individual freedom can be expressed and exercised. If freedom includes, in an important sense, the freedom to recognize hitherto unnoticed opportunities, and if, as argued, one's ability to recognize opportunities depends vitally on one's ability to seize benefit for oneself from such opportunities, then *only* a system that permits the grasping of opportunities for gain is capable of providing scope for individual liberty (other than the kind of liberty enjoyed by Robinson Crusoe).

Not only is it, then, the case that the workings of markets depend on human liberty; it turns out to be the case that only in the context of free markets is there genuine scope for human liberty in society. For the elucidation of *both* these conclusions, we have seen, an understanding of markets in terms of the market process view has been the indispensable intellectual stepping stone.

NOTES

1. This chapter draws freely on ideas developed in earlier work by the author. See especially Kirzner (1973, 1978, 1979a, 1985a). These ideas have their roots in the writing of Ludwig von Mises and Friedrich A. Hayek.

2. For a discussion of the work of E. H. Chamberlin in this regard, see Kirzner (1973: 114).

3. For an early example of such concern see Hayek (1949c). For a more recent example see Fisher (1983).

4. For an extreme version of this point of view see Stigler (1982).

5. [See "Prices, the Communication of Knowledge, and the Discovery Process" and "Economic Planning and the Knowledge Problem," in Israel M. Kirzner, *Competition, Economic Planning, and the Knowledge Problem* (Carmel, Ind.: Liberty Fund, 2018.)]

6. It should be noted that such opportunities are widely available as part of the economic environment relevant not only to pure entrepreneurs but to all market participants.

REFERENCES

Buchanan, J. M. and Vanberg, V. J. (1990) "The market as a creative process," unpublished manuscript, April.

Fisher, F. M. (1983) *Disequilibrium Foundations of Equilibrium Economics*, Cambridge and New York: Cambridge University Press.

Hayek, F. A. (1949b) "The use of knowledge in society," in *Individualism and Economic Order*, London: Routledge & Kegan Paul (originally published in *American Economic Review* 35 (4) (1945): 519–30).

—— (1949c) "Economics and knowledge," in *Individualism and Economic Order*, London: Routledge & Kegan Paul (originally published in *Economica* 4, February 1937).

Kirzner, I. M. (1973) *Competition and Entrepreneurship*, Chicago, Ill.: University of Chicago Press.

—— (1978) *Wettbewerb und Unternehmertum*, Walter Eucken Institut, Wirtschaftswissenschaftliche und wirtschaftsrechtliche Untersuchungen 14, Tubingen: J. C. B. Mohr/P. Siebeck (translation of *Competition and Entrepreneurship*).

—— (1979a) *Perception, Opportunity and Profit*, Chicago, Ill.: University of Chicago Press.

—— (1985a) *Discovery and the Capitalist Process*, Chicago, Ill.: University of Chicago Press.

Lachmann, L. M. (1986a) *The Market as an Economic Process*, Oxford: Basil Blackwell.

Lavoie, D. (1985a) *Rivalry and Central Planning: The Socialist Calculation Debate Reconsidered*, Cambridge: Cambridge University Press.

Stigler, G. J. (1982) "The economist as preacher," in *The Economist as Preacher and Other Essays*, Chicago, Ill.: University of Chicago Press.

THE MARKET PROCESS: AN AUSTRIAN VIEW

INTRODUCTION

Modern Austrian economics has, building on the work of Mises and Hayek, developed an understanding of the market economy as a process of competitive-entrepreneurial discovery.[1] This paper will survey this way of understanding the market economy, and will emphasize some of the more important implications of this view for purposes of public policy. To illustrate the distinctiveness claimed for the Austrian perspective, we shall draw on some recent work in the modern history of economic thought that has presented a strong case for revising the standard account of the celebrated interwar debate on socialist economic calculation.

We shall proceed by first introducing the Austrian view insofar as it provides a distinctive positive way of understanding the market economy. This will then enable us to appreciate how this positive view strongly suggests the adoption of criteria for normative evaluation that differ sharply from those treated as standard in mainstream welfare economics. This discussion, in turn, will lead to an unorthodox approach to the appraisal of much of the economic regulation to which modern market economies have grown accustomed.

HOW MARKETS WORK

Many writers (including many economists) have held, of course, that markets do not "work" at all, or that they do so only occasionally (or under conditions unlikely to be fulfilled in many real-world contexts). For these writers, markets are seen as likely to generate sub-optimalities,

From *Economic Policy and the Market Process: Austrian and Mainstream Economics*, ed. K. Groenvelt, J. A. H. Maks, and J. Muysken (Amsterdam: Elsevier, 1990), 23–39. Reprinted by permission.

1. The ideas in this paper have been, for the greater part, presented at greater length in various of the writer's works especially, *Competition and Entrepreneurship* (Chicago: University of Chicago Press, 1973), *Perception, Opportunity and Profit* (Chicago: University of Chicago Press, 1979), *Discovery and the Capitalist Process* (Chicago: University of Chicago Press, 1985). In those works detailed references are provided to the earlier Austrian economists, particularly Ludwig von Mises and Friedrich Hayek, whose writings provided the intellectual source for the development of these ideas.

irrationalities, disappointments, or just plain chaos. (Often the experiences of market economies during periods of economic depression are cited as exemplifying such asserted market failures). But throughout the history of economic thought the core of economic thinking has consisted in the analysis of how, or the extent to which, markets do work. With some significant reservations the Austrian view shares with the main current of modern economics an acceptance of the conclusion that, to an important extent, markets do work. Disagreement with mainstream microeconomic thought centers on what one is to understand by the assertion that markets work, and on how one is to explain and account for this systematic functioning by the market.

For mainstream microeconomics markets are held to work in the sense that they are, on standard assumptions, believed to achieve rapid market-clearing. Prices are held to respond swiftly to changes in demand and/or supply conditions, so that excess supply or shortages are rapidly eliminated. To caricature this view somewhat, one may assert that for mainstream economics the market economy is at all times at or close to, the situation corresponding to the general equilibrium configuration relevant to the respective underlying supply and demand conditions. The Austrian view, on the other hand, considers it most unlikely that the market economy is close to the general equilibrium position at any time. Moreover it is highly critical of the mainstream view (that markets are at all times in approximate balance) not merely as being descriptively inaccurate, but more importantly because this emphasis on the assumed continuous approximation of equilibrium states has tended strongly to deflect analytical attention away from the question of how, if at all, do market economies achieve tendencies *toward* equilibrium.

For most Austrian economists (including this writer) markets do typically generate significant tendencies toward equilibrium. For these Austrians the core of economic understanding consists not in the description of equilibrium states (the relevance of which all Austrians would seriously question) but in the explication of the systematic market processes set in motion, at all times, by the disequilibrium features likely to characterize markets at any given date.

From this perspective the answer to the question: "How Do Markets Work?" is briefly as follows: Markets work by providing incentives for the discovery of overlooked opportunities for mutually gainful exchanges. Markets fail to correspond to equilibrium situations because, and to the extent that, market participants have erred in their assessments concerning the presence of exchange opportunities. Such errors become translated, in turn, into opportunities for pure entrepreneurial gain; such opportunities tend to attract attention. As these opportunities are successfully noticed and exploited, the market is nudged *in the direction of* equilibrium (which is itself, in a changing world, never attained). This tendency is not a guaranteed one, since entrepreneurial endeavor may itself introduce new, additional, errors into the system. Moreover, even successful entrepreneurial endeavor proceeds against the background of spontaneously changing underlying conditions of supply and of demand; such change may not only alter what needs to be learned; it may frustrate the very learning process. Nonetheless, most Austrians would argue, markets do seem to work, and their working is to be understood in terms of the competitive-entrepreneurial discovery process here outlined. What follows represents an elaboration of this outline. We commence this outline by discussing what would be required for markets to be in the imaginary state of full equilibrium.

THE EQUILIBRIUM MARKET

We can imagine a market in equilibrium only by imagining a situation where each participant is, in effect, aware of the full extent of the willingness of every other participant to engage in exchange transactions, under all conceivable terms of exchange[2]—and has proceeded to take advantage of such willingness to the fullest possible extent. Such a market would generate a pattern of exchanges such that no conceivable opportunity for mutually gainful exchange had been passed by. If one could imagine absence of change in underlying daily conditions of demand and of supply, we could be sure that this attained array of exchanges would be repeated each day. The market would be in equilibrium; today's pattern of production, exchange, and consumption activities would be identical with those of yesterday and with those of tomorrow.

The "full-awareness" interpretation of market equilibrium itself calls for a certain degree of interpretation. To effect exchange transactions frequently calls for the expenditure of resources. The equilibrium market must then be defined in the context of the relevant transactions costs;

2. F. A. Hayek, "Economics and Knowledge," *Economica*, 1937; reprinted in *Individualism and Economic Order* (London: Routledge and Kegan Paul, 1949).

some otherwise gainful exchange may not be worthwhile after all. In particular, an important part of the costs of transacting may consist of the costs of acquiring relevant information. So that the "full-awareness" interpretation of equilibrium need not mean full knowledge of all relevant information; it may mean merely full knowledge of how to acquire (costly) relevant information. Ignorance may thus be consistent with market equilibrium to the extent that it is known that removal of this ignorance is not worth the cost of such removal.

What is not consistent with market equilibrium is ignorance, the costs of removal of which *would* be well worthwhile. That kind of ignorance would imply (as would the continued existence of any other unexploited profitable opportunity), in turn, utter ignorance of the fact that the cost of ignorance-removal is indeed worthwhile, or utter ignorance of how to proceed to remove it. It is thus "utter ignorance" that is inconsistent with market equilibrium, since it implies an unexploited opportunity for mutually gainful exchange. Notice that what is assumed, in our discussion of equilibrium, is that the existence of an unexploited opportunity for mutual gain cannot be consistent with a calmly continuing state of affairs. Sooner or later such opportunities will be grasped, utter ignorance will dissipate, stirring up the apparently placid waters (which were rendered placid only by that utter ignorance).

THE MEANING OF MARKET DISEQUILIBRIUM

But this latter observation concerning equilibrium is at the same time the clue to what we must mean by the term "market disequilibrium." At first glance it may appear tempting to deny the possibility of market disequilibrium altogether. It is tempting to say that changes in outputs, prices and adopted methods of production need not—even against the background of given tastes and conditions of production—spell disequilibrium (in the sense of a market displaying or correcting its lack of adjustment); instead it might be held that such changes arise out of the systematically changing pattern of transactions or other costs which the market experience itself generates. At each and every instant, it might be held, each market decision is the optimal one, in the light of current costs (including the costs of acquiring relevant information). As however, completed transactions operate to lower subsequent costs (including especially the costs of transacting), the pattern of optimal market transactions itself changes—even with unchanged underlying conditions of supply and of demand. The sequence of market events thus determined need contain no surprises. At each and every instant, it might be held, all achievable, worthwhile exchange opportunities are being correctly—and predictably—grasped.

Our identification of equilibrium with the absence of unexploited opportunities for gainful exchange throws light on what we are to mean by disequilibrium. Austrian emphasis upon the possibility (in fact, upon the extreme likelihood) of market disequilibrium thus corresponds to the conviction that, in the ordinary course of market events, we can almost invariably expect there to be great numbers of genuinely unexploited market opportunities. So that observed changes in outputs, prices, and adopted methods of production are likely to express the continual discovery of such hitherto overlooked opportunities (quite apart from any systematic changes generated by market-altered costs of transacting and information-acquisition). As suggested above the possibility of such overlooked opportunities' existing rests on the phenomenon of what we have called "utter ignorance"; the likelihood that overlooked opportunities will generate market agitation arises from the propensity of utter ignorance to become spontaneously dissipated.

THE NATURE AND CONSEQUENCES OF "UTTER IGNORANCE"

"Utter ignorance" differs from the kind of ignorance which, as discussed earlier, is consistent with the imaginary state of market equilibrium. Utter ignorance involves not the recognized lack of information, but the state of affairs in which the agent is blissfully unaware of such a lack. Where an agent is aware that he lacks information, we can assume that, in the agent's judgment the acquisition of the missing information is either impossible or not worthwhile; continued ignorance is thus consistent with optimizing behavior. Where an agent is "utterly ignorant," there is the strong possibility that his ignorance is distinctly sub-optimal; that is, that, when it indeed dawns upon him that he has lacked an important piece of intelligence, he will "want to kick himself" for having overlooked an obvious fact (or an obvious implication of recognized facts) staring him in the face. Much of the distinctiveness of the Austrian approach to understanding markets rests on Austrian insistence on the possibility—and ubiquity—of utter, sub-optimal, ignorance (in the face of mainstream refusal to consider this possibility, in the context of economic theorizing).

We should take note of the extraordinarily far-reaching implications of the possibility of "utter ignorance." It is not merely that utter ignorance may involve sub-optimal failure to acquire available information. Once we recognize sub-optimality in the context of information-acquisition, we are brought face-to-face with the possibility of *sub-optimality in each and every department of human decision-making*. What permits economists to place heavy reliance upon individual rationality, upon the assumption that individual decision-makers are choosing optimally in the context of given constraints, is the insight that human beings will never consciously forgo a superior option for an inferior one. Our recognition of the possibility of utter ignorance, however, compels us to consider the limits of the rationality assumption. We are confronted not simply with "bounded rationality," but with the apparently ubiquitous phenomenon of sheer sub-optimality, grounded in the open-endedness of utter ignorance.

For Austrians, however, realizations of these disturbing consequences of utter ignorance does not at all spell a sense of analytical helplessness. Quite the contrary; the phenomenon of utter ignorance turns out, for the Austrian view, to be the very foundations for our confidence in the systematic quality of market processes. This apparently paradoxically assertion draws our attention to the role of *discovery* in the market process.

SURPRISE, DISCOVERY AND THE MARKET PROCESS

As noted, the phenomenon of "utter ignorance" may correspond to an overlooked opportunity for information-acquisition. We saw that this phenomenon was not to be explained in terms of the costliness of such information-acquisition. So that one could not assert that any subsequent reduction in the costs of information-acquisition ("search-costs") might be expected to lead to any narrowing of the range of utter ignorance. It was not cost that deterred learning; it was sheer ignorance that anything existed that was waiting to be (economically) learned. From this it might appear that utter ignorance is utterly invincible; no conceivable changes can be expected to eliminate it. Were this the case one might well pronounce such ignorance to be utterly irrelevant to human affairs. What people do not know, to the extent that they will never know, and never know that they do not know, need simply not be considered. Even more to the point, were this to be the case, the Austrian perspective on market processes would have lost its foundation.

The foundation for the Austrian perspective consists in the insight that utter ignorance is the source of the phenomena of surprise, and particularly of *discovery*. It is simply not the case that the range of utter ignorance, for any given human being, remains static over time. The fog of utter ignorance has the propensity to be spontaneously dissipated. To be human is to be subjected, continually, to a stream of undeliberate, surprise learning experiences. To be human is continually to discover things that one had not noticed before. For the more alert among us such discoveries are likely to occur earlier than for those of us who are less alert. But for all of us our utter ignorance is being continually eroded by undeliberate discovery (while at the very same time, of course, the relevant range of utter ignorance may be undergoing continual spontaneous *expansion*, along other dimensions, as the result of the continually changing market environment).

While discovery is undeliberate, it is not necessarily accidental. Discovery is inspired by the prospect of gain. We are alert human beings because we are hopeful (or, which is not greatly different, because we are fearful) of what might befall us if we doze. In the market context discovery is inspired by the prospect of pure profit. The market process consists, then, in the sequence of entrepreneurial decisions that reflect the profit-inspired discoveries (or supposed discoveries) of market participants. The market process consists, thus, in a continual stream of transactions expressing newly discovered insights on the part of market participants concerning the attitudes and plans of their fellow participants. In this discovery process, as noted, pure profit provides the incentive; it is, moreover, an essential element in the notion of pure profit, that its possibility is generated precisely by that kind of utter ignorance which we have seen to constitute the basis for the phenomenon of discovery.

PURE PROFIT AND THE MARKET PROCESS

If the notion of utter ignorance has been excluded from economic analysis, the idea of pure entrepreneurial profit must present insuperable difficulties. Pure entrepreneurial profit can occur only if a given item can be sold at a price higher than that for which it (or the entire complex of factor services needed to produce it) can be purchased. But it should be apparent that, absent the possibility of utter ignorance, such an occurrence cannot even be imagined. Pure profit must simply be incomprehensible. To imagine that an item can be sold for a price higher than that at which it can be bought, is to imagine that some prospective buyers are prepared to pay more for that item than they need to. Such a situation must, absent utter ignorance, be an absurdity. Ordinary ignorance (deliberately maintained in the light of careful cost-benefit calculation) cannot account for such a situation. (If search costs are required, say, in order deliberately to ascertain the lower price at which the item can be purchased, then this means that such costs must be included in the complex of outlays needed to acquire the item.) If utter ignorance is excluded, pure entrepreneurial profit has been assumed out of existence. (Those who, already in possession of the knowledge of the price differential and of how to take advantage of it, do so take advantage would, in the absence of utter ignorance, merely be receiving the implicit rent on their superior endowment of information.) The phenomenon of pure profit, and the inspiration it provides for entrepreneurial innovative activity, rest entirely on the possibility of utter ignorance.

Buyers pay the pure entrepreneurs higher prices for given items than the latter themselves have paid, simply because those buyers have no inkling of where to obtain those items for less. Utter ignorance is completely able to account for the phenomenon of pure profit.

But, at the same time, the recognition of utter ignorance, precisely because it renders possible the concept of pure profit, provides the key to understanding what it is that markets do, and how they work. Markets are the scene of continual error, of decisions being continually made on the basis of "utter ignorance." These erroneous decisions generate continually emerging opportunities for pure profits. Since it is the lure of pure gain which activates entrepreneurial antennae, it thus turns out that it is the utter ignorance expressed in market activity that becomes translated into that market phenomenon (pure profit) which inspires discovery and correction of error. It is this systematic sequence of error, profit opportunity, discovery and correction, which constitutes the market process. It is a process which, in the light of continually changing supply and demand conditions, never ceases. It is responsible for whatever coherence and order that a market economy displays.

Not only does this market process generate systematic movements of prices and of short-run production decisions, it is also responsible for the much celebrated capacity of market economies to display spectacular long-term progress and growth. It is the entrepreneurial response to the lure of long-run pure profit that is responsible for such progress and growth. From the perspective developed here these entrepreneurial responses represent alertness to as yet untapped opportunities for technological invention and innovation, involving both scientific discoveries and the perception of new possibilities for long-term (capital) investment. Before turning to develop parallel Austrian insights into appropriate normative criteria, we pause to take note of the *competitive* character of this entrepreneurial discovery sequence that makes up both the short and the long-run market process.

COMPETITION AND THE MARKET PROCESS

Our account of the market process has, thus far, emphasized its entrepreneurial character. We have underlined how each step in this process expresses an entrepreneur's hunch that he has discovered an opportunity waiting to be grasped—whether by underselling the competition, introducing a more effective method of production, or whatever. What we wish now briefly to point out is that such an entrepreneurial market process constitutes, at the same time, a *competitive* process. It is in this sense that the market works, in the Austrian view, through the powerful agency of competition. But a certain terminological confusion, now fairly widely recognized, must first be mentioned.

For mainstream microeconomics the term "competition" has for many decades meant the state of affairs associated with the conditions of the perfectly competitive equilibrium market. That state of affairs is the one in which, for each market participant, market price is given, not subject to modification by any one agent's bids or offers. As is by now fairly generally understood, such conditions imply that the market price is *already* assumed to be the equilibrium price. This is not the place to review the "Austrian" reasons for being less than satisfied with this notion of competition as an analytical tool. Suffice it to say that the part played by competition in the above discussed entrepreneurial market process, refers to a notion of competition that is totally different from that of so-called perfect competition. For us competition refers not to a state of affairs but to a dynamic process.

The entrepreneurial market process is a competitive process in the sense that it relies on the freedom of potential entrepreneurs to enter markets in order to compete for perceived available profits. Were incumbent firms arbitrarily protected against competitive entry by government measures, the market process would be hampered or halted. Later in this paper we shall return to appraise the consequences of governmental intervention in markets, against the background of our understanding the competitive character of the unhampered market process. For us a market is competitive only insofar as it expresses the discoveries of entrepreneurial market participants each of whom is aware that, unless he stays on his toes, others may steal a march on him, and that he is himself free to take advantage of any market opportunity that he believes himself to have detected. In order to be completely competitive, in this sense, we do not require that there be many firms in any one industry; all we require is that there be complete freedom for entrepreneurial entry. No market participant enjoys the privilege of being protected against competitive entry.

In particular it will be clear that in order to be competitive we do not require that knowledge be perfect (as is, of course, required for the mainstream notion of perfect competition). Quite the contrary, we are depending on the competitive process itself to generate a flow of new entrepreneurial discoveries. It is in this sense that Hayek has referred to competition as a "discovery procedure": it is not a process in the course of which existing knowledge is brought to bear on production and market decisions, but one in the course of which new knowledge concerning market possibilities is discovered.

THE EVALUATION OF ECONOMIC PERFORMANCE

The approach we have been discussing, viewing the market as a process of competitive-entrepreneurial discovery (rather than as expressing the fulfillment of attained equilibrium conditions), offers a correspondingly distinctive approach to the *appraisal* of a market's performance. Throughout the development of modern welfare economics, economists have sought to evaluate the performance of an economy by asking, in effect, whether the allocation of resources within it corresponds to that pattern which an omniscient (consumer-oriented) central planner would select for that economy. Since Hayek's seminal work in the early 1940s,[3] Austrian economists have understood that this may not in fact be the relevant criterion for such evaluation. The economic problem facing society, Hayek taught us, is not primarily or directly that of the global allocation

---

3. See particularly F. A. Hayek, "The Use of Knowledge in Society," *American Economic Review*, 1945; reprinted in *Individualism and Economic Order, op.cit.*

of society's resources, but first that of mobilizing the dispersed bits of knowledge available in a society so that decision-making can take advantage of them. In terms of our emphasis on the competitive-entrepreneurial discovery process of the market, we may build on Hayek's insights in the following way.

Were a market to achieve instantaneous equilibrium, it would be appropriate to evaluate its performance, as mainstream welfare theory seeks to do, in terms of a comparison between (a) the allocation of resources constituting the equilibrium state, and (b) the allocation of resources that would be selected by the omniscient central planner. Equilibrium would however require the absence of what we have called "utter ignorance," whereas such utter ignorance is perhaps the most characteristic feature of the human condition; such a comparison is thus of little relevance. A more relevant normative criterion thus suggests itself as relating to the degree to which the system is able to mobilize its knowledge resources and, most especially, able to inspire that spontaneous, undeliberate discovery process upon which we must rely for the containment and constriction of such utter ignorance.

It is consistent with these insights, therefore, that Austrians in recent decades have focused attention on the concept of *coordination* as a relevant normative criterion. The social tragedy arising out of utter ignorance is surely that market participants have failed to take advantage of the opportunities awaiting each of them as a result of the attitudes and abilities of others. Utter ignorance is responsible for individual activities which are uncoordinated with each other. Coordination, therefore, offers a relevant normative standard. But a linguistic ambiguity needs to be warned against.

The term "coordination" can connote (a) the state of affairs in which decisions *are* coordinated decisions; or the same term can connote (b) the *process* in the course of which initially uncoordinated decisions come to be revised in the direction of greater mutual coordinatedness. The first of these two meanings of the term does not provide a normative criterion that differs substantively from the criterion of Pareto optimality—the workhorse of mainstream welfare economics. To judge whether a particular set of decisions are or are not fully coordinated, is to judge whether a reallocation of resources or goods could be unanimously considered an improvement (since a potential improvement implies scope for mutually beneficial exchange). It is to the second of the above two meanings that we are referring when we state that from the Austrian perspective coordination emerges as a significantly relevant normative criterion. We are interested in the extent to which an economy possesses *a capacity to induce discoveries* upon which we must depend for the identification and correction of uncoordinated sets of decisions.

These observations will be helpful in understanding the social usefulness of the market process, and in evaluating the consequences of governmental regulation of that process. An excellent introduction to these issues can be provided by a brief consideration of the celebrated controversy that raged during the 1920s and 1930s concerning the possibility of economic calculation under socialism.

THE AUSTRIAN APPROACH AND THE SOCIALIST CALCULATION DEBATE

It will be recalled that Mises argued in a 1920 article[4] that central planners must necessarily lack tools by means of which to compare the efficiency of alternative methods and patterns of production. Such comparisons can be made in the capitalist market economy by calculating comparative costs. But such calculations rely on the availability of market prices for factors of production. Under socialism such markets are excluded. Without factor prices planners have no basis for calculation. Central planners have no way by which to rank the desirability of alternative production projects. Mises' position was vigorously contested; in particular a line of argument developed in 1936 by Oskar Lange came to be widely regarded as the definitive socialist response to Mises' challenge.

A recent study by Professor Lavoie[5] has shown that the commonly accepted history of the debate has erred in several important respects. That history considers the Lange response to have decisively refuted the Misesian argument. Lavoie shows (a) that Mises (and Hayek, who strongly supported Mises' contention) never considered Lange's reasoning to have dealt seriously with the original challenge; (b) that Lange (and other socialist writers of his time) failed to realize the Austrian, market process provenance of that original challenge; so that (c) the socialist

---

4. Translated in F. A. Hayek, ed., *Collectivist Economic Planning: Critical Studies on the Possibilities of Socialism* (London, Routledge and Kegan Paul, 1935).

5. D. Lavoie, *Rivalry and Central Planning* (Cambridge: Cambridge University Press, 1985).

response to that challenge, which was conducted strictly within a mainstream understanding of markets, was based on premises commitment to which precluded appreciation for the Mises-Hayek insights. Let us see briefly how this was indeed the case.

Lange's position was that socialist decision-makers can make use, for purposes of economic calculation, of *non*-market prices for factors of production. Such non-market prices can be announced periodically by the central economic authorities, and can guide the socialist managers of state enterprises in exactly the same way as market prices guide the owners of private enterprises under the market economy. And, just as market prices adjust continually to take account of excess demands and supplies (generated by inappropriately low and high prices), so too can the socialist authorities periodically adjust the announced non-market prices to take account of revealed inadequacies in the prices announced previously. Whatever the market can achieve through market prices, the socialist economy can do through non-market prices.

As Lavoie (and others) have shown, Lange was viewing the function of market prices strictly in terms of the perfectly competitive market model. That is, his understanding of the market was built firmly and narrowly upon the comprehension of its equilibrium position. For this reason he was able to assert that the role of market prices is a "parametric" one, that is, that market participants (and, by analogy, plant managers in the socialist context) treat prices strictly as data to which they must adjust their own decisions, and over which their own decisions have no influence. But the way in which Mises and Hayek understood the role of prices in markets (and the basis for their contention that no "non-market prices" could fulfill a similar function under socialism) was altogether different.

For Mises and Hayek prices are not given features of the environment to which market participants adjust. Prices are, instead, at each moment the expressions of the active, current entrepreneurial decisions of market participants, and are continually inspired by the hunches that market participants have concerning the availability of pure profit opportunities. To argue that nonmarket prices under socialism can perform the same role as equilibrium prices in the market economy, is to ignore the role which the competitive-entrepreneurial market process plays in the discovery of the information required in order for market equilibrium to exist. To imagine that the central economic authorities under socialism can periodically adjust non-market prices in the same way as, in models of equilibrium markets, excess demands and excess supply lead to appropriate price adjustments, is to ignore the Hayekian knowledge problems that are completely begged in equilibrium models. To imagine an announced array of non-market prices that could stimulate the set of equilibrium market prices, is to imagine that the announcing authorities somehow already possess all the information which it is the function of the market process (under *dis*equilibrium conditions) to begin to reveal. These Austrian insights into the problems of socialist calculation hold important implications also for the analysis of governmental regulation of and intervention into the market economy.

THE MARKET PROCESS AND THE PERILS OF REGULATION

The Austrian insights that emphasize the discovery function of the market process, do not challenge the more traditional arguments raised by economists concerning the potential dangers inherent in government regulation. These insights do, however, add a new dimension to these arguments. The traditional economist's critique of regulations generally covers the following points: (a) government regulation may involve a paternalistic substitution of the preferences of legislators or officials in place of the wishes of the consuming public; (b) these "official" preferences may in fact be inspired by personal interests of officials, rather than by concern for the public weal; (c) apparent shortcomings in market outcomes may in fact merely express genuine social scarcities (so that the alleged need for regulation may be highly questionable); (d) even where intervention may address a genuine need, and even where its immediate objectives are in fact met, there may be unanticipated side-effects of the intervention that render it, all things considered, undesirable. The Austrian approach is in basic agreement with these criticisms; but it identifies an important *additional* line of reasoning, one that offers a serious fresh criticism of government intervention. Quite apart from—and even in the absence of the aforementioned criticism of intervention, the "discovery" approach to understanding markets suggests a potentially significant problem arising out of government regulation. This problem has to do with the propensity of government regulation to inhibit discovery. That is, we must address the question of how regulation may impact upon the incentives upon which the market depends for its functioning.

The most serious example of how this influence may be distinctly harmful occurs where regulation bars or limits the exploitation of opportunities for pure entrepreneurial profits. This is likely to take the form of a regulatory barrier to entry. Freedom of entry, for the Austrian approach, is relevant to the freedom of potential competitors to discover (and to move to grasp) existing opportunities for pure profit. Where entry has been blocked opportunities may never be discovered.

From this perspective, regulation introduced to create or maintain competition is no less harmful to the competitive-entrepreneurial process than are other forms of entry-limiting regulation. Entry of competitors need not, in the dynamic sense of the term, mean entry of firms of about equal size. Entry might, for example, refer to the *replacement*, through merger, of a number of high-cost producers, by a single, low-cost producer. Anti-trust activity designed ostensibly to maintain competition, might block this kind of entry. Such activity would thus block the capture of pure profit (in this case available through the discovery of cheaper ways of producing, through economies of scale).

Standard economics frequently draws attention to the harmful consequences of imposed prices. By fixing prices above or below their equilibrium levels, government price regulation generates artificial surpluses or shortages. But, quite apart from the discoordinating consequences (generated by such imposed prices) in the markets for *existing* goods and services, price constraints may also inhibit the discovery of wholly *new* opportunities. A price ceiling does not merely erase the upper portion of a given supply curve. Such a price ceiling may, in addition, slow down the process through which wholly unsuspected sources of supply might be discovered. (In the absence of the price ceiling, such discovery might eventually have shifted the entire supply curve to the right, or might have created wholly fresh supply curves, for products hitherto unknown and unimagined.) It is the lure of pure profit that tends to draw attention to such as yet unglimpsed opportunities. It was this kind of beneficial by-product of the free market system that the late Professor Machlup had in mind when he referred to the "fertility of freedom."

The basic insight that emerges from the foregoing relates to the unstated and profoundly false assumption underlying more traditional (and favorable) treatment of economic regulation. That assumption was that these well-meaning efforts at improving economic resource allocation can be conducted against a background of given information (including, especially, information concerning the feasibility and potential usefulness of information-increasing search). As soon as this assumption is dropped, as soon as it is recognized that economic efficiency depends on continual alertness to (i.e., the discovery of) hitherto unknown information (i.e., the very existence of which had not been suspected), the picture becomes drastically different. The writer has elsewhere identified four ways in which "discovery problems" may hamper appropriate governmental regulation.

(a) *Undiscovered Discovery*—Simply because an apparent problem manifests itself in the market, does not justify the assumption that regulatory correction is called for. After all, the market process is not instantaneous; regulation may merely frustrate the discoveries which markets might have stimulated.

(b) *Unsimulated Discovery*—The discovery process of the market cannot be simulated by regulatory activity. Given the absence of the pure profit incentive, regulators are likely not to notice those opportunities for social improvement which present themselves in the form of potential profit opportunities.

(c) *Stifled Discovery*—Since government regulation often takes the form of barring entry by potential new competitors, such regulation acts directly to discourage private discovery of existing maladjustments.

(d) *Superfluous Discovery*—Government regulation itself is likely to open up new avenues for entrepreneurial gain. Many of these avenues may not necessarily be socially beneficial. One thinks in this regard of enterprising bribery or other criminal activity, where entrepreneurial ingenuity is ("superfluously") channeled into grasping pockets of potential pure profit generated (undeliberately) by the regulatory constraints.

It should be noted that the "perils" of regulation identified in this section, have been introduced primarily for their microeconomics relevance. We have not attempted to discuss the rationale for, or possibly perilous consequences of, government intervention designed to serve as macroeconomic stabilization measures. To a certain extent such stabilization policy is likely to involve the danger we have identified in this section. Such policies characteristically exemplify what we described above as "undiscovered discovery" (i.e., the belief that macro problems perceived are unable to stimulate spontaneous market solutions). For a critical discussion of macrostabilization policies, see the paper in this volume by Professor Pascal Salin.

THE MARKET PROCESS: AN AUSTRIAN VIEW

Our survey has sought to establish the distinctiveness of the Austrian understanding of the market economy. This understanding offers an important alternative to standard positive theory, particularly in its understanding of how capitalism works. In addition, we have seen, the Austrian view offers a novel angle for a critique of the regulated market economy. This novel angle, it turns out, affords some interesting analogies with the now-classic debate on socialist economic calculation. There are grounds to believe that a fresh round in that debate may be in the offing; for any such episode, the full appreciation for the view of the market as a competitive-entrepreneurial discovery process will surely be an important prerequisite.

ECONOMICS AND ERROR

The title of this chapter, one may surmise, owes something to the title of the famous 1937 paper by Hayek, "Economics and Knowledge."[1] There was, Hayek acknowledged, an intentional ambiguity in the title of that paper: we learned there that the knowledge that economic analysis conveys depends crucially upon propositions about the knowledge possessed by the different members of society. The not-dissimilar ambiguity in the title of this chapter may, I venture to hope, suggest that a good deal of erroneous thought in economics has its source in confusion concerning the nature and role of *error* in the actions of the different members of society. It is my purpose here to dispel at least some portion of this confusion. If, in the course of this attempt, some incidental light can also be thrown on the problems raised by Hayek in his 1937 paper, this will be seen to reflect, once again not accidentally, the symmetrical ambiguities embedded in these two titles.

EFFICIENCY, WASTE, AND ERROR

Economists have traditionally been concerned with issues related to efficiency. Inefficient action occurs when one places oneself in a position one views as less desirable than an equally available alternative state. Inefficiency can therefore not be thought of except as the result of an error, a mistake, an incorrect or wrong move. Much of the work of the modern economist has the declared aim of avoiding errors, of achieving efficiency. At the same time, however, as he directs his energies toward obviating error, the contemporary economist is frequently to be found pursuing his analysis on the assumption that men do not, and will not, ever fall into error. "Waste," declares Stigler in a recent note, "is error within the framework of modern economic analysis, and it will not become a useful

Presented at the Austrian Economics Symposium, held at Windsor, England, September 1976. From *Perception, Opportunity, and Profit: Studies in the Theory of Entrepreneurship* (Chicago and London: University of Chicago Press, 1979), 120–36. Reprinted by permission; the original source is *New Directions in Austrian Economics*, ed. Louis M. Spadaro (Kansas City, Kansas: Sheed Andrews and McMeel, 1978), 57–76. © 1978 by the Institute for Humane Studies.

concept until we have a theory of error."[2] Modern economic analysis, we are to understand, lacking a theory of error, can and does proceed only by assuming it away: error and waste simply have no place in the world of economic theory. It is this position that I wish to examine critically. Is it really the case, we must ask, that economic theory requires us to abstract completely from the phenomenon of error? As a preliminary step toward the consideration of this question, it is necessary first to review a number of discussions in the economic literature in which the possibility of error has been seriously canvassed.

MISES, MARKSMEN, AND MISTAKES

In a passage in which he is concerned to explain that human action is *always* rational (in the sense of being designed to attain definite ends), Mises considers the objection that men make mistakes. This does not, Mises points out, constitute irrationality. "To make mistakes in pursuing one's ends is a widespread human weakness. . . . Error, inefficiency, and failure must not be confused with irrationality. He who shoots wants, as a rule, to hit the mark. If he misses it, he is not "irrational"; he is a poor marksman. The doctor who chooses the wrong method to treat a patient is not irrational; he may be an incompetent physician."[3] The implication here is that the incompetent physician and the poor marksman may indeed make mistakes and errors. Rational Misesian human actors *are* human enough to err. But it is clear that these errors are not inconsistent with the position (*excluding* errors) cited earlier as taken by Stigler. In fact, the reason these are not errors in the sense relevant to the Stigler position is entirely similar to the reason why these errors do not, for Mises, constitute irrationality. The mistakes made by the ill-trained doctor do not represent his failure to attain what it is within his power to attain. His failure simply reflects lack of the necessary quality of input. An error, in Stigler's sense, occurs only when an input is used in a way that fails to produce what *that* input can produce. When a poor mathematician makes a mistake in arithmetic[4] he is *not*, therefore, making an error; nor is the failure by a poor marksman to hit the mark an error. It is not an error for a physically weak man to be unable to lift a heavy weight. Nor is it an error, in the relevant sense, when one unschooled in medicine fails to prescribe proper treatment for a patient. To be sure, it may be that the incompetent physician, indifferent mathematician, and poor marksman ought not to waste their time (and their patients' lives) by engaging in tasks for which they are so definitely ill-suited. But, of course, Mises is concerned with the mistakes the physician makes in the course of the practice of medicine, not with the possible error of his attempting medicine at all.

CROCE, TECHNICAL ERROR, AND ECONOMIC ERROR

In the course of his famous correspondence with Pareto at the turn of the century (in the *Giornale degli Economisti*), Benedetto Croce did find a definite place for "economic error." Such an error, Croce explained, must be sharply distinguished from "technical error." Technical error, for Croce, consists in an error of knowledge; it occurs when one is ignorant of the properties of the materials with which one deals (such as when one places a heavy iron girder on a delicate wall too weak to support it). Economic error, on the other hand, occurs, for example, when, yielding to the temptation of the moment, one pursues a transient fancy that is not one's true goal; it is, Croce explains, an *error of will,* "the failure to aim directly at one's own object: To wish this and that, i.e., not really to wish either this or that."[5] Avoiding economic error requires that one aim at one's goal; failure to aim at one's goal constitutes, therefore, a special category of error. This error arises out of the incorrectness not of the pattern of acts taken in pursuing one's immediate aim, since these are, from the point of view of *that* aim, entirely appropriate, but of one's immediate aim itself. To pursue this aim is, from the perspective of one's "true" goals, an aberration. One places one into contradiction with oneself; one aims at what one does *not,* in fact, seek to attain.

Croce's concept of economic error has not found favor among economists. The writer has elsewhere[6] reviewed the careful analysis that Tagliacozzo many years ago made of Croce's position.[7] Briefly, the reason economists have no place for Croce's economic error is that it seems impossible, from the point of view of pure science, to distinguish between "true" goals, and erroneous, transient ones. Once we have accepted the possibility that man can discard yesterday's goals and adopt new ones toward which he will direct today's purposeful actions, we have surrendered the possibility of labeling the pursuit of any end as, on scientific grounds, an erroneous one, no matter how fleeting the "temptation" toward it may be, and no matter how permanent remorse over having yielded to it may turn out to become. Croce's economic error, it then turns out, emerges only as a result of invoking unspecified judgments of value in terms of which to classify, from a man's *own* point of view, those goals of his it is correct to pursue, and those whose pursuit he must consider an error.

Let us digress briefly to note that Mises—in whose writings one finds no room at all for the type of economic error identified by Croce—seems to have consistent scientific grounds for his unwillingness to recognize such error. It is well known that Mises denied the independent existence of a scale of values actuating human choices *apart from the acts of choice themselves* ("the scale of values . . . manifests itself only in the reality of action").[8] The notion of a given scale of values, Mises is at pains to explain, can therefore not be used to pronounce a real action at variance with that scale irrational. The logical consistency that human action necessarily displays by no means entails *constancy* in the ranking of ends.[9] Mises's insistence on the possibility of changes in adopted preference rankings is closely related to his understanding of choice as *undetermined*. Man does not choose as a *reaction* to given circumstances, on the basis of a previously adopted scale of values; he chooses freely at the time he acts, between different ends and different ways of reaching these ends. It follows that the notion of economic error as perceived by Croce has no place in economic *science*.

ERRONEOUS ACTION AND IMPERFECT KNOWLEDGE

That men frequently act on the basis of imperfect knowledge is, of course, not disputed by writers who exclude error in economic theory. In the passage cited above where Mises defends the rationality of erroneous actions, he mentions an example we have not yet cited. "The farmer who in earlier ages tried to increase his crop by resorting to magic rites acted no less rationally than the modern farmer who applies more fertilizer."[10] Men certainly engage in actions that they may regret when they discover the true facts of the situation. Croce, we have seen, termed this kind of mistake a *technical* error. Erroneous action arising from ignorance is not, however, generally seen as a serious threat to an economics that excludes error. With respect to the *perceived* framework of ends and means, error-free decision making can still be postulated. The very notion of an end-means framework, of preferences and constraints, of indifference curves and budget lines, enables the economist to confine his analysis to choice *within* the given framework. The source of error in such choices, being *outside* that framework, is thus, by the very scope of the analysis, in effect excluded from consideration.

To be sure, it is precisely this aspect of modern economics against which Lachmann and Shackle have, among other matters, so vigorously rebelled. Since action is future oriented, necessarily involving an unknown and unknowable future, men's actions are inevitably attended by what Knight called error in the exercise of judgment.[11] Such error may, if one chooses, be subsumed under Croce's technical error, but the all-pervasive and inescapable character of such errors in judgment does, in the view of these distinguished critics, seriously compromise the usefulness of abstractions depending on given, known ends-means frameworks. I will not pursue further the profound consequences with respect to modern economics that the Lachmann-Shackle critiques imply. Our discussion proceeds, instead, in the context of modes of discourse that do perceive continued relevance in theories of choice dependent on supposedly given known frameworks of preferences and constraints.

It should be pointed out that a good deal of modern theorizing proceeds along a path on which actions based on mistaken knowledge appear *not* to be errors, in a sense deeper than that so far discussed. It is not merely that an action is seen as correct within the framework of the *perceived*, but in fact in the quite wrongly perceived ends-means framework. The action is frequently seen as correct also in that the ignorance on which the mistaken perceptions are to blame, may *itself* be viewed as having been *deliberately* and quite *correctly* cultivated. Economists have long recognized that men must deliberately choose what information they wish to acquire at given prices. One who on a deliberate gamble refrains from acquiring a certain piece of costly knowledge and who then, in consequence of his ignorance, makes a mistake may indeed regret his lack of good fortune in having lost, as a result of his gamble, but he may nonetheless quite possibly feel that the chances he originally confronted when deliberating on whether or not to acquire the costly information rendered his original decision correct. The relevant ends-means framework, within which actions have been pronounced consistently errorless, has now been broadened to embrace the situation within which he chose not to buy the improved information. If Mises's incompetent physician had taken a calculated risk in deliberately not studying with sufficient care the treatment of a rare disease, his subsequent errors may indeed be seen as technical errors; they may also, as we have seen earlier, be seen simply as the entirely to be expected shortcoming in output quality consequent on the less than perfect quality of medical input. But the ignorance responsible for the technical error in medical treatment or, if one prefers, for the less than perfect quality of medical expertise available for deployment, may itself be the consistent result of a correct, deliberate choice. This way of seeing imperfect knowledge—as the correctly planned limitation on input quality—permits one to subsume errors arising out of imperfect knowledge under the general class of errors treated in the section "Mises, Marksmen, and Mistakes"—that is, as not constituting errors at all (in the sense of somehow failing to achieve an available preferred state of affairs). This way of looking at things has gained plausibility as a result of the development during the past fifteen years by Stigler and others, of the economics of information in which detailed analysis is undertaken of decisions concerning the optimum degree of ignorance to be preserved under different conditions, and of the market consequences of such decisions.

LEIBENSTEIN AND THE LACK OF MOTIVATION

Harvey Leibenstein has written an extensive series of papers developing the concept of X-inefficiency and exploring the extent to which this type of inefficiency has yet to be incorporated into standard economic theory.[12] Here we consider only those aspects of his work that bear directly on the possibility of error within the scope of economic analysis. We briefly note some of the objections raised recently by Stigler against certain aspects of Leibenstein's contribution.

For Leibenstein, X-inefficiency, as contrasted with the more conventional allocative inefficiency, is equivalent to what for others is called technical inefficiency,[13] the failure of producers to achieve, with the inputs they use, the highest level of output technically possible. Among the sources of this kind of inefficiency, in Leibenstein's view, is inadequacy of motivation and effort. "The simple fact is that neither individuals nor firms work as hard, nor do they search for information as effectively, as they could."[14] Stigler has severely criticized Leibenstein for his use of language.[15] For our purposes Stigler's objections can be stated as follows. It is certainly true that greater output could frequently be achieved by greater effort and stronger motivation. But this does not indicate error, in the sense of failing to achieve an available state of affairs more desirable than that actually achieved. If individuals are not sufficiently motivated to work harder, this presumably reflects, deliberately and "correctly," their preference for leisure. If, again, firms have not succeeded in organizing production so as to enhance worker motivation, this constitutes the firm's choice of one technology of production as against the possibility of alternative (more productivity-conscious) technologies. Choice of one technology, yielding lower physical output per week than another, does not, without our knowing all the relevant costs, warrant our asserting the presence of error in the choice of technologies. Stigler's objections are completely convincing. Leibenstein has not, in his exploration of motivational inefficiency, discovered cases of genuine error relevant to our discussion.

ECONOMICS WITHOUT ERROR?

Let us stand back and observe the position to which we have been led. This position might appear to coincide completely with that where there is no place for error in economic analysis, if by error we mean deliberately placing oneself in a situation one prefers less than another equally available situation of which one is aware. We have refused to accept Croce's terminology, in which economic error can occur when one has been temporarily seduced to aim deliberately at a goal that one in fact prefers less than another true goal. We have, with Stigler, refused to accept Leibenstein's apparent perception of inadequately motivated persons, not trying as hard as they really could, as ones who *are* in fact placing themselves in less preferred situations. We have pointed out that errors made by agents whose lack of competence or skill renders such mistakes inevitable clearly do not involve failure to achieve any attainable preferred position, since the inadequate quality of available inputs places such preferred positions out of reach. And where, as a result of imperfect knowledge, an agent achieves a position less preferred than an equally available alternative position, we have seen, too, that he cannot, within the framework of the information he believed to be relevant, be convicted of error. Moreover, we have seen that insofar as this agent deliberately refrained from acquiring more complete or more accurate knowledge, he cannot even be described as having placed himself in a less preferred situation at all, since in his view the cost of acquiring the more accurate knowledge made ignorance the preferred risk.

Our apparent conclusion that error has no place in economics does not depend on any artificial *assumption*, as does, for example, appear to be implied in Stigler. For Stigler, it seems, error is deliberately and artificially excluded by the economist from his purview on the grounds that we lack a theory of error.[16] But our own conclusions follow strictly from the insight that men are purposeful, or rational, as Mises uses the word. If men pursue purposes, it follows that, of course, they do not consciously act to place themselves in situations that are any but the most preferred of those equally available alternatives of which they are aware. If men turn out to have failed to achieve the most preferred situations, it must be either that those situations were in fact *not* available, or that, possibly as a result of deliberate, purposeful earlier decision, these agents were not aware of the full range of alternatives. Not only, that is, have we apparently been led to Stigler's conclusion that there is no place for error in economics, we have been led to this conclusion as implied directly in the very assumption of purposefulness from which we take our point of departure.[17]

Economics, it thus seems to turn out, is peopled by beings whose purposefulness ensures that they can never, in retrospect, reproach themselves for having acted in error. They may, in retrospect, indeed wish that they had been more skillful, or had commanded more inputs, or had been better informed. But they can never upbraid themselves for having acted erroneously in failing to command those superior skills or to acquire more accurate information. They must, at every stage, concede that they had, in the past, acted with flawless precision insofar as they were able. Any reproaches they may validly wish to direct at themselves—for example, for not having tried hard enough or for having succumbed to temptation—arise out of later judgments of value (concerning the significance of leisure or of the goal represented by the fleeting temptation) with which they had earlier disagreed. Such self-reproach, as we now understand, is not for having acted in error, in the sense relevant to this discussion.[18]

Indeed, the reader might reasonably claim cause for irritation at the triviality of our conclusion. Given the paramountcy accorded to purposefulness, and given a definition of error that excludes "wrong" judgments of value as well as failures ascribable to ignorance or inadequacy, whether owing to causes beyond the control of the agent or to his past purposeful choices, surely the conclusion that error is excluded is so obviously implicit in our definitions as to be completely uninteresting.

But, as I will attempt to show here, the conclusions to which we have apparently been led by our discussion thus far are not trivial at all; in fact they are not even true. Not only is there nothing, as we shall see, in the assumptions and definitions on which economic analysis is built that rules out error, it can be shown that economic analysis can hardly proceed at all without making very important use of the concept of error, as well as of the concept of the discovery and correction of error. Let us see how all this can possibly be maintained.

IGNORANCE AND IGNORANCE

Much weight was placed, in earlier pages, on our recognition that mistakes made as a result of ignorance do not qualify as errors in the sense relevant to our discussion. A person who acted with complete precision, given the knowledge he thought he possessed, could not, I maintained, be reproached with having acted in error. And where the limits to his stock of knowledge had been deliberately selected, we certainly understood him to have acted, at all times, beyond reproach. That is, the person at no time refrained from exploiting any known opportunity for achieving the most desirable situation possible. Yet surely we must recognize that, valid though these statements are within their own framework, they may *not* fully exhaust our interpretation of the situations to which they refer.

A person walks along a street and sees a store with signs offering to sell apples for one dollar; but, perhaps thinking of other things, he enters a second store where he pays two dollars for identical apples. He may have seen the signs in the first store, but his perception of them was so weak as to mean that, when he paid two dollars in the second store he did not, in fact, know that he was rejecting a preferred opportunity for one less preferred. Within the framework of his knowledge, the two-dollar apples were indeed his best opportunity; he made no error. Yet, surely, in an important sense he will, when he realizes his mistake, reproach himself for having been so absentminded as to pass by the bargain, *which he saw,* for the more expensive purchase. In this sense he *did* commit an error, the error of not acting on the information available to him, on not perceiving fully the opportunity before his very nose. He did, without the excuse of not having the necessary information available to him, consciously place himself in a less preferred position than that available to him. It is true that he was not aware of the superior alternative. But, because the necessary information *was* available to him, it was surely an error on his part to have failed to act upon it (i.e., to have remained unaware of the superior opportunity). His unawareness cannot be excused from conviction of error on the grounds of inadequacy of inputs, since the information inputs were at hand. It cannot be excused on the grounds of an earlier decision to refrain from acquiring information, since no such decision was made. This unawareness cannot be flatly excluded as impossible because of inconsistency with purposeful action because *there is nothing in purposeful action that by itself guarantees that every available opportunity must be instantaneously perceived.*[19]

In the earlier discussion, knowledge was treated as something like an input, a tool. Someone lacking this needed input could not be reproached with error for not achieving that for which this input was needed. And where this input had deliberately and correctly not been acquired because of its cost, this exemption from reproach became even more justified. But we now see that ignorance may mean something other than lack of command over a needed tool; it may be sheer failure to utilize a resource available and ready to hand. Such failure, moreover, is not inconsistent with purposefulness, since an available resource ready to hand may not be noticed; purposefulness is not necessarily inconsistent with tunnel vision. Of course one *might* insist that an agent not blessed with the alertness needed to notice resources available at hand, simply lacks, through no "fault" of his own, *another* "resource" (i.e., "alertness") necessary to take advantage of the resources with which he *has* been blessed. We cannot set down such a use of terms as *wrong*. We simply point out that while decisions can in principle be made by a person lacking any needed resources, including "knowledge," to acquire that resource he lacks, we *cannot* conceive of one who lacks alertness making a decision to acquire it. This is so because, among other reasons,[20] before a decision to acquire anything can be considered, one must *already* assume the alertness necessary for the perception that such an acquisition is needed and possible at all. Or, to put it somewhat differently, one cannot make decisions on how to use alertness, since, to make such a decision about a resource, one must *already* have been alert to its availability. Alertness thus appears to possess a primordial role in decision making that makes it unhelpful to treat it in the analysis of decisions, like any other resource. I therefore claim justification for a terminology that maintains that, where ignorance consists not in lack of available information but in inexplicably failing to see facts staring one in the face, it represents genuine error and genuine inefficiency.[21]

IGNORANCE, ERROR, AND
ENTREPRENEURIAL OPPORTUNITIES

We have seen that genuine error is not inconsistent with the fundamental postulates of economics. It remains to be shown that economic analysis *depends* on the presence of this kind of error for its most elementary and far-reaching theorems. Let us consider the theorem that Jevons correctly called "a general law of the utmost importance in economics," which asserts that "in the same open market, at any one moment, there cannot be two prices for the same kind of article."[22] Now Jevons presented this Law of Indifference as valid only where no imperfection of knowledge exists. Yet surely economists ever since Jevons have understood the law as asserting a *tendency* at all times for divergent prices of identical goods to *converge*, ceteris paribus, toward a single price. That is, the law asserts a tendency for imperfect knowledge to be replaced by more perfect knowledge.[23] Now the existence of such a tendency requires some explanation. If the imperfection of knowledge responsible for the initial multiplicity of prices reflected the lack of some resource (as the absence of the means of communication between different parts of a market), then it is difficult, without additional justification, to see how we can postulate universally a process of spontaneous discovery. If, say, imperfection in knowledge resulted from deliberate unwillingness to incur the costs of search, it is not clear how we can be confident that, in the course of the market process, such unwillingness will invariably dissipate, or that the necessary costs of search will invariably fall. Of course, one can construct models in which these costs *may* be supposed to fall. One type of theorizing concerning the nature of the market process has, following on the line of the economics of information, in effect taken this approach.

Surely our justification for asserting the existence of a tendency for the prices of identical articles to converge rests on our understanding that the imperfection of knowledge on which one must rely in order to account for the initial multiplicity of prices reflected, at least in part, sheer error. We understand, that is, that the initial imperfection in knowledge is to be attributed not to lack of some needed resource, but to failure to notice opportunities ready to hand. The multiplicity of prices represented opportunities for pure entrepreneurial profit; that such multiplicity existed means that many market participants (those who sold at the lower prices and those who bought at the higher prices) simply overlooked these opportunities. Since these opportunities were left unexploited, *not* because of unavailable needed resources but because they simply were not noticed, we understand that, as time passes, the lure of available pure profits can be counted upon to alert at least some market participants to the existence of these opportunities. The law of indifference follows from our recognition that error exists, that it consists in available opportunities being overlooked, and that the market process is a process of the systematic discovery and correction of true error. The hypothetical state of equilibrium, it emerges, consists not so much in the perfection of knowledge, since costs of acquiring knowledge may well justify an equilibrium state of ignorance, as in the hypothetical absence of error.

All this permits us to concur, in general terms, if not in detail, with that aspect of Leibenstein's concept of X-inefficiency he identifies with the scope for entrepreneurship.[24] Scope for entrepreneurship, we have discovered, is present whenever error occurs. Pure profit opportunities exist whenever error occurs. Whenever error occurs in the context of production, inputs are being used to achieve less than the optimum quantity and quality of outputs; the producer is operating inside the "outer-bound production possibility surface consistent with [his] resources."[25] X-inefficiency *is* possible; it reflects error and is necessarily reflected in the availability of entrepreneurial discovery and improvement. That our conclusion with respect to this aspect of Leibenstein's contribution apparently differs from that of Stigler, who rejects the notion of X-inefficiency entirely, is fully consistent with our refusal to join Stigler in his insistence on excluding error from economics.

MARSHALL, ROBBINS, AND THE REPRESENTATIVE FIRM

In the course of his critique of Leibenstein, Stigler has valuably recalled our attention to an old issue in the economic literature, the rationale underlying Marshall's concept of the representative firm. It was Lionel (now Lord) Robbins who in 1928[26] explained Marshall's motive in introducing the rather troublesome notion of the representative firm and who showed, with the most effective logic, that there is no need for this awkward construct at all. Our discussion thus far enables us to make several comments on the issue.

Basing his interpretation on the authoritative opinion of Dennis Robertson, Robbins explains that Marshall devised the representative firm "to meet the difficulties occurring in the analysis of supply when there is a disparity of efficiency as between different producers."[27] This disparity means that part of the total supply of each product, the magnitude of which helps determine price, is produced by producers making zero or negative profits. Consequently it appears that "the magnitude of net profit is irrelevant to the determination of . . . price." For this reason Marshall explained that price is to be understood in terms of the normal costs, including gross earnings of management, associated with the representative firm.[28]

Robbins went to great pains to show that, insofar as concerns those disparities of efficiency between firms that would not disappear in equilibrium, there is no need at all to invoke the notion of a representative firm. Such disparities in efficiency are to be traced to the presence of entrepreneurs of varying ability. "Just as units of a given supply may be produced on lands of varying efficiency, so their production may be supervised by business men of varying ability. What is normal profit for one will not be normal profit for another, that is all."[29] As Stigler put it, it is inappropriate to use variations in entrepreneurial ability to account for variations in costs among firms: "differences in the quality of an input do not lead to differences in outputs from given inputs. . . . [When] costs of firms differed because of quality of entrepreneurs (or other inputs), the differences in productivity would be reflected in differences in profits (or other input prices)."[30]

In other words, differences in costs of production arising from differences in entrepreneurial ability mean that the equilibrium prices for the various entrepreneurial inputs will be correspondingly different. When account is taken of the costs of these entrepreneurial inputs, we will see that, in equilibrium, there exist *no* cost variations between entrepreneurs. Stigler appears to conclude that Robbins's discussion justifies the neoclassical practice of viewing each producer as always at a production frontier. If, as a result of varying quality of entrepreneurial inputs, output variation occurs, this is simply because, as a result of the variance in entrepreneurial quality, each producer may have a production frontier above or below that of others.[31] There is no room, in this scheme of things, for Leibenstein's X-inefficiency, which implies the possibility that differences in output are a result of genuine differences in sheer efficiency, *not* attributable to differences in input quality.

What I want to point out here is that the portion of Robbins's critique of Marshall upon which Stigler draws is confined explicitly to the state of equilibrium.[32] Under conditions of equilibrium, we must indeed reject the possibility of genuine disparities in efficiency among firms that cannot be traced to differences in input qualities. In equilibrium, such disparities cannot be traced to sheer error. But under conditions of disequilibrium, when scope exists for entrepreneurial activity, there is no reason genuine disparities may not exist among different producers, traceable not to differences in input qualities, since we do not view alertness as an input, but to differences in the degree to which producers have succumbed to error. Robbins's critique of Marshall does *not*, therefore, imply any need to reject Leibenstein's X-inefficiency, insofar as such inefficiency coincides with the existence of a scope for pure entrepreneurship.

ERROR IN ECONOMICS: SOME NORMATIVE APPLICATIONS

My concern to defend the possibility of genuine error in economics is based on more than our wish to show that positive economic theory cannot proceed without such possibility. In addition, our concern rests upon important normative grounds. Allocative inefficiency in a society of errorless individual maximizers must, it appears on reflection, be accounted for only by the existence of prohibitive transaction costs.[33] Improvements in social well-being must, in such a world, appear possible only as a result of unexplained technological breakthroughs.

Surely such a picture of the world, a picture in which no genuine opportunities for improvement are permitted to exist, is wholly unsatisfying. Surely we are convinced that enormous scope exists at all times for genuine economic improvement; surely we are convinced that the world is chock-full of inefficiencies. It is most embarrassing to have to grapple with the grossly inefficient world we know with economic tools that assume away the essence of the problem with which we wish to deal.

But as soon as we admit genuine error into our purview, our embarrassment fades. Our world *is* a grossly inefficient world. What is inefficient about the world is surely that, at each instant, enormous scope exists for improvements that are in one way or another ready to hand and yet are simply not noticed. At each instant, because the market is in a state of disequilibrium, genuine allocative inefficiencies remain to be removed simply because entrepreneurs have not yet noticed the profit opportunities these inefficiencies represent. At each instant, available technological improvements—in some sense already at hand—remain to be exploited; they remain untapped because entrepreneurs have not yet noticed the profit opportunities embedded in them. We can ascribe many of the world's ills to genuine error, and we need an economics that can recognize this.

Only an economics that recognizes how the profit motive—by which we mean the lure of pure entrepreneurial profits—can harness entrepreneurial activity toward the systematic elimination of error can be of service in pointing the way to those institutional structures necessary for the steady improvement of the lot of mankind.

NOTES

1. F. A. Hayek, "Economics and Knowledge," *Economica*, n.s., 4, no. 13 (February 1937): 33–54.

2. G. J. Stigler, "The Xistence of X-Efficiency," *American Economic Review* 66 (March 1976): 216.

3. L. Mises, *Theory and History* (New Haven: Yale University Press, 1957), p. 268.

4. See Stigler, "Xistence of X-Efficiency," p. 215.

5. B. Croce, "On the Economic Principle," trans. in *International Economic Papers*, no. 3 (London and New York: Macmillan, 1953), p. 177.

6. I. M. Kirzner, *The Economic Point of View* (Princeton: Van Nostrand, 1960), pp. 169–72.

7. G. Tagliacozzo, "Croce and the Nature of Economic Science," *Quarterly Journal of Economics* 59, no. 3 (May 1945): 307–29.

8. L. Mises, *Human Action* (New Haven: Yale University Press, 1949), p. 95.

9. Ibid., pp. 102 ff.

10. Ibid.

11. F. H. Knight, *Risk, Uncertainty and Profit* (New York: Houghton Mifflin, 1921), pp. 225–26.

12. H. Leibenstein, "Allocative Efficiency vs. 'X-Efficiency,' " *American Economic Review* 56 (June 1966): 392–415; "Entrepreneurship and Development," *American Economic Review* 58 (May 1969): 72–83; "Competition and X-Efficiency: Reply." *Journal of Political Economy* 81, no. 3 (May/June 1973): 765–77; "Aspects of the X-Efficiency Theory of the Firm," *Bell Journal of Economics* 6 (Autumn 1975): 580–606. See also H. Leibenstein, *Beyond Economic Man* (Cambridge: Harvard University Press, 1976).

13. Leibenstein, "Competition and X-Efficiency: Reply," p. 766.

14. Leibenstein, "Allocative Efficiency vs. 'X-Efficiency,'" p. 407.

15. Stigler, "Xistence of X-Efficiency."

16. See above, note 2.

17. Put differently, our perception of the impossibility of error does not depend on any "arbitrary" assumption of utility- or profit-maximizing behavior. Error is impossible because it is inconsistent with the postulate of purposeful action.

18. The possibility for *social* "inefficiency" of any kind, in such an errorless world, would, it must appear, then rest either on the possibility that high transaction costs make the "correction" in fact uneconomic or on the highly dubious notion of an omniscient observer from whose perspective the errorless (but imperfectly omniscient) members of society are overlooking valuable opportunities for improving their positions. On all this see further, I. M. Kirzner, *Competition and Entrepreneurship* (Chicago: University of Chicago Press, 1973), chap. 6. See also the final section of the present chapter.

19. Although the extent to which available opportunities *are* perceived is not at all unrelated to the concept of purposeful action. (See also pp. 28–32 [in the 1979 source material].)

20. The other reasons include the circumstances that, were one to discover some-one whose superior alertness to profitable opportunities one wishes to hire, we would expect that other "alert one" to have already taken advantage of those opportunities or at least that he will anyway do so very shortly on his own account. (See above, p. 8 [in the 1979 source material].)

21. For further discussion of some of the issues raised in this and the following sections, see my *Competition and Entrepreneurship,* chaps. 2 and 3.

22. W. S. Jevons, *The Theory of Political Economy,* 4th ed. (1911; reprinted Pelican Books, 1970), p. 137.

23. On all this, see Hayek's pioneering contribution in his 1937 paper (see above, note 1). See also above, chap. 2.

24. Leibenstein, "Entrepreneurship and Development," and Kirzner, *Competition and Entrepreneurship,* p. 46 n.

25. Leibenstein, "Allocative Efficiency vs. 'X-Efficiency,' " p. 413.

26. L. Robbins, "The Representative Firm," *Economic Journal* 38 (September 1928): 387–404.

27. Ibid., p. 391.

28. See A. Marshall, *Principles of Economics,* 8th ed. (London: Macmillan, 1920), pp. 432 ff.

29. Robbins, "The Representative Firm," p. 393.

30. Stigler, "Xistence of X-Efficiency," pp. 214 ff.

31. Ibid., p. 215.

32. Robbins, "The Representative Firm," pp. 392–96.

33. See, e.g., G. Calabresi, "Transaction Costs, Resource Allocation and Liability Rules: A Comment," *Journal of Law and Economics* 11 (April 1968): 68.

COMMENT: X-INEFFICIENCY, ERROR, AND
THE SCOPE FOR ENTREPRENEURSHIP

Professor Leibenstein makes a valiant attempt in chapter 6 to rescue the entrepreneurial role from oblivion. In this undertaking, Leibenstein draws heavily on his well-known theory of X-efficiency, discovering that within the paradigm offered by this theory, the entrepreneurial function finds a natural place. At a number of points in the paper, Leibenstein makes brief attempts to relate his approach critically to the work that has, in recent years, proceeded in a similar direction within the Austrian tradition. Leibenstein's paper is necessarily concise in its presentation of the X-efficiency approach. For fuller understanding, one must refer to his recent book, *Beyond Economic Man*, and a series of earlier papers. However, in regard to the implications of the X-efficiency approach for the entrepreneurial role, Leibenstein's book is—somewhat strangely, one might think—virtually silent. Fortunately, a much older paper of Leibenstein's ("Entrepreneurship and Development," *American Economic Review*, May 1968) did tackle the question of the entrepreneurial role. A reading of today's new paper against the background of Leibenstein's more elaborate discussion in his earlier paper, provides a richer understanding, I believe, of Leibenstein's position.

The present discussion will seek to appraise this position from the perspective of the Austrian tradition. In particular, we will attempt to underline the points of contact between Leibenstein's work and the recent discussions within the Austrian approach, while at the same time attempting to clarify and underscore the differences between Leibenstein and the Austrian approach. It is to be hoped that this kind of discussion can make a contribution toward a more sensitive understanding of each other's work among those few economic theorists currently engaged in research on the entrepreneurial function in economic systems.

ENTREPRENEURSHIP AND DISEQUILIBRIUM

It is now well understood why neoclassical general equilibrium theory cannot find a place for the entrepreneur.[1] No matter which one of the alternative theories of entrepreneurship one wishes to follow, an entrepreneur can emerge only in a world in which he can, at least in principle, hope to discover, or create, or at any rate enjoy, opportunities for pure profit. The state of general equilibrium is simply not consistent with such a world. In general equilibrium each participant is acting successfully to place himself in the best situation available to him. The sets of prices prevailing are such that (1) each and every market participant is able to carry out his planned actions without disappointment and without regret; and (2) there is not a single pair of participants who could both have reached better situations for themselves by trading with each other at prices other than those prevailing in the market. These specifications rule out all opportunities for pure profit, and thus necessarily exclude any possibility for an entrepreneurial role. As Leibenstein has put it in his chapter, "If we want to get anywhere to solve the entrepreneurial puzzle, we have to stay away from the neoclassical general equilibrium syndrome."[2] T. W. Schultz too has recently emphasized that the entrepreneur finds his role in his "ability to deal with disequilibria."[3]

All this has, as Leibenstein recognizes, long been argued by Austrians, who have, moreover, consistently deplored the dominant trends in economic theory to exclude from consideration all but equilibrium states. Both a Schumpeter and a Mises, no matter how sharp their differences on other matters, could agree in rejecting outright the view of capitalism which fails to see it as a dynamic process. From this perspective these new signs of rediscovery of the entrepreneur point encouragingly beyond themselves to a rejuvenated economic theory in which the analysis of equilibrium conditions need no longer dominate the intellectual scene.

PROFIT OPPORTUNITIES AND THE FAILURE TO MAXIMIZE

In the world of general equilibrium, all participants are seen as successful maximizers, and, in particular, all firms are viewed as producing efficiently. In the Leibenstein world of possible X-inefficiency, on the other hand, firms do not necessarily maximize, minimum costs are not necessarily achieved. Although Leibenstein is not altogether explicit on the matter in today's paper, it seems clear that a significant explanation for the scope for entrepreneurship arises from this failure of participants to achieve efficiency. As Leibenstein explains, "[non]maximization and the operation of inertia suggest that not all entrepreneurial opportunities would be undertaken."[4] Because of X-inefficiency, "profitable entrepreneurial opportunities may be hidden" and "the entrepreneur has the function of ferreting" them out.[5] As Leibenstein put it in 1968, "[p]ersistent slack implies the existence of entrepreneurial opportunities."[6] Again it is "the difference between actual costs [not minimized as a result of X-inefficiency (I.M.K.)] and true minimum costs" that "offers opportunities for those entrepreneurs who think they can produce at lower costs."[7]

As has been recently emphasized by William Jaffé, Austrians as far back as Carl Menger have refused to view market participants as errorless maximizers, instantaneously selecting the optimum option from the array that confronts them.[8] Where there is room for error, there is surely room for the exercise of the entrepreneurial function. So that here, too, Leibenstein's paradigm might appear to be one that Austrians should find both comfortable and congenial.

A DIFFERENCE OF EMPHASIS

Despite these highly significant points of agreement joining Leibenstein's position with that of the Austrians, it seems important to identify and discuss several differences that set Leibenstein's views apart from the Austrian approach. Let us begin with what may at first glance appear as no more than a difference of emphasis. For Leibenstein, the role of the entrepreneur seems to be *far less crucial* than it is for the Austrians.

For Leibenstein, the rediscovery of the entrepreneur seems to be quite secondary. Although it is true that, as mentioned earlier, Leibenstein addressed the question of entrepreneurship carefully in his 1968 paper, it is also true that in his book (which bears the significant subtitle *A New Foundation for Microeconomics*), Leibenstein virtually ignores the role of the entrepreneur. In the book, only casual and quite incidental references are made to entrepreneurs (with the exception perhaps of two brief paragraphs on page 206 with a footnote reference to the 1968 paper), and no systematic effort (such as has been presented in the chapter here being commented on, or such as Leibenstein had himself provided in 1968) was made in the book to relate the entrepreneurial role to the X-efficiency paradigm. For an Austrian reading *Beyond Economic Man* this seems an almost extraordinary omission. And, indeed, it appears that this difference in emphasis reflects a deeper difference, between the two approaches, in the significance attached to the entrepreneurial role. For Leibenstein, entrepreneurship is merely one interesting feature of the economic landscape. It is a feature that indeed seems to come into focus when observed through the X-efficiency lens; but the X-efficiency paradigm can be presented without any special reference to entrepreneurs.

For Austrians, however, entrepreneurship is *at the very heart* of the economic process; to attempt to understand economic processes without reference to the entrepreneurial role would, for the Austrians, be a wholly misguided undertaking. This deserves some elaboration.

ENTREPRENEURSHIP AND X-INEFFICIENCY

For Leibenstein the matter seems to be as follows. In the X-efficiency paradigm we are presented with a framework for a theory alternative to that of general equilibrium. Both theoretical approaches seek to illuminate the economic world around us. The neoclassical general equilibrium approach does so by assuming that all market participants are successful maximizers. Leibenstein seeks to understand the economic world by viewing market participants as displaying, in varying degrees, X-inefficiency. As Leibenstein demonstrates in his book, his theory lends itself to numerous applications in which phenomena of the real world seem to become understandable when related to specific possibilities for X-inefficiency. In developing this theory, and in drawing implications from it to illuminate our understanding of the real world, the entrepreneurial role is not, in general, referred to. The entrepreneur is not seen as a pivotal figure in a Leibenstein world; such a world can, in Leibenstein's terms, be understood without having to rely upon the entrepreneurial function.

On the other hand, however, the X-inefficiency paradigm, as an alternative to the dominant neoclassical theory, happens to exclude precisely those features of the neoclassical framework that left no room for a neo-classical entrepreneur. Because of this, there is, in the Leibenstein world, once again, a possibility for entrepreneurial activity. In chapter 6, Leibenstein has systematically explored this possibility. In doing this, Leibenstein would presumably consider himself to be further demonstrating the richness of his general theoretical approach. He has given us no reason at all, of course, to believe that he has today revealed the ultimate mainspring—a mainspring kept carefully and successfully concealed throughout his book—for his whole theory. The situation is, for the Austrians, altogether different.

ENTREPRENEURSHIP AND THE AUSTRIANS

For Austrians, the entrepreneurial role is the key to an understanding of the course of economic phenomena. What is inadequate with an exclusively general equilibrium approach, then, is not merely that it is an approach within which we cannot seem to fit the familiar figure of the entrepreneur. Rather the neoclassical general equilibrium approach suffers most seriously in its inability to address those crucial theoretical tasks for which the notion of entrepreneurship can alone provide the key.

A state of equilibrium is one in which the decisions of all market participants are, within the given constraints, fully coordinated. Each market participant, making an offer, does so in the correct anticipation that the offer will be accepted. Each action undertaken in anticipation of coordinate actions by others, is in fact able to be successfully carried out; the anticipations are fulfilled. No pair of potential market participants between whom mutually profitable exchange activities might be carried on, fail to exploit such opportunities.

Austrians have long argued that the analysis of such equilibrium states—if not enriched by analyses of possible equilibrating processes—fails to come to grips with the problems of our world. Not only is our world one in which perfect coordination simply never exists (so that equilibrium models can have little direct relevance). In our world, the problem calling for theoretical illumination is precisely that of understanding the course of events generated by an initial *absence* of coordination. For the solution of this problem equilibrium models are distinctly unhelpful. (Moreover, from a *normative* point of view, Austrians following Hayek have consistently emphasized that the relevant task surely is not to understand how efficient an economy may be in the state of equilibrium; rather the relevant task is to evaluate the success with which an economy beset by rampant *absence* of coordination may achieve an approach toward a coordinated state. For all this the analysis of equilibrium states appears as an altogether question-begging enterprise.)

The need for a theory within which entrepreneurial activity can find its place is thus the need for a theory able to embrace the way in which uncoordinated states of affairs possibly change. The economist does, after all, understand that absence of coordination may itself generate systematic attempts to change matters. So that we can hardly avoid recognizing that what renders an uncoordinated state of affairs one of *disequilibrium* is closely related to entrepreneurial reaction to the absence of coordination.

Leibenstein refers critically on more than one occasion in chapter 6 to what he sees as the Austrian view that entrepreneurial activity propels markets strictly in the direction of equilibrium. It should perhaps be pointed out that not all Austrians in fact maintain that all entrepreneurs engage all the time in equilibrating activities. Moreover, and most significantly, what I believe most Austrians believe to be important is not so much that entrepreneurship is equilibrating (if indeed it always is) but that, if there is in fact a tendency toward equilibrium, that tendency can be understood as the result of working out entrepreneurial activity. Or, to put the same idea somewhat differently, the important thing is that the course of events in a disequilibrium setting, *whether or not that course of events converges on equilibrium,* can be understood only in terms of entrepreneurial decisions.

This aspect of the difference between Leibenstein and the Austrians may be stated concisely. For Leibenstein only a disequilibrium state provides anything for the entrepreneur to do. For Austrians it is only what entrepreneurs do that enables us to understand what happens in the disequilibrium state.

THE SOURCE OF X-INEFFICIENCY

We have mentioned earlier that one significant point of agreement between Leibenstein and the Austrians consists of the possibility of X-inefficiency. It is this possibility that, for both Leibenstein and the Austrians, provides scope for entrepreneurial activity. The escape that Leibenstein makes from a world of successful maximizers is a move that Austrians cannot but applaud. But, paradoxically enough, the particular escape-hatch through which Leibenstein makes this unorthodox exit is one that Austrians must be inclined to view with a certain coolness. This requires some clarification. Let me try:

Throughout the course of modern economics its critics have attacked some form of its central postulate—the postulate of purposeful individual action. The particular form taken by a particular piece of criticism has depended on the form in which this central postulate has been enunciated. Thus, critics of economics have denounced the notion of economic man; they have derided the postulate of rationality, or of maximizing behavior. Veblen's acid comments on the economist's view of man as a hedonistic "lightning calculator of pleasures and pains" is well known and typifies the kind of criticism to which economists have been constantly subjected.

Economists have defended themselves in one of two ways. One line of defense has been to treat the assumption of rationality as merely a useful first approximation. The alternative defense has been to argue that what seem to be examples of nonrational, nonmaximizing behavior (for example, impulsive behavior, or behavior governed strictly by adherence to custom) seem to be such only because certain important kinds of utilities or sacrifices have not been taken into account. On the first of these two lines of defense, nonefficient action is indeed possible, but is deliberately assumed away in economic theory for purposes of analytical simplicity. On the second of these lines of defense, nonefficient action *appears* possible only because the observer has—illegitimately—ignored some satisfactions that have in fact entered into the calculations of the agent.

Professor Stigler has recently taken Leibenstein sharply to task for treating X-inefficiency as inefficiency at all from the viewpoint of economics.[9] Prominent among the sources of X-inefficiency are inadequate motivation and effort. "The simple fact is that neither individuals nor firms work as hard, nor do they search for information as effectively as they could."[10] But, as Stigler points out, if individuals are not sufficiently motivated to work harder, then this presumably reflects, deliberately and correctly, their preference for leisure. If, again, firms have not succeeded in organizing production so as to enhance worker motivation, this constitutes the firm's choice of one "technology" of production, as against the possibility of alternative (more "productivity"-conscious) technologies. But choice of one technology, yielding lower physical output per week than another available technology does not, without our knowing all the relevant costs, warrant our asserting the presence of inefficiency in the choice of technologies.

Now Leibenstein has in his book already, perhaps, anticipated this line of criticism. He has explained that "the problem may be partially semantic . . . One can interpret utility in such a way that *all* behavior is subsumed under some version of utility maximization. But this would rob the concepts of utility and maximization of real meaning."[11] In other words, Leibenstein, in joining the century-old line of critics of mainstream economic theory is rejecting *both* of the above-mentioned possible defenses employed by economists. He is not prepared to broaden the notion of utility so as to render *all* action efficient. And he believes that the use of the maximizing model as a first approximation blinds us from understanding many economic phenomena, which come into focus only when we "loosen the psychological assumptions behind normal economic behavior in such a way so that rationality [does] not necessarily imply maximizing utility"—that is, only if we admit the possibility of X-inefficiency.[12] The Austrian reaction to this is somewhat complex.

AUSTRIANS AND X-INEFFICIENCY

William Jaffé has recently argued that the early Austrians, or at least Menger, were not really vulnerable to Veblen's attacks on neoclassical theory. Jaffé argues that "[m]an, as Menger saw him, far from being a 'lightning calculator' is a bumbling, erring, ill-informed creature, plagued with uncertainty, forever hovering between alluring hopes and haunting fears, and congenitally incapable of making finely calibrated decisions in pursuit of satisfactions."[13]

At the same time it has been the Austrians, in particular, Mises, who have most staunchly maintained the universal rationality of human action. Man always acts purposefully; more accurately: the very concept of human action is altogether inseparable from its purposefulness.[14] Because men pursue purposes, their actions are governed by their reason; because of this the economist, by using his own reasoning powers, can understand actions taken in the light of relevant goals postulated. Two points emerge from our consideration of Mises. First, it is clear that unless we are prepared to cut Mises off from his intellectual forbears, some effort at reconciliation with Jaffé's reading of Menger is urgently called for. Second, Mises' extensive discussions of the universality of the action-postulate and of the nature of economic reasoning, make it very clear how he (and hence modern Austrians) view Veblen-type critiques of economics. Austrians will emphatically not accept the purposefulness of human action merely as a useful first approximation. They will (as does the other of the two alternative lines of defense mentioned earlier) insist on the full validity of the postulate of purposefulness, accounting for apparent real world counterexamples by simply arguing that some significant purposes have evidently not been understood by the observing economist.

All this must seem to intensify Austrian disagreement with X-inefficiency. Surely Stigler is correct in pointing out that the cases of X-inefficiency that Leibenstein explains in terms of motivational deficiency and insufficient effort, do not qualify as aberrations from the universal purposefulness of human action. These cases can be seen as examples of inefficiency only by choosing to ignore certain purposes of which the firms and the individuals in the market take significant account.[15] Leibenstein may legitimately choose to concern himself with certain utilities to the exclusion of others. But for Austrians this does not successfully demonstrate the possibility of actions being taken that do not seek to pursue chosen goals with complete purposefulness.

On the other hand, however, Austrians do emphasize the scope for entrepreneurship. And, as stated earlier, this certainly does call for accepting the possibility of nonefficient actions. How can we reconcile the Austrian insistence on the universal purposefulness of action with the Austrian emphasis on entrepreneurship and, in particular, with Menger's recognition of *error* in human action? It is here that the possibility of a sympathetic reinterpretation of the concept of X-inefficiency becomes appealing to Austrians (if not, perhaps, to Leibenstein).

CHOICE, ALLOCATION, AND ACTION

Ever since Lord Robbins's *Nature and Significance of Economic Science* in 1932, economists have seen their discipline as concerned with the efficient disposition of means to achieve given ends. Economizing activity is that which seeks to impose upon the utilization of means, that pattern which is alone faithfully consistent with the adopted ranking of ends. Modern microeconomics is conducted very much *within* such a postulated means-ends framework. In contemporary parlance the task of *economizing* is identified with that of *allocating* scarce resources among competing uses to maximize utility, or profit, or something. And this task of allocation—itself essentially a computational task—is often described as *choice*. The selection of an optimal program of resource use with respect to a given ranking of goals is described as *choice*.

On the other hand, some contemporary economists, including not only the Austrians proper but also such critics as Shackle, have emphasized that to describe as choice the task of optimal allocation, with ends already ranked in advance, is to do violence to the nature of human decision making. True choice, or decision making, true human action, it is pointed out, must embody also the very selection and ranking of ends. More, it is argued in particular by Austrians, true choice must embrace not only the task of allocation but, at the same time, the *very perception of what ends and what means are to be relevant for allocation*. To commence an analysis of choice *after* a particular ends-means framework has been declared known and relevant, is to deal with choice in a manner that renders it completely mechanical. The *creativity* of choice, the element that makes action human, has been left out.

For Austrians, then, the role of purposefulness in human affairs goes far beyond ensuring that all actions will be efficient, with respect to adopted ends-means frameworks. Purposefulness becomes of overriding importance in inspiring man's alertness to the desirability of hitherto unknown means. For Austrians action may be genuinely in error, not in the sense of failing to optimize within an adopted ends-means context, but in the sense of having overlooked the desirability of possible ends, and the availability of ready-at-hand means. Universal purposefulness and the omnipresence of error are by no means inconsistent in the Austrian view; on the contrary they go hand in hand.

Notice that error means something other than lack of information. Information may, of course, be deliberately ignored because its acquisition is too costly. "Mistakes" made as the result of such ignorance are not true errors. They are the consequences deliberately accepted in the calculated gamble taken in not buying the costly information. But men also make mistakes in that they ignore possibly attractive opportunities not on account of deliberately avoided costs but on account of sheer failure to see what is there to be seen. Men do fail to maximize in this sense. And the notion of X-inefficiency does provide a tempting filing cabinet in which to pigeonhole this kind of error-laden action. In drawing attention to the broader notion of choice, transcending as it does the narrower concept of allocation and of economizing, the Austrian may well feel that he is roaming "beyond economic man."

ERROR AND THE ENTREPRENEURIAL ROLE

Scope for entrepreneurial activity is created in the market whenever (1) the same item is sold at different prices in different parts of the same market (or, as a special case, when the sum of prices of an input bundle is lower than the corresponding output revenue); or (2) two market participants, between whom a mutually beneficial exchange might have taken place, failed to enter into the trade. Each of these opportunities for profit cannot be imagined to emerge except as a result of error. It is thus *error* that is both responsible for absence of full coordination and to be credited with providing the incentive for its own discovery and correction.

Entrepreneurial alertness sparks the discovery of profit opportunities (and thus the elimination of discoordination). The market *process* then becomes visible as a series of innumerable changes in plans, each set in motion by the discovery of hitherto overlooked opportunities, or by the discovery of the *non*existence of opportunities previously believed to be available.

The concrete form in which a hitherto overlooked opportunity may present itself and thus the concrete tasks that an entrepreneur will undertake are of no particular consequence at this level of generality. What is of importance is that as the result both of the ignorance existing in the market at any given point in time, and of the circumstance that spontaneous and continual changes (in human tastes, resource availabilities and technological knowledge) generate a ceaseless flow of fresh ignorance, as it were, into the market—that as a result of this there is continual scope for the discovery by alert entrepreneurs of newly created opportunities.

The market offers incentives for the discovery of errors, in the profit opportunities that errors engender. Such opportunities for profit rest, in the last analysis, on the circumstance that, due to error, it may be the case that the current utilization of a unit of a resource or commodity fails to exploit its full productive or value potential. Error has generated inefficiency and thus an opportunity for entrepreneurial alertness to win profits through wiping out the inefficiency. Such inefficiency, it should be emphasized again, consists not in anyone's failure to seek allocative optimality—that is ruled out by the universal purposefulness of action; it consists in sheer unawareness of the available opportunities. Hence, the temptation (of course, only if its author so permits) to apply the term X-inefficiency (as distinct from allocative inefficiency) to these error-generated wastes in the elimination of which the entrepreneurial role consists.

At one point in his chapter,[16] Leibenstein appears to fear that X-inefficiency, by bringing about low profits or even losses, may in fact *inhibit* the entry of entrepreneurs. "In the traditional vision," Leibenstein remarks, "profits are the ideal signal" to attract entrepreneurial activity.

But, because of low profit X-inefficiency, we are given to understand, "profit opportunities may be . . . less apparent. Thus the entrepreneur has the function of ferreting out opportunities in markets where on the surface no opportunities seem to exist." I would submit that the entrepreneurial function must necessarily always be that of sniffing out opportunities that on the surface *do not* appear to exist. Once a profit opportunity has become *obvious*, it no longer retains its character of a pure profit opportunity. The market will have at once taken note of the opportunity by appropriate price changes, squeezing out the margin of pure profit. When we say that in the traditional view entrepreneurial entry is triggered by the discovery of pure profit opportunities, we must mean not so much the discovery of pure profits already made by others, as the discovery by alert, daring and far-sighted entrepreneurs, of profit opportunities in the future, as yet unnoticed and unexplored by others.

ENTREPRENEURSHIP, MARKET PROCESSES, AND THE CURRENT SCENE IN ECONOMICS

The neoclassical general equilibrium paradigm has long reigned, virtually unchallenged, at the core of economic theory. We are witnessing in our time a rather widespread dissatisfaction and disenchantment with that paradigm. It is beginning to become clear that the various proposals being made to enrich or improve or revise that paradigm cannot escape the task of grappling with the contribution that an understanding of the entrepreneurial function can provide. Austrians view these developments with very great interest indeed. It has been a pleasure to comment on one of the more imaginative proposals in this regard—the X-efficiency approach developed by Professor Leibenstein.

NOTES

1. W. J. Baumol, "Entrepreneurship in Economic Theory," *American Economic Review* 58 (May 1968): 72.

2. Chapter 6, Harvey Leibenstein, "The General X-efficiency Paradigm and the Role of the Entrepreneur," p. 129.

3. T. W. Schultz, "The Value of the Ability to Deal with Disequilibria," *Journal of Economic Literature* 13 (September 1975).

4. Chapter 6, p. 134.

5. Ibid.

6. Harvey Leibenstein, "Entrepreneurship and Development," *American Economic Review* 58 (May 1968): 75.

7. Ibid., p. 77.

8. William Jaffé, "Menger, Jevons and Walras De-Homogenized," *Economic Inquiry* 14 (December 1976).

9. G. J. Stigler, "The Xistence of X-efficiency," *American Economic Review* 66 (March 1976).

10. Harvey Leibenstein, "Allocative Efficiency vs. 'X-efficiency,'" *American Economic Review* 56 (June 1966): 407.

11. Harvey Leibenstein, *Beyond Economic Man* (Cambridge: Harvard University Press, 1976), p. 8.

12. Ibid.

13. Jaffé, "Menger, Jevons and Walras De-Homogenized," p. 521.

14. On this, *see* I. M. Kirzner, *The Economic Point of View* (Princeton, New Jersey: Van Nostrand, 1960), pp. 163–72.

15. See also B. J. Loasby, *Choice, Complexity and Ignorance* (Cambridge: Cambridge University Press, 1976), p. 119.

16. Chapter 6, p. 134.

THE ECONOMICS OF ERRANT ENTREPRENEURS

A recent stimulating *Freeman* article by Jane S. Shaw (April, 1987) provocatively drew attention to some of the benefits derived by society from
entrepreneurial daring and imagination—even when it turns out that
these are expressed in ventures that lose money and eventually fall by the
wayside. Ms. Shaw cites a spiffy and charming new restaurant in Bozeman, Montana, serving gourmet seafood. She judged the venture to be
"outlandishly extravagant and probably fool hardy," and suspects that the
opportunity she enjoys of contemplating blackened red snapper in a plea-
surable setting may turn out to be expensive for the restaurateurs, but is
grateful for the opportunity nonetheless. Ms. Shaw recognizes that no
business can operate over the long run without making a profit. But, she
concludes, "Bozeman's experience suggests that an endless succession
of businesses can operate without profits—as long as there are romantic
optimists to take up where the disillusioned leave off." Ms. Shaw sees this
as an illustration of George Gilder's conception of entrepreneurs as "giv-
ers," as economic agents who "orient their lives to the service of others."

Ms. Shaw's piece got me thinking. Most discussions of entrepreneurial energy, dating, and vision see *profitable* entrepreneurial activity
as largely responsible for capitalist success. Ms. Shaw is pointing out
that *unprofitable* entrepreneurship offers social benefits, too. Should
we, then, celebrate capitalism not only because it stimulates profitable
entrepreneurship, but because it stimulates unprofitable entrepreneurship as well? Should we indeed view entrepreneurs who lose money as
unselfish benefactors of market societies? Does the "social" perspective
suggest that young people should be encouraged to become independent
entrepreneurs—even where we judge them likely to lose money—on the
grounds that even erroneous entrepreneurs are socially beneficial?

A little thought will convince us, and I believe that Ms. Shaw would
thoroughly agree, *not* to arrive at affirmative answers to these questions

on the basis of Ms. Shaw's observations. There may be numerous benefits to society that derive from entrepreneurial error—but such benefits are likely to be far outweighed, in the judgment of most observers, by the *harm* caused by entrepreneurial errors. I shall later argue, in fact, that there is only *one* benefit to society arising out of unprofitable entrepreneurship that deserves to be treated as a fundamental advantage. All other benefits, while we may indeed be grateful for them, are likely to be enjoyed at the expense of more serious disadvantages both to others and to ourselves.

A profitable entrepreneurial venture benefits society in a way central to the logic of capitalist success. If an entrepreneur hires productive services for one million dollars and produces consumer goods that are bought for two million dollars, this means that services that might otherwise have produced goods judged to be worth not much more than one million have, in fact, produced goods that are much more valuable to market participants, as measured by money offered. An unprofitable venture, on the other hand, has *harmed* society insofar as it is likely to mean that it has used valuable, scarce social resources to produce goods worth *less* than other goods that could have been alternatively produced.

As Ms. Shaw has pointed out to us, however, it should not be thought that *no one* in society has benefited from a losing entrepreneurial venture. Clearly those who voluntarily sold to and those who voluntarily bought from losing entrepreneurs, did well for themselves—as do *all* participants in voluntary exchange transactions. Moreover, Ms. Shaw seems to suggest, not only does one who dines in an excellent, but money-losing, restaurant, gain from the venture, others do too. That is, we gather, because the parade of ever-changing opportunities offered by imaginative entrepreneurs undeterred by the losses of others, is itself a fascinating sight to watch, even if many of them, being unprofitable, are likely to disappear after a brief moment in the sun.

Despite all these benefits derived from unprofitable entrepreneurial ventures, we must recognize that few thoughtful observers are likely to judge that, all in all, the members of society should be grateful for this outpouring of entrepreneurial errors. The truth is that each and every entrepreneurial error represents a tragic waste of resources. For every beneficiary of such error, there are likely to be many whose lives, in consequence of this error, are poorer and less fulfilled than was in fact necessary. These victims of entrepreneurial error may never know that they are being harmed by these errors. In fact no one may ever know what alternative products these unprofitable ventures have precluded. As Henry Hazlitt taught us, the true costs of waste are always unseen—yet are nonetheless real and poignant.

The case for capitalism, for free entrepreneurial entry, does not and should not rest upon the possible residual benefits that some may derive from unprofitable entrepreneurial ventures. The great economic virtue of capitalism lies in its ability to stimulate vigorous and imaginative entrepreneurs who create *profitable* enterprises. In this way resources come to be deployed fully for purposes whose urgency or feasibility had hitherto been overlooked. The virtues of capitalism rest not on any supposed altruism evinced by entrepreneurs who lose money while catering to the tastes of a too-narrow group of consumers, but on the daring and judgment of entrepreneurs who see socially valuable opportunities before others do.

In fact, the one really valuable feature of unprofitable entrepreneurial endeavor lies in its crucially important role in stimulating *profitable* entrepreneurship. Only in a society where entrepreneurs are free to make errors, can we expect an outpouring of entrepreneurship to lift its economy to new, hitherto unglimpsed, heights of prosperity. Only where potential entrepreneurs are free to follow the lure of profits as *they* see them, will there be the unleashing of entrepreneurial vision, daring, and judgment that creates profits in fact—and in so doing, creates new, more valuable ways of utilizing resources.

To be sure, errant entrepreneurs suffer losses, and it is precisely because entrepreneurs with poor judgment are likely to think twice before jumping into dangerous waters, that such erroneous leaps are likely, to some extent, to be discouraged. Moreover, as Ludwig von Mises pointed out, it is likely to be those entrepreneurs who in the past have exhibited sound market judgment, who will have accumulated the capital funds that are now able to be channeled into new entrepreneurial ventures. Hence, the central social gain from losing entrepreneurial ventures is derived not by individuals unusual enough to enjoy the output of these overoptimistic ventures, but by all members of society insofar as they stand to gain from *superior* entrepreneurial judgment—a quality standard enforced by the severe discipline imposed on errant entrepreneurs, and stimulated by the freedom of market participants to follow their dreams and hunches as they, and they alone, see fit.

This freedom will, to be sure, always attract a stream of entrepreneurial fools and romantic optimists. But the incredible successes of capitalism do not depend on such follies; they depend on the stimulus the system provides to farsighted, clear-visioned entrepreneurs who are, at all times, competing away resources from foolish ventures toward more judicious, more accurate, dreams and aspirations.

THE 1975 NOBEL MEMORIAL PRIZE IN ECONOMICS: SOME UNCOMFORTABLE REFLECTIONS

On December 10, 1975, at what the *New York Times* described as a glittering Stockholm ceremony, the Nobel Memorial Prize in Economics was awarded jointly to Professor Leonid Vitalyevich Kantorovich, of the Moscow Institute of Economic Management, and to Professor Tjalling Charles Koopmans of Yale University. Their prize was awarded for their contributions to the theory of optimum allocation of resources.

Now concern with the "optimal allocation of resources" has been proclaimed in countless economics classrooms, and in innumerable economics textbooks, to be the very essence of economics. Ever since Lionel (now Lord) Robbins in 1932 defined economic science in terms revolving around men's allocative decisions, economists have seen efficiency in resource allocation as central to their discipline. It might seem then that Professors Kantorovich and Koopmans have won their Nobel prize for contributions going to the very heart of their science. Nonetheless, it is necessary to point out that, paradoxical though it may seem, in a very important sense the 1975 Nobel Prize in Economics was awarded for work having only peripheral relevance to the central contributions of economic science. What is of even greater concern, the interpretation placed by the Swedish Royal Academy on the contributions of the prize-winning scholars seems to involve implicit *denial* (if not outright ignorance) of these central contributions of economic science. These may seem surprising assertions; the following pages will attempt to provide the necessary elucidation.

It is to be hoped that, in pointing out these puzzling and disturbing circumstances, the writer will not be understood as seeking in any way to detract from the outstanding merit of the eminent men honored in Stockholm. Both of the laureates are brilliant scholars and dedicated scientists; the quality of their work undoubtedly meets the very highest standards of scientific excellence. Nonetheless, recognition of all this cannot absolve us from recognizing, at the same time, that unfortunate misunderstanding of the nature of the central problems of economic science, which appears to surround the 1975 prize.

The matter might be stated briefly, but far too superficially, in terms of a comment on the role of mathematics in economics. What both laureates—each of whom began his academic career strictly as a mathematician[1]—have devoted their lives to, it might be argued, is not, properly speaking, economics at all, but rather a special *genre* of applied mathematics. And, while questions of nomenclature might seem to be of only secondary importance, it in fact appears that, in the misunderstanding of the character and *significance* of these mathematical contributions, there lies embedded not merely semantic confusion, but also substantive unconcern with profoundly economic insights which have (at least up to the present) not proven amenable to mathematical formulation. This statement of the matter, however, while correct in itself, touches only on the surface of the issue.

ONE TECHNIQUE—MANY USES

A more thorough discussion may begin by noting that in awarding the prize jointly to a Russian and a (Dutch-born) American, the Royal Academy was intent on more than merely recognizing the international character of the scientific contributions they wished to honor. What it was evidently intended to emphasize was that the techniques of optimal resource allocation contained in modern activity analysis are in principle applicable alike to economic systems reflecting sharply divergent institutional patterns. As the *New York Times* (October 15, 1975) expressed it in the words of a distinguished colleague of Koopmans: "Activity analysis is used by economists and operations researchers to select the optimum production technique when several competing techniques are available, either at the level of the corporation, as in the United States, or at the national level, as in the planned Communist economies of Eastern Europe. . . . The indifference of these methods to the institutional arrangements of the economic system have permitted a degree of communication and intellectual exchange that could not otherwise have taken place."

This view sees economists as concerned with seeking techniques to solve resource allocation problems. These problems of securing optimum allocation of resources present themselves at a variety of levels. They present themselves, in capitalist societies, at the level of the firm; they present themselves similarly, in socialist societies, to the central planners. The techniques required to solve these allocation problems are, in principle, common to these problems regardless of institutional context. In principle the mathematical techniques employed by activity analysts to assist corporate decision making in the West, are the very same techniques needed for efficient decision making by central planners in the East. Economic science is now visible, then, as consisting of a mathematics of decision making which transcends institutional differences: what is valid for capitalist firms is valid, in principle, for socialist societies.

MISSING THE POINT

Now, we must readily concede several important elements of validity to this view. The abstract character of managerial decision making is, *given the sets of ends and means held respectively to be relevant,* indeed the same for all levels of decision making. Moreover, within a given ends-means framework, the problem facing the decision maker is indeed a mathematical one. In this context the development of activity analysis, or operations research, has been and will continue to be of extraordinary significance and usefulness. But it is a mistake to see this mathematics of optimal allocation and decision making—enormously valuable though it unquestionably is—as making up essentially the intellectual contribution of economic science. And, perhaps even more important, the uncritical assumption that application of the techniques appropriate to securing resource-allocative efficiency at the level of the firm, to the level of planning for a whole society, can achieve corresponding *social* "efficiency,"—begs entirely those questions which *are* at the heart of economics.

When Lionel Robbins in 1932 defined economic science as concerned with the implications of man's resource-allocative decisions, he did *not* mean that the central task of economics is to provide techniques for efficient allocation. Nor, it should be emphasized, was he referring at all to the concept of the "social" allocation of resources. (In fact the latter concept, while central to so many introductory textbooks and to so much work in theoretical welfare economics, is a highly dubious one.[2]) Robbins was simply defining economics as concerned with the social consequences of the circumstance that decision makers do in fact seek—each within his own framework—to achieve efficiency. Economics, in this view, is concerned not at all with how to achieve individual or social efficiency;

but rather with the social forces generated impersonally by the interaction of numerous decision makers each of whom is seeking to allocate his resources optimally. In assuming that the efficiency which firms can achieve by operations analysis, can be achieved for "society" by the use of similar techniques on the part of central planners, one is in fact *ignoring* the conclusions of Robbinsian economic science. The matter is of course vitally bound up with Mises' pioneering demonstration in 1920 of the necessary failure of socialist economic calculation. The immediate issue was perhaps most clearly stated by Hayek many years later:

> What is the problem we wish to solve when we try to construct a rational economic order? On certain familiar assumptions the answer is simple enough. *If* we possess all the relevant information, *if* we can start out from a given system of preferences, and *if* we command complete knowledge of available means, the problem which remains is purely one of logic. . . .
>
> This, however, is emphatically *not* the economic problem which society faces. . . .
>
> The peculiar character of the problem of a rational economic order is determined precisely by the fact that the knowledge of the circumstances of which we must make use never exists in concentrated or integrated form but solely as the dispersed bits of incomplete and frequently contradictory knowledge which all the separate individuals possess. The economic problem of society is thus not merely a problem of how to allocate "given" resources—if "given" is taken to mean given to a single mind which deliberately solves the problem set by these "data." It is rather a problem of how to secure the best use of resources known to any of the members of society, for ends whose relative importance only these individuals know. Or, to put it briefly, it is a problem of the utilization of knowledge which is not given to anyone in its totality.[3]

Here, in this 1945 statement by one of the 1974 Nobel laureates in economics, we have the definitive critique of the confusion we have seen to surround the award of the 1975 prizes.

THE KNOWLEDGE IS LACKING

To be able to discuss allocative decision making at all, it is necessary to presume that the decision maker has knowledge of the sets of ends and means with respect to which efficient allocation is sought. But *absence of such knowledge in centralized form* is precisely what in fact constitutes, for Hayek, the economic problem facing society. To assume, therefore, that even the most powerful and sophisticated of mathematical techniques can achieve for society the efficiency they can win for the firm, is to overlook the essence of the economic problem with which society must grapple.

One of the achievements of the market is that it generates impersonal forces which govern the size of firms. Firms which are "too small" find themselves facing opportunities for profitable expansion or merger. Firms which are "too large" find themselves at a disadvantage when facing the competition of smaller, nimbler competitors. What determines whether a firm is "too large" depends on many considerations.[4] Certainly one consideration of overriding importance has to do with the difficulty, in large organizations, of funneling the information necessary for efficient central decision making, to those entrusted with the organization's management. The market tends to limit the sizes of its decision making units to permit optimal deployment of planning techniques *within* these units, while harnessing the "invisible hand" of the market to achieve a tendency toward coordination *between* these units. All this is very much at the center of economic science,—although it shares little indeed of the mathematical character of the theory of resource allocation techniques.

AN IMPROPER ASSUMPTION

Simply to *assume* that society as a whole can be organized as a single firm, run as a centrally planned organization, and thus be able to employ the techniques of activity analysis, is to overlook what Hayek, at least, perceived, in effect, as the core concern of economic science. To be sure, the eminent scholars who pioneered in the development of mathematical allocative techniques are not, other points of possible vulnerability aside, to be criticized for assuming entirely correctly that these techniques can be useful wherever allocative decisions are in a position to be made. But we do have the obligation to point out that the economic problem facing society concerns precisely those circumstances under which, in fact, allocative decisions are *not* in a position to be made.

Economics has, ever since Mises, had a very great deal to contribute on why such circumstances are inevitable; and ever since Adam Smith economics has had a great deal to say about how, under such circumstances, the economic problem faced by society comes to be solved. Those who understand the enormous social significance of economic science as it has developed over the past two centuries, cannot therefore but be profoundly disturbed by the continued evidence that the core contributions of the discipline have simply not been noticed by those in the best position to do so. The story of the 1975 Nobel Memorial Prize in Economics suggests indeed that the light shed by economic science continues to fall on an as yet altogether incompletely illuminated intellectual landscape. All these are indeed uncomfortable, but nonetheless apparently inescapable, reflections.

NOTES

1. In fact Koopmans' footnote citation of Kantorovich's work refers to him as "the Russian mathematician" (T. C. Koopmans, *Three Essays on the State of Economic Science*, McGraw-Hill, 1957, p. 68n.).

2. On this see J. M. Buchanan, "What Should Economists Do?," *Southern Economic Journal*, January 1964.

3. F. A. Hayek, "The Use of Knowledge in Society," *American Economic Review*, September, 1945; reprinted in *Individualism and Economic Order*, University of Chicago Press, 1948, pp. 77–78.

4. See the classic paper by R. H. Coase, "The Nature of the Firm," *Economica*, November, 1937; reprinted in G. J. Stigler and K. Boulding, eds., *Readings in Price Theory*, Irwin, 1952. See also A. A. Alchian and H. Demsetz, "Production, Information Costs, and Economic Organization," *American Economic Review*, December, 1972.

HAYEK AND ECONOMIC IGNORANCE:
REPLY TO FRIEDMAN

In his stimulating and far-ranging paper, dealing with the implications of *ignorance* for human society, Jeffrey Friedman leads us across a number of disciplines. One facet of Friedman's paper draws on certain themes in Austrian (and especially Hayekian) economics, in which the economic advantages of capitalism are attributed to its ability to transcend ignorance. In particular Friedman explores the extent to which the political process might possibly achieve parallel victories over ignorance. In this comment we shall argue that Friedman's grasp of the Austrian position (and therefore of its understanding of capitalist success) is incomplete; as a result Friedman appears to have missed the principal reason why such parallel victories are not to be expected.

There are in fact *two* distinct senses in which the price system of the market tends to overcome the widespread ignorance that stands in the way of effective utilization of available resources in order to satisfy consumer needs and preferences. Friedman has focused on one of these two senses, but has, as we shall see, ignored the second.

One sense in which the price system has been seen as overcoming allocation problems attributable to ignorance, is that in which prices are *signals*. The driver of a northbound car on Road A is aware that it is intersected by Road B, running in the east-west direction. The driver of the northbound car does not, however, know whether there are cars traveling along Road B at a speed and at a time that should call for him to slow down or stop before crossing the intersection. Signal lights can help in such a situation. A green light facing our driver assures him that (in a law-abiding society) he need not fear a collision as he continues traveling north through the intersection. The green signal light conveys this information "economically"; there is no need for our driver to know any further details concerning the traffic along Road B. Market prices are, as a result of the work of Hayek cited by Friedman, widely understood in the economics profession as fulfilling a similar signaling function.

From *Critical Review* 18, 4 (2006): 411–15, ISSN 0891-3811. © 2007 Critical Review Foundation. Reprinted by permission of the publisher (Taylor & Francis Ltd., http://www.tandfonline.com).

A consumer of gasoline need not know the detailed reasons for a restriction in the oil supply; the market price of oil, which has presumably risen as a result of this supply restriction, will lead the consumer to conserve gasoline despite his ignorance of those detailed reasons. Prices thus guide production and consumption decisions to take account of relevant facts concerning which they are genuinely ignorant.

Friedman correctly identifies this function of capitalist prices. However he appears, perhaps justifiably or at least excusably, to have become somewhat confused by the way in which some economists, possibly including Hayek himself, depict the role of "trial and error" in the market process. Producers, restaurateurs, and others who have incorrectly read consumer preferences are led by the invisible hand of consumers' "unwitting" experimentation (Friedman 2005, xxix) to adjust their offerings in a way that ultimately supports the above-described "signaling" function of prices. Friedman attributes the success of capitalism to such a trial-and-error process (and finds no parallel to such a process in the political sphere).

It is here that one must protest that Friedman has not grasped the true driving force of the capitalist market process. In his trial-and-error process, according to Friedman, the market decision maker reacts "passively" to the prices he encounters. But the truth is that the market process is far more subtle in its ability to overcome ignorance than Friedman recognizes. The signaling function of prices operates, in its completest sense, only in the imaginary *equilibrium* context—in which there is no need and no scope for trial and error. It is here that we must take note of the *second* sense in which market prices have the extraordinary capacity of overcoming widespread ignorance. This consists in the capacity of (disequilibrium) market prices *to offer patterns which can be translated as pure profit opportunities*. This happens only in a market that is *not* in a state of equilibrium, and it has (almost) nothing to do with the signaling function of prices in the equilibrium state.

In the disequilibrium market (and this term is merely technical jargon to denote real-world capitalism), relevant ignorance *manifests itself in the form of opportunities for pure entrepreneurial profit*. By "relevant" ignorance we refer to situations in which resources that *could* produce more valuable outputs are being misallocated (because of ignorance) to less valuable uses. (By "more or less valuable" we refer to value as expressed in today's actual "disequilibrium" market prices.) The *central marvel* of the market process consists in the circumstance that such "inefficient" use of resources offers *at the very same time, by its very definition,* an opportunity for pure gain. When a unit of resource is currently put to a low-value use, it can be competed away from that use at a relatively low price. Where that unit of resource can be deployed to satisfy a want valued at a higher level of urgency (as reflected in output prices paid), its transferral to that more urgent use simultaneously: (a) wins pure profit for the alert entrepreneur who saw and grasped this opportunity, and (b) tends to correct the ignorance-based prior misallocation of resources. As distinct from the signaling role (of equilibrium prices) noted above, we may refer to this second sense in which market prices tend to overcome ignorance, as the *discovery* function of prices.

Signals transmit, in an economical way, already known facts. But market prices, we can now see, do far more than this. Market prices stimulate the *discovery* of earlier mistakes of which no one was aware. Market prices *attract attention* to the presence of such mistakes, by making it profitable to correct them. Entrepreneurs "smell" such opportunities; this tends to generate a continual series of discoveries, a continual tendency for ignorance to be overcome.

It should be noticed that this "discovery procedure" (Hayek's phrase),[1] which constitutes the competitive-entrepreneurial market process, is possible only because the profit opportunities that attract alert entrepreneurial notice *are* simply that very array of prices that expresses the earlier ignorance responsible for the inefficiency that the market tends to eliminate. To seize such profit opportunities *is* to move to correct those inefficiencies (i.e., to overcome the ignorance responsible for them).

What is remarkable in the market process is thus that *its very mistakes* (rooted in unavoidable, continually renewed ignorance) *contain the seeds of their own correction* (through the incentive they offer for the entrepreneurial discovery of pure profit opportunities). This remarkable circumstance has no counterpart outside the market context. Consider, for example, a socialist society. No doubt such a society offers individuals, whether government officials or plain citizens, opportunities to discover, and attempt to grasp, pure gain. "Entrepreneurial" individuals can be expected to discover and to grasp such opportunities. But nothing turns the grasping of such opportunities into useful steps in overcoming the ignorance that (the most well-meaning) social planners need to overcome in order to improve the efficiency with which they are allocating social resources.

It is this second sense in which market prices play their role in overcoming ignorance, the sense not taken note of by Friedman, which underlines *most* clearly the crucial difference between the market arena and the political arena.

NOTE

1. Friedman cites (among a number of Hayek's works) his rightly celebrated 1945 paper, "The Use of Knowledge in Society." In that paper Hayek indeed *seems* to focus (and Friedman is entirely correct in so reading him) mainly upon the signaling function of prices (at or near equilibrium). It was Hayek's mentor, Ludwig von Mises, who most clearly identified the "entrepreneurial discovery" role of (disequilibrim) market prices. That Hayek did recognize this more dynamic function of prices in the rough and tumble of entrepreneurial competition, is amply clear from, *inter alia*, his important paper "Competition as a Discovery Procedure" (delivered as a lecture in 1968; published as chapter 12 in Hayek 1978).

REFERENCE

Hayek, F. A. 1978. *New Studies in Philosophy, Politics, Economics, and the History of Ideas.* Chicago: University of Chicago Press.

There are few topics concerning which economists are currently more able to secure respectful public attention, than that of economic growth. "To foster a more rapid growth rate" has become an almost unquestioned goal of governments throughout the world. A very considerable fraction of the research efforts of economists is, and has been now for several years, directed to the problem of how this goal is to be achieved. The course of political and economic history in recent decades has focused both professional and lay attention upon the problem of growth and development, pushing out of the limelight even such long-time favorites as the problem of economic stability. Elections have revolved around economic growth, commencement day orators, columnists and editorial writers consider the topic suitable grist for their mills, and books on this supposedly esoteric subject have become popularly accepted as fare for the masses.

There are a number of points of view from which this preoccupation with growth and development appears to be based on misconception and misunderstanding. This article is concerned with the dangers which this preoccupation must seem to imply for all who are concerned with the maintenance of individual liberties. We will analyze the growth problem in order to expose those fallacies in popular thinking on the subject that are responsible for the potential dangers to a free society arising out of this preoccupation. Many of these fallacies will be seen to have their counterparts in the writings of economists themselves; this is not entirely a matter for surprise, but in any event makes our task no less pressing.

That the popular growth preoccupation carries with it implications that must seem menacing to the individualist, hardly needs elaborate demonstration. A growth policy invariably means a government policy. A growth or development policy may call, at worst, for a completely socialized economy; at best it implies a degree of regimentation forced upon an otherwise free enterprise system. Those preoccupied with growth generally believe, first, that growth is *per se* desirable; second, that the spontaneous growth of a market economy is likely to fall short of its full potential; and third, that this full potential may be achieved by

From *New Individualist Review* (Summer 1963). © 1981 by Liberty Fund, Inc.

appropriate governmental policies. Many even of those who have some understanding of the allocative functions of the price system, and who appreciate the market as an engine of social efficiency, are convinced that for growth purposes it is necessary to resort to governmental direction of economic activity. Like Keynes, they see no reason to suppose that the market seriously misemploys the factors of production which are in use;[1] perhaps, unlike Keynes, they see no reason even to believe that the market fails seriously in providing employment for all factors that can be efficiently employed, but they do nonetheless believe that the unhampered market fails to direct economic activity along the channels required for growth.[2] It is this belief that leads to the advocacy of programs of government activity that must necessarily impinge more or less heavily upon the range of opportunities open to individuals.

This article will focus critical attention on the analytical underpinnings of these beliefs, and will specifically deal with the following four aspects of the problem:

1) We will examine the view that distinguishes sharply between the current allocation of resources on the one hand, and the task of making provision for future growth on the other. It is this postulated distinction that is responsible for the possibility of a posture of simultaneous acceptance of the short-run allocational capabilities of the market, and distrust of its long-run propensities. At the same time it is to this alleged distinction that must be attributed the uncritical acceptance of growth as a goal appropriate to all situations.

2) We will examine the claim that long-run market-achieved results may be expected to be rendered inadequate because of what the economist calls "externalities" operating over time. We will examine both the claim itself, as well as the corollary drawn from it to the effect that, in consequence, government interference with the market may be desirable.

1. See J. M. Keynes, *The General Theory of Employment, Interest, and Money* (New York: Harcourt, Brace, 1936), p. 379.

2. For some recent examples of this widespread belief, see Karl de Schweinitz, "Free Enterprise in a Growth World," *Southern Economic Journal*, October, 1962; Stephen A. Marglin, "The Social Rate of Discount and the Optimal Rate of Investment." *Quarterly Journal of Economics*, February, 1963; review by Joan Robinson, *Economic Journal*, March, 1963, p. 125.

3) We will examine the uncritical use, in the growth literature, of national income (or related) figures as a means of judging and measuring the extent of achieved desirable growth.

4) We will subject to critical examination the welfare theory that is implicit in much of the current literature and discussion of growth. This theory will be scrutinized and held up for comparison with the more limited welfare propositions that are acceptable to economics seen as a science of human action, and to individualist-minded critics.

As we shall discover, these different aspects are intimately bound up with one another. Fallacies which we will expose in connection with one of these aspects, will be found to have great relevance to others. Nonetheless, for the sake of clarity, it appears expedient to deal with one matter at a time.

We turn to the first aspect: that of the postulated distinction between the goals of short-run allocation, and long-run growth. This distinction is one that is made repeatedly in the economic literature. (It is not met with quite as frequently in lay writings, probably because the allocation problem itself is poorly understood in these writings.) Many textbooks of economics inform students that allocation and the provision of growth are *separate* functions of economic systems.[3] An outstanding British economist has declared that the study of growth, rather than of allocation of scarce resources among competing ends, should be seen as the core of economic science.[4] Certain economists suggest that the Soviet economy may not be successful in allocating its resources, but is successful in achieving rapid growth.[5] And the list could easily be prolonged.

The rationale of the distinction is a simple one. At any one time an economy finds itself with given resources that set the ceiling on current productive potential. Over time the volume and composition of these resources may change, bringing about corresponding changes in the

3. For examples see Paul T. Homan, Albert Gailord Hart, and Arnold W. Sametz, *The Economic Order* (New York: Harcourt, Brace, 1958), p. 10; George J. Stigler, *The Theory of Price* (New York: Macmillan, 1952), p. 4; Richard H. Leftwich, *The Price System and Resource Allocation* (New York: Holt, Rinehart & Winston, 1960), p. 20; see also Frank H. Knight, *The Economic Organization* (New York: Kelley, 1951), pp. 12–13.

4. Peter J. D. Wiles, *Price, Cost and Output* (Oxford: Blackwell, 1956).

5. J. M. Montias, "Planning with Material Balances in Soviet-Type Economies," *American Economic Review,* December, 1959, p. 982.

productive possibilities of the economy. Two separate problems are then distinguished. First, there is the problem of squeezing the greatest possible volume of current output, in value terms, from the currently available body of resources. This is the allocation problem. Second, there is the problem of ensuring that the change over time in the volume of available resources be so arranged as to permit rapid growth.

But the superficiality of the distinction can be shown with equal simplicity. Insofar as the change over time in the volume of resources can be consciously manipulated, this second problem reduces itself immediately to an aspect of the first one. A policy today for tomorrow's resource availability must mean, if it means anything at all, a choice with respect to current production with today's resources that will have an impact on the availability of resources tomorrow. Such a choice clearly involves a particular aspect of the general problem of the allocation of today's resources.

So the writers who profess to have confidence in the ability of the market to allocate resources, but not in the ability of the market to achieve a desirable growth rate, are open to the charge of inconsistency. For the very same price mechanism through which the market system allocates current resources as between the production of shoes and the production of sausages, is available for the allocation of resources as between the production of shoes for today and the production of shoe factories for the future. In fact, the market has developed a wide range of institutions through which intertemporal exchanges can be made between individuals, in this way achieving an allocation of resources over time. There seems no obvious reason to assume the market to be any less efficient in this allocative task than in its others. Writers who wish to express doubts on this score can do so more easily by diverting attention altogether from the intertemporal allocation of resources involved in a growth policy. Their pursuance of this course must appear distinctly dangerous to individualists, if only because this procedure masks the extent to which a governmental growth policy interferes with the pattern of allocation that would emerge from the actions of free individuals acting through the market.[6]

In particular, the spurious distinction between "allocation" and "growth" must be held largely responsible for the uncritical adoption of growth as a desirable goal in all situations. And here, as elsewhere, it is the duty of the economist to point out the *costs* associated with an

---

6. See, e.g., the paper by de Schweinitz cited above, n. 2, for statements concerning the necessity to abrogate freedom for growth purposes.

otherwise desirable outcome—costs which may be of such a magnitude as to render the outcome no longer desirable at all. By implying that a growth policy is not at the same time a policy with respect to the allocation of current resources, growth writers are able to create the illusion that growth involves no cost—and is hence unquestionably desirable. By ignoring the costs required for growth, such writers are led to point accusing fingers at the performance of the market, charging that it does not achieve a sufficiently rapid growth rate. As soon as the growth problem is placed in proper perspective as an allocation problem, however, it is no longer at all obvious that growth *per se* is necessarily desirable. One no longer has the right, then, to condemn the market for not achieving a given rate of growth, when it is by no means clear *a priori* whether such a rate justifies the costs involved. In fact, the costs may be such that the most desirable goal turns out to be not to grow at all, or even to decline. The propensity to ignore the costs of achieving growth, therefore, can only facilitate government interference with the intertemporal choices of individuals through the market, by concealing this kind of cost of a growth policy altogether.

A more sophisticated rationalization for not relying on the market for growth purposes, is provided by economists concerned with external economies and diseconomies. Externalities have roughly to do: (a) with cases in which an individual is held back from undertaking a project the costs of which would be more than offset by the benefits accruing to the economy, because the project requires that while he shoulder all the costs himself, he share the benefits with many others; (b) with cases in which an individual is induced to undertake a project the costs of which fail to be offset by the accruing benefits, because he is able to escape some of these costs while reaping the full benefit for himself. Such possibilities would constitute instances in which private costs or benefits fail to coincide with "social" costs or benefits. Critics of the market economy have pointed to such cases as instances calling for government intervention to prevent an otherwise faulty allocation of "social resources."

A special example of the externalities argument occurs where a large project (or series of complementary projects), in which many people would participate jointly in both costs and benefits, would be of net benefit to each of them—but which no single individual wishes to embark upon by himself for fear that he might be left to bear all the costs while sharing the benefits with others. It is this kind of possibility that is frequently implied when the necessity for central direction of a developing economy is advocated. It is argued, that is, that the profitability of investment projects frequently hinges on the simultaneous undertaking by others of complementary investment projects. A railroad will extend a commuter line to the outskirts of a city only if a series of housing projects is expected to be built there; but the housing projects may in turn be contingent on the prospect of the commuter line extension.[7] In the words of one recent writer, "an atomistic market provides no means of breaking the deadlock: none of us is willing to invest unilaterally, each of us is prepared to if we all do."[8]

Nonetheless it is not clear that externalities and interdependence provide sufficient justification for persuading a society of free men to surrender significant degrees of their liberties. This position is based on two grounds. First, it can be shown that externalities do not render the market as impotent an engine of efficiency as might appear at first blush. Second, it can be argued that even where externalities cannot be overcome by the market process, the situation does not obviously justify coercion as a solution. We take up these two points in order.

Externalities may not seriously impair the efficiency of the market, because the market itself is able to exert forces capable of overcoming many of the obstacles raised by these externalities. The existence of interdependence sets up market forces making for conglomeration. External economies tend to become internalized by mergers of firms into larger units, or by voluntary cooperative activity.[9] This can be as true for long-range projects as for immediate ones. So long as the size of the proposed projects remains relatively small as compared with the size of the economy as a whole, this process can be carried on without seriously affecting the competitiveness of the system, and provides, in effect, a market alternative to central planning of interrelated projects.

With special regard to intertemporal allocation, too, the market is capable of considerable flexibility in developing institutions to cope with problems of interdependence. The relatively long-range plans of market

---

7. See J. de V. Graaff, *Theoretical Welfare Economics* (Cambridge: Cambridge University Press, 1957), p. 104.

8. Marglin, *op. cit.*, p. 103.

9. See Otto A. Davis and Andrew Whinston, "Externalities, Welfare, and the Theory of Games," *Journal of Political Economy*, June, 1962.

participants can interact very powerfully through intertemporal markets of all types. Forward markets, bond markets, and securities exchanges are all market institutions through which the diverse expectations of prospective investors can become mutually adjusted.

Fully as important, however, as the recognition of the capabilities of the market in overcoming problems of interdependence is the recognition of the significance of problems of this kind that still remain unresolved. Such a recognition will show that it is far from obvious that discovery of unresolved problems of interdependence constitutes an automatic case for central direction. The fact is that consideration of the hypothetical case of interdependence frequently leads one to appreciate the obvious benefits that would accrue from concerted action, without a full understanding of the associated costs. It is easy to compare one situation in which the possibilities of concerted action are not exploited, with the situation in which they are exploited, and become convinced of the resulting gains. But it is also easy to do so without taking into account the fact that the organization of concerted action involves an unavoidable cost in terms of communication of knowledge, persuasion of individuals to participate, ensuring conformity with the agreement, and so forth. These costs must, in the nature of the problem, be borne if concerted action is to take place. If these costs can be covered by the gains, there is a market basis for expecting that the task of securing concerted action will be undertaken. If the market does *not* achieve such concerted action, either through merger or cooperative agreement, this is then *prima facie* evidence that these costs are excessive and render concerted action no longer desirable on a net basis.

Under such conditions, central direction in order to achieve concerted interdependent actions by a group, becomes visible in its true light. Central direction is not a short-cut method of pushing aside the senseless obstacles to progress erected by stubborn externalities. Central direction is seen rather as involving costs of a particular kind, *alternative* to those other direct costs of achieving concerted action—costs that the market has pronounced to be so high as to make such group action not worthwhile. These particular costs involved in central direction include, of course, the liberties that must be sacrificed in the process. The argument that interdependence problems call for solution by central direction, like other such arguments, rests heavily on forgotten costs. *All* group action requires some degree of surrender of individual decision-making authority. The members of a golf club have given the club's governing body the power to make a range of decisions affecting the members. Where the market finds it unprofitable to form such clubs, this means that the costs of persuading potential members to make such a surrender are excessive and not justified by the anticipated result. Central direction does not avoid these costs; it merely substitutes its own. (After all, forcing people to join a club is not necessarily a desirable way of getting recalcitrant potential members to do what is good for them.)

A pivotal position is occupied in the literature on growth, especially that relating to proposals for a centrally directed growth program, by the *measurement* of national product, or income, or similar quantities, through such aggregative measures as national income figures. These figures, perhaps adjusted to a per capita basis, are employed to show how slow our "growth rate" has been, and thus how unsuccessful our market economy has been in this respect. It is to be stressed that only because such tools of measurement are available for use, and are widely known (by, among others, journalists), is it that the concept of a "growth rate" has gained popularity. But for the ready availability of these aggregative measures, the growth concept itself might not have been able to have been crystallized sufficiently so as to capture public attention. These aggregative figures are used in growth discussions as reflecting the level of economic well-being of a nation. It will be pointed out in this section that the indiscriminate use of such figures in the growth literature has had harmful results for two distinct reasons: (a) such aggregative measures suffer from serious (and well-recognized) limitations in respect to their ability to serve as measurements of economic well-being; (b) the use of these measures, by ignoring the serious conceptual problems which they involve, helps to create the image of a "national" rate of growth, that corresponds to no rigorous theoretical concept whatsoever.

Gross National Product figures[10] measure the annual physical output of an economy valued at market prices. Placed on a per capita basis, historical figures are frequently used to measure achieved growth, which may then be held up for comparison with similar figures for other

10. We use Gross National Product (GNP) figures for our purposes here, but other similar figures are open to similar criticism. Of course nothing in these remarks refers to the use of such figures with due awareness of their limitations.

countries. It will be pointed out here that because national product figures can necessarily measure output defined only in a particular way, their use in this manner in the growth literature—usually as indices of rising standards of economic well-being—may be highly misleading. These limitations[11] do not preclude the figures from having great usefulness, properly used. The growth problem, however, is precisely one where these limitations (or at least some of them) become crucial. These figures measure the physical output in value terms, but it is well-known that the resulting figure cannot take into consideration many important items of output that do not flow through the market; and, in addition, the output figure makes no attempt to measure the enjoyment of leisure by the members of the economy. This latter omission is, of course, not open to criticism, in a measure of output as such; but it does render the resulting figure quite misleading as a measure of economic growth, especially for comparative purposes. We are entitled to assume that the concept of economic growth, for the layman certainly, refers broadly to increases in economic well-being, rather than to increases in purely physical output. After all, as one writer has pointed out, an economy specializing in breeding rabbits could reach a very high growth rate, in physical terms.[12] But if this is granted, then a figure that reflects nothing of the leisure-dimension of well-being must seem highly distorted. Two economies growing at the same rate, according to these measurements, but which differ in the rate of addition to their leisure time, can surely in no wise be described as keeping pace with one another.[13]

The fact is that aggregate measures such as Gross National Product must necessarily fail to express sensitively many of the variations and refinements that must be taken into consideration in assessing the increase in overall economic well-being. The current fashion of measuring growth in Gross National Product terms, and of proceeding to use the resulting calculations in policy contexts, cannot fail to exert powerful constraints on the direction of subsequent individual activities. Insofar as policy is deliberately directed to accelerating growth in terms of GNP,

11. See P. T. Bauer and B. S. Yamey, *The Economics of Underdeveloped Countries* (Chicago: University of Chicago Press, 1957), Chapter II, for an excellent survey.

12. See E. Malinvaud, "An Analogy Between Atemporal and Intertemporal Theories of Resource Allocation," *Review of Economic Studies*, June, 1961, pp. 148–50, for a sophisticated critique of the "rate of growth" concept.

13. This, of course, vitiates growth comparisons between the U.S. and the U.S.S.R.

it must necessarily nudge the expansion of economic activity away from those dimensions of progress which find no expression in these aggregates, toward those which do. This may well, for example, encourage rabbit breeding at the expense of leisure, free individual preferences possibly being to the contrary notwithstanding.

Perhaps even more important, however, than the omissions that unavoidably cloud aggregates such as GNP, is the fact that the widespread use of these figures draws attention completely away from the numerous well-nigh insoluble problems involved in measuring at all the almost incredibly elusive "quantity" which GNP purports to represent, and in distilling "its" rate of growth. The truth is that the "level of economic well-being" and similar entities, during any one period, are vexingly but inescapably multi-dimensional—they involve innumerable heterogeneous goods, valued by innumerable different people. To collapse this concept into a single figure raises theoretical and statistical problems so serious that almost any use of the resulting figure in popular media can hardly fail to mislead. When this use is glibly extended to hatch out a rate-of-growth concept, it is to be feared that economists are permitting this apparently simple measure—their own creature—to foster habits of thought in their own minds and in those of the public, which would perhaps never have emerged had the intrinsic conceptual and measurement problems been borne in mind. There can be few more obtrusive examples of the tissue of fallacies that can emerge from ill-considered aggregation than this GNP-inspired notion of a "national" rate of economic growth—a notion whose appeal to the lay intellect is so suspiciously complete as to propagate an entirely new set of attitudes toward economic affairs.[14]

We turn to appraise the welfare theory that is implicit in much of the growth literature. Of all the habits of thought embedded in the growth literature, it is this that offers the most serious threat to the free society.

14. Among the more serious theoretical problems raised by the use of GNP figures as indices of growth are: (a) the aggregation of market values which individually reflect only marginal decisions and valuations; (b) the extent to which production for investment should be reflected in these measures. See J. Bonner and D. S. Lees, "Consumption and Investment," *Journal of Political Economy*, February, 1963; see also P. A. Samuelson, "The Evaluation of 'Social Income,' Capital Formation and Wealth," in F. A. Lutz and D. C. Hague, eds., *The Theory of Capital* (New York: St. Martin's Press, 1961), p. 56.

There is, in fact, a profound difficulty (from a welfare theory point of view) that seriously affects all discussions of growth "policies," and especially those relevant to long-range policies for the future. This difficulty arises from the fact that in formulating any such policy, one is necessarily involving the welfare of unborn generations; so that, before even attempting the task of policy formulation, it is necessary to clear up the problem of precisely how the welfare of as yet non-existent people is to be taken into consideration. This problem is crucially relevant to the maintenance of a free society; it is moreover relevant to the "scientific" quality of growth propositions underlying government policy in this context.

The truth of the matter is that economists are incapable of asserting *any* propositions concerning welfare that do not depend in some way on necessarily arbitrary individual judgments of value. To the extent that economists make welfare propositions, they are either acting in a non-scientific capacity, or they are *applying* scientific propositions in the context of given dominant arbitrary value judgments.[15] All this is true of welfare propositions in general; it is *a fortiori* true of propositions involving unborn generations (and thus of growth literature) in particular.

To put the matter in a different way, economists are unable to state as a scientific proposition that any given change yields a net benefit to "society." The reason for this is that ultimately no scientific meaning can be attached to the phrase "the net benefit to society."[16] The economist may be able to assert that acts freely performed by individuals have made *them* better off; but this does not preclude *others* from having been made worse off by these acts. And even if a change benefits every single individual (or benefits some without harming others), we have no scientific meaning to attach to the concept of "society's being better off," other than the fact that some *individuals* in society are better off.

"Group decision-making" can in no sense help us escape this impasse. Unless we *define* the social "good" as that emerging from some specified machinery for group decision-making, like majority rule (thereby making what seems to be a dangerous misuse of language), we cannot hope that

---

15. See the large welfare literature on these points, especially Murray N. Rothbard. "Toward a Reconstruction of Utility and Welfare Economics," in Mary Sennholz, ed., *On Freedom and Free Enterprise* (Princeton: Van Nostrand, 1956).

16. In the more important realm of metaphysics things are of course quite different.

any such group decision should "represent" the composite values of its members in a consistent fashion. To demonstrate this was the outstanding contribution of Arrow.[17]

But if all this is the case, what basis in consistent thought exists for long-range growth policies on the part of the state? We have shown in this essay that such policies can claim to be plans only if the benefits anticipated for the future are weighed against the associated current costs. But even if such a comparison is attempted, one is left facing the problem of how to *evaluate* the planned future gains. Ordinarily a plan involves a balance of yield against costs. In the growth case, not only are those who will enjoy the benefits *different people* from those who must bear the cost—these beneficiaries do not yet *exist*: their value scales are as yet nonexistent. How then can cost and benefit be meaningfully compared?

The problem can be restated in terms less skeptical of the possibility of scientific welfare propositions. Let us for the sake of argument concede that due attention to appropriate welfare criteria makes it possible to enunciate such propositions. These propositions are built out of changes in the welfare of *individuals*. Such changes can be defined only in terms of the value scales of the individuals themselves (so long as we eschew references to an absolute, metaphysical welfare). A person is made better off by a change if he prefers the new situation to the old. But such a preference can be described only against a background of *given* tastes. Should the change in situation be accompanied by a change in tastes, there may possibly exist no unambiguous meaning to the term "the preferred situation." Comparisons of benefit and cost are thus ruled out in this scheme of things, even between persons existing simultaneously; between persons not existing simultaneously, it seems hardly possible even to define what such a comparison should mean.[18]

It should be noticed that the sweeping implications of these considerations for growth "policies" have reference only to those of the state. As far as individuals are concerned, nothing need prevent them from

17. Kenneth Arrow, *Social Choice and Individual Values* (New York: John Wiley, 1951).

18. All this is well recognized in the literature. See I. M. D. Little, *A Critique of Welfare Economics* (Oxford: Clarendon Press, 1957, 2nd edition), p. 85; see also Jerome Rothenberg, *The Measurement of Social Welfare* (Englewood Cliffs: Prentice-Hall, 1961), pp. 52–58; Richard S. Weckstein, "Welfare Criteria and Changing Tastes," *American Economic Review*, March, 1962; Malinvaud, *op. cit.*, pp. 146–47.

exercising their own arbitrary judgments as to their current choices that might affect future generations. They may wish to consume all their capital and exhaust all the natural resources which they possess, leaving nothing left for posterity. Or they may conserve resources, accumulate capital, to prepare a wealthier environment for the future. It is perfectly in order that these choices be made on a non-scientific basis.

The devastating implications of the above considerations for state growth policies arise precisely from the fact that the state can hope to formulate such policies *only* as an individual does—that is, on the basis of arbitrary judgments of value. And it is here that the crucial issue for a free society is encountered. The arbitrary choices of the state can hardly fail to conflict with the arbitrary judgment of some of the citizens.

In effect, state growth policies, consciously or otherwise, require that the state set itself apart from the current wishes of its citizens, scan the future history of society, and pass judgment as to the most "desirable" inter-generation allocation of the "nation's" resources. The state becomes the guardian of the interests of its future citizens, it conserves resources for them, it deprives present citizens in order to accumulate capital for them—all this in a manner that *must* be arbitrarily different from the allocation pattern desired by at least some of the affected present citizens. Sometimes, indeed, this is explicitly recognized. Pigou deemed it the responsibility of the state to protect the long-run interests of society from the shortsighted selfishness of the current property-holders.[19]

At issue are some very fundamental questions concerning private property rights, and the proper functions, powers, and responsibilities of government. This is not the place to clarify these questions. Here it is merely desired to point out that government growth programs cannot avoid rigidly circumscribing the concept of property rights. Such programs involve the deliberate acceptance of a stewardship notion of property rights; they involve moreover the notion of a government elected by *today's* citizens, that should represent the interests also of *future* citizens (possibly in directions undesired by many of today's citizens). The implications of these matters require no elaboration.

A few final remarks concerning one further aspect of the fashionable emphasis on governmental growth policies may not be completely

19. See citations (and references to other writers) in de Graaff, *op. cit.*, p. 101.

out of place. We have referred to the pattern of development that would emerge from freely made multi-period choices of individual citizens acting through the intertemporal market. Whether growth or decline, this development may at least express the choices of today's citizens. (It may clearly be desirable in some contexts to allocate a larger portion of resources to earlier than to later periods.) Whatever the pattern of development, it depends for the success with which it reflects the wishes of the people, on the accuracy of the intertemporal market in registering the multi-period value rankings of individuals. And it is here that governmental growth (and other) policies may inhibit the desirable expression of these multi-period value rankings. An atmosphere in which individuals fear such things as chronic inflation, possible eventual abrogation of property rights, confiscatory taxation, and the like, cannot but distort the multi-period plans that individuals would otherwise make. Intervention in the intertemporal markets must, moreover, inevitably prevent them from registering individual multi-period value rankings as sensitively as possible. All this may lead conceivably to a pattern of historical development substantially different from what might have emerged from the free choices of the people working through the free intertemporal market.

THE THEORY OF ENTREPRENEURSHIP
IN ECONOMIC GROWTH

THE VALUE OF ENTREPRENEURSHIP

Why is entrepreneurship good for the economy? It is in answering this question that economics has its contribution to make. Economics explains that where there are unexploited profit opportunities, resources have been misallocated and resulted in some kind of social "waste." If a resource unit can be used to produce $15 worth of output and is currently being used to produce $10 worth of output, the current use of the resource is a wasteful one and offers an opportunity for pure profit, i.e., for entrepreneurship. A profit opportunity implies a preexisting waste. Entrepreneurship corrects waste.

Imperfect knowledge may be responsible for unexploited profit opportunities and for misallocated resources. But knowledge can be bought. If knowledge is cheaply available, how can there ever be an unexploited opportunity? The kind of ignorance responsible for profit opportunities may be an ignorance that people do not recognize. If I don't know someone's telephone number, I can expend resources to obtain the information. If, however, I don't know that this information exists, I won't be seeking information. Likewise, if I don't know that profit opportunities exist, these opportunities will remain unexploited. Entrepreneurial profit opportunities exist where people do not know what it is that they do not know, and do not know that they do not know it. The entrepreneurial function is to notice what people have overlooked.

ENTREPRENEURSHIP AND EQUILIBRIUM

In a state of economic equilibrium and perfect knowledge no misallocation would have occurred. It has been the economists' achievement to show that there are powerful forces which point toward equilibrium. Unfortunately, economists have often fallen into the trap of taking the equilibrating forces for granted and assuming that no entrepreneurial work remains to be done. On the one hand, economists are right to draw

From *Encyclopedia of Entrepreneurship*, ed. C. A. Kent, D. L. Sexton, and K. H. Vesper (Englewood Cliffs, N.J.: Prentice-Hall, 1982), 272–76. Reprinted by permission of Israel M. Kirzner.

attention to these forces. On the other hand, they are wrong to assume that the forces are so powerful and so rapid as to make the entrepreneurial process unimportant.

This can be clarified by an analogue: In any post office or bank, the lines of waiting people are of approximately equal length. The obvious explanation for this not-so-remarkable phenomenon is that whenever these lines happen to be of different length, it becomes "profitable" for someone to change from a long line to a shorter line. Were I to say that at all times lines in post offices and banks are of equal length, I would be wrong. In fact, it is precisely as a result of this imperfection that the analogue holds.

A century ago, William Stanley Jevons (1911) developed the Law of Indifference. This law declares that a commodity will not sell for two prices in the same market. The basis for the law is obvious. If the same commodity is selling for two prices, why would anybody pay the higher price? Also, why would anybody sell for the lower price? Yet it is known that the same commodity can indeed sell for two prices in the same market. It is here that entrepreneurship is involved: The successful entrepreneur buys low and sells high. This equilibrating process is set into motion precisely when the equilibrium law does not hold.

It is crucial to recognize, as economists have emphasized, the entrepreneurial role in a continuing equilibrium situation. The world is a disequilibrium world. Continuous and continual changes constantly generate new opportunities. But the stationary state of equilibrium, so important in economic analysis, is one in which the entrepreneur has no function.

Schumpeter argued that the entrepreneurial role not only exists in disequilibrium, but is in fact disequilibrating. Schumpeter's entrepreneur disrupts the existing equilibrium. Entrepreneurs may also be viewed as impinging upon a situation where equilibrium has not been achieved. When the entrepreneur makes a profit where resources have been misallocated, this tends to bring the process toward equilibrium. Markets are continually being pushed away from equilibrium by changes in the environment and brought back by entrepreneurial pressures. The entrepreneur keeps things more or less on course.

Many non-economists have ignored the insight that entrepreneurship is fundamentally a disequilibrium phenomenon. They have stressed aspects of entrepreneurial behavior which would exist in a hypothetical state of equilibrium. They have, for example, emphasized autonomy, control, and the combining of resources. Even risk-bearing, as distinct from uncertainty, which can be insured against, could exist in equilibrium. If the economist talks about entrepreneurship, he is talking about that analytical facet of behavior that cannot coexist with equilibrium. This means that, to a certain extent, economists and non-economists understand different things by the term "entrepreneur." It is important to recognize this fact if much sterile misunderstanding is to be avoided.

ENTREPRENEURSHIP IN MACROECONOMICS

Kent points out that, due to insufficient aggregate demand, equilibrium may exist in the form of unemployed resources and that entrepreneurship can correct a situation of this kind. The notion of equilibrium with unemployed resources is a fundamental denial of the scope of entrepreneurship. This is a weakness of Keynesian macroeconomics. Equilibrium with unemployed resources is, from the entrepreneurial point of view, a contradiction in terms. Unemployed resources could be used to satisfy people's wants. If these wants are not being satisfied, there is scope for entrepreneurship.

An opportunity for profit-making exists when someone needs something and is willing to pay for it, and at the same time a relevant resource is available. If something can be bought at a low price and used to produce something of higher value, there is scope for profit. As long as profit-motivated entrepreneurs are waiting in the wings, a situation with scope for pure profit can hardly be in equilibrium.

Entrepreneurs both identify and stimulate demand through advertising. This is often not properly understood by economists. One might argue that if consumers do not know they need something, they simply do not need it. But imagine consumers who, were they to know of the existence of some object, would want it. If their attention is drawn to the existence of this object, this might be described as an act of persuasion or "stimulating" demand. It could also be described as an exercise of entrepreneurship on behalf of the consumers. If the consumers were entrepreneurs on their own behalf, they would notice the opportunity and would realize that it is good for them. Not being entrepreneurs, they may notice neither the item nor its usefulness. Admittedly, there is a fine line between this entrepreneurial activity and persuasion or demand manipulation. Nonetheless, entrepreneurship through advertising may enable consumers to realize what it is that is available to them and what they would like to take advantage of.

GOVERNMENT AND ENTREPRENEURSHIP

What role can the government play as an entrepreneur? Can the government encourage innovation in a country, such as the Soviet Union, where entrepreneurship is not permitted? In a recent definitive study, J. S. Berliner (1976) concluded that there is a considerable amount of innovation in the Soviet Union, if less than in capitalist countries. However, to extol innovation in an economic system without market prices and without profit criteria comes perilously close to glorifying innovation for its own sake.

How are we to know whether, and to what extent, the innovations are socially worthwhile? It is possible to manipulate bonuses or incentives so that people will do new things, but innovation is not necessarily desirable. The entrepreneurial incentive provided by the capitalistic market serves to identify precisely those new venture activities that are useful for society. Society is willing to pay a greater price for the output than it exacts for the inputs, indicating that resource allocation has been faulty. Without the market guide of profit and prices, the whole question of innovation must be very seriously reconsidered. New methods of production may not necessarily raise efficiency; new products may be ones that no one wants.

Is entrepreneurship more useful in the wealthier countries or in developing economies? From the economists' perspective, this depends on where greater disequilibrium exists. One might assume that entrepreneurship is more important to those countries where growth in the standard of living is most urgently needed. Given the specific values, the resources, and the relevant constraints, it is conceivable that the economic system in the less developed country is already close to equilibrium. Innovative change which would move the economy out of equilibrium may not be a good thing, at least from the perspective of current social attitudes. In fact, imposing entrepreneurship and change on such an economy may be doing it a disservice. It is not likely that perfect equilibrium will exist in any economy, but to conclude that a low standard of living means scope for entrepreneurship is in error. Economists could only demonstrate scope for entrepreneurship if they knew in advance what needed to be done, if they were themselves prepared to act as entrepreneurs.

Are the hypotheses testable as proposed? If researchers are dealing with scope for entrepreneurship, they are dealing with disequilibrium, which occurs when people do not know what needs to be done. Scholars are dealing with an area of essential ignorance. If people know that a gap needs to be filled, and that it is worthwhile to fill it, the task is no longer entrepreneurial; it can be handled by competent managers through routine production methods. In such circumstances, the market will have already valued the resources necessary to produce the final product. Profit arises because the market does not know what needs to be done.

ENTREPRENEURSHIP AND ECONOMIC FREEDOM

The government can stimulate entrepreneurship by stimulating an environment of economic freedom. An eminent economist, Fritz Machlup, describes this action as the "fertility of freedom": In a free environment, there is a propensity for discovering profitable opportunities. People may know what needs to be done and can be given freedom to do it. But the primary economic question is: How do we discover what needs to be done, when this has not yet been perceived?

Hosts of opportunities are waiting to be discovered. How do they enter in the consciousness of decision-makers? It is here that the fertility of freedom becomes relevant. A free society permits profit-seeking business people to discover unexploited opportunities. The opportunities are socially important but will not be discovered unless private individuals are stimulated to notice them through the lure of entrepreneurial profit.

REFERENCES

Berliner, J. S., *The Innovation Decision in Soviet Industry*. Cambridge: MIT Press, 1976.

Jevons, William Stanley, *The Theory of Political Economy* (4th ed.). London: Macmillan, 1911. (Originally published in 1871.)

ENTREPRENEURSHIP AND THE MARKET
APPROACH TO DEVELOPMENT

It is beginning to be evident that the vast literature on growth and development conceals a yawning gap. This void refers to an understanding of the role of the entrepreneur in economic development, both at the theoretical level and at the level of past and prospective economic history. The entrepreneur, Baumol remarks,[1] has "virtually disappeared from the theoretical literature." In a penetrating essay on the entrepreneur's role in economic development, Leibenstein discovers that the "received theory of competition gives the impression that there is no need for entrepreneurship."[2]

In the literature dealing more narrowly with growth models,[3] this hiatus is almost complete and is hardly surprising in view of its predominant concern with macroeconomic relationships.[4] In contrast, the literature dealing with development proper gives some attention to entrepreneurship, although little effort has been devoted to formulating a clear theoretical understanding of the entrepreneurial role. Discussion has revolved primarily around the possibilities of an "entrepreneurial climate" emerging in hitherto primitive economies, around whether the motivation to seek profits is as weak in underdeveloped countries as frequently assumed, around the feasibility of relying upon foreign entrepreneurs, and around similar issues.[5] However valuable, these discussions appear either to lack an explicit theoretical framework within which to examine the relevant issues or, at best, to be founded rather shakily on the theory of entrepreneurship in development as expounded by Schumpeter in his justly famous work.[6] Frequent, somewhat vague references to Schumpeterian innovators and entrepreneurs are apparently considered sufficient to indicate the theoretical background that is being assumed. Consequently, the real function of the entrepreneur in a developing market

Presented at a meeting of the Mont Pelerin Society, held at Caracas, Venezuela, September 1969. From *Perception, Opportunity, and Profit: Studies in the Theory of Entrepreneurship* (Chicago and London: University of Chicago Press, 1979), 107–19. Reprinted by permission; the original source is *Toward Liberty: Essays in Honor of Ludwig von Mises on the Occasion of His 90th Birthday, September 29, 1972*, Volume 2 (Menlo Park, Calif.: Institute for Humane Studies, 1971), 194–208.

economy seems often to have been poorly understood, and the plausibility of rapid development under alternative economic systems seems to have been uncritically accepted.

I will attempt here to reconsider the role of the entrepreneur in the theory of the developing market economy. Schumpeter's approach, for all its brilliant and valuable insights, will be criticized at a fundamental theoretical level—both his approach to the notion of entrepreneurship itself and his approach to capital-using production. Finally, I will attempt to outline the far-reaching implications of these criticisms for the economic policy of developing nations.

DECISIONS AND DECISIONS

At the heart of microeconomics lies the individual decision. This decision is usually conceived of as an "economizing" one, that is, one in which the individual—whether consumer, producer, or resource owner—seeks to achieve his ends to the fullest extent possible within the constraints imposed by the available means. It involves buying where price is lowest, selling where price is highest, balancing the marginal gain from each proposed step against the associated marginal sacrifice, and so on. This essentially allocative, efficiency-oriented, economizing type of decision is the subject of exhaustive analysis in the theory of price. The theory of the market explores the extent to which economizing decisions of many independent market participants can be carried out simultaneously. The conditions necessary for all such decisions to dovetail, so that none need be disappointed, constitute the conditions for market equilibrium. The market process enables a state of affairs in which the conditions for equilibrium are absent to lead toward the state of equilibrium.

The essential feature of the economizing decision, and the feature that renders it amenable to analysis, is its "rationality" or, more helpfully, its purposefulness. But this purposefulness is viewed exclusively as imposing upon the utilization of means the importance assigned to the various relevant ends. In particular, these ends and means are viewed as given and known, the act of decision making being seen as essentially *calculative,* as though the resulting action were *already implicit* in the relationship between given ends and means.

But economists cannot confine their attention to this narrow notion of the decision. Attention must also be paid to an element in decision making that cannot be formalized in allocative, calculative terms.

Purposefulness in human decision making manifests itself along a dimension that is ignored in the analysis of economizing decision making. In addition to the exploitation of perceived opportunities, purposive human action involves a posture of alertness toward the discovery of as yet *unperceived* opportunities and their exploitation. This element in human action—the alertness toward new valuations with respect to ends, new availability of means—may be termed the *entrepreneurial* element in the individual decision.[7] Awareness of this element in human action leads to the recognition that knowledge by the outside observer of the data surrounding a decision-making situation is not sufficient to yield a prediction of the decision that will be made. The observer's calculation of the optimum choice relevant to the data may be profoundly irrelevant. The crucial question concerns what knowledge of the data is possessed— effectively possessed—by the decision maker. In fact, the essence of the entrepreneurial decision consists in *grasping* the knowledge that might otherwise remain unexploited.

EQUILIBRIUM, DISEQUILIBRIUM, AND ENTREPRENEURSHIP

It is not difficult to understand the traditional neglect by economists of this entrepreneurial element. Much economic analysis was developed against the background of an assumed world of perfect knowledge. The theory of perfect competition and, more generally, the theory of market equilibrium were developed in terms of perfect knowledge. Decisions were seen as strictly economizing decisions. Indeed, the world of perfect knowledge precludes the entrepreneurial element in decision making.

Most important, for a market to be in equilibrium, perfection of knowledge emerges as the essential condition. Equilibrium simply means a state in which each decision correctly anticipates all other decisions. In such a situation, decision making involves nothing more than the calculation of the optimum course available to the chooser, within the constraints imposed by the correctly anticipated decisions of others. No room exists for the entrepreneurial element.

In contrast, a disequilibrium market means a state of affairs in which decisions do not correctly anticipate all the other decisions being made. Clearly, scope exists here for exercise of the entrepreneurial alertness to opportunities for more advantageous decisions than those currently embraced.

It is here that the appropriateness of this concept of an entrepreneurial element in the individual decision becomes apparent. It is well known that in price theory the entrepreneur has no place in the state of equilibrium. Only in disequilibrium are there opportunities for entrepreneurial profit, for the purchase of inputs at a cost lower than the revenue obtainable from the sale of their potential output. In equilibrium all profits have been squeezed out, costs and prices have become fully adjusted. To imagine that all decisions correctly anticipate all others is to assume away all opportunities for capturing a margin between resource costs and product revenues. For the existence of such a margin is inconsistent with the knowledge assumed of resource sellers concerning the higher product revenues, and of the knowledge assumed of product purchasers concerning the lower resource costs. The perfection of knowledge, which rules out the entrepreneurial element in the individual decision, also rules out all entrepreneurial profit opportunities. The imperfection of knowledge that obtains in the disequilibrium market creates the price divergences between resource costs and product revenues that constitute the opportunities for profitable entrepreneurship in the more usual sense. And the exploitation of entrepreneurial opportunities for profit involves precisely that element in decision making that we have termed the entrepreneurial element. To win pure entrepreneurial profits, it is necessary to perceive price divergences that have gone unnoticed. What is required is an alertness to the existence of opportunities that have been overlooked—because their continued existence must mean they have been overlooked.

ENTREPRENEURSHIP—EQUILIBRATING OR DISEQUILIBRATING?

All this is elementary enough, although not always clearly perceived, and is not inconsistent with the framework within which Schumpeter develops his entrepreneur-innovator. While, unlike Schumpeter, I have couched my discussion primarily in terms of decisions (and the knowledge possessed by decision makers of others' decisions), my analysis can easily be seen to correspond to Schumpeter's discussion of the entrepreneurless circular flow and of the way the entrepreneur injects change into the system.

But the emphasis in Schumpeter's presentation, quite apart from its failure to stress the importance to decision makers of knowledge of the decisions of others, slurs over an important aspect of entrepreneurial activity. In Schumpeter it appears that the entrepreneur acts to *disturb* an existing equilibrium situation. Entrepreneurial activity *disrupts* the continuing circular flow. While each burst of entrepreneurial innovation leads eventually to a new equilibrium, the entrepreneur is presented as a disequilibrating force. "Development . . . is . . . entirely foreign to what may be observed in . . . the tendency towards equilibrium."[8]

In contrast, our discussion here indicates that the existence of an as yet unexploited opportunity for entrepreneurial profit means that the existing state of affairs, no matter how evenly it seems to flow, is a disequilibrium situation. It is a situation in which some decision makers are at least partly ignorant of the decisions being made by others. This situation is bound to change, and the existence of profit opportunities is the leaven that gives rise to the fermentation of change. Thus in our discussion the entrepreneur is seen as the equilibrating force. More precisely, we see the entrepreneur as bringing into mutual adjustment those discordant elements that constitute the state of disequilibrium. His role is created by the state of disequilibrium and his activities ensure a tendency toward equilibrium. While it is true that without him a disequilibrium state of affairs might continue indefinitely, so that one could hardly insist upon calling the situation one of disequilibrium, nonetheless it is important to recognize that the changes he initiates are *equilibrating* changes, that is, away from the maladjusted state of affairs that invites change and toward the state of affairs in which further change is unnecessary or even impossible.

This contrast, between Schumpeter's vision of the entrepreneur as a spontaneous force pushing the economy *away* from equilibrium and my view of the entrepreneur as the prime agent in the process from disequilibrium *to* equilibrium, is particularly important in the context of economic development. We must first, however, explicitly extend our discussion of entrepreneurship to the multiperiod level, in which Schumpeter's exposition suffers further.

SINGLE-PERIOD EQUILIBRIUM
AND INTERTEMPORAL EQUILIBRIUM

In an analysis confined to single-period decisions, equilibrium means the state of affairs in which all the single-period decisions made will correctly anticipate the other such decisions being made. Entrepreneurship, in single-period analysis, consists in grasping profit opportunities to buy and sell at different prices in a disequilibrium market within the same period.

In an analysis extending to multiperiod decisions, the notion of equilibrium is more complex. In such an analysis, decisions extend to plans to buy or sell in the future. A man invests now in his education, intending to sell in the future the skills he is learning. Another man erects a shoe factory now, intending to buy regular supplies of leather during the future periods of time. The equilibrium that would result from perfect dovetailing of these multiperiod plans must be an *intertemporal equilibrium*. Plans made today must fit not only with plans made by others today, but also with plans made in the past and other plans to be made in the future.[9] A state of disequilibrium will exist wherever any plan being made at any date fails to dovetail with other relevant plans of whatever date in the entire system being considered. A man who erects a shoe factory and who discovers in later periods that shoe leather is unobtainable, or that consumers no longer wish to buy shoes, made his decision in ignorance of the plans of others on which his own depended. A man who educates himself in a profession for which later demand is lacking has made a plan based upon incorrectly anticipated plans of others.

Clearly, entrepreneurship has its place in the intertemporal market in a way analogous to that occupied in the simpler single-period analysis. Where existing plans do not satisfy the conditions for intertemporal equilibrium, the relevant ignorance by the decision makers has created opportunities for entrepreneurial profit that can be grasped by those who are able to see what others fail to see. These opportunities, available to market participants with that alertness we have identified as the entrepreneurial element in individual decision making, consist in the availability of resources today at prices lower than the present value of the prices at which outputs can be sold in the future. This difference between buying prices and selling prices is similar to entrepreneurial profit in simpler contexts. This profit margin is the result of the failure by those selling the resources today at the lower prices to perceive the possibilities for selling at higher prices in the future. Entrepreneurial alertness to these opportunities will capture this difference as profit and thereby generate the universal tendency toward the elimination of profit. Their buying and selling activities in the intertemporal market will tend to bring resource prices of one date into line with output prices of later dates until only pure interest will be left separating them.

Thus, in the multiperiod context, as in the single-period analysis, the entrepreneur finds scope for his specific role in opportunities for the profitable use of resources that others have not perceived. We see him tending to bring about the exploitation of production possibilities no one has yet noticed. These insights may be extended very smoothly to encompass capital-using production plans.

ENTREPRENEURSHIP AND THE USE OF CAPITAL

Everyone knows that economic growth and development requires capital. Our discussion of the entrepreneurial role in the context of the intertemporal market will help us to understand the relation between the entrepreneur and the capitalist.

We have seen that the intertemporal production opportunities involve the acquisition of inputs at one date and the subsequent sale of products at a later date. In the context of capital-using production we say that the producer "locks up" resources in the form of capital goods, or goods in process, until the completion of the period of production. For such time-consuming, capital-using productive processes it is necessary for someone to forgo the alternative outputs available by using the inputs in less time-consuming processes of production. That is, someone must perform the capitalist role. If the input sellers—laborers—are not willing to wait for payment (wages), someone else must advance the funds for the purchase of the inputs and wait until the end of the productive process for the return of his investment. The producer who borrows the funds to finance his capital-using process of production finds it worthwhile to undertake the commitment necessary to persuade the capitalist to invest. The more productive processes of production, insofar as these involve more investment of capital, will be undertaken only to the extent that the producer sees the profitability of these processes. All this is trivial enough. But it focuses attention on the role of the entrepreneur in a way that is important for our purposes.

The technical availability of profitable capital-using methods of production and of savings to provide the necessary capital is not sufficient to ensure that these methods will be undertaken. They constitute an opportunity for intertemporal exchanges *that may never be exploited if no one is aware of it.* If, at any time, such an opportunity remains as yet unexplained, it offers opportunity for entrepreneurial profit. An entrepreneur will be able to borrow capital, buy resources, and produce output at a market value that will more than repay the capitalist's investment together with the interest necessary to persuade him to advance the capital funds. Only in intertemporal equilibrium (which, in the context of capital accumulation, certainly does *not* mean a stationary state), will capital-using methods of production yield no surplus over the resource costs plus interest. In the world of imperfect knowledge—and in the multiperiod context lack of prescience is hardly a rarity—harnessing of capital to more productive processes of production must involve entrepreneurial recognition of an opportunity that has hitherto gone unperceived.

Entrepreneurship is necessary in economic development, therefore, for the quite pedestrian purpose of ensuring a tendency toward the adoption of the socially advantageous long-term capital-using opportunities available. So far from being a kind of exogenous push given to the economy, entrepreneurial innovation is the grasping of opportunities that have somehow escaped notice. So far from Schumpeter's "spontaneous and discontinuous change in the channels of the flow," disturbing and displacing "the equilibrium state previously existing,"[10] the development generated by entrepreneurial activity is to be seen as the *response* to tensions created by unfulfilled opportunities, by the unexploited information already at hand.

SCHUMPETERIAN DEVELOPMENT: A CRITICISM

We have brought the discussion to a point where our dissatisfaction with Schumpeter's view of the role of entrepreneurship in development emerges in clear focus. Samuelson has captured the spirit of the Schumpeterian vision with an admirably apt metaphor. "The violin string is plucked by innovation, without innovation it dies down to stationariness, but then along comes a new innovation to pluck it back into dynamic motion again. So it is with the profit rate in economic life."[11] Development is *initiated* by innovators who are *generating* new opportunities. The Schumpeterian innovators stir the economy from its sluggish stationariness. The imitators compete away the innovational profits, restoring the stationary lethargy of a new circular flow, until a new spurt of innovational activity emerges to spark development once again.

In spite of the brilliance and power of Schumpeter's analysis, my own view of entrepreneurial development is quite different. For me entrepreneurship is an *equilibrating* force in the economy, not the reverse. *My* entrepreneur, whether at the single-period level or at the multiperiod level, is seen as fulfilling existing opportunities, as the one who generates the tendency toward the satisfaction of the conditions for equilibrium consistent with available information. His role is to fulfill the potential for economic development that a society already possesses.

My dissatisfaction with the Schumpeterian scheme is as follows. At all levels of human action, whether in the market economy or the centrally planned economy, we must distinguish *two* separate problems associated with ensuring that the best possible course of action will be adopted. The first concerns planning the best available course of action and is essentially a matter of calculation from the relevant data. The second problem is how to ensure that this best course of action, which *can* be carried out, *will* be carried out. At the level of the individual decision, economic analysis has all too frequently assumed that the second problem will take care of itself. The decision maker is simply assumed to seek the optimum position. In other words, the analysis overlooks the need for the entrepreneurial element in the individual decision, assuming the relevant ends and means are known. But as soon as one recognizes the problem of ensuring that the individual sees the optimum course of action, the importance of this entrepreneurial element, of ensuring alertness to and awareness of the data, becomes apparent.

When we consider the economic prospects of developing societies, the same two problems present themselves, and again we find the second problem ignored. The first problem is the determination of the best course of economic development available to the society. In principle, it is a matter of calculating, of comparing alternative possibilities consistent with available resources and technology, in the light of relevant scales of value whether of individuals or of planners, and including the relevant time preferences. No matter how elaborately this kind of calculation is carried out, the solutions obtained relate only to the first problem of determining what is best in the light of what is possible. We are still left with the second problem of ensuring that the opportunities thus computed will be fulfilled. No matter what the form of economic organization, laissez-faire or central planning or some attempted mixture, the second problem must be faced: What can ensure that the opportunities that exist will be seen and embraced? It is here, in the market case, that the entrepreneurial element comes in.

In the market system the existence of opportunities is signaled by profit opportunities in the form of price differentials. Now signals may not always be seen but the kernel of market theory is that a *tendency* exists for them to be seen. The profit incentive is viewed as the attractive force. It is a force that not only provides the incentive to grasp the opportunities once perceived, but ensures a tendency for these opportunities *to be perceived*. Entrepreneurship is seen as the *responding* agency; the alertness of the entrepreneur to profit possibilities is seen as the social mechanism ensuring that society will capture the possibilities available to it. What the entrepreneurial element in individual decision making is to the individual, the entrepreneur is to the market economy. All this is missing in Schumpeter's scheme.

The literature on growth and development consists of careful, elaborate discussions of what possibilities exist for raising the productivity of labor, for increasing the volume of resources, for accumulating physical and human capital, for making gains through foreign trade, foreign capital, and so on. The problem of entrepreneurship in this literature seems to be treated in much the same way as are economic resources in general. Although a difference is recognized between the entrepreneur and the manager, the former still appears to be treated as an element that *extends the range of possible opportunities*, rather than the element needed to ensure a tendency toward the fulfillment of opportunities available in principle without him. Schumpeter's picture of the entrepreneur as the initiator and author of development seems to be at least partly responsible for this failure to grasp the real significance of entrepreneurship. (In this regard, Leibenstein makes a valuable distinction between allocative efficiency and "X-efficiency," and recognizes entrepreneurship as being concerned with the latter rather than with the former.[12])

My objections to Schumpeter may be summed up briefly. The Schumpeterian view of development is one of spontaneous, disjointed change. The circular flow from which such change occurs is one in which intertemporal plans seem to be somehow suppressed, so that changes, say, in the capital intensity of production are associated specifically with entrepreneurial activity. This view directs attention from the possibility of intertemporal equilibrium in the sense of an economy fully adjusted, with no scope for entrepreneurship, to a definite pattern of increasingly capital-intensive activity. The role of the entrepreneur *to ensure a tendency toward the fulfillment* of such a pattern is thus suppressed. Instead of entrepreneurs *responding* to intertemporal profit possibilities through alertness to possibilities of commanding additional capital resources, the entrepreneur is pictured as *creating* profits ("the child of development").[13] Instead of entrepreneurs grasping the opportunities available, responding to and healing maladjustments due to existing ignorance, the entrepreneur is pictured as generating disturbances in a fully adjusted circularly flowing world in which all opportunities were already fully and familiarly exploited.

THE IMPLICATIONS OF THE CRITICISM

Does this criticism of the Schumpeterian view make much difference, or is it another way of seeing the same thing? There are strong grounds for insisting that our criticism does indeed have important implications.

The great neglected question in development economics concerns the existence of a social apparatus for ensuring that available opportunities are exploited. Its solution requires a way to ensure that the decision makers become aware of the existence and attractiveness of these opportunities. We have noticed that the market possesses exactly such an apparatus in the freedom with which it permits entrepreneurs to exploit opportunities for profit of which they become aware. Profit, in the market system, is not merely the incentive to lure entrepreneurs into grasping the opportunities they see, it is the incentive upon which the market relies to ensure that these opportunities will be seen in the first place. *One of the major arguments in favor of a market approach to economic development consists precisely in this crucially important element of the system.* Whatever advantage the price system possesses as a computer, facilitating an optimum intertemporal allocation of resources, these advantages depend utterly on the entrepreneurial element we have identified. And it is precisely such an element that appears to be lacking in alternative systems of social economic organization.[14] It is here, I submit, that Schumpeter's scheme fails us.

For Schumpeter's picture of economic development depends, after all, upon entrepreneurship. Yet, though he has within his grasp this enormously important insight, Schumpeter lets it go. His picture fails to bring out the power of entrepreneurship to ensure a tendency toward the fulfillment of socially desirable opportunities. It fails to throw into relief how the tension generated by the existing maladjustments draws the corrective entrepreneurial activity. It fails to reveal how it is the *market* that permits all this to occur. On the contrary, the entrepreneurship around which Schumpeter builds his system is in principle equally applicable to the centrally planned economy.[15] The notion of circular flow and the possibility of its disturbance through creative spontaneous decisions are in principle entirely relevant to the nonmarket economy. What Schumpeter's picture of innovational development fails to explain is that the existence of a possibility is not enough, that a social mechanism is needed to ensure that possibilities are perceived and embraced. Schumpeter fails to show how the nonmarket economy can grapple with this central problem.

Schumpeter's brilliant insights into the nature of innovation and entrepreneurship thus need to be recast into an ex ante mold. Instead of seeing only changes the entrepreneur has wrought, we must focus on the opportunities that were *waiting* to be grasped by the entrepreneur. Instead of identifying the profits captured ex post by the entrepreneur, we must focus attention on the profit *possibilities* that serve to attract him. Instead of seeing how the entrepreneur has disturbed the placid status quo, we must see how the status quo is nothing but a seething mass of unexploited maladjustments crying out for correction. Instead of seeing entrepreneurship as jerking the system out of equilibrium, we must see it as fulfilling the tendencies within the system *toward* equilibrium. My belief is that only such a theoretical scheme can be helpful in the great policy questions that face the developing countries of the world.

NOTES

1. W. J. Baumol, "Entrepreneurship in Economic Theory," *American Economic Review* 58 (May 1968): 64.

2. H. Leibenstein, "Entrepreneurship and Development," *American Economic Review* 58 (May 1968): 72.

3. For a survey see F. H. Hahn and R. C. O. Matthews, "The Theory of Economic Growth: A Survey," *Economic Journal* 74 (December 1964): 779–902.

4. Even Hicks's *Capital and Growth* (New York: Oxford University Press, 1965), in which the price theoretic implications of formal growth theory are pursued, is not concerned at all with entrepreneurship.

5. For a sampling of this literature see P. T. Bauer and B. S. Yamey, *The Economics of Under-developed Countries* (Chicago: University of Chicago Press, 1957), chap. 8; M. Abramovitz, "Economics of Growth," in *A Survey of Contemporary Economics* (Homewood, Ill.: Irwin, 1953), 2:157–62; H. G. Aubrey, "Industrial Investment Decisions: A Comparative Analysis," *Journal of Economic History* 15 (December 1955): 335–51; N. Rosenberg, "Capital Formation in Underdeveloped Countries," *American Economic Review* 50 (September 1960): 713–14; G. F. Papanek, "The Development of Entrepreneurship," *American Economic Review*, vol. 52 (May 1962).

6. See J. A. Schumpeter, *The Theory of Economic Development* (Cambridge: Harvard University Press, 1934).

7. See I. M. Kirzner, "Methodological Individualism, Market Equilibrium, and Market Process," *Il Politico* 32 (1967): 787–99.

8. Schumpeter, *Theory of Economic Development*, p. 64.

9. F. A. Hayek, *The Pure Theory of Capital* (London: Routledge and Kegan Paul, 1941), pp. 22 ff.; I. M. Kirzner, *An Essay on Capital* (New York: Augustus Kelly, 1966), p. 30; idem, *Market Theory and the Price System* (New York: Van Nostrand), pp. 311–20.

10. Schumpeter, *Theory of Economic Development*, p. 64.

11. P. A. Samuelson, *Economics*, 7th ed. (New York: McGraw-Hill), p. 725.

12. See H. Leibenstein, "Allocative Efficiency vs. 'X-Efficiency,'" *American Economic Review* 56 (June 1966): 392–415; "Entrepreneurship and Development," *American Economic Review* 58 (May 1968): 72–83.

13. Schumpeter, *Theory of Economic Development*, p. 154.

14. See on this the masterly passage in Hayek, *Individualism and Economic Order* (London: Routledge and Kegan Paul, 1949), pp. 201–3.

15. Schumpeter, *Theory of Economic Development*, pp. 138 ff.

KIRZNER'S THEORY OF ENTREPRENEURSHIP—
A CRITIQUE

MARTIN RICKETTS

INTRODUCTION

Over the last thirty years, no economic theorist has devoted more attention to the role of the entrepreneur in economic life than has Israel Kirzner. From his early work on the historical evolution of the "economic point of view" (1960), through his detailed analyses of the importance of the entrepreneur in the competitive process (1973, 1979), to his recent concern with the implications of entrepreneurship for distributive justice, Kirzner has consistently and forcefully argued that a correct understanding of the way capitalist economies operate requires explicit consideration of the role of the entrepreneur. His work has been radical and inevitably subversive of the "mainstream" tradition in economics. Kirzner demonstrates that the methods of equilibrium theory (whether static or dynamic) implicitly overlook the entrepreneurial role and must, therefore, present a highly distorted picture of the economic system.

Kirzner's contribution goes far beyond the mere emphasis on entrepreneurship as a key component of economic theory however. Kirzner's conception of the role of the entrepreneur is a highly distinctive one, and gives to his work a character and underlying theme that sets it apart from that of all other writers in the area. Running through the entire corpus of Kirzner's work there is a unifying "leitmotif" that the exploitation of the gains from trade will not take place automatically. To achieve the advantages of coordination through exchange requires first that these potential gains are noticed. The entrepreneurial role is to be "alert" to as yet unexploited gains from trade.

It is from this fundamentally important insight that the strengths and weaknesses in the Kirznerian system all derive. Kirzner carefully unravels the logical implications of the seemingly innocuous proposition that entrepreneurs are alert to new opportunities, and in so doing creates a

From *Austrian Economics: Tensions and New Directions*, ed. Bruce J. Caldwell and Stephen Boehm (Boston and Dordrecht: Kluwer Academic Publishers, 1992), 67–84. Reprinted by permission of Springer.

notably different theory of pure entrepreneurial profit from earlier writers on the subject.

In von Thünen's work in the first part of the nineteenth century and in Knight's (1921) work on profit can be found the idea that the entrepreneur receives a residual income. This is seen primarily as compensation for the bearing of uncertainty, however, and not as a result of "alertness." Knight (1921, 269–70) writes that "the confident and venturesome assume the risk or insure the doubtful and timid by guaranteeing to the latter a specified income in return for an assignment of the actual result." When it comes to the characteristics of entrepreneurs, it seems only fitting that Knight's should be bold, but there is no explicit recognition that they need be notably alert.

Schumpeter's (1943, 132) view of the entrepreneur, in contrast, emphasizes the forcing through of innovations. The function of the entrepreneur is "to reform or revolutionize the pattern of production by exploiting an invention or, more generally, an untried technological possibility. . . ." Schumpeter sees the personal qualities of energy, leadership, and determination as playing an important role. He compares the entrepreneurial character to that of "the medieval warlords, great or small" (133). Schumpeter's exposition has inevitably led to the impression that his conception of the entrepreneur has more in common with what the American "muckrakers" would have called the "robber barons" than with bold uncertainty-bearing knights. Neither approach, however, has quite the same flavor as that of Kirzner's, whose entrepreneur would perhaps be more likely to take the form of a humble pedlar at the fair than a contestant in the lists.

THE KIRZNERIAN ENTREPRENEUR

For the purposes of this critique it will be necessary to concentrate on a few of the salient features of Kirzner's unique approach. The following propositions represent an attempt to summarize in a few lines the most distinctive elements in his system.

1. Pure entrepreneurial profit is a return to alertness. It is quite distinct from a reward for "waiting" and from any other conception of the "return to capital." It is not the same as a reward for bearing uncertainty. Neither is it related to the compensation for undertaking the superintendence of production processes, nor is it the same as a "windfall" (a return to pure luck).

2. Unexploited gains from trade are revealed in arbitrage possibilities. By acting as a "middleman" the entrepreneur can put together new

patterns of transactions between buyers and sellers. Differences between buying and selling prices enable the entrepreneur to achieve a pure profit. Trade in resources is therefore necessary to the realization of a profit opportunity, but, Kirzner argues, it is not true that entrepreneurial profit is a return to personal wealth. Even a person totally lacking in personal wealth might, in principle, persuade a capitalist to advance the necessary funds and thus enable the entrepreneur to generate a pure profit. The return to "alertness" and the return to capital are quite different concepts. Thus "entrepreneurial profits . . . are not captured by owners, in their capacity as owners, at all. They are captured, instead, by men who exercise pure entrepreneurship, for which ownership is *never* a condition" (1979, 94).

3. The gradual discovery and realization of the gains from trade moves the economy away from disequilibrium and discoordination toward a situation of equilibrium and coordination. Neoclassical general equilibrium theory makes use of the concept of an imaginary "auctioneer" *outside* the system who, by a process of trial and error, establishes a set of prices that clear every market. Kirzner substitutes the entrepreneur *within* the system as the agent with the motivation and alertness to uncover the opportunities available. This process he perceives as a movement toward equilibrium. Thus "we have seen that the movement from disequilibrium to equilibrium is nothing but the entrepreneurial-competitive process. . . ." (1973, 218). Again, in the context of economic development Kirzner comments that "this contrast between Schumpeter's vision of the entrepreneur as a spontaneous force pushing the economy *away* from equilibrium and my view of the entrepreneur as the prime agent in the process from disequilibrium *to* equilibrium, is particularly important. . . ." (1979, 112).

4. Any ethical appraisal of capitalism requires that the nature of entrepreneurial profit is understood. Kirzner emphasizes that income generated by pure entrepreneurship is *discovered* income. It is not, as in the traditional textbook accounts of production, the result of the application of known means to the achievement of given ends, but the result of noticing new opportunities. If entrepreneurial profit represents a "find" rather than something that is "produced," it is possible to argue that ethical appraisal should take account of its special character. In particular, Kirzner argues that, to the extent that the "finders-keepers" ethic is accepted, it should apply to entrepreneurial profit.

In the following sections several issues raised by these propositions are discussed. Section three takes issue with Kirzner's treatment of the capitalist and argues that, from the perspective of his own system, the pure capitalist is never an entrepreneur. In section four it is argued that the distinction between equilibrating and disequilibrating entrepreneurs is difficult to sustain within a subjectivist framework and that Kirzner's approach to the entrepreneur could survive without reference to the concept of equilibrium. In section five similar arguments lead to the conclusion that the rent seeker and the Kirznerian entrepreneur cannot be distinguished in the absence of clear agreement about the existing distribution of property rights. Section six takes up Kirzner's views on the justice of entrepreneurial profit, while in section seven further practical reflections on the relevance of Kirzner's approach to the processes of economic development are presented. A few suggestions are also mooted concerning the relationship between Kirzner's entrepreneurial processes and the behavioral and evolutionary approach to economics.

ENTREPRENEURSHIP, UNCERTAINTY, AND THE CAPITALIST

As has already been noted, Kirzner is quite clear that the entrepreneur and the capitalist are analytically distinct categories. He writes that "the key point is that *pure* entrepreneurship is exercised only in the *absence* of an initially owned asset" (1973, 16). Yet, Kirzner is equally clear that the capitalist cannot avoid exercising an entrepreneurial function. "The Misesian insight that every capitalist must at the same time be an entrepreneur permitted us to see how entrepreneurial competition among capitalists plays a vital role in the selection of which would-be entrepreneurs shall be entrusted with society's scarce and valuable capital resources" (1979, 105).

Now, this statement is open to differing interpretations. The words "every capitalist must . . . be an entrepreneur" might suggest that the proposition is either axiomatic or some logical inference from earlier propositions. It might, for example, derive from the Misesian view that "in any real and living economy every actor is always an entrepreneur" (1949, 253). Everyone is an entrepreneur and the capitalist is no exception. Alternatively, it might reflect an implicit process of reasoning such as—the entrepreneur is alert to unexploited gains from trade; all capitalists must, by the nature of their business, be alert to unexploited gains from trade; ergo all capitalists are entrepreneurs. Finally, it might reflect an empirical judgment such as "in practice, although the return to capital and entrepreneurial profit are theoretically quite distinct analytical categories, every capitalist's income contains elements of both."

It would seem reasonable, given the prominence accorded to the idea that capitalists must be entrepreneurs, to infer that this goes beyond an assertion of the Misesian view that all human action is inherently entrepreneurial. Further, it is not entirely clear why Kirzner should concur in such a view. It is, after all Kirzner himself who in pursuit of pure (Crusonian) profit carefully constructs alternative hypothetical situations in which the castaway luckily receives a windfall or carefully calculates the return to his effort and thereby receives income that "calls for nothing entrepreneurial in Crusoe's character" (1979, 160). For Kirzner, entrepreneurial profit requires the recognition of error, that is, that there exist alternative courses of action that will produce superior results to those derivable from existing ones. To the extent that it is accepted that some component of human action does not derive from a recognition of error, but can reasonably be seen as the result of a process of Robbinsian calculation or indeed of the perpetuation of mere routine, every actor is presumably *not* "always an entrepreneur." There is a big difference between the claim that any person *may* act as an entrepreneur and the view that every action is entrepreneurial.

The tension that can be sensed in Kirzner's work between the Misesian view that entrepreneurial action is all pervasive, and the view that it comprises only some portion of human action (though a crucially important and neglected one) is a theme that will recur throughout this critique. For the moment, we consider the possibility that the statement that all capitalists must be entrepreneurs is a reflection of the empirical judgment that, in practice, a "pure capitalist" will never be observed. As Kirzner would be the first to point out, such a statement leaves the analytical categories of entrepreneur and capitalist quite intact. The fact that the overall return to a capitalist's activities will comprise some component of pure entrepreneurial profit, as well as a return to uncertainty bearing and the simple provision of capital resources, does not prevent us from disentangling these components as a conceptual exercise. It would still be true that the pure Kirznerian capitalist, artificial construct though he or she may be, receives no entrepreneurial profit. In practice, after all, the pure Kirznerian entrepreneur is likely to be no less elusive. All entrepreneurs will be capitalists to some degree, even if their contribution of resources is limited to the cost of a telephone call to the capitalist, or indeed the opportunity cost of the time taken up in buttonholing him in the street.

We are left now with the alternative that every capitalist decision must, by its very nature, involve an entrepreneurial element. There is some evidence that Kirzner wishes to be interpreted in this way. He writes that "the decision to lend capital is itself partly an entrepreneurial one, because it involves the possibility that the borrower may be unable to carry out his side of the contract" (1979, 97). This has always appeared to the present writer to sit uneasily with Kirzner's emphasis on *alertness* as the defining characteristic of the entrepreneur. It would seem more compatible with a Knightian conception of the entrepreneur as a person who shoulders uncertainty. Consider Crusoe's predicament as Friday appears on the scene. Friday rapidly notices the hunting potential of Crusoe's musket and realizes that a certain type of edible bird that lives unknown to Crusoe on the other side of the island, and that has hitherto been out of reach of the available technology, will become easy game. He therefore suggests to Crusoe that a hunting party would be mutually beneficial. No doubt Crusoe may be uncertain about how much reliance to place on Friday's vision of the future. Is it a realistic possibility or the result of a deceptive calenture? But it is difficult to see where any particular alertness on Crusoe's part is involved. Like all capitalists he will have to assess Friday's character and credibility and will be uncertain about the outcome, but any entrepreneurial profit generated by the plan would more reasonably be labeled Fridavian than Crusonian.

Several writers have noted the fact that Kirzner's analytical framework insulates the entrepreneur from uncertainty bearing. Although Kirzner (1982) attempts to refine his concept of alertness to avoid the implication that the entrepreneur discovers immediate and certain gains, there is still no possibility within his system that the entrepreneur can incur losses. As High (1982, 166) notes in his comment on Kirzner's (1982) paper, Kirzner "has not particularly emphasized the role of losses in the market process." High goes on to ask the rhetorical question "if entrepreneurship is completely separate from ownership, is it meaningful to speak of entrepreneurial loss?" (166). There would appear to be no escaping the conclusion that entrepreneurs cannot lose *as entrepreneurs*. If I think that I have made a "find" that turns out to be worthless, I have lost nothing unless I have used my resources in attempting to develop it. In Kirzner's system, resource owners bear uncertainty, not the entrepreneur.

ENTREPRENEURSHIP AND EQUILIBRIUM

In this section we consider the role played by the concept of equilibrium in Kirzner's theory of the entrepreneurial process. It was noted above that Kirzner is consistent in regarding the entrepreneur as a coordinating force. "My own treatment of the entrepreneur emphasizes the equilibrating aspects of his role" (1973, 73). Yet, it is by no means clear that, when taken together, all the components that go to make up Kirzner's approach to the market process are compatible with such an "equilibrating" conception of the entrepreneur.

The essential difficulty is in deciding whether the entrepreneur should be seen as operating within a given technological, scientific, and perhaps legal background—discovering all the opportunities for exchange latent in a certain "state of the arts"—or whether entrepreneurial alertness can be responsible for changing this background. In terms of neoclassical "textbook" concepts, Kirzner suggests that the entrepreneur moves the economy to a suitable point on the "production possibility frontier" where no further gains from trade exist. The frontier itself, which represents all the social possibilities attainable with given resources, is not objectively known by anyone and has to be discovered by entrepreneurial alertness, but there is a sense in which it exists, and in which its existence does not depend upon its discoverer. "I view the entrepreneur not as a source of innovative ideas ex nihilo, but as being *alert* to the opportunities that exist *already* and are waiting to be noticed . . . as responding to opportunities rather than creating them" (1973, 74).

This conceptualization of the entrepreneurial process has its drawbacks. In the first place it implies a tendency for the economic system to "run down" as opportunities are discovered unless some outside force intervenes to "create" more and more potential entrepreneurial discoveries. Second, this outside force, which we might call invention or scientific advance, has to be seen as nonentrepreneurial in character. Yet, much technical advance would appear to be quite entrepreneurial in Kirzner's sense of requiring alertness to new possibilities. When technical progress is called "induced," it is implied that existing market prices stimulate entrepreneurial efforts to do things in new ways. A famous historical example is the invention of Hargreaves' "spinning jenny," which has been related to high prices of yarn occasioned by developments in weaving. Such inventions, it could be argued, did not come "out of the blue" as a result of pure luck, neither did they arise from a purely Robbinsian process of maximization, but they required alertness to the possibility of an unexploited opportunity. Price signals are perceived *ex post* as being important in appearing to "induce" the innovation, but this should not lead us to think of the process as being automatic. If ex ante prices and ex post profits appear to "explain" the pattern of technical change, this may simply reflect the point that big opportunities are more likely to be noticed than small ones.

I do not claim here that all scientific or technical advance is the result of entrepreneurial discovery. Perhaps great technical changes can derive from the findings of "basic research," which involves the pursuit of pure scientific knowledge rather than pure entrepreneurial profit. Once it is accepted that some component of innovation and even invention is entrepreneurial in Kirzner's sense, however, the idea of the equilibrating entrepreneur is no longer sustainable unless one is prepared, as Shackle puts it, to "rule a line under the sum of human knowledge, the total human inventive accomplishment" (1982, 255). As in section three, the issue here concerns the domain of entrepreneurship, whether it relates to all human action, including technical innovation, or whether it is possible to confine our conception to a more limited sphere. In section three it was argued that, in principle, human action could be envisaged that was non-entrepreneurial in Kirzner's, if not in Mises' sense. In contrast, I am in this section arguing that Kirzner's conception of entrepreneurship makes a clear distinction impossible between movements *toward* and movements *of* the production possibility curve, and that his implicit attempt to confine entrepreneurial movements to the former is unsuccessful.

It should be recognized that a wider reading of Kirzner suggests that he is himself unwilling to draw a very definite line between entrepreneurship and technical innovation, and that he has a rather broad conception of the role of the entrepreneur. For example, Kirzner writes that "it is the essence of our position throughout this book that exactly the same competitive-entrepreneurial market process is at work whether it manifests itself through prices adjusting toward general (or partial) equilibrium patterns or through the adjustment of commodity opportunities made available, techniques of production, or the organization of industry" (1973, 129). Further, in his later work he appears to move away from an explicitly "noncreative" conception of the entrepreneur. Quite the contrary—"the human agent can, by imaginative, bold leaps of faith and determination, in fact *create* the future for which his present acts are designed" (1982, 150: emphasis in original). In his work on distributive justice (1989, 40–44) Kirzner is even more explicit. He refers to "the basic unity shared by genuinely creative artistic and technological innovation on the one hand, and the more simple acts of discovery . . . on the other. To discover an opportunity, I have implied, is to create it (40)."

There would seem no way that the earlier simple view of the equilibrating entrepreneur can be made compatible with this later conception. On the other hand, Kirzner appears anxious to retain the notion of the entrepreneur as a coordinating force and distances himself from Shackle's nihilism. Shackle refers (1979, 31) to "the anarchy of history," whereas Kirzner wishes to draw attention to "the benign coordinative powers of the human imagination" (1982, 157). For Kirzner, it is unrewarding to see the world either as utterly chaotic or as a process of remorseless drive toward a final static equilibrium. It would, therefore, seem that the very notion of equilibrium is unhelpful and misleading when discussing the Kirznerian entrepreneur.

Kirzner's conception fits more into an evolutionary approach to economics than the standard neoclassical one, although it is to the latter that Kirzner most often directs his comparisons. Just as the natural world is in a perpetual state of change, change that is neither easily predictable nor entirely chaotic, so economic life may be envisaged, by analogy, to exhibit similar properties. The evolutionary models of Nelson and Winter, for example, generate time paths of economic variables on the basis of a "substitution of the 'search and selection' metaphor for the maximisation and equilibrium metaphor" (1982, 227). Firms, in their approach, adopt "routines" (the genetic material of the institution), which given the environment in which they are placed, result in varying levels of profit. Profits influence the expansion or contraction of the firm, again through the application of rules, while these routines may themselves be modified by the process of "search"—the counterpart of genetic mutation in evolutionary theory" (18). As it stands, this is far from being a Kirznerian conception. Search for Nelson and Winter has itself a "routine" aspect that would appear to make the "mutation" analogy extremely forced. If the comparison with "mutation" is to be used, however, it might well be thought that mutation through the intervention of Kirzner's entrepreneur is a more reasonable interpretation. This would emphasize that, in the case of the economic system, "blind watchmakers" do not make good metaphors.[1] The evolutionary process is not completely "blind," but is influenced by the ability of entrepreneurs to peer ahead and "to formulate an image of the future" (Kirzner 1982, 149) in a conscious attempt to create it.

ENTREPRENEURSHIP, RENT-SEEKING, AND EFFICIENCY

Kirzner devotes very little attention to rent seeking. Given his emphasis on alertness to gains from trade as the defining characteristic of the entrepreneur, the lack of interest in behavior that involves no such gains might seem understandable. But other writers, neither ignorant of nor unsympathetic to subjectivist traditions in economics,[2] have noted that alertness to the possibilities of *personal* gain may not always imply *social* gain. It may instead simply result in the "discovery" of ways of diverting resources from one person to another. In the following paragraphs it is argued that Kirzner's lack of interest in rent-seeking leads him to attach the term "entrepreneurship" to activities that may not justify it.

The analysis of monopoly is an area in which this dispute has been particularly intense. Kirzner points out (1973, ch. 5) that it would be a mistake to consider monopoly from an entirely static point of view. An entrepreneur may gain control of the entire supply of some resource. From the point of view of the present moment he is a monopolist and his return is monopoly rent. But from a longer run and more dynamic perspective this rent may derive from a thoroughly *entrepreneurial* decision to appropriate the resource—a decision not imitated by others and presumably unnoticed. This part of Kirzner's argument is entirely compatible with Littlechild's (1981) critique of the misleading nature of calculations of the social cost of monopoly. Taking issue with Cowling and Mueller's (1978) estimates, Littlechild pointed out that their methodology implied that all monopoly profit represented efficiency losses. Cowling and Mueller made absolutely no allowance for the Kirznerian possibility that the observed profit was an entrepreneurial return and actually represented social gains, gains that in the absence of the entrepreneur would have remained entirely unexploited.

It is one of the most enjoyable features of Kirzner's writing that he tries out his ideas even under the most unfavorable circumstances, rather as a physical component of a new product might be tested to destruction to assess its reliability. Kirzner (1979, 222–23) considers the appropriation by one of a group of travelers (by means of racing ahead of the others) "of the unheld sole water hole in the desert which *everyone* in a group of travelers knows about." Even this, argues Kirzner, might be seen as entrepreneurial discovery. To the present writer, however, it seems that if this can be seen as entrepreneurial discovery, there is *nothing* that cannot be seen as entrepreneurial discovery. The other travelers, argues Kirzner, might equally have raced ahead. Perhaps this indicates the want of alertness or the lack of appreciation of the "true market value of the unheld water." Perhaps they wrongly assumed that no one could get to the water before them, or they overestimated the quantity of water available, or "gave the water no thought at all."

Perhaps the root of my disagreement with Kirzner at this point concerns his lack of any close attention to the nature of property rights. He describes the water as simply "unheld" although known to everyone. The physical existence of the water had presumably been discovered at an earlier time and the knowledge of its whereabouts distributed to all potential users. In these circumstances I would assert that it is inconceivable that the group of travelers would regard the water as "unheld" and therefore available for entrepreneurial appropriation. They would instead regard the water as a communal asset with a clear right of individual *use* implied. Kirzner is able to come to his startling conclusions only by postulating a set of circumstances that are mutually incompatible, namely general knowledge of both the existence and economic uses of an asset combined with lack of *any* conception of rights to its use. Of course, it may well be true that *private and exchangeable* rights to the asset are not held, but Kirzner is led into error by the implicit assumption that property rights either take this strong private form or otherwise are entirely absent.

Once the existence of weaker "communal" rights to resources is recognized, even if supported, as Alchian (1965, 129) puts it, "by the force of etiquette, social custom, (and) ostracism," rather than any more specific coercive powers of the State, the activities of the fleet-footed water grabber are revealed as rent-seeking. By appropriating the water, he has infringed the property rights of the other travelers.

It must be admitted, however, that the case can still give rise to difficulties. Suppose that the water resource is being overused by travelers exercising their communal rights. The quality and quantity of the water is deteriorating, the surrounding verdure is wilting, and the general amenity value of the watering place is declining. A person contacts each of those in the group that, by custom, is considered to have a right of use and persuades them to relinquish any claim. This person, unlike other members of the group, may have spotted the great economic value of a properly managed resource, and should he gain control through agreement, some of the social gains will appear as pure entrepreneurial profit. No rights have been infringed, and the social gains from greater coordination achieved.

Now suppose, however, that the resource is not overused, and that it bestows its benefits on all passersby freely and efficiently as a gift of nature. Along comes our putative entrepreneur and by some noncoercive means manages to gain control. He does not run ahead of the other travelers but merely gets them drunk by the camp fire and so induces them to part with their rights. Is this person a Kirznerian entrepreneur? He has certainly been more alert than the others. He may certainly have perceived the possible market value of the water if only access could be restricted. Further, my objection concerning the infringement of implied property rights no longer applies.

There is a genuine (and possibly irresolvable) dilemma here. Since no property rights have been coercively challenged, the returns in this case could be seen as entrepreneurial. Yet we might be tempted to argue that this entrepreneur can gain only by restricting the use of the water, reducing the use of this particular route across the desert, and diverting the consumers' surplus, hitherto enjoyed by the traveler to himself in the form of a payment for what had always been received without charge. The entrepreneur, it might be claimed, has been alert merely to the possibilities of successful deception, and the other members of the group will have received less in payment for their rights than they will in future be returning to the entrepreneur for water supplies.

Once it is clear that no uncompensated transfers of property rights have taken place, however, Kirzner is in a stronger position to counter these points. The problem with this reasoning is that it introduces an "objectivity" into the situation that is not warranted. How do we know that deception has anything to do with the case? Perhaps the exchanges negotiated between the entrepreneur and the other members of the group reflected the true judgments of all the participants. Further, the implicit assumption of the "objectivist," that there can be no net social advantage derivable from the pattern of exchanges described and that, therefore, there *must* be some legerdemain involved, may be untrue. Perhaps the entrepreneur has spotted the potential of the surrounding land for the purposes of tourism or agriculture, and recognizes that the entrepreneurial profits will be greater, and imitation more difficult, if he can secure control of the supplies of necessary water.

To summarize, rent-seeking can either be defined in terms of activities that infringe established property rights, or in terms of activities that result in social losses. Kirzner is a consistent subjectivist and his writing clearly implies the impossibility of identifying social waste objectively. But his somewhat casual treatment of concepts of property seems to the present writer to lead to a neglect of the possibility of rent-seeking (interpreted as action that infringes property rights) and to the impression that all alertness may be entrepreneurial, even the alertness of the shoplifter. The Kirznerian entrepreneur can act only within a given structure of rights. This status quo may be difficult to define and may give rise to disagreement, but without a careful appraisal of the nature and distribution of property rights within a community it will be impossible to distinguish the Kirznerian entrepreneur from the rent-seeker. Further consideration is given to this point at the end of section seven.

ENTREPRENEURSHIP AND DISTRIBUTIVE JUSTICE

In his treatment of distributive justice, Kirzner uses the special nature of entrepreneurial profit to question the applicability of conventional "end state" concepts of justice to the ethical evaluation of capitalist income. Most treatments of distributive justice, he argues, are based on the analogy of sharing out a given pie. Even those more sophisticated treatments that link the size of the pie with the distributive rule adopted, see the problem as one of choosing among various alternatives that are already known, and that imply predictable maximizing behavior on the part of economic agents. This approach cannot cope with the justice of a form of income that depends upon the *discovery* of new opportunities. A finders-keepers ethic would be more applicable to this situation. Indeed, Kirzner goes further to argue that it is possible to reconsider the philosophical problem of establishing original just title to natural resources by accepting the discovery element inherent in their appropriation.

Kirzner makes it clear, however, that his major interest is not to take issue with the ethics of existing discussions of distributive justice, but to establish that they are based on a mistaken view of capitalist income.

He writes, "My disagreement with the existing literature will, then, turn out to be not a disagreement in ethics but a disagreement in economics" (1989, 3). The existing approaches are not based on a "valid positive understanding" of the way capitalism works because they overlook the importance of pure entrepreneurial profit and the return to alertness.

Produced versus Discovered Pies

A major problem that Kirzner appears not to resolve, however, is the quantitative significance of his observation. Kirzner's economics may be "positive" in that it is concerned with how capitalism actually works, but his subjectivist methodology does not permit the identification and measurement of empirical counterparts to theoretical concepts such as pure profit. How are we to tell at any point in time what part of a person's income is the result of entrepreneurial alertness, and what part is the result of Robbinsian maximizing behavior? The question would appear to be irresolvable. At some points Kirzner writes as if all income is in a meaningful sense "discovered." "Every penny which the resource owner in fact obtains in exchange for his resources is thus a 'find' " (1989, 116). At other points, the Kirzner of the early chapters of *Competition and Entrepreneurship* reasserts himself. "Resource incomes present aspects both of discoveries and of simple entitlement-generated resource proceeds" (1989, 126). "I would not . . . deny that, besides these discovery elements in capitalism, inextricably intertwined with them, are elements of fairly stable repetitive patterns" (176).

Much of the tension in Kirzner's work between the view that all income is discovered and the alternative view that only a certain proportion represents newly discovered gains from trade derives, it might be argued, from the issues discussed in section three. The Misesian argument that every decision is inherently speculative might well lead to the designation of all income as entrepreneurial in nature. Yet, I have already argued that the specifically Kirznerian insight that entrepreneurial income is *discovered* does not, in spite of Kirzner's attempts, necessarily result in such a conclusion. When a resource owner agrees to sell, argues Kirzner (1989, 116), "he is taking a daring entrepreneurial gamble"; perhaps he is missing better opportunities elsewhere; or his decision "may be, in an entrepreneurial sense, an embarkation on a *losing* venture." But what have the acceptance of daring gambles and the risk of *losses* to do with alertness? Is this not the job of the capitalist and resource owner? Kirzner appears at these points to risk confounding the distinctions, so painstakingly established, between alertness to new opportunities and the bearing of inevitable uncertainty. If, after all, Kirzner has concluded that these distinctions are unsustainable, his system loses many of its distinctive properties.

The Market and the Graspers-Keepers Ethic

Suppose for the moment that a return to conscious, purposeful, alertness can be distinguished from other types of income. It is still not clear that the alert discoverer of an opportunity will gain the profit. *Realization* of an entrepreneurial opportunity requires resources, so that it is by no means obvious that the first discoverer of an opportunity will reap the reward. Kirzner draws the analogy with the pursuit of an animal and argues that apportioning legal rights between original pursuer and final slayer is a matter of convention. He offers the opinion, however, that "the first one taking possession should, I would argue, really be recognized as the first genuine discoverer of the economic value of the unowned resource" (1989, 172). Where the quarry is not some physical resource, but "the gains from new patterns of exchange," it is difficult to see how these could accrue to anyone *but* the final person who *realizes* the opportunity. In market processes, the spoils go to those who grasp them rather than to those who first notice them. Yet, somehow the phrase "graspers-keepers" has a less persuasive appeal as an ethical principle than "finders-keepers," even though it more accurately reflects the realities of the market. Kirzner circumvents the problem by defining it away. The grasper *is* the finder. Without the grasp, where is the evidence that anything has been found? The distinction between finder and grasper may still have significance in the moral thinking of many people, however.

Consider the celebrated recent takeover battle between Guinness and Argyll for control of Distillers in the United Kingdom. The chairman of Guinness, Ernest Saunders, was found to have misappropriated Guinness shareholders' funds in his efforts to fund a share support operation, thus keeping the price of Guinness shares "artificially" high. He won the battle for control of Distillers but was later imprisoned. A Guinness shareholder wrote to *The Times* (August 30, 1990) that, as a direct result of the takeover of Distillers, the company had gone from strength to strength and that he could not see any sense in which he could be said to have suffered a loss by theft. Further "Ernest Saunders was the one who saw the opportunity and went for it." James Gulliver, the defeated

Argyll chairman replied the following day "A letter in *The Times* yesterday talks about Ernest Saunders identifying the opportunity. He did not. It was identified, analysed and a strategy developed by Argyll" (23). As far as Gulliver was concerned it was not the Guinness shareholders but those of Argyll who were robbed. His complaint mainly concerned the means used by his opponent to gain victory, but it is impossible to mistake the implicit extra claim that prior discovery gave Argyll some sort of additional title to the quarry.

SOME CONCLUDING COMMENTS

Kirzner's insights concerning the role of entrepreneurship in economic development are of more than purely philosophical significance. The persuasiveness of his approach rests not on its coherence as a purely metaphysical system, but on its ability to make sense of our observations of the world. As we survey the ruins of the planned economies in Eastern Europe, their failure cannot be explained merely by reference to technological considerations. They failed because their structure ignored Kirzner's "positive understanding" of the way the market economy they were supposed to replace and supplant actually worked.

An entrepreneurial perspective also helps in the understanding of other historical cases. From 1965 to 1980 Rhodesia was faced with economic sanctions imposed by the United Nations. Over the period, however, it diversified its agriculture, attained the highest rate of growth in Africa, and developed export markets in a whole range of new crops (Harris, 1990). If necessity is said to be the mother of invention, it seems equally true that adversity is often the precursor of entrepreneurship. On the other hand, as Witt (1989, 414) points out, Kirzner gives us no well-articulated theory of alertness to explain these and other phenomena. His attention is so focused on the *rationale* of the entrepreneur that the circumstances most favorable to the realization of entrepreneurial talent are not really explored. "A more profound theoretical basis could indicate which factors possibly affect the incentive to be alert, to search for new opportunities, or the time it takes for competition to erode the 'alertness' rent."

It is less easy to see how Kirzner's theory of entrepreneurship can be used normatively as an aid to policy formulation. Clearly, the exercise of entrepreneurship requires the ability to trade in property rights. But there are other important questions to address. For example, although a regime of purely private and exchangeable property rights is most conducive to entrepreneurial alertness, does it follow that alternative regimes are necessarily less desirable? Is greater scope for entrepreneurship always preferable to less?

Because Kirzner's conception of the entrepreneur is so intimately associated with the gains from trade, it is easy to assume that the greater the recognition of "error" the better. But the arbitrage conception of the entrepreneur requires that the *durability* of exchange relationships is always precarious and may be disturbed at any time by alert entrepreneurial intervention. This disturbance may harm none if everyone accepts that agreements are entered into only for the duration of each moment. If, however, long standing agreements to trade in a certain way are in existence, and if assurances concerning the durability of such agreements were required to make them initially acceptable, entrepreneurial intervention could prove very destructive. Kirzner's theory of the entrepreneur, in other words, does not take account of the *relational* or *obligational* aspects involved in long-term contract.[3]

Even though the entrepreneur may achieve pure profits from putting together new exchange relationships, he may not have recognized true "error" in Kirzner's sense. Recontracting may have harmed some of those who invested specific resources in the existing relationship. If the entrepreneur's profit is not sufficient to compensate those harmed, it is difficult to argue that any error would have been involved in resisting change. Even if the newly spotted opportunity is so productive that *all* could be compensated, and real Kirznerian error would be associated with continuing with present arrangements, grasping the new prospect may not be socially desirable unless compensation is actually paid to the losers. In the absence of such compensation, economic agents would be less prepared to tolerate a position of dependence on others. Establishing rights in such situations may be extremely difficult, however, and we again see the importance of correctly establishing the framework of property rights and social conventions within which the entrepreneur is assumed to operate. A society in which new opportunities are always immediately graspable may be one that is incapable of achieving the benefits of long term associations because no one will be prepared to commit specific resources to maintaining them. An agreement *not* to trade with a newcomer over a certain period of time may be necessary if the confidence to make specific investments and endure economic vulnerability is to be developed. The corollary of this observation is that economic progress depends not only on giving scope for entrepreneurial alertness and the recognition of error, but also, in appropriate circumstances, on giving protection from entrepreneurial intervention and encouraging a certain degree of acceptance of error.

NOTES

1. The metaphor is used by Dawkins (1986).

2. See, for example, Buchanan et al. (1980).

3. The problems of trading frequently over long periods in the presence of "asset specificity" have figured prominently in the work of writers such as Oliver Williamson who argue that such factors determine the form of "governance" required for transactional relations. See, for example, Williamson (1985) and Goldberg (1976).

REFERENCES

Alchian, A. A. 1965. "Some Economics of Property Rights," *Il Politico* 30(4): 816–29.

Buchanan, J. M., Tollison, R. D. and Tullock, G., (eds.) 1980. *Toward a Theory of the Rent Seeking Society.* College Station: Texas A&M University Press.

Cowling, K. and Mueller, D. C. 1978. "The Social Cost of Monopoly Power," *Economic Journal* 88(4): 727–48.

Dawkins, R. 1986. *The Blind Watchmaker.* New York: Longman.

Goldberg, V. 1976. "Toward an Expanded Economic Theory of Contract," *Journal of Economic Issues* 10, 1: 45–61.

Gulliver, J. 1990. "How Scotland Lost Out to Hammersmith Flyover," *The Times,* August 31, 23.

Harris, M. 1990. *Economic Sanctions and Rhodesia.* Unpublished M. Phil Thesis, University of Buckingham.

High, J. 1982. "Alertness and Judgment: Comment on Kirzner." In *Method, Process, and Austrian Economics,* Kirzner, I. M. (ed.) Lexington, Mass.: D. C. Heath, 161–68.

Kirzner, I. M. 1960. *The Economic Point of View: An Essay in the History of Economic Thought.* Kansas City: Sheed and Ward.

———. 1973. *Competition and Entrepreneurship.* Chicago and London: University of Chicago Press.

———. 1979. *Perception, Opportunity, and Profit: Studies in the Theory of Entrepreneurship.* Chicago and London: University of Chicago Press.

———. 1982. "Uncertainty, Discovery and Human Action: A Study of the Entrepreneurial Profile in the Misesian System," In *Method, Process, and Austrian Economics,* Kirzner, I. M. (ed.) Lexington, Mass.: D. C. Heath, 139–59.

———. 1989. *Discovery, Capitalism and Distributive Justice.* Oxford: Blackwell.

Knight, F. H. 1921. *Risk, Uncertainty and Profit.* Boston: Houghton Mifflin.

Littlechild, S. C. 1981. "Misleading Calculations of the Social Cost of Monopoly Power," *Economic Journal* 9(2): 348–63.

Mises, Ludwig. 1949. *Human Action*. London: William Hodge.

Nelson, R. R. and Winter, S. G. 1982. *An Evolutionary Theory of Economic Change*. Cambridge, Mass.: Harvard University Press.

Schumpeter, J. A. 1943. *Capitalism, Socialism and Democracy*. London: Unwin University Books.

Shackle, G. L. S. 1979. "Imagination, Formalism and Choice." In *Time, Uncertainty, and Disequilibrium: Exploration of Austrian Themes*, Rizzo, Mario J. (ed.) Lexington, Mass.: D. C. Heath, 19–31.

———. 1982. "Means and Meaning in Economic Theory." *Scottish Journal of Political Economy* 29(3): 223–34.

Williamson, O. E. 1985. *The Economic Institutions of Capitalism: Firms, Markets, Relational Contracting*. London: Collier Macmillan.

Witt, U. 1989. "Subjectivism in Economics—A Suggested Reorientation." In *Understanding Economic Behaviour*, Grunert, K. G. and Ölander, F., (eds.) Dordrecht: Kluwer Academic Publishers, 409–31.

COMMENTARY: ENTREPRENEURSHIP, UNCERTAINTY, AND AUSTRIAN ECONOMICS

I am most grateful for Martin Ricketts' perceptive and generous critique of my work on the theory of entrepreneurship. I must also express similar appreciation for Martin Ricketts' recent review of my *Discovery, Capitalism, and Distributive Justice;*[1] the ideas expressed in this commentary have been valuably stimulated by both of these essays.

Ricketts has raised a number of highly interesting, often subtle points in his critique. It will not be possible to address all of them in this response, and I apologize for this. It seems wisest for me to try to restate certain aspects of my understanding of the entrepreneurial role from a somewhat fresh perspective. This restatement may prove to be helpful in addressing several of the key objections raised by Ricketts, by emphasizing certain debatable features of his (otherwise superb and accurate) presentation of my position.

OPPORTUNITIES: NOTICED AND UNNOTICED

Standard microeconomics proceeds by postulating an array of known, alternative opportunities for action confronting the individual decision-maker—permitting him, indeed requiring him, to adopt the optimal one. The very existence of opportunities is treated as synonymous with their having been already perceived. The optimizing or maximizing requirement thus ensures that the best opportunity will in fact be exploited. The entrepreneurial perspective on human action emphasizes the arbitrariness of this set of assumptions. In particular it calls attention (1) to the possibility that an opportunity may exist but not have been perceived to exist, and (2) to social and market forces that tend to make it, nonetheless, reasonable for economists to postulate a *tendency* for available opportunities to become perceived by those for whom they are in fact attractive.

It will be useful to examine some differences between the meaning of a perceived opportunity and an unperceived opportunity. If an individual

From *Austrian Economics: Tensions and New Directions*, ed. Bruce J. Caldwell and Stephen Boehm (Boston and Dordrecht: Kluwer Academic Publishers, 1992), 85–102. Reprinted by permission of Springer.

perceives an opportunity *with certainty*, this means that he sees the pleasant outcome offered by the opportunity as *already within his grasp* (contingent only on his taking appropriate action). Although the actual enjoyment promised by the opportunity has of course not yet been experienced, he already "possesses" it, since he fully controls the ability to enjoy it at will. It is as if he has ice cream in his freezer, available for consumption whenever he chooses. It is, as it were, "in his pocket."

Consider someone who sees with certainty how he can acquire ice cream. He does not have ice cream in his freezer, but he has money in his wallet, a well-functioning car in his driveway, and a well-stocked supermarket a short distance away; if he has complete confidence in his wallet, his car, and his supermarket, then he already *now* feels, within his grasp, the power to consume the ice cream (or, at least, to do so in about a half hour). When he in fact consumes the ice cream, the enjoyment he experiences is simply the actualization of a fully anticipated, and assured, experience. No element of happy surprise whatever is attached to it. A plan has been successfully completed, that is all. The certainty with which that success had been anticipated ensures the absence of any sense of pleasant novelty in its successful outcome.

The unperceived opportunity is, of course, quite different. So long as it remains wholly unperceived, the opportunity simply does not exist—at any rate for the unsuspecting potential beneficiary. At the moment when this opportunity comes to be noticed, its existence impinges upon its potential beneficiary as a flash of light, as a discovery. This flash of light transforms the enjoyment (afforded by the opportunity) from being nothing more than the fully anticipated outcome of a plan always believed to promise success with certainty—into a fortunate, even exciting, surprise. The glimpsing of this unanticipated enjoyment lifts one out of the routine sequence of everyday experience. It is in the nature of a windfall—with one crucial difference.

This crucial difference arises out of the purely lucky character of the windfall, contrasted with the human discovery source of the suddenly perceived opportunity. When we think of a windfall, we are thinking of a fortunate situation enjoyed by its beneficiary without it being in any way traceable to that beneficiary's actions or discoveries. But the newly discovered opportunity opens up an avenue for an enjoyment that its discoverer can justly attribute, at least in part, to his own "entrepreneurial" alertness. Had it not been for his alertness, this opportunity may have remained forever hidden and unexploited. He, not blind luck, is to be credited with the successful outcome.

Because we attribute to human beings a tendency—an "entrepreneurial" tendency—to notice that in their environment which is likely to be of use to them, we find the idea of a *permanently* unnoticed opportunity difficult to swallow. Sooner or later, we are sure, this opportunity will come to be discovered. The dark night of sheer ignorance that is responsible for the unnoticed character of an opportunity, will sooner or later give way to the light of dawn. At that moment it will "dawn" on the individual decision-maker that he has available to him a hitherto unnoticed prize. And it is because of our confidence in this tendency for opportunities to be noticed, sooner or later, that we employ the metaphor of equilibration to the process of opportunity discovery. An unnoticed attractive opportunity is, in the context of the individual, a disequilibrium phenomenon. In this sense the discovery of an opportunity is seen as an equilibrating step. It is of course true that at any given moment, for each individual, there will exist many opportunities that he has as yet not perceived. We do not really find it easy to imagine an individual in full equilibrium (that is, with no fog of ignorance preventing him from realizing all available opportunities). Nonetheless, it seems useful to recognize the tendency for human beings to come to notice that which it is in their interest to notice, as an equilibrative tendency. A good deal of the changing patterns of human activity can, we believe, be explained in terms of this all-pervasive entrepreneurial tendency.

Thus far, we have contrasted the case of the opportunity already perceived with certainty with that shrouded in *complete* ignorance. The discovery of this latter kind of opportunity, we saw, was in the nature of a flash of light illuminating a scene otherwise hidden in complete darkness. We hasten to emphasize that these two cases (that of complete certainty, and that of complete ignorance) are merely polar cases in a continuous spectrum. The uncertainty of life is unlikely to leave many cases in which an opportunity is perceived as being one hundred percent assured of success. On the other hand relatively few of our actions are inspired by the flash of light that impinges on *complete* darkness. Most of our decisions, taken indeed under uncertainty, are nonetheless inspired, in part, by a fairly confident general assessment of the relevant possibilities. Most of our actions, taken indeed with reasonable assurance of success, are nonetheless beclouded by our awareness of how little is certain in this world. Let us more carefully consider these more realistic classes of opportunities perceived through a cloud of subjective uncertainty.

THE OPPORTUNITY SEEN WITH UNCERTAINTY

The typical example is something like the following. At 2:45 A.M. a person, suddenly craving ice cream, considers whether he should drive to the twenty-four-hour supermarket to buy some ice cream. At 3:00 A.M. he finally decides to do so. There has been no sudden flash of light illuminating any utter ignorance. Everybody knows that the supermarket is two miles away, and is open twenty-four hours a day. Everybody knows the approximate cost of a pint of ice cream. Everybody knows how to get to the supermarket by car. Nonetheless, there may have been good reason for the prospective ice cream patron to have decided at 3:00 A.M. *not* to buy ice cream (quite apart from the obvious possibility that he might, at 3:00 A.M. especially, have ranked sleep more highly than ice cream). After all, the supermarket might (for some reason yet unknown to him) in fact turn out to be closed (or, at any rate, to have run out of ice cream); or the price of ice cream may, just possibly, have increased so as to render it a substantially less attractive buy; or the chances of one's car breaking down (or of becoming involved in an accident caused by some inebriated party-goer returning home); or the ice cream found to cause cancer, are perhaps not entirely negligible. The uncertainties combine to make the opportunity to buy ice cream at 3:00 A.M. in the supermarket something less than an altogether sure desirable, thing. It is possible that our ice cream afficionado might have decided *not* to drive to the supermarket because of these uncertainties. But we have supposed that eventually he does decide to drive to the supermarket after all—and successfully brings home the ice cream. His earlier failure to drive to buy ice cream is revealed to have been a mistake. The uncertainties that fueled that failure are now revealed to have obscured the true state of affairs.

What has happened, clearly, is (1) that the opportunity to drive to the store and buy ice cream at 3:00 A.M. did in fact exist, and (2) that our insomniac ice cream enthusiast did finally correctly perceive this opportunity— despite the uncertainty surrounding it. At 2:45 A.M. he had, because of these uncertainties, not quite made up his mind to forage for ice cream; we may wish to say that he had, at 3:00 A.M., discovered an opportunity he had previously not quite fully perceived. The fog of uncertainty had rendered him blind, or at any rate, hazy-sighted, to the real possibility of buying ice cream in the early hours. While his "discovery" at 3:00 A.M. was thus somewhat short of being a case of illuminating a previously total darkness (since the principal elements making up the opportunity were fully known long before 3:00 A.M.), nonetheless, it is reasonable to recognize that something of a discovery did occur at that time. Up until then the uncertainties surrounding the drive to the supermarket had appeared to be so menacing as to render this opportunity no opportunity at all (since there was a sufficient chance of failure to cancel out the opportunity value of any attempted drive to the store). At 3:35 A.M. our insomniac saw (as it turned out correctly) that an attempted drive to buy ice cream was, despite the uncertainties, a worthwhile venture, after all. His enjoyment, at 3:45 A.M., of his nocturnally acquired ice cream was not really an anticipated possibility at 2:45 A.M. (since at that time he had not yet become convinced that the drive to the store was a good idea; at 2:45 A.M. he did not believe—with sufficient confidence to undertake the expedition—that such a trip would provide ice cream for 3:45 A.M. consumption).

The "discovery" that inspired the 3:00 A.M. decision was thus in the nature of *overcoming* uncertainty, of *seeing through* the fog of uncertainty. It is not that our hero has accepted the burden of uncertainty but that he has conquered it. He does not shoulder uncertainty; he shoulders it aside. Where pure entrepreneurial discovery (of an opportunity hitherto hidden by utter ignorance) is in the nature of a flash of light illuminating what had previously been complete darkness, the decision finally to act in an uncertain situation constitutes the discernment of an opportunity which has, up until now, been revealed (through the fog of uncertainty) only in incomplete outline. If we see the essence of entrepreneurial discovery to consist in the glimpsing of that which was previously not seen, then we should recognize an entrepreneurial element, at least, in the decision made under uncertainty. This entrepreneurial element consists in finally being able to see the complete contours of a worthwhile opportunity where, until now, significant segments of these contours had not been glimpsed through the fog.

The achievement attained through successfully grasping an opportunity in the face of uncertainty can hardly be viewed as a complete, exciting, surprise (as was the case, we saw, with the success won through a suddenly perceived opportunity hitherto shrouded in complete darkness). Even at 2:45 A.M. (when our insomniac had not yet clearly seen the decisive worthwhileness of driving to the store for ice cream) he certainly realized that such a trip *could* quite possibly lead to ice cream. So the ice cream he acquires soon after 3:00 A.M. is hardly in the nature of a totally unexpected pleasure. This is quite true. But we must also emphasize, on the other hand, that we can hardly view the enjoyment of this ice cream (or the success achieved through any opportunity grasped under uncertainty) as merely part of a routinely expected future that is unfolding in preordained and fully anticipated pattern. There *is*, after all, an *element* of surprise, or at least of discovery, in the achieved success. When our sleepless ice cream seeker enjoys his purchase, he can congratulate himself on having seen an opportunity that had not been completely visible. Apparently, the successful outcome of an opportunity grasped under uncertainty, is *both* surprising *and* unsurprising; it bears the characteristics both of the unanticipated discovery *and* of the deliberately adopted goal.

Notice that this inherent ambivalence cannot be resolved into two clearly defined, separable portions. One cannot say that one portion of the ice cream was fully anticipated, and the remaining portion is a total surprise. *All* ice cream is, in some degree, anticipated: *all* the ice cream is, in some degree, discovered. The presence of the entrepreneurial element in the case of the uncertain opportunity (expressed in the successful grasping of the opportunity *despite* the uncertainty) has transformed the successful outcome—all of it—into a (partial) discovery. Each ounce of ice cream consumed partakes, to a degree, of the character of an entrepreneurial discovery.

Once we have recognized this discovery element in the successful outcome of the opportunity grasped under uncertainty, we should also recognize the operation of that same "equilibrative tendency" of which we took earlier notice (in the context of the discovery of the hitherto wholly unperceived opportunity). If there is a tendency for individuals to notice that which it is in their interest to notice, then it is plausible that this tendency be operative also in the case of the opportunity, hitherto only partially glimpsed through the fog of uncertainty. The entrepreneurial propensities possessed by individuals enable them to live reasonably successfully in an uncertain world by continually revealing to them the worthwhileness of emerging opportunities hitherto (or otherwise) shrouded in the fog of uncertainty (if not in the night of utter ignorance). The incentive that switches on the entrepreneurial alertness that enables individuals to overcome uncertainty is the prospect of gaining that which had not been clearly anticipated. Uncertainty indeed discourages many worthwhile undertakings (or, at any rate, undertakings which hindsight reveals to have been worthwhile). But life must go on even under uncertainty; individuals are in fact compelled to do the best they can in peering ahead through the fog, and it is their entrepreneurial sense that guides them, in the face of uncertainty, to undertake the actions that do in fact make it possible for life to go on with reasonable success.

Until now our discussion of opportunities, perceived and unperceived, brightly etched in an imagined certainty, or shrouded in the realistic fog of uncertainty, has been conducted entirely from the perspective of the individual. We have not considered the impact of these perceptions (or lack of perception) upon any social economic processes. (Although we talked of an individual contemplating buying ice cream in a store at 3:00 A.M., we might just as well have been talking of a Crusoe contemplating an expedition, in the dead of night, to the other side of his island, to forage for strawberries). But our interest in the entrepreneurial element (which, in the context of the individual, consists in noticing the existence of real opportunities despite the presence of discouraging uncertainties) in fact stems from our conviction as economists that it is upon this entrepreneurial element that the working of the market process depends. The opportunities that market entrepreneurs perceive and exploit are created by earlier coordination failures among market participants. The tendency for such opportunities to be noticed and exploited is (not only the process through which individual entrepreneurs come to notice what is profitable for them, but also) the process through which the market tends to coordinate the actions and decisions of countless market participants. Let us take note of certain peculiarities that surround the idea of an opportunity within the social context.

OPPORTUNITIES IN SOCIETY: THE
ROLE OF RIGHTS AND INSTITUTIONS

In the Crusoe context an opportunity exists in the configuration of physical resources and available and known technological possibilities. But in the social context an opportunity (available to a given individual) is marked out not only by the configuration of physical possibilities but also by the configuration of the anticipated actions of others (and by the individual's own convictions concerning the ethical significance of the interplay between his own actions and those of others). The actions that others are likely to take is partly a function (and expression) of the institutions that these others support and/or take as given. (The same is true concerning the individual's own ethical evaluations.) In particular the rights of property are crucial in marking out what constitutes an available opportunity and what does not. Where an individual recognizes the private property rights of others, he will perceive opportunities only as these are marked out by the relevant rights (of himself and of others). Where an individual fails to see a well-enforced rights system (and where his own ethical constraints do not lead him to respect such a system) he may see and grasp opportunities for what others might consider and denounce as theft. Or, again, where an individual sees the possibility of profitably *modifying* an existing institutional structure we must recognize such institutional change as an entrepreneurial opportunity for him.

A similar ambiguity may also relate, it should be observed, to the welfare economist assessing the social efficiency of a given pattern of resource allocation. To the extent that the economist accepts some specified societal assignment of rights as an unquestioned, morally relevant given, he may assess the efficiency of a market generated pattern of resource allocation only against the background and within the framework of that pattern of rights assignment. From this perspective it will be idle and irrelevant—in fact, almost meaningless—to speculate concerning the possible welfare advantages to society of abolishing or modifying the rights system itself. But it may be that the welfare economist does *not* take the existing system of rights as a given. He will then assess the welfare consequences not merely of economic changes that leave that rights system intact, but also of possible modifications in that rights system itself.

All this has relevance for the question of whether to describe the entrepreneurial process in the market context as socially equilibrative[2] (in the same way that we saw that the exercise of entrepreneurship could be considered equilibrative at the individual level). Social equilibration and coordination are notions that depend, for their meaning, upon the given social framework within which they are being defined and considered. If one wishes to consider the possibility of changes in this given framework itself, one can talk of an equilibrative character of such changes (or absence of such a character) only in the context of some meta-framework. The possibility of such a meta-framework (and even the possibility that changes in the data be seen as disequilibrative with respect to such a meta-framework) does not in any way diminish the possible relevance of the circumstance that these changes may, within the *originally* given social framework, be equilibrative in character.

But the ideas expressed in the previous paragraph may be turned around. Once we appreciate how the entrepreneurial grasping of an opportunity by an individual can be understood as equilibrative (in the "individual" sense explained in an earlier section), and once we appreciate how the entrepreneurial process (carried on within a given market-institutional framework of private property) can be understood as socially equilibrative (within that given social-institutional framework), we should be able to recognize that the "evolutionary" perspective and the "equilibrative" perspective are mutually complementary rather than mutually substitutive. The analytical power conferred by our insights into the equilibrative character of market processes, need not be surrendered in order to appreciate the possibly evolutionary character of those (longer-run?) processes through which institutional frameworks may themselves change. Moreover, a sensitivity to the analytical fruitfulness of the equilibrative perspective can alert us to the possibility that evolutionary changes in frameworks may themselves be understood as *possibly* "equilibrative"—within the context of relevant even-more-primordial social meta-frameworks.

It is quite true that individual entrepreneurial acts may take "rent-seeking" forms that may include the exploitation of weaknesses in the institutional guarantees for private property rights. Certainly such entrepreneurial acts may be judged to be categorically different, in their social-welfare implications, from those acts of arbitrage whose socially coordinative properties this writer has emphasized. No one claims that all opportunities grasped entrepreneurially must be socially coordinative. But it remains the case, surely, that a tendency toward the grasping of arbitrage opportunities, as they emerge *within the institutional framework of a market system,* does represent a socially coordinative tendency, *viewed from the perspective of that institutional framework.* In much of my own work, dealing with the operation of the market, entrepreneurship has been explored against the background of that institutional framework which permits markets to function. It followed, therefore, that a primary example of entrepreneurial opportunity perception was that of the successful arbitrageur, and it was in the tendency for arbitrage profits so to be competitively eroded that we saw the typical operation of the market coordinative process. Moreover, our concentration on the market context meant that the coordinative (i.e., the "gains-from-trade") advantages of that entrepreneurial process coincided with the plausible applicability of a finders-keepers ethic for justification of the entrepreneurial profit so won. It came to appear that entrepreneurship is necessarily identified with an entrepreneurial gain which is both directly justifiable on ethical grounds and socially beneficial in the coordinative sense. This work may fairly be criticized, perhaps, for failing sufficiently to emphasize that these apparently benign ethical and social consequences of entrepreneurship arise strictly within the market-institutional context. But a careful understanding of these benign consequences of market entrepreneurship should not, surely, lead one to infer similarly benign consequences for the entrepreneurial grasping of opportunities within other institutional contexts. Where property rights are not well defined, not fully protected, or otherwise not complete enough to satisfy the conditions for a fully private enterprise economy, opportunities for gain may be noticed by alert entrepreneurs where the gain may indeed be able to be denounced as infringing on the rights of others. Certainly, it is a legitimate research objective for Ricketts to explore the exercise of entrepreneurial alertness within property rights frameworks that provide scope for rent-seeking behavior.

THE PURE CAPITALIST AND THE PURE ENTREPRENEUR

The foregoing discussions presented key aspects of this writer's view of entrepreneurship and the entrepreneurial process, in a way seeking to respond, directly or indirectly, to a number of the points raised critically and valuably by Ricketts. In particular, our discussion of the meaning of equilibration, both at the level of the individual and at the societal level, was designed to address at least some of the questions posed, on subjectivist grounds, by Ricketts' fourth section. And our discussion of the role of the institutional (and, in particular, the property rights) framework within which equilibration is being defined, was designed to throw some light on the extent to which entrepreneurship and the entrepreneurial market process can be held to be socially beneficial, in response to criticisms expressed in Ricketts' fifth and seventh sections. In the present section and in the next one, we pursue some implications of our preceding discussions in order explicitly to address matters raised by Ricketts in his third section. This will warrant special and explicit attention because in Ricketts' view these matters involve a theme that recurs throughout his critique, viz. the tension that he senses in my work "between the Misesian view that entrepreneurial action is all pervasive, and the view that it comprises only some portion of human action (though a crucially important and neglected one)." This theme gains additional importance by having been also prominently noted in his review article (mentioned at the outset of this essay) of a recent book of mine. Ricketts has, indeed, identified an apparent ambiguity (if not an outright inconsistency) in my treatment of the entrepreneurial role. I believe, however, that no inconsistency is involved and that this apparent ambiguity can be clarified. I shall attempt to provide this clarification in this section and the next.

The problem identified by Ricketts is the following one. Especially in my earlier work on the entrepreneurial role, use was made of a model of the market process in which there were two kinds of players, pure "Robbinsian" decision-makers and pure (Misesian) entrepreneurs. Robbinsian decision-makers made their "mechanical" maximizing decisions within given frameworks of certain prices. No ounce of entrepreneurship was called for in order to make these maximizing decisions; the analysis began with these given frameworks having already been revealed to these decision-makers with certainty. These Robbinsian decision-makers were seen to include all resource owners and all consumers. The second kind of players, the pure entrepreneurs, were, in this model, seen as alertly taking advantage of price discrepancies implicit in the diverse expectations of the Robbinsian resource owners and consumers. That is, the pure entrepreneurs bought inputs from resource owners at prices which, offered to resource owners as certain and unalterable options, added up to costs of production possibly lower than the prices (similarly certain and unalterable) at which these entrepreneurs offered to sell the product to consumers. Within this model the income earned by the resource owner was a pure productivity return, containing no element of entrepreneurial profit. While the model admitted only these analytically pure categories of decision-makers, the model was presented as somehow capturing important features of real-world markets. In these real-world markets there are, of course, no pure Robbinsian resource owners, and no *purely* entrepreneurial intermediators between resource owners and consumers. All resource owners and all consumers, in the real world, do exercise at least some entrepreneurial alertness to changed opportunities. All real-world entrepreneurs do own, to some extent, some factor services of their own (and, moreover, recognize some aspects of their environment as relatively stable, offering little to the alertest of opportunity-watchers). So that, from the point of view of these analytical models of the market, a real-world resource owner's gross income would include (besides the more significant component of purely nonentrepreneurial marginal productivity return) some component of pure entrepreneurial profit. Most significantly, however (for the problem identified by Ricketts), the major portion, or at the very least, an important portion of the real-world resource owner's income is seen as consisting in a pure "Robbinsian" resource revenue component, containing no element of pure profit. The significant portion of the real-world resource owner's income could not, in this perspective, be explained, or ethically justified, along the lines that might be used, in particular, for the explanation and/or ethical justification of pure profit.

It is as against this picture of the real world—one seen as a collage formed out of analytically pure roles, both entrepreneurial and nonentrepreneurial—that Ricketts finds a second, rather different picture of the real world set out (or implied) in other parts of my work. In this second picture the entrepreneurial aspect inevitably present in the activity of any real-world decision-maker—in particular the inescapable radical uncertainty confronting real-world decision-makers—transforms the *entire* resource revenue earned by real-world resource owners into a form of entrepreneurial profit. Every penny of the wages earned by the laborer in the real world can, from this perspective, be seen as a species of entrepreneurial profit, calling, at least to some degree, for the very same economic and ethical evaluations accorded to the category of pure entrepreneurial profit itself. Although this latter perspective has been articulated only in my more recent work, Ricketts apparently finds (what he believes to be) disturbing premonitions of this view already in an earlier paper of mine[3] on entrepreneurship, in which I pointed out, following Mises,[4] that every real-world capitalist must, in the nature of his activities, be exercising entrepreneurship. Ricketts is puzzled and disturbed by this assertion of mine, which he apparently reads as being at variance with my own insistence (at least in my earlier writings on entrepreneurship) on the importance, for analytical purposes, of the notion of the pure capitalist role as distinct from that of the pure entrepreneur. In particular, he finds this assertion confusing in the light of his attribution to me of the (Schumpeterian[5]) position that "resource owners bear uncertainty, not the entrepreneurs."

Now, while the above mentioned ambiguity that Ricketts detects in my work certainly warrants attention (see the following section in this commentary), it should be pointed out that the passage cited (from my 1979 book) to the effect that each real-world capitalist is also, to some degree, an entrepreneur, should in no way be seen as tainted by that ambiguity. Although Ricketts, rather surprisingly, canvasses an array of apparently alternative interpretations[6] of this latter cited passage, the simple interpretation of it (viz., that it draws attention to the conflation in the real-world make-up of the typical "empirical" capitalist investor, of elements both of the pure capitalist and of the pure entrepreneur) is in fact made abundantly clear in the paper from which the passage was cited. There is nothing in that cited passage that might obscure the identification of a pure resource-revenue income with the pure resource owner's role (and of pure entrepreneurial profit with the pure entrepreneurial role).

Nonetheless, it will be useful to refer to aspects of Ricketts' discussion of this cited passage of mine (attributing a significant element of entrepreneurship to the real-world capitalist) in order to help clear up the above cited ambiguity that Ricketts has perceptively noted as arising out of some of my recent work in this area. To this we now turn.

THE PURE AND THE IMPURE: A CLARIFICATION

As mentioned, Ricketts has interpreted me as seeing the pure entrepreneur—he who is alert to new opportunities—as in no way bearing uncertainty. He finds this at odds, however, with a recent passage[7] in which I point out that a resource owner is, typically, taking a daring entrepreneurial gamble. (Because when a resource owner sells, he knows that he may be missing better selling opportunities elsewhere, that is, he may be embarking upon a losing venture.) What, Ricketts asks, "have the acceptance of daring gambles and the risk of *losses* to do with alertness?" I submit that not only is there a straightforward answer to this question, but that this answer can direct us toward the clarification of the apparent ambiguity in my position, identified in the preceding section.

It is true that exposing oneself to the risk of a loss is not at all the same thing as being alert to a new opportunity. However, it is also true that the very notion of being alert to opportunities is conceivable only in the context of an uncertain world, that is, in a Knightian world within which one is inevitably exposed to the uninsurable risk of loss. And here is the nub of the matter. Although the essence of the entrepreneurial function does not lie in the bearing of the burden of sleepless nights (occasioned by worry about losses), this function would evaporate entirely in a world unclouded by uncertainty. One can act entrepreneurially only in an uncertain world; conversely, as we shall see, to act in an uncertain world must mean to exercise, at least to some degree, one's capacity for entrepreneurship. As Mises put it (in explaining why, in the real world, everyone is an entrepreneur), "one must never forget that every action is embedded in the flux of time and therefore involves a speculation."[8]

Now, as discussed in one of the earlier sections of this commentary, action in the face of uncertainty does seem to involve exactly that same notion of discovery as occurs in the case of a hitherto unglimpsed opportunity suddenly being noticed by the alert entrepreneur. Uncertainty obscures key features of a developing situation; what is in fact a gainful opportunity may not be seen as such, the chances of costly failure may loom so prominently in the vision of the prospective agent that it may appear prudent *not* to attempt to grasp for possible gain. To act in the face of uncertainty is thus to believe—correctly or otherwise—that one *has* seen a genuine opportunity through the fog that almost obscured it. Such action in the face of uncertainty requires, that is, a degree of alertness to what is "around the corner" (i.e., hidden behind the fog of uncertainty)—in other words, it requires the exercise of the human entrepreneurial propensity.

It follows that in our real world of uncertainty, every action by a resource owner is, at least to some extent, in the nature of an entrepreneurial gamble; that is, it consists in the alert grasping of an opportunity dimly perceived through the fog of radical uncertainty. It is true that the entrepreneurial function of exercising alertness (to hitherto existing but unperceived opportunities) is not, in itself, a matter of being exposed to the risk of losses. But, on the other hand, it is also true that wherever such uninsurable risk of loss exists, action must presuppose the exercise of entrepreneurial alertness.

What we wish to emphasize, however, is not so much this insight itself, but rather the difficulties this insight must entail for the model (outlined in the preceding section) in which the world of uncertainty is pictured as a collage formed exclusively out of analytically pure roles, entrepreneurial and nonentrepreneurial, respectively. Can we still maintain that the real-world investor is part pure entrepreneur and part pure capitalist? Can we still maintain that his income consists of one distinct pure profit component together with a second distinct pure interest component? The position developed in my more recent work, in which I have argued that every penny of a resource owner's income in an uncertain world can be seen to some extent as being the fruit of entrepreneurial alertness (and, thus, defensible on the basis of the same ethical principles used to defend the legitimacy of pure entrepreneurial profit), clearly answers these latter questions in the negative. Are we then to reject completely that model of the market process (used particularly in my own earlier work on entrepreneurship) in which pure entrepreneurs who owned no resources whatever were conceived of as offering deals to pure "Robbinsian" resource owners and consumers (who display no entrepreneurship whatsoever)? I wish to submit that we do not need to, and should not, reject that model out of hand. There are analytical purposes for which that model is illuminating and instructive—despite those features of it that render it incompletely faithful to and expressive of the complex realities of the real world of uncertainty. But, I further submit, at the same time we must be careful not to permit use of that model, valuable though it may be for its own purposes, to mislead us into overlooking those features of the real world that that model suppresses—in contexts where it is precisely those features which may be of significance. In other words, there are some analytical purposes that are usefully served by viewing real-world resource owners *as if* they are combination pure "Robbinsian" resource owners and pure entrepreneurs; there are other purposes for which, such a fiction would obscure significant features of reality. The ambiguity Ricketts has identified is a real one, but it involves no tension; it presents no inconsistencies and no problems. All this warrants some elaboration.

In order to understand the entrepreneur-driven market process, it is useful to focus on the pure entrepreneurial role. Such a focus is the more sharply attained if we adopt the device of treating resource owners and consumers as exercising no entrepreneurship whatsoever. Nothing is lost, in regard to our understanding of how markets work through continual entrepreneurial discovery (of gaps in existing market coordination), by imagining that, at each instant, the pure entrepreneurs are offering the nonentrepreneurs deals with complete certainty.

But there are other purposes—such as that of reaching an adequate ethical evaluation of real-world resource owners' incomes—where it will simply not do to treat resource owners as if they operated in a world different from what it really is. For these purposes it is necessary to recognize that no one, in the real world, can wholly escape uncertainty. As Mises taught us, in the real world of uncertainty each acting human being *is* an entrepreneur. And, to the extent that resource owners do operate in the real world of open-ended, uninsurable uncertainty, their incomes— every penny of their incomes—must be recognized as partaking, to some degree, of the discovered quality we attribute to pure entrepreneurial profit. As noticed at length in an earlier section of this commentary, most real-world situations display aspects of unanticipated discovery *and* aspects of plan-fulfilling attainment of anticipated outcomes. However, as explained in that section, the nature of the ambivalence (inherent in most real-world situations) is such that it does *not* permit one to identify, in the revenue won through action in the face of typical uncertainty, a purely routine component and a distinct, purely entrepreneurial component. The Misesian insight that all human action is entrepreneurial has thus led us to recognize that all market incomes—every penny of them— display, to greater or lesser degree, the character of pure profit.[9]

The considerations we have advanced to clarify the ambiguity noticed by Ricketts may perhaps be usefully summarized as follows:

1. Real-world situations in which market participants act offer us aspects in which these acts are (as a result of uncertainty) in the nature of the spontaneous grasping of hitherto unanticipated discoveries, and also offer aspects in which these acts constitute the plan-fulfilling attainment of anticipated outcomes (because the uncertainty is seen as being bounded).

2. Economics seeks understanding of what occurs in real-world market processes by reference to models of market equilibrium, and also seeks to derive concepts of market processes of equilibration (as they may occur in the real world of disequilibrium).

3. Models of equilibrium can in no way reflect those aspects of real-world situations that arise out of the uncertainty of disequilibrium and the entrepreneurial grappling with such uncertainty; such models can reflect only those aspects (of real-world situations) that express the boundedness of uncertainty (even in disequilibrium).

4. In order to understand those aspects of the real world that arise out of the boundedness of uncertainty, we therefore focus on the way those aspects would in fact constitute the *whole* of the situations portrayed in our models of equilibrium. Resource owners' incomes are thus portrayed as pure marginal productivity incomes.

5. In order to understand market processes that arise in real-world disequilibrium, we focus precisely on those entrepreneurial (i.e., uncertainty-driven) elements that have *no* place in the equilibrium models. In order to highlight these entrepreneurial elements we generally conceive the *non*-entrepreneurial elements in the real world as if these were in fact *purely* nonentrepreneurial. But in so doing we are, inconsistently, conflating an equilibrium picture with a disequilibrium picture. For purposes of conceptualizing the dynamic market process such a conflation does no harm. This conflation is designed to focus analytical attention on one real-world element—the key element that drives the market process; it does so with greater impact by deliberately imagining away certain real-world aspects of the resource owner and consumer roles. In this context resource owner incomes appear as purely Robbinsian, purely nonentrepreneurial outcomes.

6. When we wish to consider the ethics and economics of real-world resource owner incomes in their own right (that is, not merely as part of an effort with the primary objective of understanding the market process itself), it becomes necessary to recognize those entrepreneurial aspects of real-world resource ownership from which it had been expedient (in seeking understanding of the market process) to abstract. It is then no longer possible to see resource owners' incomes—not even any fraction of them—as wholly planned outcomes; an element of entrepreneurial discovery is seen as attached to every penny of such incomes.

THE ENTREPRENEURIAL PERSPECTIVE
AND AUSTRIAN ECONOMICS

It may be useful to conclude these rather rambling observations, inspired by Ricketts' valuable critique, by pointing out how the emphasis on entrepreneurship in much of the modern Austrian literature reinforces and deepens those insights that have, from its earliest Mengerian roots, characterized the Austrian School. The subjectivism of Austrian economics meant that it saw economic phenomena, market prices, incomes and resource allocation patterns rather differently than other schools of economic thought. For Austrians these were seen, not as inevitable consequences of physical needs and resource constraints, not as the outcome of an interplay between physical resources and human rankings of preference—but as the results of the ways in which deliberate human decisions, both in isolation and in society, impinge upon and shape a given physical world.

There were times, during the twentieth-century history of Austrian economics, when this vision was confined to a "Robbinsian" understanding of human decisions, that is, with human beings seen as entering the economic arena with preassigned perceptions of the possibilities open to them. It was the signal merit of Mises's notion of human action that it deepened the Austrian vision to include, as a dominant factor influencing economic outcomes, that active element in human decision making that perceives and identifies what the possibilities and options for choice are seen to be. As a result of this work of Mises, and of a distinct series of insights concerning knowledge explicated by Hayek, modern Austrian economics has come to recognize that this entrepreneurial element (identified by Mises) plays the crucial role in achieving the market's tendencies toward coordination. It is not merely that awareness of the entrepreneurial element enhances our appreciation for the subjectivist perspective central to the Austrian tradition. It is our awareness of the entrepreneurial element that enriches our understanding of the coordinative properties of markets. As Ricketts has identified the central theme that has inspired my own work on entrepreneurship, "the exploitation of the gains from trade will not take place automatically. To achieve the advantages of coordination through exchange requires first that these potential gains are noticed." The deepened Austrian subjectivism that recognizes the manner in which economic phenomena express such noticing of potential gains, is at the same time the source of our deepened Austrian understanding of the social process of "coordination through exchange" which markets make possible.

NOTES

1. *Journal des Economistes et des Etudes Humaines*, Vol. 1, No. 2, June 1990, 179–82.

2. Whereas we have, somewhat idiosyncratically, used the notion of an "equilibrative tendency" at the level of the individual to refer to the tendency of an individual sooner or later to come to realize what it is in fact best for him to do, we use here the notion of an "equilibrative tendency," in the social context, in a far more conventional manner. In the market context the equilibrative tendency consists in those many entrepreneurial steps of mutual discovery through which market participants are led more accurately to anticipate what others are able and motivated to do, thus bringing the pattern of exchanges gradually closer to that pattern that would exhaust all possible mutually gainful opportunities. (It will be noticed that this social process of equilibration is made up of series upon series of individual opportunity discoveries, with each such discovery being the manifestation of the equilibrative tendency we found operating at the individual level.)

3. *Perception, Opportunity, and Profit.* Chicago: University of Chicago Press, 1979, ch. 6.

4. L. Mises, *Human Action.* New Haven: Yale University Press, 1949, 254.

5. See, for example, Joseph A. Schumpeter, *The Theory of Economic Development.* Cambridge: Harvard University Press, 1934, 75, 137.

6. However, see Note 9.

7. Israel M. Kirzner, *Discovery, Capitalism, and Distributive Justice.* Oxford: Basil Blackwell, 1989, 116.

8. L. Mises, *Human Action,* op. cit., ibid.

9. It should be noted that the Misesian insight that, "in any real and living economy every actor is always an entrepreneur," is simply an implication of what it means to live in a real world of radical uncertainty. The empirical circumstance of ubiquitous uncertainty entails the impossibility of finding, in real life, individuals whose decisions wholly fit those of the pure "Robbinsian" maximizer (for whom the ends-means framework is given with certainty). It thus follows that the alternative interpretations Ricketts suggests for this writer's assertion that real-world capitalists are engaged in entrepreneurial competition, in fact, all turn out to be simply different ways of expressing the identical circumstance—the inescapable uncertainty surrounding the human condition.

ON THE RELEVANCE OF POLICY TO
KIRZNERIAN ENTREPRENEURSHIP

STEPHEN SHMANSKE

I. INTRODUCTION

Israel Kirzner (1985 and 1973) suggests that neoclassical theory, in concentrating its attention on equilibrium states, neglects the role of the entrepreneur, particularly the role of entrepreneurial discovery. Kirzner, therefore, argues for a widening of traditional analysis to include this discovery process. Kirzner pursues this endeavor vigorously and is led to conclusions wholly in favor of decentralized, free-market, capitalist systems.

While in substantial agreement with the conclusions regarding the efficacy of free and open competition, this paper discusses two related frustrations caused by Kirzner's analysis. First, in my view, the free-market conclusions reached by Kirzner are already implied by the optimizing behavior present in traditional analysis. Kirzner accepts the legitimacy of such Robbinsian maximization but seems bored by its mechanistic flavor and, regardless, believes that it is not enough. The second frustration is, perhaps, more problematic. In my view, Kirzner does not and cannot derive his conclusions from the view of entrepreneurship he espouses. By insisting on costless discovery through alertness rather than on costly, purposive search, Kirzner is actually analyzing the part of an environment where economizing behavior is irrelevant and where policy that attempts to influence outcomes by altering economic costs or benefits will be impotent. In examining these two issues, this essay will attempt to show, first, that the extent to which policy can influence entrepreneurship is a topic covered by standard economic analysis in the models of search, public choice, rent-seeking and property rights, and second, that to the extent which a Kirznerian entrepreneur is different from the actors in these models, few, if any, policy directives follow.

From Stephen Shmanske, "On the Relevance of Policy to Kirznerian Entrepreneurship," in *Advances in Austrian Economics,* Volume 1, ed. Peter J. Boettke, Israel M. Kirzner, and Mario J. Rizzo (Greenwich, Conn., and London: JAI Press, 1994), 199–222. Reprinted by permission.

A part of my argument rests on an explanation and critique of an overly simplified understanding and portrayal of the import of equilibrium in standard economic analysis. This is presented in the next section. That different views exist regarding the relevance of equilibrium is not a new theme. Kirzner (1985, pp. 7–10) himself recognizes two polar views roughly corresponding to the ideas of T. W. Schultz (1975) and G. L. S. Shackle (1972). A similar dichotomy is presented by Roger Garrison (1986), who uses Robert Lucas and Ludwig Lachmann as representatives of the polar views. The Schultz/Lucas pole corresponds to a neoclassical world in continuous equilibrium. Kirzner asserts that the true essence of entrepreneurial behavior is absent in this world. The opposite pole of Shackle and Lachmann rejects the notion of equilibrium altogether. Entrepreneurial behavior may be present in this world, and may be valued in and of itself, but it does not lead anywhere in particular. Kirzner rejects both poles arguing that truth lies in the middle ground:

> The neoclassical view implies exclusion of all true novelty and surprise from our explanations; the alternative view points to the exclusion of explanations other than those that run in terms of the novelty, spontaneity, and intrinsic unpredictability of human choices. . . . The sections that follow seek to show how the "alertness" view of entrepreneurship mentioned earlier in this chapter enables us to adopt a middle course (1985, p. 10).

I will argue that a proper understanding of what is meant by equilibrium allows one to see that what is valuable in Kirzner's middle ground is, in fact, already included in the equilibrium pole. What is left is precisely "intrinsically unpredictable" and, therefore, vacuous with respect to policy.

Despite its flaws, Kirzner's analysis is valuable. His discussions of the entrepreneurial element in the market process are clear, innovative, and insightful. His understanding of the competitive process of arbitrage and his exposition of it in *Competition and Entrepreneurship* was a primary catalyst to my own thinking on the subject. Kirzner's ability to see arbitrage in untraditional settings, that is, in settings other than simple simultaneous purchase and sale at different prices, is unsurpassed. His intuitive explanations of the implications of uncertainty and incomplete information clearly illustrate the difference between risk taking and pure discovery. In fact, I believe there is nothing in Kirzner's analysis or policy conclusions that is inconsistent with my understanding of standard neo-classical analysis except his insistence that such equilibrium analysis is lacking.

A theme implied by the last paragraph deserves mention here, but will not be expanded in this paper. By distancing himself from standard analysis, Kirzner makes it easier for the mainstream to ignore his arguments. Charles Baird has noted a similar tendency in his paper comparing Austrian economics with the economics of James Buchanan: "Austrians are often dismissed by practitioners of neoclassical orthodoxy as free-market ideologues who cannot count" (1989, p. 202). Baird goes on to defend the Austrians: "[i]f mainstream economists will not take them seriously, the Austrians cannot be faulted for 'talking only to converts' " (1989, p. 202). Rather than give up center stage to a mainstream view which is misleading or incorrect, however, I would prefer to incorporate what is good in Kirzner's work or that of other Austrians into the mainstream where it will necessarily displace that which is misleading. In the case of Kirzner, I believe this can be done readily. Of course, one's style of argumentation is somewhat a matter of taste. The issue of whether Kirzner's message would be more widely internalized today if he had argued differently is moot. However, the issues of whether economics leads to free-market or interventionist policy prescriptions and of whether policy regimes affect the amount of entrepreneurship are still hotly debated.

After the discussion of the nature and meaning of equilibrium in Section II, Section III of this paper presents and highlights several passages from Kirzner's writings. For each passage I will attempt to show how Kirzner's analysis is either misleading or unfruitful. The final section is a brief summary.

II. EQUILIBRIUM

In this section, I trace the development of the notion that markets can be examined as if in a continual state of equilibrium. The issues of statics versus dynamics, coordination of plans, arbitrage, uncertainty, contingent plans, equilibrium versus disequilibrium, intervention, subjectivity, and optimality are treated in turn.

A. Simple Equilibrium Notions

The simplest notion of equilibrium that we usually encounter first in economics is that of an equilibrium, market-clearing price. Even in this setting, one can talk about plan coordination, absence of arbitrage, stability conditions and the like. There are several "stories" we tell our principles students when the idea is first introduced. One such story emphasizes that it is useful to study equilibrium because markets once in equilibrium will remain in equilibrium. This story refers to the *definition* of equilibrium as a state in which there is no pressure to change. Coordination of plans is central in this view because it is precisely the fact that actors in the model can achieve what they set out to do, that is, buy and sell at the market-clearing price, that eliminates any pressure for the price to change. Another story emphasizes that if not in equilibrium, then the pressures to change are toward the equilibrium state. This story relates to the *stability* of equilibrium. If the price is not at its equilibrium level, then plans cannot be coordinated, there will be either excess demand or excess supply, and arbitrage possibilities for pure profit will exist. A third story views the establishment of a market-clearing price as a thought experiment. This story concerns the *existence* of equilibrium. Different prices are considered, and the logical implications of such a price or set of prices are deduced to determine whether or not that price does clear the market. If it does, we have equilibrium; if it does not, another price is considered.

As a matter of positive economics, knowing the characteristics of the equilibrium state is useful for prediction. For policy prescriptions, however, it is necessary to compare the equilibrium with some notion of an optimal state of affairs. Thus, as a normative matter, we are concerned with the *optimality* of the equilibrium. Invisible-hand theorems generally show that the equilibrium reached in such models is Pareto optimal. This result is usually developed as an indirect proof with an accompanying story. The story shows how nonmarket clearing prices lead to arbitrage, which can benefit some people without hurting others. When the market clearing prices are established, the arbitrage possibility disappears. Note at this juncture that the indirect proof of the optimality of the equilibrium relies as much, if not more, on the absence of arbitrage as on the coordination of plans. I will return to this point below.

Each of these stories plays an integral part in traditional theory and in Kirzner's writings. Kirzner, perhaps, pays least direct attention to the existence of equilibrium. Indirectly, however, equilibrium is important as the direction in which the market is moving, spurred on by the equilibrating tendencies of entrepreneurial arbitrage. If equilibrium does not exist, a different set of problems arises and a different basis upon which to formulate policy must be developed. Kirzner is most concerned with the stability of equilibrium. Indeed, the only "action" in this simple static equilibrium world would concern the arbitrage that would occur in disequilibrium in order to bring about the equilibrium. Implicitly, Kirzner is also concerned with the definition and the optimality of the equilibrium. If the static equilibrium were not optimal, then presumably we would not be so concerned about the speed with which it is reached, or whether it is reached at all.

B. Static Equilibrium versus Dynamics

The schizophrenic view outlined above, that is, static, timeless equilibrium versus disequilibrium (but equilibrating) action through time, is at the root of the misunderstanding of the import of equilibrium. Perhaps the most common view is that it is only partially possible to incorporate time and dynamics within the simple equilibrium setting. Surely, one can easily talk of coordinated plans in a series of discrete periods. Indeed, once any static equilibrium is reached, one could envision a future that reproduces that equilibrium over and over again in each period. In fact, Kirzner embraces this view:

> In equilibrium, it turns out, all market decisions have somehow come already into complete mutual coordination. . . . So long as the underlying present consumer attitudes and production possibilities prevail, it is clear that we can rely on the very same set of decisions being made in each of an indefinite number of future periods (1985, p. 43).

As most would admit, this approach does not come close to capturing real world, real time economic behavior. However, one must not be too quick to dismiss equilibrium because there are more sophisticated views which come closer.

Continuous time can be modeled by interpreting quantities as rates of production and consumption to be replicated continuously. This approach can also be expanded to allow for seasonality and/or growth so that the identical (through time) prices, production rates and consumption rates need not be a characteristic of the equilibrium. If there were perfect foresight, the whole future could be fully arbitraged, and a set of equilibrium, time-dependent prices established that will clear all markets in a general equilibrium established once and for all as in the time-dated claims approach.[1]

In any of these approaches, however, the question of how the market comes into equilibrium remains. If there is first a "trading period" in which thought experiments are conducted to simultaneously show existence of and arrive at equilibrium, we have not overcome our original schizophrenic problem. Note that if markets are interpreted as always being in equilibrium, this problem disappears. But, how is such an interpretation justified?

C. Equilibrium: Prices versus Behavior

The problem stems from Kirzner's asking a model of general equilibrium prices to do more than it is designed to do. Remember that the model as I outlined it is occupied with defining and showing the existence, stability, and optimality of equilibrium *prices*. It is inappropriate to ask this model to also describe behavior in disequilibrium states. Indeed, as far as existence of equilibrium is concerned, such models are nothing more than logical thought experiments to trace the implications of certain sets of prices. It is legitimate to ask what behavior would look like in equilibrium, and we could highlight coordinated plans and the absence of arbitrage. However, it is stepping outside the bounds of this model to question how these prices come about.

It would seem that I am making Kirzner's case for him. The static equilibrium models are not enough because they do not pay enough attention to the human process behind the formation of such equilibrium prices. But, to leave the analysis here is to make a straw man of neoclassical theory. Indeed, to criticize a model for not doing something it did not set out to do misses the point of the model entirely. The general equilibrium models do show that plans can be coordinated, resources allocated, and goods distributed by a set of market clearing prices. These models also show how the resulting equilibrium is optimal in some sense. These models, however, do not show how those prices come about. But other, solidly neoclassical models do. Indeed, standard neoclassical theory, in models of consumer and producer behavior, does go behind the scenes of the demand and supply schedules to examine the maximizing or optimizing *behavior* leading to such schedules. Other models, such as monopoly, oligopoly, bargaining models, and Edgeworth boxes, examine the price setting process. Kirzner recognizes these models as describing a type of behavior he calls Robbinsian maximization. But, he repeatedly dismisses these models, asserting that something more is required.

D. Coordination, Discoordination and Arbitrage

Kirzner and other Austrian economists following the lead of Hayek (1948) are led to a preoccupation with the shortcomings of the general equilibrium models because of their view of equilibrium as a mutual coordination of plans. The crucial issue in this view concerns the kind of institutions, if any, which lead the individual members of society to use their resources (including their information) in some kind of coordinated way. Indeed, given a taste for fish and meat, we would not want everyone to become hunters. The price/exchange system, of course, provides information in a useful and economic form to consumers and producers who combine the market information with their own private information and make optimizing decisions given their own particular tastes and constraints. The question of coordination of plans boils down to one of existence of equilibrium. The desirability of coordinated plans boils down to a question of the optimality of the equilibrium. But still, the issue of the movement to equilibrium is glossed over. One needs to address squarely what happens if plans are not coordinated, that is, what happens at disequilibrium prices.

The discussion at this point usually changes from talking about plans to talking about arbitrage. Rather than address the implications of frustrated or unfulfilled plans to the people making those plans, attention is now given to the entrepreneur who can discover and act. Entrepreneurs, however, do not act because others' plans are frustrated. Rather, they act because of a potential profit from arbitrage.

In one sense arbitrage and plan coordination are opposite sides of the same coin. In equilibrium, plans are coordinated and there is an absence of arbitrageable opportunities. In disequilibrium, plans are not coordinated and profit from arbitrage is possible. In another sense, however, they are different and I believe that the differences favor the use of the arbitrage interpretation, especially when trying to examine disequilibrium. Essentially, this is because arbitrage deals with behavior, while plan coordination describes a state of affairs. In particular, arbitrage deals positively, or actively with behavior in disequilibrium, whereas plan coordination deals negatively with such a situation by talking about the absence of plan coordination. Alternatively, plan coordination deals positively with equilibrium in addressing all the desirable properties and implications of coordinated plans, while in equilibrium we talk of the absence of arbitrage. Because arbitrage directly deals with behavior, it is more apparent to everyone whether or not they have an arbitrageable opportunity, than whether or not plans are coordinated. Indeed, in a world of uncertainty it is hard to imagine how a market participant would ever distinguish between uncoordinated plans and stochastic events which are, probabilistically speaking, planned.

In essence, the plan coordination view is too Walrasian. In focusing on plan coordination, one is predisposed to use a model designed to show the existence and optimality of some equilibrium, market-clearing prices. These, of course, are necessary steps because if the equilibrium does not exist, or is not optimal in some sense, we would be less concerned with whether or not we reached or approached it. Such a model develops the characteristics of the equilibrium as a thought experiment, but gives little attention to whether an external auctioneer, or market participants are actually setting and changing the prices. Alternatively, the arbitrage/absence of arbitrage view focuses directly on the behavior of the market participants.

In my view, a related clear benefit of the arbitrage/absence of arbitrage view is that is provides the kernel for the understanding of the view that markets are always in equilibrium. Simply ask yourself or anyone if there are arbitrageable, pure profit opportunities that exist. If the answer is yes, then the person is not maximizing unless they are carrying out the arbitrage. If they are not carrying out the arbitrage because of some cost, then the situation appearing to allow for arbitrage profit is essentially nothing more than a mirage. If the person is maximizing and not engaged in arbitrage for pure profit, the reason must be that the market is in equilibrium vis-à-vis the behavior of that person. The fully arbitraged world is a world in equilibrium.[2] Whereas it is believable to think that people, naturally, would know profitable arbitrage if they saw it, how is anyone to know whether or not plans are coordinated, except by reference to such arbitrage?

E. Uncertainty and Coordinated Plans

Unemphasized so far is the role of uncertainty. An immediate effect of trying to consider the dynamic passage of time is that uncertainty must be incorporated into the model. It is obviously impossible to know the future with certainty. Indeed, the whole basis of Kirzner's entrepreneurial discovery is the finding out or noticing of something previously unknown. In a world of certainty, this could never happen.

The effect of uncertainty on behavior needs to be carefully considered. Alchian (1950), for example, emphasizes that straightforward maximization no longer makes sense because any action would lead to a distribution of outcomes, and one cannot maximize a distribution. One can, however, maximize some utility function that depends on the parameters, for example, the mean and variance, of a distribution. Alchian claims that such an endeavor may be impossible because of the mathematical or computational complexity of the problem. This is a curious approach, because it is ordinarily understood that maximization of utility automatically means *constrained* maximization. If it is costly to go through the maximizing calculus to its fullest (unconstrained) degree, then it is not optimal to do so. The agent maximizes, subject to all relevant constraints.

At this point, Kirzner would highlight that it is not even possible to consider all of the possible outcomes of any action, even in a probabilistic sense. After all, where is one to come up with an exhaustive list of possible outcomes with related probabilities summing to one? Certainly there is no objective way to do so. Again, however, it is curious why one should require a completely specified (as opposed to economically specified) probability distribution. Presumably, people attempt to subjectively determine, to the best of their ability, the probabilistic outcomes of any action. People are subject to scarcity in this endeavor as much as in any other endeavor and continue to the point on the margin where the costs start to outweigh the benefits. If there are any costs at all to this process, the person stops before developing an exhaustive list of the possibilities. To continue would waste scarce resources. There is no pathology imbedded in this process. People do the best they can with what they have. As far as each individual is concerned, such maximization means they have exploited all pure profit, arbitrage situations and are left in a situation that can be described as continual optimization. Such a situation leaves no arbitrage opportunities for the individual and thus is a (continual) equilibrium. This implies that plans are coordinated, but the plans may not look like what one is used to seeing in the Walrasian model.

The following three examples will illustrate the preceding arguments.

1. Example One: Contingent Plans

I have suggested above that the identification of unfulfilled plans is a nettlesome business. Consider the example of a traveler who wants to go from point A to point B. There are two roads, although one is admittedly better (faster, safer, shorter, smoother and/or more scenic) than the other. The traveler does not have perfect foresight and it is possible that either road may be completely blocked. Our traveler chooses the better road and, indeed, finds it to be blocked, requiring a return to point A to start down the other road.

Now, consider the following questions in turn. In what senses is or is not the traveler's plan fulfilled? At what point is or is not the traveler in equilibrium? In what sense is or is not the traveler optimizing? Are any entrepreneurial discoveries made? Is there an arbitrage opportunity?

It is tempting to think that the traveler's plan was simply to travel down the better road from point A to point B. Since it becomes impossible, the plan is thwarted. In a world of uncertainty, this view would lead to every plan being thwarted except plans made by a clairvoyant or a very lucky plan maker. Such a view of what is necessary for a plan to be fulfilled is too restrictive. Essentially, this view of what is required for a plan to be fulfilled comes from the static, full information Walrasian model which discusses what is required about prices to allow plans to be fulfilled. This notion of plan fulfillment must be discarded in a continuous time model with imperfect foresight.

I prefer to think of the traveler as making or having contingent plans. That is, the traveler's plan is to travel down the better road from A to B, unless it turns out to be impassable, in which case the plan is to return and travel down the other road. In this sense, the plan is fulfilled. In this sense, all contingent plans are always fulfilled and we are always in equilibrium. It should be clear that this approach is superior to the naive, static view of equilibrium, which requires that the traveler reach B before attaining equilibrium. Such a view does not allow for any *action* to be consistent with equilibrium. (Note that even if the person had been able to fulfill the naive plan directly, the person would still be in disequilibrium until reaching B.) This view, however, is not useful in a real time model. My view is that the person is in equilibrium by nature of the continuous optimization that occurs.

There is no Kirznerian entrepreneurial discovery in this example. The traveler is simply maximizing his/her subjective utility and reacting to the surrounding stochastic world. A slight change in the premise of the example, however, and the discovery process highlighted by Kirzner can be illuminated. Something completely unpredictable must happen. Anything that is conceivably possible is already accounted for in the contingent plans of the traveler. Up until the moment of the discovery of the unpredictable event, the traveler is optimally following the plan with all its contingencies. The traveler is in equilibrium. I do not think it makes sense to say that the traveler is in disequilibrium because he/she has not yet made a discovery about to be made. The traveler could have made the discovery at an earlier time but evidently it was too costly to do so. In fact, since the discovery was completely unpredictable a priori, the *expected* cost of making such a discovery would be infinite. To have invested any effort into making the discovery sooner would have been a misuse of resources.[3]

At the moment of discovery, the cost of making the discovery suddenly falls to zero. The traveler realizes that the previous plan with all its contingencies is no longer an optimal one. For an instant, the person is in disequilibrium but only for an instant. Immediately, the traveler formulates a superior plan, which compared to the old plan yields greater expected utility. So, instantaneously, the traveler is back on an optimizing path, back in equilibrium. (Note that if plan reformulation is costly or takes time, the traveler does not formulate a new plan in an instant; rather, he/she starts to formulate or starts to think about formulating a new plan in an instant. This traveler is still instantaneously following a new plan, the first step of which is to formulate the rest of the new plan in an economically optimal way.)

The arbitrage opportunity in this final example is coincident with the unexpected discovery. Doing things one way, that is, following the old plan, is unequivocally inferior to doing things a different way, that is, following the new plan. There is a pure gain in expected utility at the moment in which the discovery is made, the old plan scrapped and the new plan formulated. The fact that the actual gains come only through time as the new plan with its contingencies is followed, is consistent with Kirzner's view of the discovery process. In Kirzner's view a discovery is made about how to do something better, and from that point on, it is Robbinsian maximization that follows through on the discovery.

2. Example Two: Equilibrium, Disequilibrium and Intervention

There are two groups of buyers and sellers who do not know about each other. The individuals in the groups are buying and selling and planning to buy and sell and their plans are fulfilled. The groups, however, are exchanging the same good at different prices. Should this situation be considered an equilibrium or not? Kirzner thinks not. In fact, Kirzner (1985, pp. 158–159), uses precisely this example and argues that it represents "incompleteness of coordination." But, there is no buyer or seller in either market whose plan is not reaching fruition, given the relevant prices, that is, the prices they face. Any omniscient observer could, however, point out some profitable arbitrage opportunities. But, if no agent in the model ever discovers the price discrepancy, essentially because it is costly to have all information that might be useful, then this situation could persist. Taking into account the information costs, we would have to conclude that there were no profitable arbitrageable opportunities and that the markets were in equilibrium.

Once an entrepreneur discovers the price discrepancy, he/she can earn pure profit by buying in the low price market and selling in the high price market in the familiar arbitrage story. Because this story is familiar, however, the details often get glossed over. Indeed, is the market now in equilibrium or disequilibrium? If in disequilibrium, how long will it take for equilibrium to be reestablished? How fast is the arbitrage? I submit that the only sensible answer is that equilibrium is reestablished instantaneously.

I do not mean that prices immediately jump in the two markets from preexisting static equilibrium values to new static equilibrium values. Nor is it the case that rates of consumption and production in the two markets immediately switch to new long-run values. Changing one's production rates and delivery schedules is costly, as is the act of simultaneously buying and selling. Presumably, the faster one tries to make these changes, the more costly it is. The agents make these changes and the entrepreneur pursues the arbitrage in an optimizing, economic manner, balancing the benefits of faster action with the related costs. This, of course, is just how they make all decisions. They are still in equilibrium, producing, buying and selling at optimal rates, given the constraints they face. Prices or other constraints or conditions may change through time, but changing prices are not evidence of disequilibrium as can be illustrated easily in the continuous time, general equilibrium models.

Some would view this example as an instance of a market starting in equilibrium, then disturbed (destructed) by the creative discovery of the entrepreneur.[4] The desire to view the disturbed market as a disequilibrium comes from the inability of real world prices and production to immediately settle on new, constant, equilibrium values as predicted in a model. This view, however, opens the door for intervention. If the desirable welfare properties come from the Pareto optimality of the equilibrium state, a world in disequilibrium is susceptible to improvement by interventionist policy. Rather than calling this a disequilibrium, and opening the door for intervention because of the market's failure to achieve equilibrium, I would call this a model failure, because the model is too highly stylized.[5] The model abstracts from adjustment costs and information costs in order to simplify the analysis. When the real world does not live up to the predictions of the abstract model, such as instantaneous price adjustment, the fault lies with the model not with the market. If we attempted to make the model more realistic by the inclusion of adjustment costs and the like, we would find that the results of our model look more and more like the achieved results in reality. After all, the actors in the model and the actors in the real world are assumed to do the same thing, that is, to continually optimize.

Others would view this as a case where the market was originally in disequilibrium and where the profit seeking on the part of the entrepreneur creates a process through which the market moves toward an equilibrium. The market may or may not get there before some other underlying information changes or comes to light. But, this market is only in disequilibrium with reference to some perfect information benchmark; this perfect information does not exist in the hands of the relevant actors in the market and, therefore, is irrelevant.

I view this as a case of a market beginning in equilibrium. At some moment a discovery is made which makes the existing equilibrium irrelevant, much as an exogenous change in some condition in a comparative static model. The actors then immediately set out to optimize, that is, to establish and follow new contingent plans. As such, the market participants immediately jump to a new time path of equilibrium, optimizing behavior with implications for price and quantity changes.

3. Example Three: Uncertainty, Subjectivity and Optimality

This example illustrates how the direct application of results from a certainty model to a world with imperfect foresight and subjective expected utility maximization leads to incorrect implications for policy. Consider the case of two individuals considering exchanging one unit of some good. The potential buyer is willing to pay as much as six units of currency, while the prospective seller is willing to part with the item for as little as three. Standard analysis suggests that the individuals should exchange the good for any price between three and six. If what is known as the small numbers bargaining problem prevents the trade from occurring, a so-called market failure results. Such a view could lead to the establishment of some interventionist policy, perhaps binding arbitration, that will bring about the exchange.

The bargaining problem occurs when the buyer thinks that there is a sizable probability that the seller will eventually give in and sell for a price of three. Meanwhile, the seller thinks the buyer will eventually offer six. If the probabilities associated with these expectations are high enough, the best strategy for each trader, in terms of maximizing subjective expected utility is to hold out and try to wait for the other to give in. The market failure interpretation is supported because the modeler with omniscience knows that both subjectively determined probabilities cannot be "true" in the objective sense from the point of view of perfect information. The interventionist position implicitly assumes that policy makers have this perfect information and can use it effectively to bring about the exchange.

There are several avenues of attack on this interventionist position. Hayek (1945) points out that it is virtually impossible for the public sector decision makers to have better information about the relevant values and probabilities than the actual people involved. Following up on this theme, Demsetz (1969) warns of the "nirvana approach," that is, comparing the decentralized market with its incomplete information and subjective probabilities to an intervening government sector with perfect information. A complementary attack on the interventionist position comes from the Public Choice school. This attack states that even if it were possible for the government to have the information required, it would not have the incentive structure to use the information properly.[6]

Kirzner essentially agrees with the tone of these attacks. The incentives for entrepreneurial action by workers in the private sector are dulled by too much government intervention. Also, the incentives for entrepreneurial action by workers in the public sector are dulled by the absence of private property rights in the outcomes of their decisions and malaligned by the political rent seeking existing in government. To Kirzner, Hayek, and Demsetz, the best system to bring about the equilibrium requires freedom from government intervention and regulation.

These attacks on the interventionist position, however, create the impression that there is a market failure to correct. The argument is reduced to the best way to approach the equilibrium, that is, to bring about the trade.

I interpret this situation as another example of the misapplication of the model. Indeed, the traders are mutually maximizing their subjective, expected utilities. If it would be better for them to delegate the authority to a third party to bring about the exchange, perhaps through binding arbitration, then they would do so, *voluntarily*. If they do not do so, we must assume that they are following expected utility maximizing plans, and that they are on an equilibrium time path. Our traders get higher expected utility by waiting for the other side to give in than by making the exchange for an intermediate price. To make them split the difference and trade against their wills would actually make them worse off.

In this view, the market is already in the relevant equilibrium. The relevant expected utilities are being maximized. There is no market failure to correct. It is not required that the individuals reach some perfect information standard of coordinated plans and by so doing achieve some static notion of Pareto optimality. The individuals, as far as they are concerned, are already following maximizing plans and are already achieving the relevant, dynamic notion of optimality that following optimal plans implies. It is not a question of the institutions that will lead to the quickest resolution of the "disequilibrium," because there is no relevant disequilibrium. As long as the individuals are not forced or coerced to do something against their wills, which would be the case in any interventionist action by the state, optimality is achieved.

III. KIRZNERIAN ENTREPRENEURSHIP AND PUBLIC POLICY

The preceding arguments have illustrated how correctly interpreted standard equilibrium models lead to policy conclusions showing that government intervention is unnecessary and perverse. The following few excerpts are designed to show first, how Kirzner's approach, to the extent that conclusions are forthcoming, mimics these arguments, and second, how Kirzner's approach, to the extent that it explicitly rejects the standard neoclassical models, leads to no conclusions in particular.

A. Kirzner's Middle Ground
It appears as if Kirzner has foreseen and addressed my criticisms from the outset. Consider the following passages:

> My view of the role of entrepreneurial discovery rejects, further, the thesis that recognition of entrepreneurial activities obscures the rel-

evance of equilibrium configurations or that such relevance can be preserved only by compressing entrepreneurial activities, too, into the equilibrium mold. I hold, on the contrary, that entrepreneurial discoveries are the steps through which any possible tendency toward market equilibrium must proceed. . . . I must reject the view that requires us to hold *either* that agents already possess relevant items of knowledge (with this option including, as a special case, possession by agents not of the relevant items of knowledge themselves, but rather, and altogether equivalently, their possession of knowledge of how to search for and obtain those relevant items of knowledge) or not only that agents are grossly ignorant at any given time, but also that they must, except as a matter of sheerest luck, necessarily continue to remain ignorant of the relevant items of knowledge. I maintain, rather, that human alertness at all times furnishes agents with the propensity to discover information that will be useful to them. Without resorting to any assumption of systematic, deliberate search; and without relying on sheer luck, I postulate a continuous discovery process (1985, pp. 11–12).

Kirzner rejects the equilibrium pole in rejecting the view that "agents already possess relevant items of knowledge." The key word here is "relevant." If relevant means, "objectively true in some full-information, long run equilibrium sense," then Kirzner is rejecting the naive, static notion of equilibrium, that is, a straw man. Clearly the market is not and will never achieve equilibrium in the sense of having *all* information, nor should it, because having *all* information is too costly. Whether or not some analyst assumes that he/she has all the information in some model, to expect the agents in the real world to match the outcome of the model would be to misapply the model. On the other hand, if relevant means "subjectively available in an optimizing and economizing on the part of the decision maker sense," then indeed, this is precisely the information that the agents possess. Kirzner, no doubt, would reply that he meant neither of these choices, but, rather, something in between. Yet, I and other neoclassical economists admit to no middle ground, and between the two choices given, choose the latter.

There are many other such passages where Kirzner asserts the relevance of his view. However, there never is a proof. The lack of a proof puts Kirzner's critics at somewhat of a disadvantage. How does one prove in a concise manner that someone never did something? Kirzner gets a lot of mileage out of "alertness" but I have yet to discover an example or application of this idea leading to noninterventionist policy that could not be explained by reference to optimizing search.

B. Search Versus Alertness

The parenthetical phrase in the last quoted passage hints that Kirzner distinguishes entrepreneurial alertness from neoclassical search, by suggesting that the search models are equivalent to the equilibrium models. More to the point, Kirzner insists that "we distinguish sharply between pure alertness, on the one hand, and 'deployable' scarce inputs that may be useful in decision making, for example, time, technical knowledge, managerial expertise, on the other" (1985, p. 24). For Kirzner, search takes time, has costs, produces benefits, and can be analyzed in an equilibrium context. Alertness, however, is different; "we recognize the quality of entrepreneurial alertness as something which *somehow emerges into view at the precise moment when decisions have to be made*" (1985, p. 24, emphasis in original).

In my view, this departure from the neoclassical orthodoxy is unfortunate. "Something which somehow" is not much to go on.[7] By staying within the bounds of equilibrium analysis, one can pose and answer such policy relevant questions as "how much search is optimal?" Straightforward analysis leads to free market policy conclusions by showing how subsidized search generally leads to too much search and discovery from an economic standpoint, while taxes on profits cut into the benefits of search and lead to a suboptimal amount. To my knowledge, Kirzner never has directly posed and answered in a meaningful way, "How much alertness is optimal?" When analyzing search, a well-understood cost-benefit calculus applies, but the same is not true for alertness.

Kirzner seems to imply only that more alertness is always preferred to less. At the very least, there are numerous statements about the advantages and desirability of alertness and not one example indicating that it is possible, economically speaking, to have too much. Free market policy recommendations would be consistent with desiring more alertness if two conditions were true. First, government tax and/or regulatory policy would have to dampen entrepreneurial alertness (as Kirzner argues throughout his work) and second, government would necessarily be incapable of doing anything, other than diminishing its intervention, to promote alertness (a point on which Kirzner, for the most part, is consistent). If, as in my view, alertness is taken to be the same thing as search, the first condition is true, as I argued above. The second condition would also seem to be true, if alertness were the same as search. This follows as a straightforward extension of Hayek's knowledge problem. Unfortunately, with Kirzner's formulation of alertness, the first condition does not follow. Meanwhile, Kirzner occasionally embraces the possibility of proactive government policy to stimulate alertness, but, compared to the first condition, this is a minor point.[8] The first condition does not follow, essentially because Kirzner, in his zeal to distinguish alertness from search, has repeatedly insisted that entrepreneurial alertness is costless.

C. Costless Discovery
Kirzner must view entrepreneurial alertness and discovery as costless, because to do otherwise is to equate alertness with neoclassical search and all its equilibrium properties. This one facet, more than any other, is the unsteady foundation that ultimately leads to the crumbling of his analytical structure. Consider the following passages.

> [E]ntrepreneurship is costless. In using any quantity of a scarce resource (in the usual sense of that term) the decision maker is always viewed as choosing between alternative goals to which the scarce resource might be applied. The goal foregone is the cost of using the resource for its present purpose. In the case of entrepreneurial alertness, however, a decision maker never considers whether to apply some given potential alertness to the discovery of opportunity A or opportunity B. As already argued, the opportunities (or any one of them) are either perceived or not perceived; alertness is not something about which a decision can be made *not* to deploy it (1985, p. 24, emphasis in original).

> I have described entrepreneurial alertness as in principle, inexhaustible, I have also been careful to notice that potential alertness may be (and so often is) untapped and inert (1985, p. 25).

> That in the real world we encounter innumerable instances of faulty and inadequate entrepreneurship must be interpreted, therefore, not as evidence of the absolute scarcity of entrepreneurial alertness (with the existing stock of it having been applied elsewhere), but as evidence that the alertness costlessly available has somehow remained latent and untapped (1985, p. 25).

To my knowledge, Kirzner never satisfactorily addresses the following question. If entrepreneurial alertness is costless, and if it provides some benefit to the entrepreneur, why is not all entrepreneurial alertness exercised? Also, how can any policy which effects the potential benefit of any valuable discovery (excepting a policy which lowers the potential benefit from some positive amount to zero or negative) influence *costless* alertness or discovery? As long as the benefit remains positive, the cost-less discovery will be made. In fact, if discovery is truly costless, then one would even "discover" opportunities that would be profitable, except for onerous taxes or regulations which render them unprofitable. One may question whether, in such a case, a "discovery" has been made.

Kirzner never really does more than assert that all alertness is not exercised. In the first passage, he asserts that an opportunity may be "not perceived," in the second, "alertness may be (and so often is) untapped and inert," and, in the third, "in the real world we encounter innumer-able instances of faulty and inadequate entrepreneurship." But, by what criteria can anyone ever know these things? Would not a better interpre-tation be that the potential expected cost of perceiving any opportunity outweighs the potential expected benefit, therefore making the opportu-nity economically irrelevant? Such an interpretation fits squarely within standard theory and still allows the policy conclusions that Kirzner sup-ports. Furthermore, such an interpretation explains in an economizing framework why some potentially valuable discovery can remain undis-covered. The best Kirzner can do is to assert that "alertness costlessly available has *somehow* remained latent and untapped" (emphasis added).

Costless alertness, or anything for which scarcity does not apply, does not admit to too much in the way of economic policy. Logically speaking, as long as the potential benefits to the entrepreneur remain positive, taxes or regulations can be heaped on and discoveries will still be forthcoming. Of course, taxes and regulations may turn some potentially profitable discov-eries into losing propositions, so that even if a discovery is made, it will not be acted upon. This result adds nothing to the neoclassical search position that agents compare expected costs of search with expected benefits. Taxes and regulations can obviously influence expected benefits, but whether those benefits are compared to costly search or costless alertness, the same decision calculus applies. If anything, the view that costs are zero would seem to be an unrealistic and unhelpful narrowing of the traditional theory.

In other passages, however, Kirzner seemingly denies the idea of cost-less alertness. He claims, "It can be stated with considerable confidence *that human beings tend to notice that which it is in their interest to notice*" (1985, p. 28, emphasis in original). Why, if alertness is costless, don't human beings notice everything? There must be a cost to noticing some things, maybe in the form of not noticing others. The fact that one notices something which it is in his/her interest to notice, simply means that the benefits outweigh the costs for that discovery. Again, the interpretations and implications that Kirzner wants to highlight come from standard search theory, and not from costless entrepreneurial alertness and discovery.

D. The Role of Uncertainty

Kirzner is further led to embrace the costless alertness view because of his interpretation of part of what is known as "the knowledge problem." According to Kenneth Boulding, searching for information contains a paradox,

> implicit in the very concept of knowledge, that we have to know what we want to know before we can start looking for it. There are things that we ought to know, and which we do not know that we ought to know, that remain largely unknown and unsought for (1968, p. 146).

Because of the knowledge problem, two wholly different methods exist for learning or knowing something. One can deliberately search for some information, or one can spontaneously, undeliberately absorb it. The extent to which one believes that information is deliberately searched for, influences how one will think about equilibrium. If all information is acquired through search, we can see the world as in continuous equilibrium. Neoclassical economic theory is relevant. Alternatively, if all or almost all information comes to us in a spontaneous bombardment over which we have no control, we see the world as in continual disequilibrium, and, therefore, equilibrium theory is irrelevant. These are the poles to which we referred earlier, the poles that Kirzner rejects.

Essentially, Kirzner rejects the equilibrium pole because some relevant information can only be absorbed undeliberately. It is impossible to search unless,

> one *already* knows enough about the territory to be able to calculate rewards and costs. So that, if we are to view the acquisition of knowledge as deliberately undertaken, one must postulate some prior knowledge *not* acquired through deliberate search. . . . The knowledge upon which the very first decision to search for knowledge depended was itself *not* acquired deliberately (1979, p. 142, emphasis in original).

In this passage, Kirzner effectively proves that at least the very first acquisition of knowledge was absorbed undeliberately. After that first acquisition, which might be at birth or even in the womb, the issue of how to interpret all the rest of information acquisition remains. Indeed, just how much does one need to know about the territory to be "enough"? This, essentially, is an economic question. As discussed above, to require one to know the exact, objective probabilities of each possible outcome (with respect to discovery of knowledge) is to apply too literally the assumptions made in the context of a model that is trying to illustrate the phenomenon of how search works. All that is really required, is that the individual have some subjective, economically specified probability distribution over what might happen. Implicit in such a specification is the realization that the individual never will truly know the exact territory over which he/she searches, and so will never have a completely specified probability distribution. There will be a realization on the part of the agent that something completely unexpected might happen, and this possibility will be given due weight, subjectively, in the individual's optimization. Since the possibility is completely unexpected, it is not clear what weight to attach to it, but at least the decision maker will keep such possibilities in mind.[9] In this view, the information that the consumer does have is the economically relevant information.

The extent to which one thinks information is discovered through the specified portion (as opposed to the unknowable portion) of the probability distribution colors one's view as to whether purposeful search and equilibrium or undeliberate discovery and absence of equilibrium dominate. This section concludes with the discussion of two complementary arguments implying the dominance of the equilibrium view. The first argument shows that search is more important because it is the activity to which agents devote more of their time (infinitely so) as compared to undeliberate discovery. The second points out that what is called undeliberate discovery probably has a necessary, and costly, deliberate component, thus bringing it within the scope of search.

E. Search, Undeliberate Discovery and Time

I believe that it is consistent with Kirzner's views that search activity is carried out in real time, although any actual discovery that is made through the search takes place in an instant, specifically, the instant before the shriek of "eureka, I've found it." This is because search represents *behavior,* while a discovery is an event. Also consistent with this interpretation is the fact that undeliberate discovery is a timeless, discrete event. These views fit nicely in a world in which search and optimizing behavior in continuous time are punctuated by discrete instants of pure discovery, much as a number line is punctuated by the discrete points known as the rational numbers, or much as our traveler from an earlier example is continually optimizing except for the instant he/she discovers that the old plan is nonoptimal due to some unexpected event. Mathematical analysis of the real number line (which, in this case, measures time) indicates that any finite number of such discrete points add up to a length of zero, as compared to the continuous open-ended intervals between the points. In this view, the undeliberate discoveries are unimportant in the relevant sense in describing the behavior of the optimizing agents.

The discoveries, of course, will be very important in terms of causing alterations in previously planned behavior of the individuals. Unless this previously planned behavior was visible or known in some way, however, it will generally be impossible, empirically, to tell whether any visible behavior represents the following of some maximizing, contingent plan, or represents the response to the undeliberate discovery, that is, a new maximizing, contingent plan. The agent's behavior through real time is still best understood by reference to optimizing, maximization, and search, and in this sense, the undeliberate discoveries are unimportant.

Even if there are an infinite number of discoveries, unless there are enough of them so that they are close enough together to no longer be discrete, (compactness) their importance wanes in comparison to the rest of the time when agents are purposefully optimizing. If there were enough undeliberate discoveries so that they do continuously fill the time space, as in Shackle's view, as quoted in Kirzner (1979, p. 143, emphasis in original) that "*being* consists in continual and endless fresh *knowing*," then the view of the agent as a purposeful maximizer is brought into question. If we want to view the agent as a purposeful optimizer, then Shackle's pole should be rejected, putting us at the equilibrium pole, except for *instants* of unplanned discovery.

F. Costly Search, Costless Alertness: A Reconciliation

The discrete moments of unplanned discovery imbedded into a continuous optimization problem support the position that the "exercise" of alertness is costless. Indeed, as several of the above excerpts have indicated,

Kirzner holds that alertness is not something that can be deployed like other resources. The discovery only takes an instant and in that sense entails no opportunity cost. But, Kirzner's analysis creates a riddle where there is none. The riddle is how, when, or why something can remain unnoticed. Where does the faulty alertness come from?

I believe that the answer to this riddle involves considering two dimensions of alertness.[10] Alertness, instead of being a scarce *resource* which is used up when deployed, has a non-rival character to it so that it is not used up, either wholly or partially, when a discovery depending on that alertness is made. It is in this sense that alertness is costless. But these comments refer only to the application or utilization of alertness. There is another relevant dimension relating to the production of alertness.

In this second dimension, alertness, instead of being an endowed trait or, as Kirzner says, a "gift individuals enjoy in quite different degrees" (1979, p. 148), is viewed as a produced characteristic or a state of awareness that takes effort and expenditure to produce, and possibly also to maintain. It is the necessary expenditure of effort to create alertness that explains why some have it and others do not. Thus, alertness in this dimension is costly, and is subject to all the analysis that would normally apply to any scarce input or valuable output. It is possible to think of a stock of alertness that is created by costly investment over time and yielding a flow of alertness services. More investment makes one more alert. Meanwhile, making a discovery that depends on that alertness does not necessarily use up any of the stock.

Consider a mathematician who has spent many hours learning his/her field. The mathematician knows that the knowledge of mathematics may be useful someday, but does not really know how or when. At some point, the mathematician is alert enough to make an unexpected discovery, of a type that would have been impossible without a certain level of mathematical training. On the one hand, the mathematician's alertness does not get used up in the discovery, but on the other, without the costly training, he/she would not have been alert enough to make the discovery. Essentially the same example could be developed for a business-related entrepreneurial discovery that depended on some aspect of Robbinsian maximization which was not intuitively self-apparent, for example, the requirement that marginal rates of technical substitution be equalized across production facilities. Costly study heightens alertness.

Now the crux of the matter is upon us. Is the discovery of the mathematician or the business entrepreneur deliberate or spontaneous? Should we say that anything that was not explicitly planned is a surprise that can only be addressed analytically via a metaphysical "alertness"? Or should we say that the discovery was one of countless possibilities that were created and set in progress when an optimizing, searching decision to make a costly investment in education was made? The former view makes us victims of our environment. The latter view makes us masters of our destiny. The former view is silent on public policy except to say that alertness is good, but that we do not know how to encourage it. The latter view leads directly to laissez-faire policy conclusions once a correct cost-benefit analysis of the costly investment in creating alertness is made. The former view is Kirzner's. The latter view is wholly consistent with neoclassical search in a world in continual equilibrium.

Unfortunately, Kirzner never addresses the possibility of a two-dimensional alertness, that is, a costly production of alertness, and a costless utilization of it. By focusing on the costless nature of alertness and implicitly assuming that it is just a natural trait or gift that people hold in varying degrees, Kirzner misses the substantial message that neoclassical economics carries with it regarding the production of alertness. Indeed, all of Kirzner's free market conclusions (such as no taxation of entrepreneurial profits, no interference with profitable arbitrage, etc.) come directly from a standard analysis of the optimal investment decision in costly alertness. If, for example, profits are taxed (or even if there is the expectation that future profits might be taxed), then a suboptimal investment in producing alertness, and probabilistically speaking, a suboptimal time path of future discovery will be the outcome.

IV. CONCLUDING COMMENTS

This paper has argued several related points. First, the world and individual behavior in the world can be viewed fruitfully as being in continual equilibrium, in the sense of being fully arbitraged with respect to all economically relevant costs and benefits. Second, this continuous time world may be punctuated with discrete moments of planned and unplanned discovery, moments which account for none of the actual continuous time in the world. Third, what might be seen as unplanned, undeliberate discoveries can also be interpreted as the results of prior constrained optimizing investments in being alert. Fourth, the ability to make costly investments to increase alertness (even to the extent of learning reading, writing, arithmetic and economics), allows for standard neoclassical interpretations of Kirzner's discovery process, interpretations running along the lines of optimal search. Fifth, the correct neoclassical interpretations allow for normative policy conclusions wholly in favor of free markets and private property. Sixth, Kirzner's formulation of the discovery process based on costless alertness leads to these same conclusions only to the extent that such alertness is analyzed as in neoclassical search models. Seventh, a literal interpretation of Kirzner's beneficial but costless alertness and discovery actually opens the door for interventionist policy to increase such alertness.

Why is Kirzner so willing to downplay, but not discard standard equilibrium analysis? The following passage hints at a possible reason.

> With the economics of general equilibrium fully developed by the 1970s, it was perhaps understandable that theorists began to turn their attention to facts that did not fit easily into the equilibrium mold. . . . other economists, growing impatient with the *patently implausible* assumption that the world is at all times in the neighborhood of equilibrium (1985, p. 5, emphasis added).

Equilibrium analysis (except for monopoly, for which the Austrian economists had another story) was associated with Pareto optimality. But if the world was not in equilibrium, as it *apparently* was not, at least, by comparison to static Walrasian models, then the possibility of government intervention seemed justified. Kirzner, believing in the efficacy of free market institutions, kept the equilibrium analysis (with all its Robbinsian maximization) as the normatively justified direction in which the economy was moving. But, perhaps being swept along with the current, he also kept the disequilibrium. Such disequilibrium could only be overcome by the equilibrating arbitrage resulting from free market exercise of entrepreneurship. Free market institutions remained justified because they led to the quickest discovery and exploitation of relevant arbitrageable opportunities. In a nutshell, if free markets could not be defended on the basis of equilibrium, they could be defended on the basis of efficacious equilibration.

In my view, Kirzner is too quick to agree that equilibrium was "patently implausible." What seems "implausible" is most often a case of improper analogizing from truncated models to real-world situations. Instead of moving the argument to the unsteady ground of undeliberate discovery and costless alertness where it is ignored by the mainstream, it seems fruitful to stick to equilibrium models which, when properly deployed, still generate invisible-hand theorems.

With what are we left? If the world is always in equilibrium and completely arbitraged in the relevant sense, and if equilibrium and optimality coincide, what is the role of any normative inquiry? While this is the subject of another complete paper, I will briefly hint at an answer to close this one. It is true that individuals, through their continuous optimization, continuously achieve the dynamic version of Pareto optimality, subject to all the relevant costs, as long as they are free to act and transact voluntarily. Government intervention has an influence by changing property rights, broadly conceived. For example, government action can raise costs by requiring a license. A (property) right to free entry which used to be held by all potential entrants is now taken away. As Coase (1960) suggests, in a world of no transactions costs and no wealth effects this would not matter. But in a realistic world, relative wealth positions will be influenced, and economic decisions will be changed depending on the nature of the transactions costs and how transactions costs change when rights are redefined.

Consider the two worlds, one with the licensing restriction and one without. Each will appear to be in equilibrium, given the relevant costs and constraints; each will appear optimal, given the relevant costs and constraints.[11] But, an extra and completely artificial cost is imposed in one of the worlds, lowering the total utility or welfare in that scenario. We would probably like our government to choose the set of institutions that avoids unnecessary costs, and to assign property rights to minimize the transactions costs associated with their exchange. Unfortunately, because of the Hayekian knowledge problem, and public choice incentive problems in the public sector, there is little hope that government action will efficiently carry out this goal.

ACKNOWLEDGMENTS

I wish to thank Marian L. Stevens and Shyam Kamath for their comments on an earlier draft. Versions of this paper were presented at the 1992 WEA International meetings in San Francisco, in a session organized and published by the Smith Center for Private Enterprise Studies, at the Workshop in Economic Research at California State University,

Hayward, and at the Austrian Colloquium at New York University. Helpful comments were received at these workshops from Charles W. Baird, Roger Garrison, Mario Rizzo, Israel Kirzner, and Sanford Ikeda. I am also grateful for the financial support at the Smith Center. Any remaining errors are due to scarcity and information costs and are consistent with equilibrium.

NOTES

1. For an exposition see, Jack Hirshleifer (1965).

2. I attribute this view to graduate seminars in microeconomic theory conducted at UCLA in the 1970s by Armen A. Alchian.

3. To look ahead, think about whether Kirznerian alertness requires any effort.

4. This interpretation is closest to Schumpeter's.

5. Really, this is an application failure. There is nothing wrong with the model, as far as it goes. The problem arises because of an inappropriate attempt to apply the model where it does not belong.

6. Not only will government bureaucrats not have the correct incentives, they will have the wrong ones, due to rational ignorance and agency problems.

7. At another point, Kirzner implies that it is not incumbent upon him to explain more fully. He asks rhetorically, then answers: "How can an *unnoticed* potential outcome, no matter how attractive, affect behavior? How can the attractiveness of an unknown opportunity that awaits around the corner possibly inspire one to peer around the corner? It would be presumptuous and misleading to suggest that I know how to answer these questions" (1985, p. 109, emphasis in original).

8. For the most part, the only policies that Kirzner endorses are those which eliminate taxes or regulations, or eliminate laws and institutions that tend to muddle property rights. But, consider his favorable paraphrasing from Arthur Seldon: "Arthur Seldon has remarked that the qualities that make for entrepreneurial alertness (such as restive temperament, thirst for adventure, ambition, and imagination) may be nurtured or suppressed" (1985, p. 89).

9. Note that a system of free markets and private property give the decision maker the correct incentive to assess the potential importance and impact of unpredictable possibilities as long as the decision maker gets to privatize the associated benefits and privately incurs any costs.

10. See Stephen Shmanske (1982) and (1991).

11. See Harold Demsetz (1982), who shows that the licensing restriction does not fit any of the standard definitions of an entry barrier.

REFERENCES

Alchian, Armen A. 1950. "Uncertainty, Evolution and Economic Theory." *Journal of Political Economy*, 58(3, June): 211–21.

Baird, Charles W. 1989. "James Buchanan and the Austrians: The Common Ground." *The Cato Journal,* 9(1, Spring/Summer): 201–230.

Boulding, K. E. 1969. "Knowledge as a Commodity," p. 146 in *Beyond Economics: Essay on Society, Religion and Ethics.* Ann Arbor: University of Michigan Press.

Coase, Ronald H. 1960. "The Problem of Social Cost." *The Journal of Law and Economics,* 3(October): 1–44.

Demsetz, Harold. 1969. "Information and Efficiency: Another Viewpoint." *Journal of Law and Economics* 12(1, April): 1–22.

———. 1982. "Barriers to Entry." *American Economic Review,* 72(1, March): 47–57.

Garrison, Roger W. 1986. "From Lachmann to Lucas: On Institutions, Expectations, and Equilibrating Tendencies," pp. 87–101 in *Subjectivism, Intelligibility and Economic Understanding,* edited by Israel Kirzner. New York: New York University Press.

Hayek, Friedrich A. 1945. "The Use of Knowledge in Society." *American Economic Review,* 35(4, September): 519–30.

———. 1948. "Economics and Knowledge." Reprinted in F. A. Hayek, *Individualism and Economic Order,* pp. 33–56. Chicago: Henry Regnery.

Hirshleifer, Jack. 1965. "Investment Decision Under Uncertainty: Choice Theoretic Approaches." *Quarterly Journal of Economics,* 79(November): 509–536.

Kirzner, Israel M. 1973. *Competition and Entrepreneurship.* Chicago: The University of Chicago Press.

———. 1979. *Perception, Opportunity, and Profit.* Chicago: The University of Chicago Press.

———. 1985. *Discovery and the Capitalist Process.* Chicago: The University of Chicago Press.

Schultz, T. W. 1975. "The Value of the Ability to Deal with Disequilibria." *Journal of Economic Literature,* 13(3, September): 827–46.

Shackle, G. L. S. 1972. *Epistemics and Economics: A Critique of Economic Doctrines.* Cambridge, Cambridge University Press.

Shmanske, Stephen. 1982. "Public Goods, Product Quality Determination and Dimensionality of Consumption." *Public Finance,* 37(3, Fall): 387–403.

———. 1991. *Public Goods, Mixed Goods and Monopolistic Competition.* College Station, Tex.: Texas A&M University Press.

A TALE OF TWO WORLDS: COMMENT ON SHMANSKE

Professor Shmanske has written an insightful and thoroughly consistent critique of the economic worldview which I have sought to project in my writings on the entrepreneurial role. In this brief comment I shall attempt to crystallize and sharpen the difference between that economic worldview and the alternative worldview which Shmanske's thoughtful paper expresses. The purpose of this exercise is, naturally, to persuade the reader of the superior plausibility and analytical serviceability of the former way of seeing things.

The view of the world which Shmanske expresses is one which fits modern neoclassical economics, when consistently pushed, as Shmanske indeed wishes to push it, to its logical extreme. In a 1976 paper I once described a world similar to this neoclassical world in the following terms. Such a world, I wrote,

> is peopled by beings whose purposefulness ensures that they can never in retrospect, reproach themselves for having acted in error. They may, in retrospect, indeed wish that they had been more skillful, or had commanded more inputs, or had been better informed. But they can never upbraid themselves for having acted erroneously in failing to command those superior skills, or to acquire more accurate information. They must, at every stage, concede that they had, in the past, acted with flawless precision insofar as they were able (Kirzner 1979, p. 128).

From Shmanske's perspective, the failure to notice an opportunity staring one in the face is to be seen not as an error, but as the unfortunate but nonetheless deliberately accepted cost, planfully incurred in an earlier rational decision (to refrain from further investing in the special skill of "noticing opportunities"). The tragedy of missed opportunities is under no circumstances (except, it seems to be conceded, at the stage of the very first steps taken from the cradle) to be attributed to any pure

From Israel M. Kirzner, "A Tale of Two Worlds: Comment on Shmanske," in *Advances in Austrian Economics*, Volume 1, ed. Peter J. Boettke, Israel M. Kirzner, and Mario J. Rizzo (Greenwich, Conn., and London: JAI Press, 1994), 223–26. Reprinted by permission.

mistake—a notion which has been consistently banished from Shmanske's world—but is to be attributed entirely to the paucity of one's stock of alertness, a paucity rationally and deliberately arranged during earlier stages of investment decision making. (From this perspective there is, therefore, in fact *no* tragedy to be seen in missed opportunities.) A prime advantage[1] which Shmanske sees in this way of understanding the world is that it "explains" missed opportunities (and also grasped opportunities) in terms of the economist's tools of deliberate, constrained-maximization analysis, without recourse to any "metaphysical" notion of an unexplained "alertness" somehow imported as deus ex machina into the world of the economist.

The view of the world which I have advanced in a series of writings on entrepreneurship during the past two decades, is a sharply different one. While this view certainly recognized the critical explanatory role fulfilled by deliberately adopted plans (including planned investments in resource acquisition), it emphasizes at the same time that in the real world of radical uncertainty, such explanations do not and cannot *fully* account for economic events. Such events also, almost invariably, reflect the results of decisions made *in error*—with the blamed errors considered as being in a special and narrow sense,[2] "inexcusable" (i.e., "unexplainable in terms of any cost benefit calculus").

The extent to which agents successfully avoid such "inexcusable errors" is seen, in this "Austrian" view, as residing in the quality of alertness, in such manner as to render the constrained-maximization analysis of the economist entirely irrelevant. In no way can the successfully alert entrepreneur ascribe his *pure* profit to wise past planning; in no way can the unsuccessful entrepreneur excuse his losses as somehow being part of the planned price paid for earlier economizing in investment in human or other capital. (It is this irrelevance of the planning paradigm, so dear to the economist's heart, which moves Shmanske to set down this alertness as "metaphysical").

It may be immediately conceded to Shmanske, of course, that very often the detection and grasping of opportunities *may* certainly and correctly be attributed to deliberately cultivated skills which were acquired as a result of careful cost-benefit calculations. What the Austrian view contends, however, is that in an open-ended world fraught with Knightian uncertainty, one in which, to quote Shmanske, "something completely unexpected might happen" at any time—there must always be a role for alertness (and for the absence of alertness), in the sense of a quality in regard to which rational planning is fundamentally irrelevant.

Now, each of these two worldviews is *logically* coherent. One cannot choose between them merely on the basis of comparing their internal consistency. However, there *is* a question of fact—not merely one of perspective—which separates these two views of the world. One's choice between them must and can be based on one's judgment concerning this question of fact. (The difficulty lies in the empirical elusiveness of the factual difference which separates these two views of the world.) For Shmanske, the ex post discovery of a missed opportunity always constitutes an event which was foretold and accepted (in the sense similar, at least, to the sense in which any decision made in a risky situation "anticipates" the possibility of the eventuality that was gambled *against*). The decision maker's regret over the missed opportunity refers not to *his* failure to notice the opportunity *at the moment when it might have in fact been noticed,* but (if indeed there *is* room for regret at all) to the *circumstances* which led him, *in the past,* to invest in alertness in a manner which deliberately generated "insufficient" alertness at the moment of the missed opportunity. For the "Austrian" view of the world, such an ex post discovery of a missed opportunity may well, when hindsight has revealed that opportunity to have stared one in the face, lead one to regret one's "blindness"—without excuses. To be sure, it is extremely difficult to devise an empirical test through which to decide this question of fact. The reader may, on the basis of introspective evidence, come to his own conclusions.

Let it be emphasized once again that, because this question of fact can hardly be decided on empirical grounds, it is possible to adopt Shmanske's perspective in a manner which can ostensibly account, in consistent fashion, for the entire complex of economic decisions and events. There need be no internal logical flaw in the coherency of this *picture of the world*. But, this observation entails a corollary: the internal consistency of this worldview—a consistency which Shmanske finds to be eminently satisfying—does not in any way establish its validity. Shmanske charges that the Austrian view of the world has not provided proof of its truth, only assertions thereof. Perhaps this is correct, but Shmanske's assumption that the burden of such proof rests upon the Austrian view appears itself to rest upon no more substantial a foundation than the *assumption* that the economist's paradigm of constrained maximization is *universally* and *exhaustively* applicable—an assumption which, of course, simply begs the entire question at issue.

Again, while no logical incoherency necessarily flaws Shmanske's neoclassical worldview, nonetheless it does entail a logical dilemma all its own. This logical dilemma is a simple and devastating one *for the enterprise of economic theorizing. If* the world is accepted as an errorless world in relevant equilibrium at each and every instant, then this acceptance has at once abandoned the traditional backbone of economic science—the thesis that systematic market processes tend toward market-clearing prices. There is nothing, in Shmanske's world of continuous equilibrium, to drive prices in the direction of conventional supply-demand equality—*because supply-demand equality* (appropriately defined) *obtains at each and every instant.* It has indeed been the central contention of the Austrian view associated with this writer's articulation of the entrepreneurial role, that an understanding of such systematic processes *requires* stepping outside the confining framework of perfect (relevant) information.

The reader must therefore choose between two views of the world. In one of these views, (a) there is no room whatever for error and ex post regret, and (b) we are confined by the assumption of equilibrium at each and every instant, leaving no scope whatever for systematic equilibration of any kind. The second of these views, by contrast, offers a world in which true error and pure entrepreneurial profit and loss exist at every turn, and thus a world in which we can understand the process of equilibration which governs price movements (and which constitutes the most impressive empirical feature of real-world market economies).

The signal merit of Professor Shmanske's paper is that he has spelled out his own worldview with an unsurpassed consistency and starkness. It is this starkness which can now help the reader determine whether this worldview fits either the introspective world of his own experience, or his experience of the outer world of systematic market price movements.

NOTES

1. Shmanske also repeatedly refers to an advantage which he claims for his perspective, in that it more easily produces laissez-faire policy conclusions. Although I do not, in fact, accept this latter contention, I prefer to present the choice between the two worldviews as one which focuses on their relative intrinsic validities, rather than upon their abilities to satisfy any prejudged policy position.

2. For further decision of this "special sense," see Kirzner (1989, p. 32; 1992, pp. 21–22).

REFERENCES

Kirzner, Israel M. 1979. *Perception, Opportunity and Profit.* Chicago: University of Chicago Press.

———. 1989. *Discovery, Capitalism, and Distributive Justice.* Oxford: Basil Blackwell.

———. 1992. *The Meaning of Market Process. Essays in the Development of Modern Austrian Economics.* London: Routledge.

THE LAW OF SUPPLY
AND DEMAND

THE LAW OF SUPPLY AND DEMAND

The theory of supply and demand is recognized almost universally as the first step toward understanding how market prices are determined and the way in which these prices help shape production and consumption decisions—the decisions that make up not only the skeleton but also the flesh and blood of the economic system. Austrian economics thoroughly agrees with this. However, when we dig just a little below the surface of the "law" of supply and demand, we encounter difficulties that have, directly or indirectly, led Austrians to explain the determination of prices differently from how it is often, at least implicitly, presented. I will try to explain the sense in which Austrians are unhappy with the textbook presentations of supply and demand—and are yet fully in agreement with the *general* emphasis on supply and demand as being the key to economic understanding.

THE BASIC PROPOSITION

The basic insight underlying the law of supply and demand is that at any given moment a price that is "too high" will leave disappointed would-be sellers with unsold goods, while a price that is "too low" will leave disappointed would-be buyers without the goods they wish to buy. There exists a "right" price, at which all those who wish to buy can find sellers willing to sell and all those who wish to sell can find buyers willing to buy. This "right" price is therefore often called the "market-clearing price."

Supply-and-demand theory revolves around the proposition that a free, competitive market does in fact successfully generate a powerful tendency toward the market-clearing price. This proposition is often seen as the most important implication of (and premise for) Adam Smith's famed invisible hand. Without any conscious managing control, a market spontaneously generates a tendency toward the dovetailing of independently made decisions of buyers and sellers to ensure that each of their decisions fits with the decisions made by the other market participants. Were this tendency to be carried to the limit, no buyer (seller) would be misled so as to waste time attempting to buy (sell) at a price below (above)

From *The Freeman* 50, 1 (January 2000): 19–21. Reprinted by permission of the Foundation for Economic Education.

the market-clearing price. No buyer (seller) would in fact pay (receive) a price higher (lower) than necessary to elicit the agreement of his trading partner. To the extent that this proposition is valid, free competitive markets achieve what F. A. Hayek has justifiably called a "marvel." But it is in regard to the validity of this proposition (and in particular to our reasons for being convinced that this proposition is both valid and relevant) that Austrians differ sharply with mainstream textbook economics. And it is precisely because of the universally acknowledged centrality of the supply-and-demand proposition for all of economics that this disagreement is so important.

THE ROLE OF KNOWLEDGE

The mainstream textbook approach to this proposition is, in one way or another, explicitly or implicitly, based on the assumption of perfect knowledge. The Austrian approach does not make the perfect-knowledge assumption the foundation for this proposition; quite the contrary, Austrians base the proposition squarely on the insight that its validity proceeds from market processes set in motion by the inevitable *imperfections* in knowledge, which characterize human interaction in society.

In certain respects the mainstream view is not unreasonable. In many contexts we generally take it for granted that human beings are aware of the opportunities available to them. When economists believe, for example, that a price increase will cut the quantity people seek to purchase, and a price decrease will stimulate sales, this belief is based on the reasonable assumption that such price increases or decreases are in fact likely to become known to prospective buyers soon enough to make a difference.

The mainstream view takes this not unreasonable assumption and pursues it relentlessly, in effect, to its logical—but no longer quite so reasonable—conclusion. This conclusion is that in any free market, the market-clearing price is *instantaneously* (or, at least, *very* rapidly) established. If every market participant knows what every other market participant is prepared to do (including, especially, the quantity he is prepared to buy or sell at any given price), it follows that any price higher than the market-clearing price cannot emerge (since prospective sellers would realize that they would be left with unsold goods). It follows, similarly, that any price lower than the market-clearing price cannot emerge (since prospective buyers would realize that they will be left without the goods they wish to buy and for which they are in fact prepared to pay a higher price if necessary). The proposition that free-market prices are thus inevitably market-clearing prices proceeds inexorably from the belief that market prices are, in effect, instantaneously known to all potential market participants.

THE DANGEROUS ASSUMPTION

The assumption that all market participants are always fully aware of market opportunities in which they might be interested is often presented, in mainstream textbook expositions, as part of the assumption of so-called "perfect competition." Perfect competition *explicitly* presumes universal market omniscience. One way of expressing the Austrian unhappiness with the mainstream textbook treatment is to point out that to start supply-and-demand analysis by assuming that competition is "perfect" (in the textbook sense) is not only to be wildly (and therefore unhelpfully) unrealistic; it is in fact also to rob the analysis of all significant economic content—since the principal results sought to be shown turn out to be simply statements repeating the governing assumption in slightly different language.

To demonstrate that the interplay of supply and demand in a free market generates a powerful tendency toward the market-clearing price is to meet a daunting analytical challenge. To demonstrate that in a perfectly competitive market the only possible price is the market-clearing price is simply trivially to identify what has already been planted in the initial assumption. To unpack the mathematically implied properties of a definition *may*, of course, be a significant (mathematical) contribution. But to demonstrate the attainment in free markets of the market-clearing price by restricting analytical attention to the situation in which this price is the only one permitted to be conceivable, is, as a matter of *economic* analysis, a hollow triumph indeed.

This difficulty that Austrians find with the textbook discussions of supply and demand can be presented in somewhat different terms. The traditional classroom blackboard demonstration of the law proceeds by drawing the classic supply-and-demand diagram—a downward sloping demand curve intersecting an upward sloping supply curve. (For present purposes we forgo the details surrounding the construction of this diagram; it is one familiar to the hosts of students who have ever been exposed to elementary economics.) The core of the classroom analysis generally consists of discussion showing, first, that any market price higher than that indicated by the intersection of the two curves (that is, a price higher than the market-clearing price) must tend to produce competitive pressure toward a decrease in price (since the high price will generate a surplus of unsold merchandise); and second, that any market price lower than that indicated by the point of intersection must produce competitive pressure toward an increase in price (since the low price will generate a shortage of goods offered for sale, as compared with the quantities prospective buyers wish to buy).

Austrians do not have serious disagreement with such discussions in themselves; they simply point out that those discussions are utterly inconsistent with the assumption of perfect competition (which textbook analysis takes as its operative assumption). A little careful analysis of the perfect-competition assumption (which analysis can, however, unfortunately *not* be fitted into this space) suffices to show that under perfect competition *there cannot in fact exist two curves* (the demand curve intersecting with the supply curve). Under perfect competition the supply-and-demand diagram shrivels instantly *to a single point*—the point where the two curves *would* have intersected (*had* the curves themselves existed!). This is so because any point on a market supply curve or on a market demand curve that is *not* that intersection point can have analytical existence only by suspending some or all of the conditions that define the state of perfect competition. The diagram (valuable though it certainly is!) is simply not consistent with the assumed conditions under which it is supposed to be operating.

Our discussion has unfortunately been overwhelmingly negative. We have pointed out problems that Austrians have with mainstream supply-and-demand analysis—but we have not suggested how an alternative approach might avoid these difficulties. Subsequent articles in the present series will attempt to fill this gap. For Austrians, the law of supply and demand, properly explained, is at least as centrally important for economic understanding as it is for mainstream economics. We will show how Austrians deploy insight into the *entrepreneurial* character of dynamically competitive markets (insights that can have no place within the mainstream textbook paradigm) to explain the law of supply and demand in an intuitively and analytically satisfying way.

ENTREPRENEURIAL DISCOVERY
AND THE LAW OF SUPPLY AND DEMAND

Last month we promised to explain how Austrian economics presents its understanding of the law of supply and demand by invoking the *entrepreneurial* character of dynamically competitive markets. The key element in this Austrian understanding is the appreciation that individual buying and selling decisions are examples of what Ludwig von Mises called *human action*. For Mises, each human being is, in a very important sense, an entrepreneur. (See Ludwig von Mises, *Human Action*, 3d ed., 1966, p. 252.) And it is the entrepreneurial element in those decisions that is responsible, in the Austrian view, for that crucially important tendency toward market-clearing that (for Austrians as well as for non-Austrians) constitutes the heart of the law of supply and demand.

THE MEANING OF HUMAN ACTION

The Misesian notion of *human action* is significantly richer than the mainstream-economics notion of the *economizing decision*. An economizing decision is seen as the selection of the most desirable option out of *an array of given alternatives with a given ranking of what is more desirable and less desirable*. Since both the alternatives available and the ranking are already identified *prior* to the act of decision, such decision-making consists essentially of the solution to a mathematical maximization exercise; the outcome is predetermined: it is implicit in the given context within which the decision is to be made.

For Misesian human action, on the other hand, the action is, most importantly, seen as *including* the determination of both what the available alternatives are and what ranking of relative desirability is to be adopted. Determining these elements inevitably exposes the agent to the uncertainties of an open-ended future (in a sense absent in the context of the standard "economizing decision"): action is the present choice between future alternatives that must, in the face of the foggy uncertainty of the future, now be *identified* in the very act of choice. It is this aspect of human action that renders it, for Mises, essentially entrepreneurial. Mathematical expertise in solving maximization problems is of very limited help in choosing among courses of action when the very alternatives must be "created," as it were, by the agent's entrepreneurial imagination and creativity, by his daring and boldness.

THE ENTREPRENEURIAL ROLE

For Austrian economics the entrepreneurial role is, despite—or more accurately, precisely because of—its analytical "fuzziness," responsible for the systematic character of market processes ("fuzzy" since no economist can "model" the creative imagination of the entrepreneur acting under open-ended uncertainty). Going beyond the context of the entrepreneurial elements in each individual human action, Austrian economics focuses on the role of the businessman-entrepreneur in the dynamic market process. The successful businessman-entrepreneur "sees" what other market participants have not yet seen; the entrepreneur sees opportunities to buy at one price and to sell at a higher price. To see such opportunities will typically call for (a) superior imagination and vision (since the perceived opportunity to sell at the higher price is likely to exist only in the future) and (b) *creativity* (since such a profit opportunity is likely to take the form of selling what one buys in an innovatively different form, and/or different place, than was relevant at the time of purchase).

It is because Mises saw each human being as, to some extent, an entrepreneur that he understood the powerful tendencies that exist in free markets for profit opportunities to be sensed and exploited (and thus eliminated) by profit-oriented entrepreneurial market participants. In a dynamically changing world, new profit opportunities are continually emerging, and their emergence continually generates the incentives toward their discovery and exploitation. It is this ceaseless re-creation and discovery of entrepreneurial opportunities that make up the market process we observe in the world around us.

THE LAW OF SUPPLY AND DEMAND RECONSIDERED

For Austrians, the law of supply and demand is simply an insight into one particular (but central) element in this more comprehensive, dynamic, entrepreneur-driven market process. For any particular commodity, the market forces acting on the prices at which it will be bought and sold (and thus the market forces acting on the decisions made to produce and to buy it) tend to identify and exploit the opportunities (structured by the technology and the economics of its production on the one hand, and by the urgency with which potential consumers wish to consume it, on the other hand) and thus to ensure that the quantities which are simultaneously worthwhile for producers to produce and for consumers to buy will in fact tend to be produced, offered for sale, and purchased.

If, for example, current production of this commodity is "too low," this means that opportunities exist for additional units to be produced at an outlay below the highest price potential consumers would be prepared to pay; it is "worthwhile" to produce these additional units. Entrepreneurial producers will tend to discover and act on such opportunities. If, on the other hand, current production is "too high," this means that the production outlay for at least some units exceeds the highest price potential consumers are prepared to pay for them; these units were produced as a result of entrepreneurial error. Entrepreneurial producers will tend to discover these (marginal) losses and cut back on production.

The entrepreneurial forces acting on the market for any one commodity are thus continually pushing that market toward the market-clearing point—that is, to where (a) the quantity produced is such that (only) all units "worth producing" are indeed produced, and (b) the market price for this commodity is just high enough to make it, as a practical matter, worthwhile for producers to produce this quantity, and is just low enough to make it worthwhile for consumers to buy it.

Clearly, these forces would, were all other dynamic changes in market conditions to be suspended, tend to achieve exactly those outcomes identified, in more conventional mainstream formulations of the law of supply and demand, by the intersection of the supply curve and the demand curve. It is for this reason that we have described Austrian economics as basically in agreement with mainstream economics in its emphasis on the centrality of the law of supply and demand. It is worthwhile, however, briefly to ponder the sense in which the Austrian version of the "law" *avoids* reliance on any presumption of universal perfect market knowledge (a presumption that, as seen in the preceding article, pervades much standard economics).

THE ROLE OF IGNORANCE AND LEARNING IN THE ENTREPRENEURIAL MARKET PROCESS

As Austrian economist F. A. Hayek emphasized, the market process we have been describing in entrepreneurial terms can also usefully be understood in terms of *learning*. The process through which the market tends to generate the "right" quantity of a commodity, and the "right" price for it, can be seen as a series of steps during which market participants gradually tend to discover the gaps or errors in the information on which they had previously been basing their erroneous production and/or buying decisions. Buyers who had overestimated the willingness of producers to produce and sell the commodity had been "incorrectly" refusing to offer higher prices (that they would indeed have been prepared to pay); those who had underestimated that willingness were "incorrectly" offering higher prices than were in fact needed to inspire sellers to produce. Sellers who had overestimated the willingness of buyers to buy were "incorrectly" asking higher prices (and were producing more units of the commodity than it was "really worthwhile" to produce), and so on. The market process is one in which, driven by the entrepreneurial sense for grasping at pure profit opportunities (and for avoiding entrepreneurial losses), market participants, learning more accurate assessments of the attitudes of other market participants, tend toward the market-clearing price-quantity combination.

Two concluding observations are in place at this point. First, we should emphasize, once again, that this "law" is simply an element in the more general dynamic, entrepreneurial market process that is continually at work not only (as in the narrowly defined law of supply and demand) within a particular industry but also between industries. It is this that renders understanding of the law so important for the broader and deeper understanding of the role of free markets generally in achieving socially effective economic outcomes.

Second, we should emphasize the extent to which the law of supply and demand is being continually buffeted and interrupted—and continually reasserted and re-created—in the real world of dynamic change. (The circumstance that these dynamic changes typically take the form of forces acting on a particular commodity market from *other* commodity markets reinforces the observation made in the preceding paragraph.)

Next month we will again explore the dynamic entrepreneurial free-market process with particular concern for the nature of and role for *competition* in this process, and for the implications in regard to antitrust policy.

ISRAEL KIRZNER ON SUPPLY AND DEMAND

JAMES C. AHIAKPOR

Israel Kirzner misrepresents mainstream economics by his assertion that in explaining market price determination by supply and demand curves, it always assumes "perfect competition," worse yet, perfect knowledge.[1] "The mainstream textbook approach . . . is, in one way or another, explicitly or implicitly, based on the assumption of perfect knowledge" and in which the "market-clearing price is *instantaneously* (or, at least, *very* rapidly) established." In contrast, "the Austrian version of the law [of supply and demand] *avoids* reliance on any presumption of universal perfect market knowledge (a presumption that . . . pervades much standard economics)."[2]

Mainstream economics uses the upward-sloping supply and downward-sloping demand curves simply to reflect the basic self-interested pursuit of net gains by market participants: sellers looking for higher prices in order to offer more quantities for sale per unit of time, and buyers looking for lower prices in order to purchase more quantities per unit of time. All such bargains are made by the market participants with as much knowledge as they may possess, but there is no insistence on complete or perfect information on the part of sellers or buyers.

Thus to say that there is an upward-sloping market supply curve for "capital" or savings in the financial market simply means that people or financial institutions would be willing to offer more funds on loan if offered higher interest rates. Similarly, to draw a downward-sloping demand curve for "capital" or savings is to suggest that more loans would be taken by borrowers if they were offered at lower interest rates. It is from such contrary tendencies of lenders and borrowers that classical and neoclassical economists explain that the rate of interest is determined by the supply and demand for "capital" or loanable funds (an explanation many Austrians fail to recognize[3]). The same model of supply and demand may be used to explain the determination of wage rates in different occupations or rental rates in different housing markets, but without invoking the assumption of perfect knowledge.

Few mainstream economists believe that the model of price determination in a "perfectly competitive" market is a satisfactory representation of real market situations, and few invoke the assumption of perfect knowledge. Rather, they consider oligopolistic and monopolistic competition as the norm. As George Stigler points out, "it seems improper to assume complete knowledge of the future in a changing economy. Not only is it misleading to endow the population with this gift of prophecy but also it would often be inconsistent to have people foresee a future event and still have that event remain in the future."[4] Several textbooks now talk about price-taking firms rather than perfectly competitive firms. Paul Samuelson and William Nordhaus, after teaching the perfect competition model and without invoking the assumption of perfect knowledge, also remark, "By the strict definition, few markets in the U.S. economy are perfectly competitive," and "If you look out the window at the American economy, however, you'll find that such cases [of perfect competition and complete monopoly] are rare; you are more likely to see varieties of imperfect competition between these two extremes. Most industries are populated by a small number of firms competing with each other."[5]

MARSHALL AND MILL

Classical economists and such early neoclassical economists as Alfred Marshall also discussed equilibrium market-price determination by the forces of supply and demand but without invoking the assumption of "perfect competition." Thus, summarizing classical value theory, J. S. Mill notes that:

> if a value [price] different from the natural value [long-run average cost, including normal profits] be necessary to make the demand equal to the supply, the market value will deviate from the natural value; but only for a time; for the permanent tendency of supply is to conform itself to the demand which is found by experience to exist for the commodity when selling at its natural value. If the supply is either more or less than this, it is so accidentally, and affords either more or less than the ordinary rate of profit; which, under *free and active competition*, cannot long continue to be the case.[6] (emphasis mine)

Marshall talks about "free competition, or rather, freedom of industry and enterprise" and by "competition" means "the racing of one person against another, with special reference to bidding for the sale or purchase of anything."[7]

It is also well known that the modern perfectly competitive model is one in which firms or sellers do not compete—they can't change prices or product quality, two of the principal means of competition: "it is one of the great paradoxes of economic science that every *act* of competition on the part of a businessman is evidence, in economic theory, of some degree of monopoly power, while the concepts of monopoly and perfect competition have this important feature: both are situations in which the possibility of any competitive behavior has been ruled out by definition."[8] Moreover, "the theoretical concept of [perfect] competition is diametrically opposed to the generally accepted concept of competition."[9]

For his strictures to be useful, Kirzner needs to justify his insistence that the use of market supply and demand curves to illustrate equilibrium price determination in mainstream economics always must entail the assumption not only of perfect competition but also of perfect knowledge.

NOTES

1. See Israel M. Kirzner, "The Law of Supply and Demand," *Ideas on Liberty*, January 2000, pp. 19–21.

2. See Israel M. Kirzner, "Entrepreneurial Discovery and the Law of Supply and Demand," *Ideas on Liberty*, February 2000, pp. 17–19.

3. James C. W. Ahiakpor, "Austrian Capital Theory: Help or Hindrance?" *Journal of the History of Economic Thought*, Fall 1997, pp. 261–85.

4. George J. Stigler, "Perfect Competition, Historically Contemplated," *Journal of Political Economy* 65 (1) 1957, pp. 1–17.

5. Paul A. Samuelson and William D. Nordhaus, *Economics*, 16th ed. (New York: Irwin-McGraw-Hill, 1998), pp. 155, 170.

6. John Stuart Mill, *Collected Works*, vol. 3, J. M. Robson, ed. (Toronto: University of Toronto Press, 1965), p. 457.

7. Alfred Marshall, *Principles of Economics*, 8th ed. (Philadelphia: Porcupine Press, 1990 [1920]), pp. 10, 4.

8. Paul McNulty, "Economic Theory and the Meaning of Competition," *Quarterly Journal of Economics* 82 (4) 1968, p. 641.

9. S. Charles Maurice, Christopher R. Thomas, and Charles W. Smithson, *Managerial Economics*, 4th ed. (Homewood, Ill.: Irwin, 1992), p. 431.

A PUZZLE AND ITS SOLUTION:
REJOINDER TO PROFESSOR AHIAKPOR

I was at first puzzled by Professor James C. W. Ahiakpor's charge that I had misrepresented mainstream economics (by my statement that mainstream economics' use of its supply-and-demand apparatus relies on the assumption of perfect competition, and thus perfect knowledge). I was puzzled because mainstream textbooks are quite explicit on this point.[1]

Upon rereading Professor Ahiakpor's comment, especially his quotations from Stigler and other mainstream writers who emphasize the unrealistic nature of the assumptions of the perfectly competitive model, and particularly its assumption of perfect knowledge, I believe that I can put my finger on the source of Professor Ahiakpor's misunderstandings. In fact, I will use several passages from Stigler's textbook on price theory (not the source of Professor Ahiakpor's Stigler quote) to attempt to clarify matters.

As a prelude to his discussion of how demand and supply determine price, Stigler carefully articulates the conditions (especially that of perfect knowledge) needed for perfect competition.[2] He then proceeds to address possible misgivings concerning these conditions. "If the reader bristles at the acceptance of assumptions such as perfect knowledge . . . he is both wrong and right. He is wrong in denying the helpfulness of the use of pure, clean concepts in theoretical analysis: they confer clarity and efficiency on the analysis, *without depriving the analysis of empirical relevance.* He is right if he believes these extreme assumptions are not *necessary* to the existence of competition. . . ." (Italics in original.)

Clearly, Stigler's position can be stated in three points: (a) the real world is not perfectly competitive; it is not characterized by perfect knowledge; however, (b) the economist is best able to explain price determination in the real world by referring to a "pure and clean" analytical model of supply and demand under conditions of perfect competition; and (c) this pure and clean model is then useful in understanding the real world because the degree of competition and of perfection of knowledge in the real world is sufficiently close (to the pure and clean concepts

From *The Freeman* 50, 7 (July 2000), 25–26. Reprinted by permission of the Foundation for Economic Education.

of the analytical model) as to render *that analytical model* a useful basis for understanding price determination in the real world.[3] Ahiakpor has focused exclusively, it seems, on points (a) and (c), and somehow concluded that mainstream explanations for price determination do not depend analytically on perfect-knowledge assumptions. But surely this conclusion is quite mistaken; point (b) can *not* be denied.

For mainstream economics (and particularly for Stigler) the *applicability* of the pure and clean analytical model of supply and demand to the *real* world of imperfect knowledge is based entirely on the belief (hope?) that the degree of such imperfection in knowledge is not serious enough to compromise the applicability of the pure model. But the analytical basis for such application remains the pure and clean model itself. *Any explanation of real world price determination rests, in mainstream economics, on the validity of the explanation for price determination offered by the pure and clean model of supply and demand, under conditions of perfect knowledge.* The Austrian critique points out the internal, *analytical inadequacy* of that pure and clean model (quite apart from the unrealism of its assumptions).[4] As Hayek and the modern Austrians point out, the true explanation for the emergence of the market price refers strictly to *those very imperfections of knowledge that mainstream economists find it necessary to downplay.*

THE MODEL'S USES

I would like to make a concluding observation. The asperity of Professor Ahiakpor's comment suggests that he has read my pieces as expressing complete dismissal of mainstream economics and as doing so with complete hostility toward it. This is by no means the case. Speaking strictly for myself (rather than on behalf of Austrian economists), I can say that there certainly are important uses for the mainstream perfect knowledge model. For many rough and ready purposes of applied economics, it is *this* model that is the most useful practical tool. I have often stated that if students had to be exposed to only one lecture in economics, I would hope that that lecture would be the mainstream supply-and-demand lecture. But, I must insist, such usefulness, *as a matter of pure science*, is severely limited. For adequate understanding of how markets work it is necessary to go beyond the perfect competition/perfect knowledge analysis, and to explore the *processes* that flow from imperfect knowledge and from the entrepreneurial decisions set in motion by such imperfection of knowledge. The truth is that recognition of this scientific insight turns out to be of utmost importance for developing enlightened public policy. For as Austrian economists know, it is in and through *these* processes that free markets make their contribution to human well-being.

NOTES

1. I list here three examples, at different levels of sophistication: George J. Stigler, *The Theory of Price*, 3d ed. (New York: Macmillan, 1966), pp. 87–89 (leading into his discussion of price determination through demand and supply); J. M. Henderson and R. E. Quandt. *Microeconomic Theory: A Mathematical Approach* (New York: McGraw-Hill, 1958), chapter 4 (and especially p. 86, leading into the discussion of market equilibrium in terms of supply and demand analysis); and D. Salvatori, *Microeconomics* (New York: HarperCollins, 1991), p. 26.

2. Stigler (p. 87) treats perfect competition as equivalent to the state in which each market participant faces infinitely elastic supply or demand curves—the state which corresponds to the price-taking assumption to which Professor Ahiakpor refers.

3. Many mainstream economists would follow Milton Friedman in arguing that the absence of realism in the assumptions of the perfectly competitive model is almost irrelevant to the usefulness of the model in predicting real world outcomes. For Friedman's well-known position on this see his *Essays in Positive Economics* (Chicago: University of Chicago Press, 1953), pp. 14f.

4. It was Hayek who, in his brilliant 1946 critique of the perfectly competitive model, identified its central flaw as an explanation for price determination. The model cannot explain how price *comes* to be that which the model predicts. The model can only, given its assumptions, postulate that that *is* the price. The model *assumes* the result the *emergence* of which we are seeking to explain. See F. A. Hayek, *Individualism and Economic Order* (London: Routledge and Kegan Paul, 1949), pp. 93f.

entrepreneurship theory: Austrian
tradition summarized, 3–11,
358–59; development approaches,
13–23, 98
entrepreneurship theory, Ricketts's
critique and Kirzner's response:
overviews, 323–26, 358–60;
behavior definition question,
332–35; capitalist category problem,
325, 326–28, 336–37, 351–58;
distributive justice question, 325,
335–38, 348–51; equilibriating
concepts, 329–32, 344, 359n2;
institutional framework argument,
348–51; methodology issues,
336–37, 356–58; policy applicability,
338–39; rent-seeking problem,
332–35, 350–51; uncertainty
problem, 327–28, 344–48
entrepreneurship theory,
Schumpeterian vs. Kirznerian:
automobile innovation example,
61–63; coordinative/equilibriating
perspectives, 60–63, 71–73,
78–79; creativity vs. alertness
misunderstanding, 74–80;
discovery's role, 51–52, 53–54, 59–
60, 72; disruption/disequilibrium
perspectives, 52–53, 61, 71, 313–14;
reconsiderations summarized,
50–51, 64–65; reviewer critiques,
54–56; semantics obstacle, 63–64,
65n11, 77–78; significance of
temporal framework, 56–59,
66n21, 76, 314–16; uncertainty's
role, 56–59, 66n21
entrepreneurship theory, Shmanske's
critique: overview, 361–63, 384–86;
alertness concept problems, 376–
81, 383–84; equilibrium analysis
problems, 363–75; Kirzner's
reply to, 389–93; relevance claim

problem, 375–77; search vs.
discovery arguments, 380–84
entry barriers, economic harms,
239–40, 244–45, 386
equilibrium analysis: and
entrepreneurship theorizing,
14–16, 18–19; significance of
temporal periods, 314–16
equilibrium analysis, Shmanske's
critique of Kirzner: overview,
361–63, 384–86; arbitrage vs.
coordination interpretations,
367–68; bargaining individuals
example, 373–75; buyer-seller
groups example, 371–73; price
vs. behavior examination, 366;
simple setting for, 363–65; static
vs. dynamic conditions, 363–65;
traveler's plan example, 369–71;
uncertainty factor, 368–69
equilibrium models: analytical
limitations, 6–7, 72–73, 127,
409–10; as artificial world, 220–21,
268; as distorted perception of
capitalism, 86–87; as dominant
theory, 214–16; entrepreneurship's
exclusion, 72–73, 98–101,
265; ignorance removal costs,
215–17, 221–23, 234; and Law
of Indifference, 26–27; logic
vs. empirical analysis, 142–46;
perfect knowledge assumption,
151–52, 157–58, 214–15, 233–34, 312,
405–6, 408–9; price determination
problem, 125–27, 128–29, 138–40,
216–17, 232; treatment of processes
question, 137–40, 215–16. See also
disequilibrium condition
equilibrium models, entrepreneur's
function: exclusion problem,
70–73, 98–101, 305–6; Schultz's
concept of special abilities,

This book is set in Scala and Scala Sans, created
by the Dutch designer Martin Majoor in the 1990s.

This book is printed on paper that is acid-free and
meets the requirements of the American National
Standard for Permanence of Paper for Printed Library
Materials, z39.48-1992. ♾

Book design by Richard Hendel, Chapel Hill, North Carolina
Typography by Apex CoVantage, Madison, Wisconsin
Index by Sherry L. Smith, Bend, Oregon
Printed and bound by Thomson-Shore, Dexter, Michigan